Practical Usage of ISPF Dialog Manager

Springer

London
Berlin
Heidelberg
New York
Barcelona
Budapest
Hong Kong
Milan
Paris
Santa Clara
Singapore
Tokyo

Anthony S. Rudd

Practical Usage of ISPF Dialog Manager

With 62 Figures

 Springer

Anthony S. Rudd, MS(Hons)
Datev eG
Paumgartnerstrasse 6-14
D-90426 Nuremberg, GERMANY

ISBN-13:978-3-540-19950-2

British Library Cataloguing in Publication Data
Rudd, Anthony S.
  Practical usage of ISPF Dialog Manager. - 2nd ed.
  1.ISPF Dialog Manager (Computer program)   2.Computer programs
  I.Title
  005.3'29
  ISBN-13:978-3-540-19950-2   e-ISBN-13:978-1-4471-3040-6
  DOI: 10.1007/978-1-4471-3040-6

Library of Congress Cataloging-in-Publication Data
A catalog record for this book is available from the Library of Congress

Typesetting: camera ready by author

34/3830-543210 Printed on acid-free paper

Preface

The title of this book "PRACTICAL USAGE OF ISPF DIALOG MANAGER" reveals the purpose I had in writing it: a concise, complete, source of information necessary for the development of applications using IBM's ISPF Dialog Manager package. Furthermore, this book is hopefully more than a mere reference; it contains tips and notes I and my colleagues found out the hard way. I have tried to present this practical information in such a form that it is easy to find and use. I hope this will enable readers to spend more productive time developing, rather than trying to find out why something works in a particular way.

The original book was based on courses I have conducted for ISPF Dialog Manager over a number of years, and many of the students' criticisms and comments have been incorporated into the examples and explanations. This second edition has been extended to cover windowing, the CUA (Common User Access) standard as applied to ISPF, Library Management, and ISPF Client/Server. Because a full discussion of DTL (Dialog Tag Language) would exceed the scope of this book, it is not covered in detail. Similarly, some specialised features (such as Double-Byte Character Set) are not covered.

To reflect the change of emphasis in the procedural language, the CLIST chapter has been removed, and many examples illustrate the use of REXX.

And who should read this book? Both beginners and experts. Beginners are lead through the steps required to develop dialogue applications; complete worked examples, large enough to be practical but devoid of superfluous detail, enable the Dialog Manager novice to see what is necessary to write a simple application. Experts have a compact reference for ISPF Dialog Manager.

Table of Contents

1

Introduction

1.1 HISTORICAL DEVELOPMENT

The development and characteristics of Dialog Manager can only be appreciated by considering how programming has been done on IBM mainframe computers in the past.

Program development in the 1960s and early 1970s was still performed using punched cards as input medium. Alterations to programs were made offline and submitted for batch compilation. Tests were similarly conducted in batch mode and the results printed. Altogether, this was a very time consuming and non-productive procedure. IBM provided with TSO (Time Sharing Option) under the MVT (a forerunner to MVS) Operating System a significant improvement on systems operating. TSO, as the name says, was an option for time sharing. This enabled programmers to prepare and submit programs on their own terminals. TSO resulted in significant gains in productivity, however, only line-oriented terminal devices, or devices operating in this mode, were supported. Around the mid-1970s visual display devices, which supported screen-oriented processing, were starting to become popular. IBM responded to this trend by announcing SPF.

SPF (Structured Programming Facility), as the acronym implies, was originally released as a dialogue package for program development. The "structured" being derived from the powerful editor which supported several commands for structuring source text. In addition, SPF offered full-screen support for the program development environment. Although SPF was only available as a complete package, dialogue applications were developed using the dialogue support functions.

```
┌─────────────────────────────────────────┐
│                    SPF                   │
│       STRUCTURED PROGRAMMING FACILITY    │
└─────────────────────────────────────────┘
```

In 1981 these dialogue support functions were officially released as the Dialog Manager; the original SPF becoming the Program Development Facility (PDF), both packages being part of the Interactive System Productivity Facility (ISPF).

```
┌─────────────────────────────────────────┐
│                   ISPF                   │
│     INTERACTIVE SYSTEM PRODUCTIVITY FACILITY │
├──────────────────────┬──────────────────┤
│   DIALOG MANAGER     │  PROGRAM         │
│                      │  DEVELOPMENT     │
│                      │  FACILITY        │
└──────────────────────┴──────────────────┘
```

In 1982 Dialog Manager and Program Development Facility became two separate packages, with Dialog Manager being part of ISPF and PDF running as an application of ISPF. Indeed, Dialog Manager and ISPF have become synonymous. Most literature, this book included, uses ISPF to refer to the Dialog Manager components.

Version 3 brought limited workstation-like functionality in the form of pop-up windows and pull-down menus. The DTL (Dialog Tag Language) was introduced as an alternative means of creating dialogue panels.

Version 4 provided a GUI (Graphical User Interface) that permitted a simple porting of the user-interface for mainframe applications to a workstation. ISPF and ISPF/PDF were recombined to form a single product, ISPF. However, ISPF/PDF is still usually considered to be the program development interface (editor, compilation dialogue, etc.). With the exception of the Dialog Manager Test Facility, this book restricts itself to the programming interfaces.

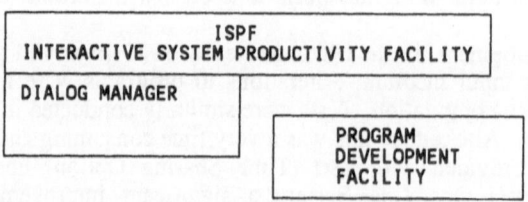

To summarise, Dialog Manager (ISPF) is a vehicle for implementing dialogue applications. One such application is PDF, which itself can be used as a tool in the development of dialogue applications.

1.2 GENERAL APPLICATION AREA

ISPF is primarily used for the implementation of decentralised dialogue applications. A decentralised application is self contained and executed in the user's own address space, in this case, TSO region. Such applications are normally used by a limited number of people. Applications using ISPF are characterised by the ease with which they can be implemented. The use of ISPF is especially appropriate for personal dialogue systems, although many ISPF applications have been successfully implemented for large numbers of users.

In general, ISPF is a dialogue management system best suited to the implementation of individual (personal) dialogue systems and those systems which are required to run from the TSO/ISPF environment. ISPF is also ideally suited for prototyping.

ISPF offers two interfaces:

·   an interpretive interface;
·   a programming interface.

The interpretive interface is used by command procedures (REXX execs or CLISTs).

The programming interface is used from conventional programming languages:

·   Assembler
·   C/370
·   COBOL
·   FORTRAN
·   Pascal
·   PL/I.

1.3 COMPARISON WITH OTHER DIALOGUE SYSTEMS

As mentioned previously, ISPF is a decentralised system with each user being responsible for his dialogue application. However, this responsibility can be transferred to a central authority for general applications. IBM products such as CICS (Customer Information Control System) and DB2 are by comparison centralised (dedicated) systems and require a Data Administrator for their supervision. This central authority has both advantages and disadvantages.

Centralised systems have as an advantage the improved control of resources and the simplified passing of information between users of the system. The price for this efficiency is normally paid for by the complexity of implementing such applications and the bureaucratic overhead necessary to define the system environment. Figure 1.1 shows the differences between centralised and decentralised systems.

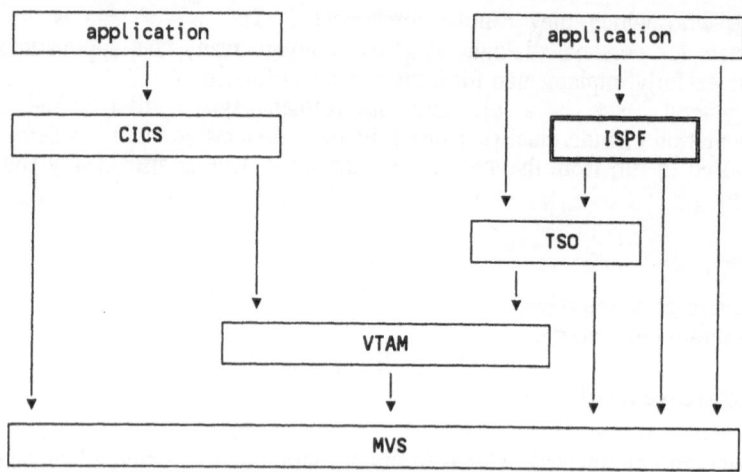

Figure 1.1 - Comparative dialogue systems and their interaction with the operating system

1.4 THE FUTURE OF ISPF

In 1987 IBM announced the concept of Systems Application Architecture (SAA) as its future strategy. In simple terms, SAA aims to present a common interface, independent of the operating environment (hardware and software), to the user. User is not restricted to being the end-user, but also includes the application developer. The SAA definition of the interface for dialogue applications is contained in the Common Programming Interface (CPI). And CPI Dialog Interface is essentially ISPF. Furthermore, many important IBM products (e.g. QMF) themselves use ISPF as an interface.

ISPF Version 4 has brought major changes to the functionality of ISPF by introducing client/server components. These very significant changes signal IBM's continuing commitment to the product.

2

General Concepts

2.1 DEFINITION OF DATA PROCESSING

Data processing is, according to an IBM definition, the systematic execution of operations on data.

And what are data? **Data** are a representation of information in a formalised manner suitable for processing. Thus each concept of data and processing is defined in terms of the other concept, and, as such, of limited use. However, a clear appreciation of the concept of data (and its processing) is a prerequisite for understanding this book.

The concept of data can best be described empirically with an example. The value "90210" is only useful, and as such represents data, when it is associated with a meaning (e.g. post code, salary). This pragmatic definition of data, **value with an associated meaning**, will be used in this book.

Conventional (batch) data processing defines data items implicitly by means of their position and length in a record. Such a data item has no global identifier and each processing program may refer to data items as it pleases. This, naturally, has repercussions for data consistency and maintenance. If the length or position of a data item in a record changes, then all programs using the data item must be changed.

More modern data processing systems (e.g. data base systems) define data items and their characteristics globally in an external index or data dictionary.

ISPF adopts a compromise by using global names for data elements, known as **variables**, but without having a central index. ISPF is primarily concerned with the management of variables at the elementary and aggregate level. Aggregates of variables constitute records in batch data processing and the various dialogue components in the ISPF environment. ISPF is responsible for the processing of these components.

2.2 DEFINITION OF DIALOGUE

A **dialogue**, in the data processing sense, is the interaction of a person (user) with an application currently being executed on the computer.

2.3 DIALOGUE COMPONENTS

It will now be shown how ISPF components are used in a dialogue application.

As stated previously, a dialogue, in the data processing sense, is the interaction of a person with an application currently being executed on the computer. On modern computer systems, this interaction takes place using a visual display unit (VDU) as **output device** and a keyboard (light pen, mouse, etc.) as **input device**. Obviously, the user does not input data blind but in response to a request. This request in the ISPF context is in the form of a **panel** display. A panel is the formatted description of the display (layout, processing to be performed before the panel is displayed, processing to be performed after the panel is displayed, etc.). As in batch processing, the panel layout consists of fields. Field content may be either fixed or variable. Fixed fields are **text** fields; variable fields are either **input** or **output** (output fields are **protected** against being altered). Each field is prefixed by an **attribute character** which specifies the field's characteristics. A unique variable name identifies input and output fields.

The following figure depicts a simple panel as it is displayed. The following convention has been adopted:

italics	output fields
underscore	input fields
other	text fields.

```
----- PERSONNEL INFORMATION SYSTEM ----- 12:08

PERSONNEL-NO. ===> _____
SURNAME       ===> _____
```

Note: The input fields are shown as being empty, they could, however, have contained predefined data.

Panel definitions are contained in the **panel library**. A panel library is a partitioned data set allocated to the **panel file** (ISPPLIB). The **panel name** is the **member name** in the library. The values of the variables specified for input and output fields are automatically fetched from a **variable pool** prior to the panel being displayed. There are three hierarchies of variable pools: **function pool**, local data; **shared pool**, data to be retained during the current ISPF session; **profile data**, data to be retained across ISPF sessions.

A panel is displayed on the terminal using an ISPF display service (DISPLAY, SELECT PANEL, TBDISPL) as depicted in the following schematic diagram:

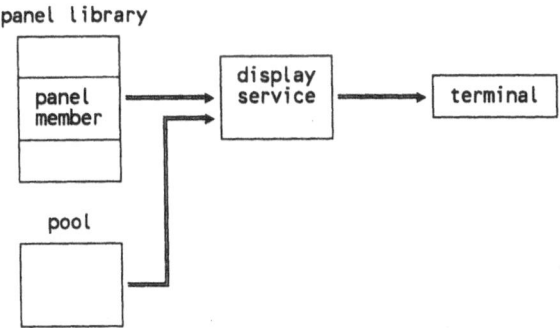

Panel definitions are entered into the panel library using a standard text editor (e.g. ISPF/PDF EDIT) or SDF2. SDF2 has the advantage that the panels can be easily transferred to other systems supported by it (e.g. CICS), but does not support all ISPF features. If SDF2 is not used, either native statements or DTL (Dialog Tag Language) can be used for the panel definitions. The dialogue elements are described in detail in this book. DTL permits a higher-level, platform-independent definition for panels, which had more significance when there was an OS/2 implementation of Dialog Manager; Section 2.4 provides a more detailed introduction to DTL.

Subsequent processing of panels can be optimised by using a special ISPF utility program to **preprocess** the panels.

Input data may be entered into input fields. The data are automatically transferred to the function pool. The panel definition can specify processing to be performed before control is returned to the point of invocation. Typically the input is formally validated, a re-input can be forced by issuing an error **message**.

Messages are grouped together as members of the **message library**. The message library is a partitioned data set allocated to the **message file** (ISPMLIB). A message definition may have up to three levels of information: short text, which is displayed initially; long text, which is displayed in response to pressing the help key; a tutorial, which is displayed in response to the further pressing of the help key.

ISPF uses **tables** as principal storage medium. A table is a two dimensional array. The columns are variable names and the rows contain the corresponding values. Two table forms exist: **temporary** and **permanent**. Temporary tables contain working data and exist only in main storage, permanent tables exist as members of a **table library**. Data for our sample panel could be stored according to the following scheme:

PNO	SURNAME	
1234	ALPHA	column names
2456	BETA	column data

Although dialogue systems use the terminal as the standard output device, there is often the need to produce "normal" output files. ISPF uses the concept of **file tailoring** to generate parameterised output files (reports, job control statements, etc.). File tailoring uses **skeletons** (members of the **skeleton library**) as input. A skeleton consists of control statements and data. Control statements can specify table input, conditional processing, etc. Both data and control statements may make use of dialogue variables.

These items are the principal ISPF components. The question now arises: how are these various components put together to form a practical **application**? Command procedures (REXX execs or CLISTs) provide the necessary dialogue environment for ISPF. The various ISPF services can either be directly invoked from a command procedure (ISPEXEC is the command procedure interface to ISPF) or from a program or a **selection panel** (also known as menu) which has been initiated from a command procedure (ISPLINK is the program interface to ISPF). command procedures, programs or selection panels directly invoked using ISPF services are known as **functions** and have their own function pool for local variables. A function may invoke further functions. An application is an aggregate of one or more functions.

The members, except tables and load modules, are entered into the libraries using a standard editor program. Tables are created and maintained using ISPF services. Load modules are stored with the Linkage Editor (or Binder). The standard file names for each component type are listed in the following list:

ISPPLIB	panel library
ISPMLIB	message library
ISPSLIB	skeleton (input) library
ISPTLIB	table (input) library
ISPTABL	table (output) library
ISPFILE	file tailoring output file
ISPPLIB	load module library

SYSPROC (CLISTs) and SYSEXEC (REXX execs) are not explicit ISPF libraries, but normally are required for Dialog Manager applications.

These libraries are either preallocated (static definition) before ISPF is invoked or allocated by the application itself (dynamic definition). The application-oriented allocations, using the LIBDEF service described in the next chapter, may use non-standard file names.

Figure 2.1 shows the schematic interaction of the various ISPF components. —>> represents explicit data flow; —> represents implicit data flow. ISPXXXX (SYSPROC) is the standard file name for the library.

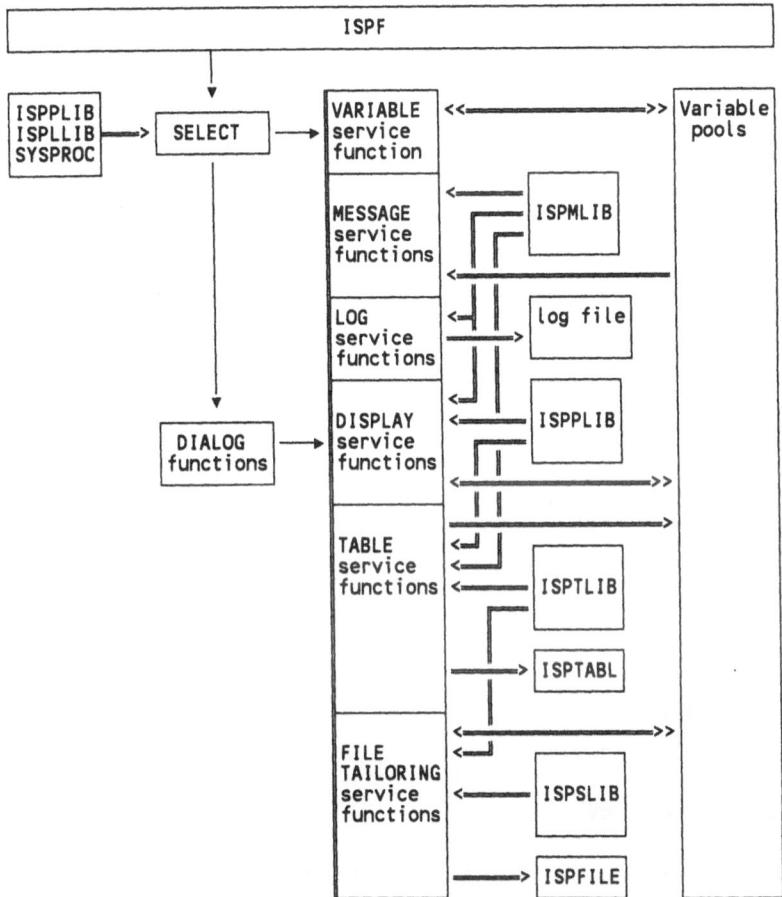

Figure 2.1 - Schematic interaction of ISPF components

2.4 INTRODUCTION TO DTL

DTL differs in several aspects from the dialogue elements described in detail in this book. Whereas the dialogue elements define individual panels, etc., DTL is more suited to define the panels in an application (or part of an application). DTL offers more flexibility, for example with regard to panel layout. DTL also can define those elements that are directly related with panel processing, for example, the preliminary command processing. For small applications, the additional overhead required to define the application environment (e.g. variable classes) may not be warranted.

3

Invocation

3.1 INTRODUCTION

An ISPF **application** consists of one or more functions. An ISPF **function** is a
program, command procedure or selection panel which has been invoked using an
ISPF service. Such functions may use ISPF services (e.g. display a panel), invoke
host environment services (e.g. TSO commands) or invoke a further function. The
method of invoking an ISPF function depends on whether the function is being
called from within the ISPF environment. Although ISPF usually runs as a dialogue
application, it can operate in batch provided no interaction is required.

3.2 INVOCATION SERVICES

ISPF provides two means of invoking an ISPF function:

· ISPSTART   Initiate the ISPF environment and invoke the function.
· SELECT   Invoke the function.

ISPSTART is a command procedure statement. ISPSTART must be used to initiate the
ISPF environment. From within the ISPF environment, SELECT can be invoked to
start another ISPF application. SELECT may be invoked from a selection panel,
program or command procedure.

3.2.1 ISPSTART - Initiate ISPF Environment and Invoke Function

ISPF is invoked and control passed to the specified function (application). Optionally, the application can be invoked in GUI (graphical user interface) mode.

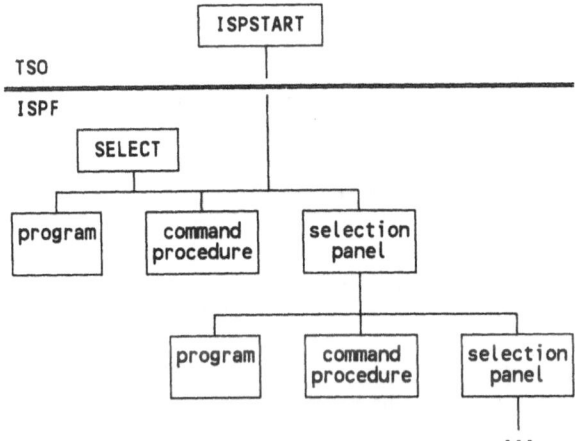

Figure 3.1 - Invocation of an application

Syntax:
```
ISPSTART
       ( PANEL(panelname) [OPT(option)]}
       ( CMD(command [parameter] ...]) [LANG(APL|CREX)]}
       ( PGM(programname) [PARM(parameter)]        }
       [NEWAPPL[applicationid | ISP )]]
       [TEST | TESTX | TRACE | TRACEX]
       [GUI(LU:display|IP:display)] [TITLE(title)]
       [GUISCRW(width)]
       [GUISCRD(depth)]
       [FRAME(STD|FIX|DLG)]
       [NOLOGO|LOGO(logopanelname)]
       [BATSCRW(width)]
       [BATSCRD(depth)]
       [BDISPMAX(maxdisplays)]
       [BREDIMAX(maxredisplays)]
       [DANISH|ENGLISH|GERMAN|JAPANESE|PORTUGUE|SPANISH|
       KOREAN|FRENCH|ITALIAN|CHINESET|CHINESES|SGERMAN]
```

PANEL(panelname)
> Invoke the selection panel **panelname**.

OPT(option)
> The **option** is passed as initial option; this option is processed as if it had been entered manually, however, the panel is not displayed.

Example:
```
ISPSTART PANEL(SPAN000) OPT(2)
```
This statement initiates ISPF and invokes the SPAN000 selection panel with option 2.

CMD(command [parameter]...)

The **command** is the name of the command processor to be invoked. Any specified **parameters** are passed to it. A command processor is a special program stored in the assigned program load library.

LANG(APL|CREX)

APL: The APL2 environment is to be initiated.

CREX: A compiled REXX procedure is to be initiated. This parameter does not apply for (the usual) interpreted REXX procedures.

Example:
```
ISPSTART CMD(%XCMD ALPHA BETA)
```
This statement initiates ISPF and invokes the command procedure XCMD with two parameters: ALPHA and BETA; the % appended to the command name ensures that only a member of the command library is invoked and that the load libraries allocated to the ISPLLIB file are not searched (reduced overhead).

PGM(programname)

Load the program with the name **programname** from the program library and pass control to it.

PARM(parameter)

Pass **parameter** to the program.

Note: The parameter is passed to the program in the form of an "EXEC PARAMETER", i.e. a character string preceded by a halfword containing the length of the following parameter.

Example:
```
ISPSTART PGM(PGM00) PARM(ALPHA BETA)
```
Initiate ISPF and invoke the program PGM00 with the parameter ALPHA BETA. The parameter has the form:

| 10 | ALPHA BETA |

NEWAPPL(applicationid)

The application is assigned the **applicationid**. The following profile members and command table are assigned to the application:

user profile	*aaaa*PROF
Edit profile	*aaaa*EDIT
command table	*aaaa*CMDS

aaaa is the **applicationid**. Default: ISP.

Note: The user profile contains variables explicitly stored there using the VPUT service with the PROFILE parameter. The edit profile contains various settings used by the ISPF/PDF editor. The command table (see Chapter 13) specifies how commands are to be interpreted.

TEST

ISPF is to operate in TEST mode:

The current panel and message definitions are always re-fetched from the library. In normal mode the addresses of the definitions in the library are stored in a resident table and these addresses are only updated when ISPF is exited and the members subsequently accessed;
Help panels are displayed with current panel name, previous panel name and the previous message id in the bottom line of the display;
Screen print-outs include line numbers, panel name and message id.

Note: Chapter 20 contains a detailed description of debugging facilities.

TESTX

ISPF is to operate in extended TEST mode. **Extended TEST mode** is the same as TEST mode, except messages written to the ISPF log file are also displayed on the terminal.

TRACE

ISPF is to operate in TRACE mode. TRACE mode operates as TEST mode except a message is written to the ISPF log file for every ISPEXEC service requested.

TRACEX

ISPF is to operate in extended TRACE mode. **Extended TRACE mode** is the same as TRACE mode except messages written to the ISPF log file are also displayed on the terminal.

GUI(LU:display | IP:display)

The GUI keyword specifies that application is to be invoked with the graphical user interface.

LU:display

Display is the workstation's APPC network name.

IP:display)

Display is the workstation's TCP/IP hardware-level IP address.

TITLE(title)

Title is the text (truncated to 255 characters) to be displayed in the title bar. If ZWINTTL or ZAPPTTL is non-blank, they take precedence.

GUISCRW(width)

Width is the display width that overrides the screen width.

GUISCRD(depth)

Depth is the display depth that overrides the screen depth.

FRAME(STD|FIX|DLG)

The form of the first window frame that is displayed.

STD: Standard. A GUI window can be resized.

FIX: Fixed. A GUI window cannot be resized, but has max/min buttons.

DLG: Dialogue. A GUI window cannot be resized and does not have max/min buttons. Pop-up panels are always displayed in dialogue frames.

NOLOGO|LOGO(logopanelname)

The LOGO keyword specifies the logo panel that is displayed when the application is initiated.

BATSCRW(width|80)

Width is the batch mode screen width.

BATSCRD(depth|32)

Depth is the batch mode screen depth.

BDISPMAX(maxdisplays|100)

Maxdisplays the maximum of displays in the batch session.

BREDIMAX(maxredisplays|2)

Maxredisplays the maximum of redisplays for a .MSG-redisplay loop in a batch session.

DANISH|ENGLISH|GERMAN|JAPANESE|PORTUGUE|SPANISH|KOREAN|FRENCH|ITALIAN|CHINESET|CHINESES|SGERMAN

The language that is to override the session language.

The service always sets the return code to 0.

3.2.2 SELECT - Invoke Function

The specified function (application) is invoked. The function may be a hierarchy of selection panels (menus), a program or a command procedure. A new function pool is created, the significance of the function pool is discussed in Chapter 6.

Syntax:
```
ISPEXEC SELECT
        { PANEL(panelname) [OPT(option)] [ADDPOP] }
        { CMD(command [parameter] ...])
                       [LANG(APL|CREX))]
                       [MODE(LINE|FSCR)]
                       [BARRIER]
                       [NEST]                        }
        { PGM(programname) [PARM(parameter)]
                       [MODE(LINE|FSCR)]              }
        {([NEWAPPL[applicationid|ISP]] [PASSLIB]} | [NEWPOOL]} [SUSPEND]
```

PANEL(panelname)

Invoke the selection panel **panelname**.

OPT(option)

Pass **option** as initial option. This option is processed as if it had been entered manually. However, the panel is not displayed.

ADDPOP

The panel displayed with the SELECT service is displayed in a window. A corresponding REMPOP is performed automatically at the end of the display.

Example:
```
ISPEXEC SELECT PANEL(PAN000) OPT(2)
```
Invoke the selection panel PAN000 with option 2.

CMD(command [parameter]...)

The **command** is the name of the command processor to be invoked. Any specified **parameters** are passed to it.

LANG(APL)

Initiate the APL2 environment.

LANG(CREX)

The command is a compiled REXX procedure.

MODE(LINE)

Line mode is to be entered when a command or program function is selected.

MODE(FSCR)

Full-screen mode is to be entered when a command or program function is selected.

BARRIER

Commands are not pulled from the REXX data when the command invoked with the SELECT service terminates.

NEST

Commands invoked with the SELECT service will be nested.

Example:
```
ISPEXEC SELECT CMD(%XCMD ALPHA BETA)
```
Invoke the command procedure XCMD with two parameters: ALPHA and BETA. The % prefixed to the command name ensures that only a member of the command procedure library is invoked.

PGM(programname)

Load the program with the name **programname** from the program library and pass control to it.

PARM(parameter)

The **parameter** to be passed to the program.

Note: The parameter is passed to the program in the form of an "EXEC PARAMETER", i.e. a character string preceded by a halfword containing the length of the following parameter.

Example:
```
ISPEXEC SELECT PGM(PGM00) PARM(ALPHA BETA)
```
Invoke the program PGM00 with the parameter ALPHA BETA. The parameter has the following form:

| 10 | ALPHA BETA |

NEWAPPL(applicationid)

The application is assigned the **applicationid**. The following profile members and command table are assigned to the application:

user profile	*aaaa*PROF
Edit profile	*aaaa*EDIT
command table	*aaaa*CMDS

aaaa is the **applicationid**. Default: ISP.

Note: If the NEWAPPL keyword is not specified, the current application-id is retained.

NEWPOOL

A new shared pool is to be created. The current shared pool is restored on completion of the function.

PASSLIB

Pass any application-level ISPF libraries to the selected application.

SUSPEND

All pop-up winds in the logical screen are removed from the display.

The SELECT service sets one of the following return codes:

0	Normal completion; the function was terminated with END.
4	Normal completion; the function was terminated with RETURN or EXIT.
12	The specified panel could not be found.
16	Truncation error in storing a variable.
20	Severe error; e.g. program could not be found, command procedure could not be found.

3.3 MISCELLANEOUS ENVIRONMENTAL SERVICES

A number of ISPF services are available to set environmental attributes for applications. These services are:

- CONTROL   Set processing modes
- LIBDEF   Allocate application libraries
- LIST   Write data to ISPF list dataset
- LOG   Write message to ISPF the log dataset
- QLIBDEF   Query LIBDEF information.

The LOG service is described in Chapter 6.

3.3.1 CONTROL - Set Processing Modes

The CONTROL service sets processing options for the dialogue environment.

Syntax:
```
ISPEXEC CONTROL
        [ DISPLAY ( LOCK )
                  ( LINE [START(linenumber)] )
                  ( SM [START(linenumber)] )
                  ( REFRESH )
                  ( SAVE | RESTORE ) ]
        [ NONDISPL [ ENTER | END ] ]
        [ ERRORS [ CANCEL | RETURN ] ]
        [ SPLIT ( ENABLE | DISABLE ) ]
        [ NOCMD ]
        [ SUBTASK ( PROTECT | CLEAR ) ]
```

DISPLAY LOCK
> The next display output will lock the keyboard. The displayed panel will be processed as if the ENTER key had been pressed.
>
> **Tip**
> DISPLAY LOCK is useful to inhibit input while long-running processing is in progress.

DISPLAY LINE [START(linenumber)]
> Terminal line-mode (e.g. TSO) output is expected. The screen is rewritten on the next display.
>
> **linenumber** is the line (line number 1 is the top line of the screen) where the line-mode output is to be placed.
>
> Default: The line after the end of the body display of the current panel.

DISPLAY SM [START(linenumber)]
> The screen display is to be controlled by the TSO Session Manager when the next line-mode output is made.

linenumber is the line (line number 1 is the top line of the screen) where the line-mode output is to be placed.

Default: The line after the end of the body display of the current panel.

DISPLAY REFRESH

ISPF will rewrite the whole screen for its next display. This parameter should be used after other products (e.g. GDDM graphics system) which perform full-screen formatting have been invoked. REFRESH is necessary because normally only the updated fields are rewritten to the screen.

DISPLAY SAVE

The control information pertaining to the current screen display is to be saved. This is necessary when the DISPLAY, TBDISPL, BROWSE or EDIT services are invoked from the current display.

DISPLAY RESTORE

The control information previously saved by DISPLAY SAVE is to be restored.

Note: CONTROL DISPLAY RESTORE without CONTROL DISPLAY SAVE causes an error condition. Similarly, SAVEs and RESTOREs must be paired, otherwise a subsequent RESTORE will restore incorrect control information.

NONDISPL [ENTER | END]

The next panel display request will not be displayed. ENTER specifies that the panel will be processed as if the ENTER key had been pressed; END specifies that the panel will be processed as if the END key had been pressed. Default: ENTER.

Tip
This option can be useful for performing validation processing in a (dummy) panel.

ERRORS [CANCEL | RETURN]

CANCEL specifies that errors resulting from service requests will cause cancellation of the function.
RETURN specifies that errors resulting from service requests will cause a return to the calling function.
Default: CANCEL.

Note: An error is signalled by a return code greater than or equal to 8.

Tip
The ERRORS setting is retained for the duration of the function, unless changed.

SPLIT ENABLE

Enable the split screen option. The enabling of split screens can have significant repercussions for the application, e.g. it is then possible to run the same application in the second screen with the result that datasets could be incorrectly allocated, etc. This option remains in effect until disabled.

Tip
If SPLIT ENABLE is enabled, then the application developer must take the appropriate precautions if his application is to be robust. Programs linked with the REUS option will cause an unlimited wait if they are invoked twice concurrently.

SPLIT DISABLE
Disable the split screen option. This option remains in effect until enabled.

NOCMD
In the next panel display, any command (or PF key) entered will not be processed. This option remains in effect for the redisplay of a panel.

SUBTASK {PROTECT|CLEAR}
These are specialised options and are not discussed here.

Note: The CONTROL service has many option combinations, some of which are mutually exclusive, e.g. CONTROL SPLIT ENABLE and CONTROL SPLIT DISABLE. Each CONTROL service invocation may only specify one option. If multiple options are required, then CONTROL must be invoked a number of times. Example:

```
ISPEXEC CONTROL NONDISPL ENTER
ISPEXEC CONTROL ERRORS RETURN
ISPEXEC CONTROL SPLIT DISABLE
```

The service sets one of the following return codes:

    0   Normal completion; the function was terminated with END.

    8   Screen display is currently in split mode but SPLIT DISABLE requested; screen remains in split mode.

  20   Severe error.

3.3.2 LIBDEF - Define Application Libraries

The LIBDEF service can be used to define ISPF libraries for a particular application.

ISPF supports two classes of libraries:

· Static library definitions made before ISPF is invoked - these include the standard IBM and installation libraries.
· Application-level library definitions made by the application itself - these definitions precede the static library definitions. If static library definitions are to precede the application-level library definitions, then the following file names must be used:

· ISPMUSR   user message library
· ISPPUSR   user panel library

- · ISPSUSR   user skeleton library
- · ISPTUSR   user table input library
- · ISPTABU   user table output library
- · ISPFILE   user file tailoring output library
- · ISPLUSR   user load module (program) library.

The LIBDEF service is used to allocate application-level libraries. Table 3.1 contains a summary of the search order.

Syntax:
```
ISPEXEC LIBDEF filename
        [ DATASET ID(datasetname [datasetname] ... )
          | LIBRARY ID(ddname)
          | EXCLDATA ID(datasetname [datasetname] ... )
          | EXCLLIBR ID(ddname)]
        [COND|UNCOND]
```

filename

The file name (DDname) for which the allocation is to be made. One of the following **filenames** may be specified:

- · ISPMLIB   message library
- · ISPPLIB   panel library
- · ISPSLIB   skeleton library
- · ISPTLIB   table input library
- · ISPTABL   table output library
- · ISPFILE   file tailoring output library
- · ISPLLIB   load module (program) library
- · libname   library name specified in LIBRARY parameter of table or file tailoring service.

If no further parameter is defined, then the application-level definition is removed.

Example:
```
ISPEXEC LIBDEF ISPPLIB
```
This statement removes the application-level definition for ISPPLIB.

DATASET ID(datasetname [datasetname] ...)

A concatenation of dataset names; a maximum of 15 dataset names may be listed.

Example:
```
ISPEXEC LIBDEF ISPPLIB DATASET ID('ISPF.ISPPLIB',USER.ISPPLIB)
```
This statement defines a concatenation of two datasets.

EXCLDATA ID(datasetname [datasetname] ...)

An **exclusive** concatenation of (load library) dataset names; a maximum of 15 dataset names may be listed. ISPF uses only those ISPLLIB-libraries explicitly defined in the concatenation.

Example:
```
ISPEXEC LIBDEF ISPLLIB EXCLDATA ID('ISPF.ISPLLIB',USER.ISPLLIB)
```
Define an exclusive concatenation of two datasets.

LIBRARY ID(ddname)

Ddname identifies the name of a previously allocated DD statement which defines the concatenated dataset names.

Example:
```
ALLOC FILE(ALPHA) DSN('ISPF.ISPPLIB',USER.ISPPLIB) SHR
  ...
ISPEXEC LIBDEF ISPPLIB LIBRARY(ALPHA)
```

The LIBDEF statement assigns the datasets allocated to file ALPHA as an ISPPLIB library.

EXCLLIBR ID(ddname)

The name of a previously allocated DD statement which defines the **exclusive** concatenated (load library) dataset names; ISPF uses only those ISPLLIB-libraries explicitly defined in the concatenation.

Example:
```
ALLOC FILE(BETA) DSN('ISPF.ISPLLIB',USER.ISPLLIB) SHR
  ...
ISPEXEC LIBDEF ISPLLIB EXCLLIBR(BETA)
```

The LIBDEF statement assigns the datasets allocated to file BETA as an exclusive ISPPLIB library.

COND

The application-level library is to be **conditionally** defined, i.e. only when no application-level library of this type currently exists.

UNCOND

The application-level library is to be **unconditionally** defined.
Default: UNCOND.

The service sets one of the following return codes:

- 0   Normal completion.
- 4   No application-level definition of this type exists.
- 8   An application-level definition of this type already exists; COND specified.
- 12   Invalid **filename**.
- 16   **Ddname** not allocated or invalid **datasetname**.
- 20   Severe error.

Table 3.1 - Library search order

	LIBDEF				no LIBDEF
	EXCLDATA	EXCLLIBR	DATASET	LIBRARY	
Panels	-	-	ISPPUSR libdef ISPPLIB	libdef ISPPLIB	ISPPLIB
Messages	-	-	ISPMUSR libdef ISPMLIB	libdef ISPMLIB	ISPMLIB
Table Input	-	-	ISPTUSR libdef ISPTLIB	libdef ISPTLIB	ISPTLIB
Table Output	-	-	ISPTABU libdef	libdef	ISPTABL
File Tailoring Output	-	-	ISPFILU libdef	libdef	ISPFILE
Table Services Input LIBRARY	-	-	library* libdef	libdef library*	library*
Table Services Output LIBRARY	-	-	library* libdef	libdef	library*
File Tailoring Output LIBRARY	-	-	library* libdef	libdef	library*
Programs	JPA* libdef LPA* LINKLIB	JPA* libdef LPA* LINKLIB	JPA* ISPLUSR libdef ISPLLIB STEPLIB LPA* LINKLIB	JPA* libdef ISPLLIB STEPLIB LPA* LINKLIB	JPA* ISPLLIB STEPLIB LPA* LINKLIB

```
        - = invalid
     JPA* = Job Pack Area
     LPA* = Link Pack Area
 library* = allocated library
```

3.3.3 LIST - Write Data Lines to ISPF List Dataset

The LIST service writes to specified data lines to the list dataset assigned to ISPF. The data lines are specified as dialogue variables.

Syntax:
```
ISPEXEC LIST BUFNAME(variablename) LINELEN(linelength)
        [PAGE]
        [SINGLE|DOUBLE|TRIPLE]
        [OVERSTRK]
        [CC]
```

BUFNAME(variablename)
> **variablename** specifies the name of the dialogue variable that contains the data to be passed to the list dataset.

LINELEN(linelength)
> **linelength** specifies the length of the data to be passed to the list dataset.

PAGE
> The first data line for this service request is written to the list dataset preceded by the page skip print control character.
>
> This parameter is ignored if the CC parameter is specified.
>
> **Tip**
> The first entry into a new list dataset always forces a page skip, unless the CC parameter has been specified. However, the ISPF list dataset may be used by other applications (e.g. PDF) and so it is recommended that applications always sets either the PAGE or CC ('1') parameter for the first output line.

SINGLE
> The data lines are written to the list dataset preceded by the single space print control character.

DOUBLE
> The data lines are written to the list dataset preceded by the double space print control character.

TRIPLE
> The data lines are written to the list dataset preceded by the triple space print control character.
>
> Default: SINGLE.
>
> The SINGLE, DOUBLE or TRIPLE parameter is ignored if the CC parameter is specified.

OVERSTRK

The data line is to be written using overstrikes, i.e. the data line is highlighted.

This parameter is ignored if the cc parameter is specified.

CC

The first character of the dialogue variable written as data line is a print control character.

This parameter overrides any PAGE, SINGLE, DOUBLE, TRIPLE or OVERSTRK parameter specified for this service request.

Note: The length specified by the LINELEN operand must include a count of one for the control character.

Note: The following system variables can be referenced (but not modified):

ZLSTNUML   number of lines that have written to the current page;
ZLSTLPP   maximum number of lines that may be written on a page.

The service sets one of the following return codes:

    0   Normal completion; the function was terminated with END.
    8   Maximum record length for the list dataset exceeded; data truncated.
  12   Specified dialogue variable not found.
  20   Severe error.

Example:
```
SET &ALPHA = &STR(SAMPLE OUTPUT LINE)
SET &L = &LENGTH(&STR(&ALPHA))
ISPEXEC LIST BUFNAME(ALPHA) LINELEN(&L)
```
This command procedure writes the text SAMPLE OUTPUT LINE with single spacing (default) into the ISPF list dataset.

3.3.4 LOG - Write a Message to the ISPF Log Dataset

The LOG service writes the short and long message text for the specified message identifier to the log data set defined for ISPF. The message is prefixed with the current time. Substitutions are performed for any symbolic variables in the message text.

Syntax:
```
ISPEXEC LOG MSG(messageid)
```

MSG(messageid)

messageid identifies the message for which the information is to be retrieved.

The service sets one of the following return codes:

  0 Normal completion.

  12 No message for the specified message identifier is contained in the message library.

  20 Severe error.

Example:
```
ISPEXEC LOG MSG(TSSPF002)
```

If the TSSPF002 massage has the following definition:

```
┌─ message TSSPF002 ──────────────────────────────────┐
│ TSSPF002 'empno. &PNO missing' .HELP=&H .ALARM=&A    │
│ 'employee no. &PNO not defined'                      │
└─────────────────────────────────────────────────────┘
```

Then the text "empno. &PNO missing" and "employee no. &PNO not defined", where &PNO is replaced by the current value for the variable, are written to the ISPF log dataset.

3.3.5 QLIBDEF — Query LIBDEF Information

The QLIBDEF service returns the current LIBDEF definition information.

Syntax:
```
ISPEXEC QLIBDEF libtype [TYPE(typevar)] [ID(idvar)]

CALL ISPLINK ('QLIBDEF ',libtype,[,typevar][,idvar])
```

libtype
> The LIBDEF type to be queried: ISPPLIB, ISPMLIB, ISPSLIB, ISPTLIB, ISPLLIB, ISPTABL, ISPFILE, or a generic name.

typevar
> The (optional) name of the dialog variable that the QLIBDEF service sets to contain the type of the corresponding LIBDEF definition. One of the following values is returned: DATASET, EXCLDATA, LIBRARY or EXCLLIBR. The variable is set only if a corresponding LIBDEF exists.

idvar
> The (optional) name of the dialog variable that the QLIBDEF service sets to contain the identifier of the associated file (DDname) or dataset. Dataset names are returned fully qualified. Multiple dataset names are returned separated by a comma. The variable is set only if a corresponding LIBDEF exists.

The service sets one of the following return codes:

    0   Successful processing.

    4   No associated LIBDEF definition.

   12   Invalid libtype.

   16   Truncation.

   20   Severe error.

Example:
```
/* REXX */
ADDRESS ISPEXEC
"LIBDEF ISPTABL DATASET ID(user.isptlib)"
...
"QLIBDEF ISPTABL TYPE(vt) ID(vid)"
SAY RC vt /* DATASET */
SAY RC vid /* 'userid.USER.ISPTLIB' */
```
Where **userid** is replaced by the current user-id.

3.4 ISPF SERVICE INVOCATION

ISPF services are invoked from within the ISPF environment that the ISPSTART command initiated. The ISPF services can be invoked directly from a command procedure or from a program.

- A CLIST procedure uses the ISPEXEC command to invoke a service. For example, ISPEXEC DISPLAY PANEL(TXPAN).
- A REXX exec invokes a service from the ISPEXEC environment. For example, ADDRESS ISPEXEC "DISPLAY PANEL(TXPAN)". The REXX exec can set a global environment, for example, ADDRESS ISPEXEC; "DISPLAY PANEL(TXPAN)";. It is more efficient to set the environment globally.

3.4.1 Error Message Variables

If the ISPF services set an error condition (return code greater than 8), the following system variables contain further information on the cause of the error:

ZERRALRM Alarm indicator: YES or NO.

ZERRHM   The name of the associated help panel.

ZERRLM   Long message.

ZERRMSG   Message-id.

ZERRSM   Short message.

Note: By default, ISPF handles errors by displaying an error message panel and terminating the application. If the application is to handle errors, it must use the CONTROL ERRORS RETURN service to get control. The worked example in Section 17.4 shows an example of error processing.

Example:
```
ADDRESS ISPEXEC
"LMINIT DATAID(did) DATASET(my.file) ENQ(SHR)"
IF rc > 0 THEN SAY ZERRLM /* if error, display long msg */
```

3.5 BATCH INVOCATION

ISPF services can operate in batch TSO. Batch invocation can be appropriate in the following circumstances:

· No interaction required, although interactive services (e.g. DISPLAY) can be used if any required input is supplied by the application.
· Long running application.
· Printed report required (although ISPF listing services also can be used to produce a report).

GDDM services cannot be invoked in batch. Batch TSO is invoked with the Terminal Monitor Program (by default IKJEFT01). The batch TSO job must allocate the required TSO and ISPF libraries with the appropriate DD statements. As usual, the ISPSTART command (in the SYSTSIN input data stream) initiates ISPF. The TSO PROFILE command can be used to assign the userid.

3.5.1 Panel Input in Batch

When an ISPF application runs in batch, any panel displays must either be suppressed (with CONTROL NONDISPL END) or the END condition simulated (by setting the .RESP control variable or the panel command field to END). Any input that normally would have been made to the displayed panel must be made by setting the appropriate dialog variables.

3.5.2 Sample Batch JCL

```
//TSOSTEP  EXEC PGM=IKJEFT01
//STEPLIB  DD   DSN=...,DISP=SHR
//SYSHELP  DD   DSN=SYS1.HELP,DISP=SHR
//SYSPROC  DD   DSN=...,DISP=SHR
//ISPTLIB  DD   DSN=...,DISP=SHR
//ISPTABL  DD   DSN=...,DISP=SHR
//ISPPLIB  DD   DSN=...,DISP=SHR
//ISPMLIB  DD   DSN=...,DISP=SHR
//ISPSLIB  DD   DSN=...,DISP=SHR
//ISPLIST  DD   SYSOUT=A,DCB=(BLKSIZE=1210,RECFM=FBA,LRECL=121)
//ISPLOG   DD   ...
//ISPPROF  DD   DSN=...,DISP=SHR
//SYSUADS  DD   DSN=SYS1.UADS,DISP=SHR
//SYSTSPRT DD   SYSOUT=A
//SYSLBC   DD   DSN=SYS1.BRODCAST,DISP=SHR
//* application program files
//SYSTSIN  DD   *
 PROFILE PREFIX(BATUSER)
 ISPSTART CMD(%LM02) NEWAPPL(XYZ)
 END
```

Note: The ISPPROF dataset must be available for exclusive use.

4

Command Procedures

4.1 INTRODUCTION

A **command procedure** is a sequence (list) of commands and subcommands together with control statements. Command procedures were written originally as CLISTs (command lists), but which have been largely superseded by REXX execs. Command procedures usually are interpreted, although a REXX compiler is now available. Although such a command procedure is not strictly an ISPF component, there are very few ISPF applications which do not use command procedures. Similarly, basic TSO commands for file allocation, invocation of procedures, etc. are required in many ISPF applications. As such, a basic knowledge of command procedures and TSO commands is a prerequisite for writing ISPF applications. This chapter briefly discusses command procedure concepts and syntax; the appropriate reference manual should be consulted for more detailed information.

A command procedure is the natural language for implementing ISPF applications, especially at the prototype level (certain high-performance applications may have to be written using program calls). The ISPEXEC command provides the command procedure interface to ISPF. The command procedure language can be classified as being a high-level language combining TSO commands and subcommands with ISPF services. With exception of the "Program Environment" (Chapter 14), all examples in this book are described in REXX syntax.

4.2 CLIST FEATURES

The CLIST language has the following features:

· use of variables (an ampersand (&) prefixes CLIST variables, other than target variables)
· logical operations
· arithmetic operations
· commands to support structured programming constructions
· elementary file processing
· built-in functions (primarily concerned with basic string processing)
· direct interface to ISPF (common variable pool).

4.2.1 CLIST Syntax Summary

The following items summarise the CLIST syntax:

· A CLIST is a physical sequential dataset or a member of a partitioned dataset. By default, the SYSPROC file specifies the CLIST library.

· CLIST statements have a free format.

· A line may contain only one CLIST statement.

· A CLIST statement may be continued onto the following line(s) with a minus ("-") or plus ("+") as the last character of the line to be continued. The plus ignores leading blanks on the continued line.

· Comments are defined by the two character pairs "/*" and "*/", example: /* this is a comment */. The terminal "*/" is necessary only for comments embedded within a statement.

· Every CLIST statement sets the return code (in the LASTCC variable). Statements used to invoke programs and command procedures set the return code passed back from the invoked component.

· CLIST statements may be written in either lowercase or uppercase, with the exception of control statement operations which must be written in uppercase.

Example:
```
SET &pn = PANO1
ISPEXEC DISPLAY PANEL(&pn)
```

4.3 REXX FEATURES

Although REXX has many similarities with CLIST, it is much more powerful and not restricted to being used for procedures — REXX can be used for many general programming tasks.

The following items summarise the most important REXX features.

·   use of variables
·   logical operations
·   arithmetic operations
·   commands to support structured programming constructions
·   elementary file processing
·   large library of built-in functions (primarily concerned with string processing)
·   host environments (e.g., TSO, ISPEXEC)
·   external functions
·   extendibility (third-party (or user-written) host environments and external functions)
·   REXX and ISPF have a common variable pool.

4.3.1 REXX Syntax Summary

The following items summarise the REXX syntax:

·   A REXX procedure (exec) is a physical sequential dataset or a member of a partitioned dataset. By default, the SYSEXEC file specifies the REXX library. Any REXX procedures contained in the CLIST library must be identified as such with a REXX comment (i.e. a comment that contains the word REXX) as the first statement.

·   REXX statements have a free format.

·   A REXX statement can be either implicitly or explicitly continued onto the following line. Implicit continuation arises from the statement syntax (for example, an IF clause must be followed by a THEN clause). A comma (,) specifies explicit continuation.

·   Comments are defined by the two character pairs "/*" and "*/", example: /* this is a comment */. Comments can be nested.

·   Any statement that is not recognised as being a REXX instruction or comment is passed as a command to the current host environment. Commands set the return code (in the RC special variable).

·   REXX statements may be written in either lowercase or uppercase, with the exception of control statement operations which must be written in uppercase.

·   Although a REXX variable has by default its (uppercase) name as content, this feature should not be used; literals should be written expressly as such (within single or double quotes).

Example:
```
pn = 'PAN01'
ADDRESS ISPEXEC 'DISPLAY PANEL('pn')'
```

4.4 TSO COMMANDS

From the large number of TSO commands, only the following are of particular relevance for ISPF applications:

- ALLOC   Allocate dataset or DD statement (file)
- CALL   Execute program
- EXEC   Execute procedure
- FREE   Release dataset or DD statement
- SUBMIT   Submit JCL statements for batch execution.

TSO dataset names have two forms:

- **Explicit dataset name**. The dataset name is enclosed within apostrophes, e.g. 'TEST.LOAD'.
- **Implicit dataset name**. The dataset name is not enclosed within apostrophes and will be prefixed with the current TSO prefix.

Example: If the current TSO prefix is TSOUSER, the implicit dataset name TEST.LOAD is equivalent to the explicit dataset name 'TSOUSER.TEST.LOAD'. Some TSO commands use an implicit final qualifier when the dataset name is not fully qualified (such qualifiers are described in the text).

4.4.1 ALLOC - Allocate Dataset or File

The ALLOC statement makes the specified dataset or file (DD statement) available for use by the procedure or program. The ALLOC statement is equivalent to the JCL DD statement in batch.

The ALLOC statement has a large number of parameters, only those parameters appropriate for ISPF applications are listed here.

Syntax:
```
ALLOC[ATE] {FILE(filename) | DDNAME(filename)}
        [{DATASET | DSNAME}((*) | (datasetname ...) | DUMMY)]
        [ OLD | SHR | MOD | NEW | SYSOUT(sysoutclass) ]
        [VOLUME(volumeserial)]
        [SPACE (primaryquantity [,secondaryquantity])
        { BLOCK(value) | AVBLOCK(value) | TRACKS | CYLINDERS }]
        [BLKSIZE(blocksize)]
        [DIR(directoryblocksnumber)]
        [REUSE]
        [UNIT(unittype)]
        [ KEEP | DELETE | CATALOG | UNCATALOG ]
        [LRECL(logicalrecordlength)]
        [RECFM({{F | V} [B] [A | M]} | U})]
        [DSORG( DA[U] | PO[U] | PS[U] )]
```

Example:
```
ALLOC F(SYSPRINT) DA(*)
```

4.4.2 CALL - Execute Program

The CALL statement loads the program from the specified library and executes it.

Note: The low level qualifier LOAD is suffixed to a non-explicit library name.

Syntax:
```
CALL librarydsname[(programname) | (TEMPNAME)] ['parameter']
```

Example:
```
CALL 'PROD.LOAD(MYPGM)'
```
Execute MYPGM from 'PROD.LOAD'.

```
CALL TEST(MYPGM)
```
Execute MYPGM from 'userid.TEST.LOAD'.

4.4.3 EXEC - Execute Command Procedure

The EXEC statement executes a command procedure. Unlike an ISPF SELECT, a TSO EXEC does not create a new ISPF environment.

Note: The low level qualifier CLIST is suffixed to a non-explicit library name. A procedure contained in the SYSPROC library can also be executed with the %procedurename command.

Syntax:
```
{ EX[EC]datasetname[(procedurename)]|%implicitprocedurename}
        ['parameterlist']
        [ LIST | NOLIST ]
        [ PROMPT | NOPROMPT ]
        [ EXEC | CLIST ]
```

Example:
```
EXEC TEST(MYPROC)
```
Invoke MYPROC from 'userid.TEST.CLIST'.

4.4.4 FREE - Release Dataset or File

The FREE statement releases the specified dataset or DD statement (file) available for use by the procedure or program.

Syntax:
```
FREE {FILE(filename)|DDNAME(filename)|DATASET(datasetname ... )
    | DSNAME(datasetname ... )}
        [HOLD|NOHOLD]
        [KEEP|{DELETE[SYSOUT(sysoutclass)]}|CATALOG|UNCATALOG]
```

Example:
```
FREE F(SYSPRINT)
```

4.4.5 SUBMIT - Submit Job Control Statements for Batch Execution

The SUBMIT statement passes the job control statements to the internal reader for batch execution. A job card is optional in the job control statements. A job card is generated according to installation standards, the jobname is the userid suffixed with an identifying character.

Note: The submitted job control statements must have the following dataset attributes:

- RECFM=F [B]
- LRECL=80

Syntax:
```
SUB[MIT] (datasetname[(membername) ... ) | *
         [ NONOTIFY | NOTIFY ]
```
The * operand submits a job from the input stream.

Example:
```
SUB JCL.CNTL(MYJOB)
```
Submit MYJOB member from 'userid.JCL.CNTL'.

4.5 COMMAND INVOCATION

Whereas in CLISTs, TSO and ISPF commands are in effect directly incorporated into the language, in REXX commands are passed to the currently active host environment.

4.5.1 CLIST Command Invocation

Because TSO and ISPF commands are in effect directly incorporated into the CLIST language, such statements are written directly in the CLIST command procedure.

Example:
```
PROC 0
ALLOC F(ISPTABL) DA(USER.TABLE) SHR
IF &LASTCC > 0 THEN EXIT
ISPEXEC CONTROL ERRORS RETURN /* receive control of errors
ISPEXEC TBOPEN TEMP LIBRARY(ISPTABL)
IF &LASTCC = 0 THEN DO
 /* processing */
END
```

4.5.2 REXX Command Invocation

In REXX, commands are passed to the current host environment. The ADDRESS instruction sets the host environment. The host environment can be set either globally, which applies for all subsequent commands (until changed), or temporary, which applies only for the current ADDRESS instruction (the command on the ADDRESS instruction is passed to the specified host environment). It is more efficient to set a global environment.

Example 1 (temporary environment):

```
/* REXX */
ADDRESS TSO "ALLOC F(ISPTABL) DA(USER.TABLE) SHR"
ADDRESS ISPEXEC "CONTROL ERRORS RETURN" /* receive control of errors */
ADDRESS ISPEXEC "TBOPEN TEMP LIBRARY(ISPTABL)"
IF RC = 0 THEN DO
 /* processing */
END
```

Example 2 (global environment):

```
/* REXX */
ADDRESS TSO
"ALLOC F(ISPTABL) DA(USER.TABLE) SHR"
ADDRESS ISPEXEC
"CONTROL ERRORS RETURN" /* receive control of errors */
"TBOPEN TEMP LIBRARY(ISPTABL)"
IF RC = 0 THEN DO
 /* processing */
END
```

5

Panels

5.1 INTRODUCTION

A **panel** is a member of the panel library (ISPPLIB). A panel describes the form of the display, the processing to be performed on fields before and after it is displayed, and if it is redisplayed.

Panels can be displayed in full-screen mode or windowed as **pop-up panels**; see Figure 5.1.

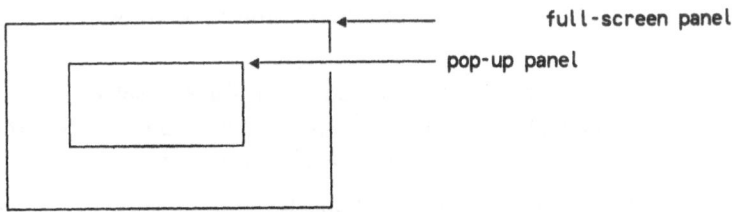

Figure 5.1 — Panel display modes

Within a panel, if an action bar has been defined, the selection of an action bar entry displays the associated **pull-down menu**; see Figure 5.2.

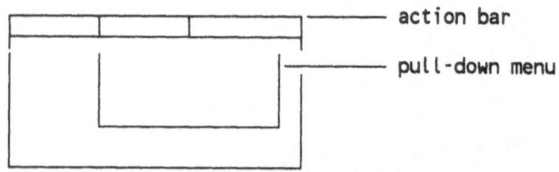

Figure 5.2 — Action bar and pull-down menu

5.2 PANEL DEFINITION

ISPF has four panel types:

· Display Panel
· Selection Panel
· Table Display Panel
· Information Panel (Help).

A panel definition always has the same basic structure which consists of a number of **sections**. Depending on the panel type, certain sections are mandatory, whereas other sections are optional. The ")" character followed by the appropriate keyword at the start of a line indicates the start of a section. Sections must be defined in the following sequence:

)PANEL   The Panel Section (optional). The panel section indicates that the panel is to be displayed in CUA mode and specifies the associated keylist.

)ATTR   The Attribute Section (optional) defines those special characters (attribute bytes) which are to be used to identify field types in the Body Section. There are default attribute characters for input and text fields.

)ABC   Action Bar Choice section (optional).

)ABCINIT   Action Bar Choice Initialisation section (required if)ABC has been specified).

)ABCPROC   Action Bar Choice Processing section.

)BODY   The Body Section (mandatory) defines the format of the panel as it will be displayed.

)MODEL   The Model Section (mandatory for Table Display Panels, must not be present for other panel types) specifies the display format of one logical row from the corresponding ISPF table.

)AREA   Scrollable Area section (optional).

)INIT   The Initialisation Section (optional) defines the processing which is to be performed before the panel is initially displayed.

)REINIT   The Reinitialisation Section (optional) defines the processing which is to be performed before the panel is redisplayed. A redisplay occurs after an "error" condition has been signalled or when the data for a selected row in a table display panel is retrieved.

)PROC   The Processing Section (optional) defines the processing which is to be performed after the panel has been displayed.

)PNTS   The Point-and-Shoot Section (optional) defines the processing which is to be performed on point-and-shoot fields.

)HELP   The Help Section (optional) specifies the help panels associated with fields.

)END   The End Section (mandatory) terminates the panel definition.

Figure 5.3 shows the schematic representation of a panel definition. Figure 5.4 shows the schematic representation of the recommended panel layout (the bold entries are mandatory). To permit a complete screen display in split-screen mode, the panel should have at most one less line than the screen.

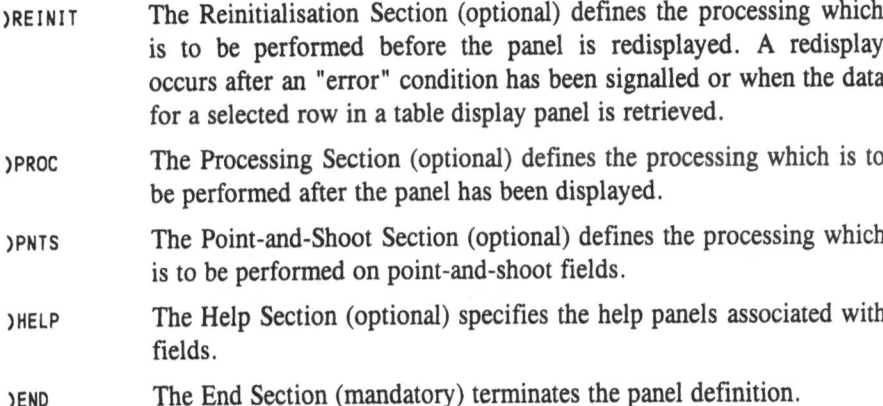

Figure 5.3 - Schematic panel representation

The displayed panel consists of fields or so-called panel areas, or a combination. The fields can be either input, output or text. The panel areas are either dynamic (either scrollable or non-scrollable), scrollable, or graphical; a graphical area contains a GDDM diagram.

The panel processing described in Chapter 8 applies to all types of panel, with the exception of the model section, which is only used in table display panels. However, each type of panel has special requirements as described in the following section.

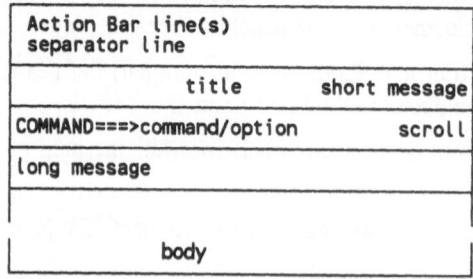

Figure 5.4 - Recommended panel layout

The following services are concerned with panel display:

· ADDPOP   Display pop-up panel
· DISPLAY   Display data input panel
· REMPOP   Revoke pop-up panel display
· SELECT   Display selection panel
· TBDISPL   Display table.

Help panels are displayed indirectly.

5.2.1 ADDPOP — Pop-Up Panel Display

The ADDPOP service is used to display panels in pop-up mode. Each ADDPOP invocation creates a new pop-up hierarchy. All subsequent panel displays are made at this pop-up level until revoked with the REMPOP service. A title for the pop-up windows can be set into the ZWINTTL variable.

The pop-up panel can be positioned relative to a field in the original panel or at an absolute position.

Syntax:
```
ISPEXEC ADDPOP
        [POPLOC(fieldname)]
        [ROW(row)]
        [COLUMN(column)]
```

POPLOC(fieldname)

Position the pop-up panels next to the specified field (fieldname) in the original panel. If no fieldname is specified, the pop-up panel is positioned near the top of the original panel (by default 1 row and 2 columns from the upper-left edge).

ROW(row)

The **row** specifies the displacement in rows of the left-upper edge of the pop-up panel from the original panel. By default, 1 row is used.

COLUMN(column)

The **column** specifies the displacement in columns of the left-upper edge of the pop-up panel from the original panel. By default, 2 columns are used.

Example:
```
/* REXX */
ADDRESS ISPEXEC
"DISPLAY PANEL(XPAN1)"
ZWINTTL = 'LEVEL 1'
"ADDPOP"
"DISPLAY PANEL(XPAN2)"
ZWINTTL = 'LEVEL 2'
"ADDPOP"
"DISPLAY PANEL(XPAN3)"
"REMPOP ALL"
```

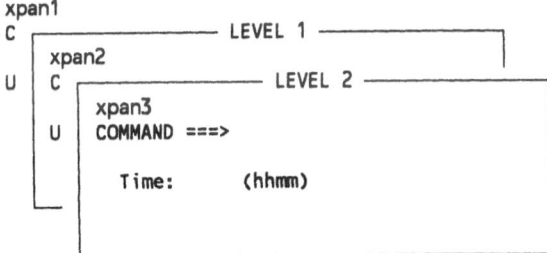

The service sets one of the following return codes:

    0   Normal termination.

  12   ADDPOP already active at this level.

  20   Severe error.

5.2.2 DISPLAY — Data Input Panel

A data input (**display**) panel is a general purpose panel used for display and data input. A **display panel** is invoked with the ISPEXEC DISPLAY service. Control is returned to the invoking function at the end of the display. Figure 5.5 illustrates display panel invocation. Table 5.1 summarises display panel processing

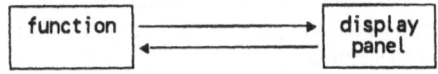

Figure 5.5 - Display panel invocation

Table 5.1 - DISPLAY processing

PANEL	MSG	processing
x	x	panel retrieved MSG displayed)INIT processed
x		panel retrieved)INIT processed
	x	panel redisplayed with MSG)REINIT processed
		panel redisplayed)REINIT processed

x = present

Syntax:
```
ISPEXEC DISPLAY [PANEL(panelname)]
        [MSG(messageid)]
        [CURSOR(fieldname)]
        [CSRPOS(cursorposition)]
        [COMMAND(stackname)]
        [RETBUFFR(returnname)]
        [RETLGTH(returnlengthname)]
```

PANEL(panelname)
> The panel **panelname** is displayed. If omitted, the current panel is redisplayed.

MSG(messageid)
> The message associated with **messageid** is displayed.

CURSOR(fieldname)
> The cursor is positioned at the panel field with the name **fieldname**. If omitted, the cursor is positioned in the first input field (unless the panel specifies cursor positioning).

CSRPOS(cursorposition)
> The cursor is positioned at **cursorposition** in the panel field at which the cursor is placed; 1 is the first (leftmost) character of a panel field. The default is 1, which also applies if the cursor-position is not within the bounds of the panel field.

COMMAND(stackname)
> The variable **stackname** contains a chain of commands which are to be executed before the panel is processed. The panel is processed as if CONTROL NONDISPL ENTER had been specified, i.e. the panel is not displayed.

RETBUFFR(returnname)
> The variable **returnname** contains the remainder from the chain of commands in the variable **stackname** (including the command in error) should an error occur in the command stack.

RETLGTH(returnlengthname)

    The variable **returnlengthname** contains the number of characters contained in the variable **returnname.**

If the .MSG control variable is set by panel processing, the panel is automatically redisplayed, otherwise the control is returned to the point of invocation with one of the following return codes set:

    0   Normal termination.

    4   One or more commands contained in the command stack could not be found in the active command table.

    8   The user terminated the panel display with the END or RETURN command.

    12   The specified panel, message or cursor field could not be found.

    16   A truncation or translation error (VDEFINE) occurred while performing variable processing.

    20   Severe error.

Note: A display panel must not set the ZSEL system variable. Although a display panel cannot invoke other functions, a command field (ZCMD) should be defined to enable commands to be directly called while in the panel display, unless this is not wanted for some reason.

Example 1:

```
ISPEXEC DISPLAY PANEL(TUPAN000) MSG(TUMSG001) CURSOR(PNO)
```

The panel TUPAN000 is displayed with message TUMSG001, the cursor is positioned at the panel field PNO.

Example 2:

```
ISPEXEC DISPLAY PANEL(TUPAN000) COMMAND(ALPHA)
```

If the variable ALPHA contains the string "KEYS;TSO TIME", the ISPF KEY definitions panel will be displayed, the TSO TIME command executed and finally the processing specified in panel TUPAN000 performed (the panel itself is not displayed).

Sample display panel:

```
)BODY
+--------------------- title ---------------------
+COMMAND ===> _ZCMD

+Employee Number%===> _PNO +
+            Name%===>_NAME              +

)INIT
)PROC
VER(&PNO,NONBLANK,NUM)
VER(&NAME,NONBLANK)
```

Figure 5.6 - Sample display panel

5.2.3 REMPOP — Revoke Pop-Up Panel Display

The REMPOP service revokes the display of panels in pop-up mode at the current level. Each ADDPOP invocation creates a new pop-up hierarchy, which the corresponding REMPOP invocation revokes. The REMPOP service can revoke all pop-up hierarchies.

Syntax:
```
ISPEXEC REMPOP [ALL]
```

ALL

> The ALL keyword revokes all active pop-up levels, i.e. all subsequent displays are made in non-windowed mode.

Example:
```
ISPEXEC ADDPOP
ISPEXEC DISPLAY PANEL(USPAN01)
ISPEXEC DISPLAY PANEL(USPAN02)
ISPEXEC REMPOP
ISPEXEC DISPLAY PANEL(USPAN03)
```
Whereas USPAN01 and USPAN02 are displayed as pop-up panels, USPAN03 is displayed normally.

The service sets one of the following return codes:

- 0   Normal termination.
- 12   No pop-up active at this level.
- 20   Severe error.

5.2.4 SELECT — Selection Panel

A **selection panel** is invoked with the ISPEXEC SELECT PANEL service and itself invokes either a program, a command procedure or a further selection panel. Generally, a selection panel will contain a list of options, one of which is to be chosen. The selection panel sets the ZSEL system control variable to contain the name of the program, command procedure or selection panel to be invoked; this invoked function returns to this original selection panel.

A selection panel may be classified as being a **primary option menu** (by specifying &ZPRIM=YES in the panel definition), in which case the RETURN command by-passes intervening any selection panels until the previous primary option menu is reached.

The specified function is invoked, provided no errors have been detected in the initial selection panel. The function may be a hierarchy of selection panels (menus), a program or a command procedure. A new function pool for variables is created. Figure 5.7 is somewhat simplified because programs and command procedures can also invoke selection panels.

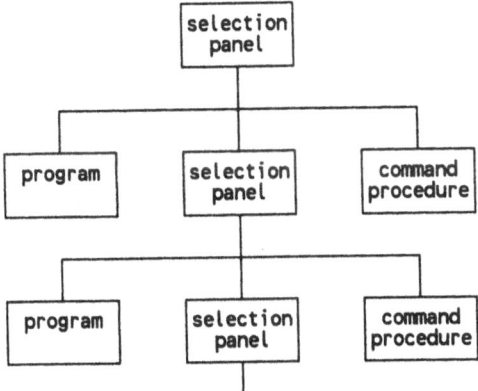

Figure 5.7 - Selection panel hierarchy

A select panel is subject to certain constraints:

- A select panel must have at least one input field in which the user can enter a selection option. To conform to standards, this field should be the command field zCMD and the first input field in the panel. Note: The user can set the ISPF/PDF options to place the command field at the bottom of the screen.
- A select panel must set the zSEL system variable to contain the calling sequence of the function to which control is to be passed. This function may be a selection panel, a program or a command procedure.

Syntax:
```
ISPEXEC SELECT
        ( PANEL(panelname) [OPT(option)] [ADDPOP] )
        ( CMD(command [parameter] ...))
                       [LANG(APL|CREX))]
                       [MODE(LINE|FSCR)]
                       [BARRIER]
                       [NEST]                              )
        ( PGM(programname) [PARM(parameter)]
                       [MODE(LINE|FSCR)]                    )
        (([NEWAPPL[applicationid|ISP)]] [PASSLIB]) | [NEWPOOL]) [SUSPEND]
```

The parameters are described in detail in Section 3.2.2.

zSEL can be assigned a string having one of the following forms:
```
    ( 'PANEL(panelname) [OPT(option)]
    [NEWAPPL[applicationid | ISP ) ]] | [NEWPOOL]' )

    ( 'CMD(command [parameter] ...)) [LANG(APL)]
    [NEWAPPL[applicationid | ISP ) ]] | [NEWPOOL] [NOCHECK] [LANG(APL)]' )

    ( 'PGM(programname) [PARM(parameter)]
    [NEWAPPL[applicationid | ISP ) ]] | [NEWPOOL] [NOCHECK]' )

    EXIT
```

PANEL(panelname)

Invoke the selection panel **panelname**.

OPT(option)

The **option** is passed as initial option; this option is processed as if it had been entered manually, however, the panel is not displayed.

Example:
&ZSEL = 'PANEL(TUPAN000) OPT(2)'
Invoke the selection panel TUPAN000 with option 2.

CMD(command [parameter]...)

Invoke the command procedure **command, parameters** are passed to the command procedure.

Example:
&ZSEL = 'CMD(%TSCMD ALPHA BETA)'
Invoke the command procedure TSCMD with two parameters: ALPHA and BETA; the % appended to the command name ensures that only a member of the command library is invoked.

PGM(programname)

Load **programname** from the program library (ISPLLIB) and pass control to it.

PARM(parameter)

Pass **parameter** to the program.

Note: The parameter is passed to the program in the form of an Exec parameter, i.e. a character string preceded by a halfword containing the length of the following parameter.

Example:
&ZSEL = 'PGM(TUPGM00) PARM(ALPHA BETA)'
Invoke the program TUPGM00 with the parameters ALPHA BETA. The parameter has the form:

| 10 | ALPHA BETA |

NEWAPPL

The application is assigned the default application-id, ISP. The following profile members and command table are assigned to the application:

user profile   ISPPROF
Edit profile   ISPEDIT
command table   ISPCMDS

NEWAPPL(applicationid)

The application is assigned the **applicationid**. The following profile members and command table are assigned to the application:

user profile	*aaaa*PROF
Edit profile	*aaaa*EDIT
command table	*aaaa*CMDS

aaaa is the **applicationid**.

Note: If the NEWAPPL keyword is not specified, the current application-id is retained.

NEWPOOL

Create a new shared pool. The current shared pool is restored on completion of the function.

PASSLIB

Pass any application-level ISPF libraries to the selected application.

NOCHECK

Disable the checking of the program or command procedure parameter.

Selection panels may be arranged in a hierarchy. Panels in this hierarchy can be selected directly by specifying the option in each hierarchy, provided each panel separates out its option and places the remainder in the .TRAIL system variable. Example: "2.4.2" specifies option 2 at level 1, option 4 at level 2, and option 2 at level 3.

In the case of a program or command procedure, the NOCHECK parameter disables the normal validity checking, and the dialogue function is itself responsible for the interpretation of the lower level option.

```
Example:
&ZSEL = TRANS(TRUNC(&ZCMD,'.')
       1,'PANEL(...)'
       2,'CMD(...) NOCHECK'
       3,'PANEL(...)'
       4,'PGM(...) NOCHECK')
&REST = .TRAIL
```
The nested option is delimited by "."; lower nesting levels are set into the REST variable, which the command procedure or program must interpret appropriately.

EXIT

EXIT is used only in the ISPF primary option menu and causes the ISPF session to terminate using the standard options for LIST and LOG output.

The following ZSEL contents are interpreted in a special manner:

- " " (blank), the message "ENTER OPTION" is displayed;
- "?" (question mark), the message "INVALID OPTION" is displayed.

The special processing associated with ZSEL is normally coded as follows:

```
&ZSEL = TRANS(&TRUNC,'.')
          1, ...
          2, ...
          ...
          ' ',' '
          '*','?')
```

The example selection panel Figure 5.8 allows the user to make one of four valid input selections in the COMMAND field:

- 1   pass control to the TUCMD01 CLIST
- 2   invoke the TUPGMD00 program
- 3   display the TUPAN002 selection panel
- X   terminate the function.

5.2.5 TBDISPL — Table Display Panel

The TBDISPL service is used to display the contents of an ISPF table using a panel definition; either the whole table or selected rows from the table can be displayed. The information which is displayed is not restricted to what can fit on a single screen, but may be scrolled vertically.

```
)BODY
+----------------------- title -----------------------
+COMMAND ===>_ZCMD

+1   data acquisition
+2   data display
+3   print report

+X   EXIT (terminate)
)INIT
&ZPRIM = NO
)PROC
&ZSEL = TRANS(TRUNC(&ZCMD,'.')
               1,'CMD(%TSCMD01)'
               2,'PGM(TUPGMD00)'
               3,'PANEL(TUPAN002)'
               X,EXIT
               ' ',' '
               '*','?')
```

Figure 5.8 - Sample selection panel

A table display panel is subject to certain constraints:

- A table display panel must have a model section (")MODEL") which defines the display form of a single table row, the table name is specified as parameter to the TBDISPL service. The model section may contain up to 8 lines.
- A table display panel should have a command field, the first input field in the panel.
- A table display panel should have an input field containing the scroll amount as the second input field in the panel, this field must have length 4. The scroll

amount specifies the size of the vertical scroll increment (e.g. PAGE, HALF or a number of lines).

The display for a table display panel has two parts:

- a fixed part (")BODY" section)
- a scrollable part (")MODEL" section).

The model section may contain the following field types:
- input
- output
- text

A **variable model line** is the name of a variable preceded by ampersand ("&"), and may be the only data in the line and must commence in column 1. The variable may contain any data which is valid in a model definition line, i.e. input, output and text fields. If this variable contains the special character string "OMIT", the model line will not be displayed.

The table display panel has a fixed form, although certain features of the display may be changed by the application developer.

- The row number of the first line currently displayed and the total number of lines in the table appears in the short message field:

    ROW m OF n

    m is row number of the first displayed row
    n is row number of the rows in the table.

This text may be replaced by the application developer's own text, the message-id identifying the message containing the text is set into the ZTDMSG system variable. The short message text (or long message text, if no short message text exists) associated with this message-id is displayed as text, substitutions will be performed for any variables contained in the message definition.

Example:
```
SET &TABNAME = PERSTAB
SET &ZTDMSG = TUMSG096
```

```
┌─ TUMSG09 member ──────────────────────┐
│ TUMSG096 'TABLE &TABNAME DISPLAY'      │
│ ' '                                    │
└───────────────────────────────────────┘
```

displays the text: TABLE PERSTAB DISPLAY at the top of the table display panel.

Note
A message definition which contains neither short message text nor long message text will result in no text being displayed.

The following standard text is displayed after the last table row:

*** BOTTOM OF DATA ***

The application developer can replace this text with text he has placed in the
ZTDMARK system variable. Example:
    SET &ZTDMARK = &STR(LAST TABLE ROW)
This statement causes the text: LAST TABLE ROW to be displayed.

The)MODEL header has two optional parameters:
)MODEL [CLEAR(varname [,varname]...)]
           [ROWS(ALL|SCAN)]

CLEAR(varname)

Clear the **varname** extension variable in the table display before each table
row is formatted. If CLEAR is not used, variables which appear in model lines
but are not present in the table row will remain on the display.

Example:
)MODEL CLEAR(ALPHA,BETA)
This statement clears the two variables ALPHA and BETA.

ROWS(SCAN)

Perform a selection of rows using the search argument that was specified
with the TBSARG service before the table was displayed.

Default: ROWS(ALL), all table rows are to be displayed.

Note: Specifying ROWS(SCAN) in the model header without the corresponding
TBSARG results in a severe error when the TBDISPL service displays the panel.

Syntax:
    ISPEXEC TBDISPL tablename
            [PANEL(panelname)]
            [MSG(messageid)]
            [CURSOR(panelfieldname)]
            [CSRROW(tablerownumber)]
            [CSRPOS(cursorposition)]
            [AUTOSEL(YES| NO)]
            [POSITION(crpname)]
            [ROWID(rowidname)]

The use of TBDISPL is discussed in detail in section 8.4.4. Figure 5.9 depicts a
typical table display panel. Figure 5.10 illustrates table display parameters.

```
)ATTR
a TYPE(OUTPUT) SKIP(ON)
)BODY
+----------------------- Title -------------------------
+COMMAND ===> ZCMD
+  EMPNO   Surname
)MODEL
 ZaPNO     aNAME
)INIT
.ZVARS='(OP)'
.HELP=TUPANH01
)PROC
VER(&OP,LIST,s,S)
```

Figure 5.9 - Sample table display panel

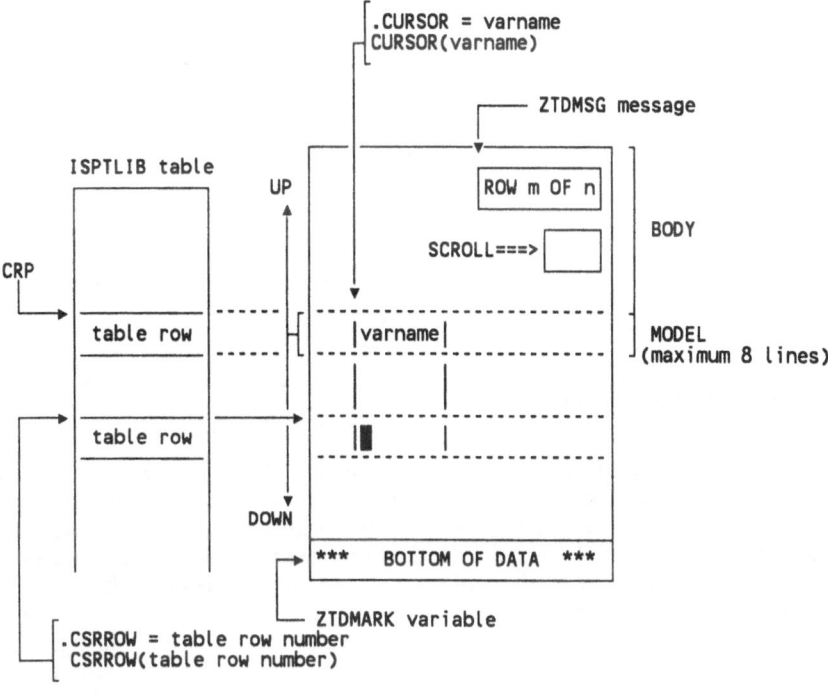

Figure 5.10 - Table display parameters

5.2.6 Help Panel

Help panels are displayed as a result of entering the help environment. Help panels can be directly associated with messages and panels, and with panel fields (**field help** and **reference phrase**). In addition, help panels can be arranged to form a tutorial and/or index for the application. Help panels normally only display information. However, they are in no way limited to being display-only; they can contain ISPF variables, etc. Help panels have similarity with select panels in that ZSEL contains the name of the next help panel to be displayed.

The help environment also can be directly entered by invoking the tutorial program with the name of the help panel to be displayed as parameter:

```
ISPEXEC SELECT PGM(ISPTUTOR) PARM(panelname)
```

Help panels and the help environment are described in detail in Chapter 15.

Help panels can be displayed directly by entering the HELP command or pressing the PF-key associated with the HELP command (usually PF1 or PF13). A field help is displayed if a field-help panel has been assigned to the field in which the cursor is currently positioned and the HELP PF-key is pressed. A reference phrase help is displayed if a reference phrase panel has been assigned to the field in which the cursor is currently positioned and the HELP PF-key is pressed.

```
)BODY
+---------------------- title -----------------------
+COMMAND ===> ZCMD
+
+The selection panel may be used to select one or more
+rows; rows are selected by placing "s" is the operation
+column.
+
+Further help information may be obtained by pressing
+ENTER.
)PROC
&ZSEL=TUPANH02
```

Figure 5.11 - Sample help panel

5.3 PREPROCESSED PANELS

Panels created with a standard text editor or SDF2 are stored as text in the panel library; DTL-generated panels can be stored in text form. This has the advantage that panel definitions can be easily changed, but with the disadvantage that the panel definitions must be interpreted each time they are used. The time-consuming interpretation of panels can be minimised by **preprocessing** the panels. Preprocessed panels have the further advantages of being significantly smaller than non-preprocessed panels and offer increased-protection against being changed by users. A panel library may contain both preprocessed and non-preprocessed panels.

Panels that contain the following items cannot be preprocessed:

·)BODY header using a dialogue variable in the WIDTH keyword;
· EXTEND(ON) parameter for DYNAMIC or GRAPHIC area;
· model line which is defined as an ISPF variable.

The preprocessing program is invoked by either:

· entering ISPPREP as command;
· directly calling the ISPPREP program.

Tip

Panels should be stored in preprocessed format only after they have been fully tested.

The ISPPREP program displays the following initial panel:

```
---------------- PREPROCESSED PANEL UTILITY --------------------
COMMAND ===>


SPECIFY "FROM" AND "TO" DATA SET NAMES BELOW:


  PANEL INPUT DATA SET:
    DATA SET NAME ===>
    MEMBER        ===>                ( * for all members )
    VOLUME SERIAL ===>                ( If not cataloged  )

  PANEL OUTPUT DATA SET:
    DATA SET NAME ===>
    MEMBER        ===>                ( blank or member name )
    VOLUME SERIAL ===>                ( If not cataloged      )

  REPLACE LIKE-NAMED MEMBERS ===> NO   ( YES OR NO )
```

The input fields of this panel are largely self explanatory. However, the same member name may not be specified for the same input and output library.

The required parameters may be passed to ISPPREP directly invoked as a program:

```
ISPEXEC SELECT PGM(ISPPREP)
          [PARM(INPAN(inputlibraryname[(inputmembername)])
          ,OUTPAN(outputlibraryname[(outputmembername)])
          [,INVOL(inputlibraryvolume)]
          [,OUTVOL(outputlibraryvolume)]
          [,( NOREPL|REPLACE )])]
```

INPAN(inputlibraryname[(inputmembername)])
> **Inputlibraryname** is the dataset name (TSO convention) of the input library. **Inputmembername** is the name of the input member; if omitted, the complete input library is processed.

OUTPAN(outputlibraryname[(inputmembername)])
> **Outputlibraryname** is the data set name (TSO convention) of the output library. **Outputmembername** is the name of the output member; if omitted, the name from the input library is used.

INVOL(inputlibraryvolume)
> **Inputlibraryvolume** is the volume of the input library, only required if the input library is not catalogued.

OUTVOL(outputlibraryvolume)

Outputlibraryvolume is the volume of the output library. This is only required if output library is not catalogued.

NOREPL

This keyword causes a member in the output library having the same name not to be replaced. Default: NOREPL.

REPLACE

This keyword causes a member in the output library having the same name to be replaced.

Example:
```
ISPEXEC SELECT PGM(ISPPREP) PARM(INPAN(EX.ISPPLIB(PAN1)), +
    OUTPAN(EXP.ISPPLIB))
```
Convert the PAN1 member from the EX.ISPPLIB input panel library into the EXP.ISPPLIB output library. The converted member retains its name from the input library.

The ISPPREP service sets one of the following return codes:

    0   Normal termination.
    4   Panel definition cannot be processed; member already exists in output library (NOREPL specified).
    8   Panel definition contains syntax errors; panel is currently being used (ENQ failure) or panel not found.
  12   Syntax error in invocation PARM; data set not found.
  16   Data set allocation error.
  20   Severe error.

6

Variable Services

6.1 INTRODUCTION

The **variable** is the basic data item in the ISPF environment and consists of a name
and value. There are two classes of variables: **system** and **user**. System variables
are those variables defined by ISPF and concerned with its operational
environment. System variables are themselves subdivided into two groups:
modifiable and **non-modifiable**; all system variables have names which
commence with "z" (e.g. ZDATE, ZUSER).

The Variable Service Functions are concerned with processing variables at the
elementary level, the other service functions are used for processing of aggregates
(panels, etc.). The Variable Service Functions are used for the explicit transfer of
variables between the various **pools**.

The pools are arranged in a **hierarchy**. The initiation of an ISPF **function**
creates a new **function pool (intra-function** pool) in the hierarchy. The function
pool for the previous function is restored if control is returned to that function,
only one function pool is active at any one time. The **shared pool** contains
variables as the next higher **hierarchy level**. This pool retains variables between
functions (**inter-function** pool). The **profile pool** is at the top of the hierarchy and
is used to store variables across ISPF sessions. Each function may be assigned an
application identifier, the profile pool is then created for this application.

6.2 SYNTAX

The form of a variable is described by the following syntax diagram:

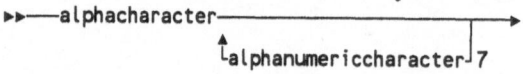

Tip

Variables with names beginning with "z" are reserved for system variables and can cause unexpected results if used as user variables.

6.3 VARIABLE POOLS

ISPF has five variable pools:

· function pool
· shared pool
· profile pool
· read-only profile pool
· command procedure pool.

6.3.1 Function Pool

A function pool is created when a function is initiated and restored to its original state, provided control is returned to this function. A function is a processing complex (program, command procedure or selection panel) initiated by the ISPEXEC SELECT service; a TSO EXEC command can invoke a command procedure without creating a new function pool. Only one function pool is active at any one time.

Note: In the program environment (discussed in Chapter 14), ISPF is called directly from a program. The VDEFINE service defines variables in an additional function pool, called the **defined function pool**. The defined function pool exists together with the normal function pool.

6.3.2 Shared Pool

The shared pool is used to store or pass variables between functions. A single shared pool exists during the ISPF session.

6.3.3 Profile Pool

Each initiated function is assigned an application identifier. If no application identifier is explicitly specified, the current application identifier is retained. A profile pool is created for the application and stored as a member in the ISPPROF library. The profile member is assigned the member name *appl*PROF, where *appl* is the application identifier. Profile pools are retained across ISPF sessions, provided the session terminates normally.

Tip

Profile pools are best suited to store application-oriented parameters (e.g. user name).

6.3.4 Read-Only Profile Pool

The **read-only profile pool** is related to the normal profile pool, but the variables it contains cannot be (directly) changed by the function. The read-only profile pool can be used to store global parameters for an application, etc. The read-only profile pool is an ISPF table, the name of which is stored in the ZPROFAPP system variable contained in the profile member for the application. The values for the required read-only variables are stored in the table using the usual table processing services (TBADD, etc.). A subsequent VPUT for a read-only variable will cause the variable to be stored in the normal application profile pool (which then takes precedence over the variable in the read-only profile pool). Table processing services must also be used to update the read-only profile member. The processing of read-only profile variables is shown in Figure 6.1.

Example:
The command procedure to create a read-only profile member:

```
PROC 0
SET COMPANY = ASR
SET COMPUTER = &STR(IBM/3090)
ISPEXEC TBCREATE ROPROFIL
ISPEXEC TBADD ROPROFIL SAVE(COMPANY COMPUTER)
ISPEXEC TBCLOSE ROPROFIL
SET ZPROFAPP = ROPROFIL
ISPEXEC VPUT (ZPROFAPP) PROFILE
```

This command procedure creates a read-only profile member ROPROFIL containing two variables:

```
COMPANY    'ASR'
COMPUTER   'IBM/3090'
```

The following command procedure statement accesses one of these variables:

```
ISPEXEC VGET (COMPANY)
```

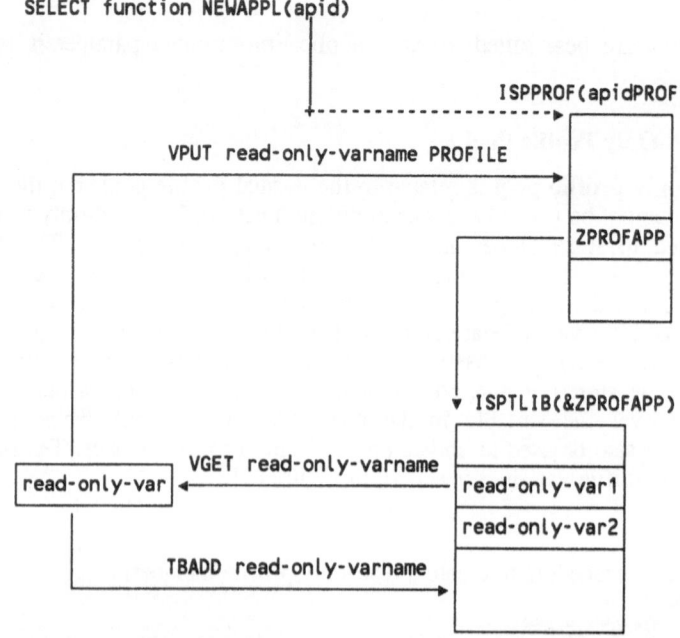

Figure 6.1 - Read-only profile variable relationships

6.3.5 Command Procedure Pool

Variables defined (set) in a command procedure are automatically made available to the ISPF function pool.

Command procedure system variables (SYSTIME, SYSUID, etc.) are not available in the ISPF environment. However, there are equivalent ISPF variables, e.g. ZTIME, ZUSER.

Note: A new command procedure pool is created when a command procedure calls another command procedure or sub-procedure.

6.4 ACCESS TO VARIABLES AND POOLS

Variables can be assigned a value only in the function pool. The following means of assigning a value to a variable are available:

·	command procedure	SET statement (CLIST) or assignment statement (REXX)
·	panel	explicitly by the assignment operator (=) or implicitly by inputting a value into a panel field
·	skeleton	)SET statement
·	table	read operation

The variable can then be passed to another pool using the VPUT statement (ISPEXEC VPUT from a procedure). Similarly, a variable can be explicitly retrieved in a procedure from a pool with the ISPEXEC VGET statement.

Variables referenced implicitly (in panel, procedure, etc.) are retrieved from the pool hierarchy, in the sequence: function pool, shared pool and profile pool. Figure 6.2 depicts the various pool relationships.

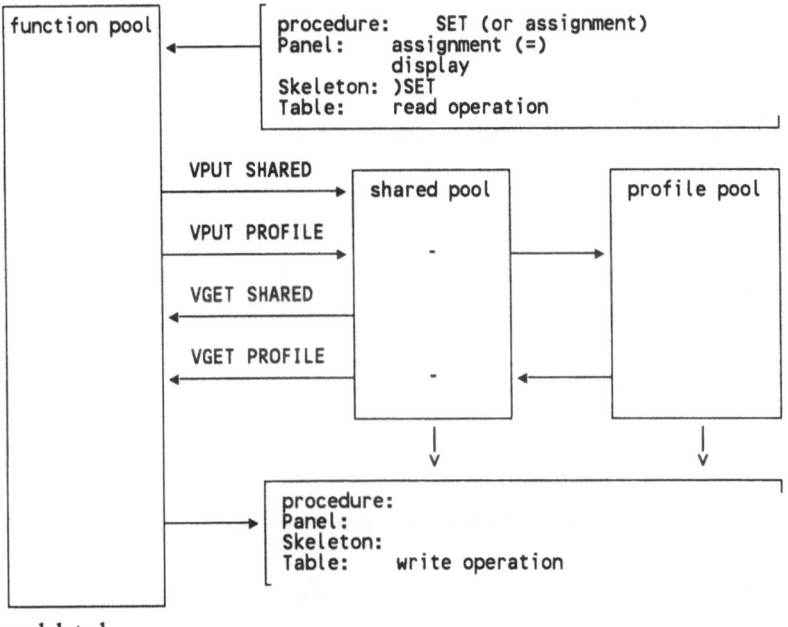

- entry deleted

Figure 6.2 - Pool relationships

6.5 VARIABLE SERVICES

ISPF has three variable services that can be invoked from procedures:

· VERASE   Delete Variable
· VGET   Get Variable from a Pool or Profile
· VPUT   Put Variable into a Pool or Profile.

These service also are available as program calls (see Chapter 14).

6.5.1 VERASE - Remove Variable from Shared or Profile Pool

The VERASE service removes the named variables from the specified pool.

Syntax:
```
ISPEXEC VERASE (variablename [,variablename] ...)
       [ASIS|SHARED|PROFILE|BOTH]
```

variablename

> The name of the variable which is to be deleted from the specified pool.

ASIS

> Delete the variable(s) from the first pool in which it is found. Pools are searched in the order: shared pool, profile pool. Default.

SHARED

> Delete the variable(s) from the shared pool.

PROFILE

> Delete the variable(s) from the profile pool.

BOTH

> Delete the variable(s) from both the shared and profile pool.

The service sets one of the following return codes:

> 0   Normal completion.
> 8   One or more variables do not exist.
> 20   Severe error.

Example:
```
ISPEXEC VERASE (PNO,PNAME) BOTH
```
Delete PNO and PNAME from both shared and profile pools

6.5.2 VGET Get Variable from a Pool or Profile

The VGET service retrieves a variable or variables from the shared or profile pool into the function pool, as appropriate. If the named variable already exists in the function pool, it is updated, otherwise it is created.

Syntax:
```
ISPEXEC VGET (variablename [,variablename] ...)
      [ ASIS | SHARED | PROFILE ]
```

variablename

> The name of variable which is to be copied into the function pool from the specified pool.

ASIS

> The variable is to be copied into the function pool from the pool where it is first located; the pools are searched in the following sequence: shared, profile. ASIS is the default.

SHARED

> The variable is to be copied into the function pool from the shared pool.

PROFILE
>   The variable is to be copied into the function pool from the profile pool; the variable is removed (set to null) from the shared pool, should it exist there.

The service sets one of the following return codes:

>   0   Normal completion.
>   8   One or more of the specified variables does not exist in the specified pool.
>   20 Severe error.

Example:
```
ISPEXEC VGET (PNO) ASIS
```
Copy the variable PNO from the pool in which it is first found (the shared pool being searched before the profile pool) into the function pool.

Tip
To avoid unexpected results the source pool should always be specified. For example, assume that the variable FLAG contains status information which is to be retained across ISPF sessions (this implies that this variable is to be stored in the profile pool), a VGET statement which does not explicitly specify the source pool could retrieve a variable having the same name from the shared pool but having nothing to do with the status FLAG. Remember, variables are identified exclusively by name, it is the user's responsibility to assign a value to a variable and to place that variable in the required pool. A variable with the same name but having different values can coexist in the three pools (function, shared and profile). Within the program environment (Chapter 14) it is possible to have more than one occurrence of the same variable in the program function pool.

6.5.3 VPUT - Put Variable into a Pool or Profile

The VPUT service passes a variable or variables from the function pool to the shared or profile pool, as appropriate. If the named variable already exists in the destination pool, it is updated, otherwise it is created.

Syntax:
```
ISPEXEC VPUT (variablename [,variablename] ...)
        [ ASIS | SHARED | PROFILE ]
```

variable-name
>   The name of variable which is to be copied from the function pool into the specified pool.

ASIS
>   The variable is to be copied from the function pool into the pool where it currently occurs; if the variable does not exist in any pool, it is stored in the shared pool. ASIS is the default.

SHARED

The variable is to be copied from the function pool into the shared pool.

PROFILE

The variable is to be copied from the function pool into the profile pool; the variable is removed (set to null) from the shared pool, should it exist there.

Note: Parentheses may be omitted for a single variable.

The service sets one of the following return codes:

  0   Normal completion.
  8   One or more of the specified variables do not exist in the function pool.
  20   Severe error.

Example:
```
ISPEXEC VPUT (PNO,PNAME) SHARED
```
Copy the two variables PNO and PNAME from the function pool into the shared pool.

6.5.3 Passing Variables Between Applications

To avoid unexpected results, the destination pool should always be specified. This is especially important if the source pool is not explicitly specified in the VGET statement.

To maintain flexibility when variables are passed between applications, the variables can be passed (and retrieved) in two steps (the first step passes the names of the variables, see example — this avoids the receiving application from having to know the names of the variables).

Example:
```
/* sending procedure */
vn = 'alpha beta'
ADDRESS ISPEXEC "VPUT (vn alpha beta)"

/* receiving procedure */
ADDRESS ISPEXEC "VGET vn"
ADDRESS ISPEXEC "VGET ("vn")"
```
The VN variable contains the names of the actual variables (here ALPHA and BETA).

6.6 SYSTEM VARIABLES

System variables are variables used by ISPF to communicate with the application, and vice versa. System variables usually have names beginning with "z". There are two types of system variables: modifiable and non-modifiable; modifiable variables can be set by the application. The pool in which the system variable is contained depends on the variable.

The bracketed entry that follows each description has the form: [length, type, pool], although some entries are omitted. If the type is omitted, it is read-only.

6.6.1 General Variables

Z	Null variable [0]
ZACCTNUM	The current TSO account number [max. 40]
ZAPLCNT	APL invocation count in the logical screen [4]
ZAPPLID	Application identifier [8]
ZAPPTTL	In GUI mode, the window frame title (ZWINTTL is used as title in a pop-up window) [in]
ZCS	NLS currency symbol [5]
ZDECS	NLS decimal separator character [1]
ZENTKTXT	In GUI mode, the Enter button inscription [12, in]
ZENVIR	Environment description [32]:
	aaaaaaaabbbbbbbbccccccccdddddddd
	aaaaaaaa = product name and version [8]
	bbbbbbbb = operating system name (MVS) [8]
	cccccccc = operating environment (TSO, BATCH) [8]
	dddddddd = reserved.
ZGUI	Workstation address or name (blank = not GUI-mode) [68]
ZISPFRC	Return code set by invoked dialog [8, in]
ZKEYHELP	Keys help panel identifier [8, in]
ZLANG	Session language [8]
ZLOGO	Logo display indicator (NO|YES)
ZLOGON	TSO logon procedure stepname [8]
ZPLACE	Command line placement (ASIS|BOTTOM) [7, i/o, profile]
ZPREFIX	TSO user prefix [8]
ZPROFAPP	Name of application profile pool extension table [8, in, profile]
ZSYSID	The IEASYSxx SYSNAME [8]
ZTEMPF	Name of temporary data set for file tailoring output [44]
ZTEMPN	DD-name of temporary data set for file tailoring output [8]
ZTHS	NLS thousands separator character [1]
ZTS	NLS time separator character [1]
ZTSICMD	ISPF invocation command [max. 32767]
ZTSSCMD	SELECT portion of the invocation command [max. 32767]
ZUSER	Userid [8]
ZVERB	Command verb [8]
ZWINTTL	Pop-up window title [in]

6.6.2 Time and Date Variables

ZDATE	Current date (8)
ZDATEF	Current date in the national language date format (8)
ZDATEFD	Current date in the national language date format (8)

ZDAY	Day of month (2 digits)
ZJDATE	Date in day-of-year format (yy.ddd)
ZMONTH	Month of year (2 digits)
ZSTDYEAR	4-digit year
ZTIME	Time of day (hh:mm)
ZYEAR	2-digit year

6.6.3 Terminal Function and PF Key Variables

ZCOLORS	Number of colours supported by the terminal [4]
ZDBCS	DBCS terminal capability (YES | NO)
ZFKA	Current function key area setting (LONG, SHORT, OFF) [8]
ZHILITE	Extended highlighting availability (YES | NO)
ZKEYS	Number of function keys [4, out, profile]
ZPFCTL	PFSHOW command authorisation [5, i/o, profile]
ZPFFMT	Number of function key definitions per line [4, i/o, profile]
ZPFSET	Function key definition set displayed [4, i/o, profile]
ZPFSHOW	PFSHOW command status [4, i/o, profile]
ZPFnn	Function key setting; nn = 1,..., 24 [max. 255, i/o, profile]
ZPFLnn	Function key label setting; nn = 1,..., 24 [8, i/o, profile]
ZPRIKEYS	Primary function key setting [4, i/o, profile]
	LOW: PF1 to PF12
	UPP: PF13 to PF24
ZSCREEN	Logical screen number (1, 2, 3, or 4)
ZSCREEND	Screen depth available for dialog use [4] *
ZSCREENW	Screen width available for dialog use [4] *
ZSCRMAXD	Maximum available screen depth [4] *
ZSCRMAXW	Maximum available screen width [4] *
ZSPLIT	Split-screen mode in effect (YES | NO)
ZTERM	Terminal type [8, out, profile]

* These variables represent the physical screen dimensions and not the logical screen dimensions (i.e. split is not taken into account). Exceptions:

· 3290 Display: A screen with physical width of 160 which has be vertically split yields ZSCREENW = 80;
· 3278/5 Display: If screen format has been defined as being STD, ZSCREENW and ZSCREEND yield 80 and 24, respectively (rather than 132 and 27).

6.6.4 Scrolling Variables

ZSCBR	BROWSE service scroll amount [4, i/o, profile]
ZSCED	EDIT service scroll amount [4, i/o, profile]
ZSCML	Member list scroll amount [4, i/o, profile]
ZSCROLLA	Scroll amount (PAGE, MAX, number) [4, out]
ZSCROLLD	Default scroll amount [4, in]
ZSCROLLN	Scroll amount computed as number [4, out]

6.6.5 TBDISPL Service Variables

ZTDADD	More rows needed to satisfy scroll request (YES | NO) [3, out, func]
ZTDAMT	Number of rows needed to satisfy scroll [3, out, func]
ZTDLROWS	Number of rows in the logical table [6, in, func]
ZTDLTOP	Map current top row in physical table to its position in logical table [6, in, func]
ZTDMARK	User-defined bottom-of-data text [in]
ZTDMSG	User-defined message-id for top of table [8, in]
ZTDRET	[8, in, func]
ZTDROWS	Number of displayed table rows [6, out, func]
ZTDSCRP	CRP of top row to be displayed after scroll [6, i/o, func]
ZTDSELS	Number of selected table rows [4, out, func]
ZTDSIZE	Size of scrollable section [4, out, func]
ZTDSRID	Row-id of the row pointed to by ZTDSCRP [6, out, func]
ZTDTOP	Row number (CRP) of top row displayed [6, out, func]

6.6.6 Dialogue Error Variables

ZERRALRM	Message alarm indicator (YES | NO) [3, out, func]
ZERRHM	Name of associated help panel [8, out, func]
ZERRLM	Long error message text [512, out, func]
ZERRMSG	Error message-id [8, out, func]
ZERRSM	Short error message text [24, out, func]
ZERRTYPE	Error message type [8, out, func]
ZERRWIND	Error message window type [6, out, func]

6.6.7 Control Variables Used in Selection Panels

ZCMD	Command input field*
ZPARENT	Parent selection panel name (when in explicit chain mode)
ZPRIM	Primary option selection panel (YES | NO)
ZSEL	Command input field truncated at first period

* This variable may also be used in a non-select panel.

6.6.8 Control Variables Used in Help Panels

ZCONT	Name of next continuation panel
ZHINDEX	Name of first index panel
ZHTOP	Name of top panel
ZIND	Index page indicator (YES | NO)
ZUP	Name of parent panel

6.6.9 List Service Variables

ZLSTLPP	Line count for the list data set [4]
ZLSTNUML	Number of lines on the current list data set page [4]
ZLSTTRUN	List data set record length truncation value [4]

6.6.10 List and Log Dataset Variables

ZLOGNAME	Log data set name [44]
ZLSTNAME	List data set name [44]

6.6.11 System Variables as Panel Control Variables

A number of panel control variables (special variable names prefixed with ".", example .ALARM) can be used within a panel to control processing. The following system variables can be used outside panels to achieve the same result:

```
ALARM      .ALARM
AUTOSEL    .AUTOSEL
ATTR       .ATTR
ATTRCHAR   .ATTRCHAR
CSRPOS     .CSRPOS
CSRROW     .CSRROW
CURSOR     .CURSOR
HELP       .HELP
MSG        .MSG
PFKEY      .PFKEY
RESP       .RESP
TRAIL      .TRAIL
ZVARS      .ZVARS
```

7

Message Services

7.1 INTRODUCTION

The message services are used to access a message or message text stored in the Message Library. This is either explicitly to use the text so obtained or implicitly to pass a message identifier to ISPF which then displays the corresponding text at the appropriate time.

7.2 FORM OF MESSAGE

Each definition always consists of two or more lines.

First line:
```
messageidentifier ['shortmessage']
        [.HELP=panelname|*]
        [.ALARM=YES|NO]
        [.WINDOW=RESP|NORESP|LRESP|NOLRESP]
        [.TYPE=NOTIFY|WARNING|ACTION|CRITICAL]
```

Long message line (subsequent line), continued:
```
        'longmessageline' +
```

Last long message line:
```
        'longmessageline'
```

Each line extends from column 1 through column 80; the message-identifier and the long-message-text must commence in column 1. Long message text lines can be continued with a plus (+). Each logical message defined in the message library may be separated from one another using one or more blank lines or a comment (/*) starting in column 1.

Tip

A special case of message definition is a message which does not have any text. For example,

```
APPLX999
  '  '
```

This dummy message can be used where message processing is required but no message text is to be displayed, e.g. it can be used to force a panel redisplay.

messageidentifier

The **messageidentifier** uniquely identifies the message and has the form:

prefix   one to five alphabetic characters;
number   three numeric characters;
suffix   an alphanumeric character (optional).

The message-identifier has a maximum length of eight characters; if the suffix is not omitted, the prefix may only contain a maximum of four characters.

Examples:

APPLX000   valid (prefix: 5 characters, suffix omitted)
APPLX00A   invalid (prefix: 5 characters, suffix one character, number only two characters).

shortmessage

Shortmessage, if present, is displayed as standard at the right-hand end of the first line on the display. A short message, after substitution, is truncated to 24 characters.

Note: The two messages (short-message and long-message) are not fields in the usual ISPF context and so require no variable to be defined in the panel where they are to be displayed.

HELP=panelname | *

Panelname is the name of the panel which is displayed when the tutorial mode is entered. "*" means that the HELP panel associated with the panel currently being processed will be displayed. Default: *.

ALARM = YES|NO

An acoustic signal will sound when the message is displayed. Default: NO.

Tip
Use the acoustic signal consistently, e.g. sound for messages which require
the operator's intervention.

WINDOW = RESP | NORESP | LRESP | NOLRESP

The WINDOW keyword specifies that the message is to be displayed in a pop-
up window. The RESP and NORESP operands specify that both short and long
messages are to be displayed. The LRESP and NOLRESP operands specify that
only the long message is to be displayed. The RESP or LRESP operand
specifies that a response to the displayed message must be made before
processing can continue (modal display).

TYPE = <u>NOTIFY</u> | WARNING | ACTION | CRITICAL

The TYPE keyword specifies the severity of the displayed message. The
severity determines the colour of displayed message and the symbol
displayed in GUI-mode. Default: NOTIFY.

longmessage
The **longmessage** is displayed after the short message if the HELP key is
pressed. The long message is displayed as standard at the left-hand end of
the third line of the display. The long message is displayed in place of the
short message, should no short message be present.

Messages are grouped according to the message identifier and these groups are
stored as members of the message library; the member name is formed by
truncating the message identifier after the second character of the number part.

Example:
messageid	member name
APPLX001	APPLX00
TS001	TS00

This means that the member APPLX00, for example, contains the messages
APPLX000,...,APPLX009.

Tip
If the ISPF/PDF Editor is used for the definition of messages, the option NUMBER OFF
should be specified to avoid line numbers being placed in columns 73 through 80.

7.2.1 Variable Substitution

Symbolic variables may be specified in the message definition and will be replaced
with the value for the variable. Whereas for the SETMSG service, the substitution for
the variable is made when the message is displayed, the substitution is made when
the service is invoked.

A keyword is a constant identifying an entry, e.g. ".HELP=" . The symbolic variables so used must contain a valid value at the time of invocation.

Two special characters have particular significance when used in variable substitution:

· A period separates a variable from a concatenated literal. For example, &VAR.AB; AB is appended to the current value of VAR. Two periods must be specified if a single period is to appear after substitution, e.g. &VAR..AB.
· If an ampersand (&) is to appear after substitution, two ampersands must be paired, e.g. &&XYZ.

Example:
The following APPLX001 message definition uses four symbolic variables: &PNO (twice), &H and &A.

```
┌─ message APPLX001 ─────────────────────────────
│ APPLX001 'empno. &PNO missing' .HELP=&H .ALARM=&A
│ 'employee no. &PNO not defined'
└─────────────────────────────────────────────────
```

This message could be displayed using the following statements:
```
SET &PNO = 1234
SET &H = TSPAH001
SET &A = YES
ISPEXEC SETMSG MSG(APPLX001)
```

Tip
To avoid having to define a large number of messages a generalised message "torso" containing symbolic variables may be defined:

```
┌─────────────────────────────────────────────────
│ APPLX000 '&SMSG' .ALARM=&ALRM
│ '&LMSG'
└─────────────────────────────────────────────────
```

The three symbolic variables &SMSG, &LMSG and &ALRM are replaced by the appropriate text for "short message", "long message" and alarm condition (ON or OFF), respectively, when the message is displayed. The user must himself weigh up the advantages and disadvantages compared with a larger repertoire of fixed messages.

7.3 MESSAGE PROCESSING

Messages are displayed in conjunction with panels. The message identification may be specified explicitly when the panel is displayed or implicitly by means of the SETMSG statement (and takes effect when the next panel is displayed).

The short message is displayed first in the right-hand side of the top line of the display. If no short message is defined, the long message is displayed in the left-hand side of the third line of the display. However, these default locations may be changed in the panel definition or by the user specifying that the command line is to be placed at the bottom of the display. The following pseudo code illustrates the message processing:

```
If short-message defined
  then display in 1st display line (right-justified)
  If Help-key pressed
    then display long-message in 3rd display line (left-justified)
    else display long-message in 3rd display line (left-justified);
  If Help-key pressed
    then display Help-panel;
```

7.4 MESSAGE SERVICES

ISPF provides the following explicit message services:

· GETMSG   Get a message.
· LOG   Write a message to the ISPF log dataset.
· SETMSG   Set a message.

Messages can also be set in conjunction with panel display, with certain panel processing functions or with the .MSG panel variable (see Section 7.6).

7.4.1 GETMSG - Get a Message

The GETMSG service obtains the message from the message library. The information fields associated with the message are returned as the specified variables and substitutions are made for any symbolic variables specified in the message.

Syntax:
```
ISPEXEC GETMSG MSG(messageid)
        [SHORTMSG(shortmessagename)]
        [LONGMSG(longmessagename)]
        [ALARM(alarmname)]
        [HELP(helpname)]
        [TYPE(typename)
        [WINDOW(windowname)
```

MSG(messageid)
    Messageid identifies the message for which the information is to be retrieved.

SHORTMSG(shortmessagename)
    Shortmessagename is the name of the variable which is to contain the short message text.

LONGMSG(longmessagename)
    Longmessagename is the name of the variable which is to contain the long message text.

ALARM(alarmname)

> **Alarmname** is the name of the variable which is to contain the alarm indicator. The alarm indicator is either "YES" or "NO". The value "NO" is returned if no alarm indicator has been specified for the message.

HELP(helpname)

> **Helpname** is the name of the variable which is to contain the name of the help panel. The value "*" is returned if no help panel name has been specified for the message.

TYPE(typename)

> **Typename** is the name of the variable which is to contain the type of the help panel. The type is one of the values: NOTIFY, WARNING, ACTION, or CRITICAL.

WINDOW(windowname)

> **Typename** is the name of the variable which is to contain the window mode of the help panel. The window mode is either RESP or NORESP, depending on whether or not a response to the displayed message is to be made.

The service sets one of the following return codes:

> 0   Normal completion.
>
> 12   No message for the specified message identifier is contained in the message library.
>
> 20   Severe error.

Example:
```
SET &PNO = 1234
ISPEXEC GETMSG MSG(APPLX001) SHORTMSG(SNAME)
WRITE &SNAME
```
These statements return in variable SNAME the short text for message APPLX001. For the previous example, "empno. &PNO missing", where &PNO is replaced by the current value for the variable. That is, "empno. 1234 missing" will be displayed here.

Tip

The GETMSG service can be used to pass parameters, such as display heading, to an application.

Example:
```
ISPEXEC GETMSG MSG(TSMSG011) LONGMSG(LMSGTEXT)
```
that uses the message definition

```
┌─ message TSMSG011 ───────────────┐
│TSMSG011 ' '                      │
│'report heading'                  │
└──────────────────────────────────┘
```

stores the long message text from message TSMSG011 into the variable LMSGTEXT.

7.4.2 LOG - Write a Message to the ISPF Log Dataset

The LOG service writes the short and long message text for the specified message identifier to the log data set defined for ISPF. The message is prefixed with the current time. Substitutions are performed for any symbolic variables in the message text.

Syntax:
```
ISPEXEC LOG MSG(messageid)
```

MSG(messageid)
Messageid identifies the message for which the information is to be retrieved.

The service sets one of the following return codes:

   0   Normal completion.
   12 No message for the specified message identifier is contained in the message library.
   20 Severe error.

Example:
```
ISPEXEC LOG MSG(APPLX002)
```
that uses the message definition:

```
 ─ message APPLX002 ──────────────────────────────
 APPLX002 'empno. &PNO missing' .HELP=&H .ALARM=&A
 'employee no. &PNO not defined'
```

writes the text "empno. &PNO missing" and "employee no. &PNO not defined", where &PNO is replaced by the current value for the variable, to the ISPF log data set.

7.4.3 SETMSG - Set a Message

The SETMSG service specifies the message from the message library which is to be used when the next panel is displayed. SETMSG may be repeatedly called before the next panel is displayed, the last specified message is the one actually used. If an explicit message is specified for the panel display, that message takes precedence over any messages set by the SETMSG service. If the message contains symbolic variables, substitutions are made using the values for these variables at the time of invocation not at the point of display.

The message remains pending until the next physical display is performed, i.e. the CONTROL NONDISPL request has no effect on any messages which have been previously set.

If the message specifies a help panel, then substitutions for any symbolic variables contained in this panel are when the HELP command is processed and not when the SETMSG is issued.

Syntax:
```
ISPEXEC SETMSG MSG(messageid)
        [COND]
        [MSGLOC(messagefieldname)]
```

MSG(messageid)

Messageid identifies the message which is to be displayed.

COND

The message is displayed only if there is no pending SETMSG message request.

MSGLOC(messagefieldname)

Messagefieldname identifies the message which is to be displayed.

The service sets one of the following return codes:

0   Normal completion.
4   COND SETMSG issued while a SETMSG is pending.
12   No message for the specified message identifier is contained in the message library.
20   Severe error.

Example:
```
ISPEXEC SETMSG MSG(APPLX001)
```
The text associated with the APPLX001 message will be used for the next panel display. The symbolic variable is replaced by the value current at the time of invocation.

7.5 SYMBOLIC PARAMETERS

```
message-identifier 'short-message'  .HELP=panel-name .ALARM=code
'long-message'
```

Figure 7.1 - Use of symbolic parameters in message definition

```
GETMSG MSG(message-id)
       SHORTMSG(short-message-name)
       LONGMSG(long-message-name)
       ALARM(alarm-name)
       HELP(help-name)

LOG MSG(message-id)

SETMSG MSG(message-id)
```

Figure 7.2 - Use of symbolic parameters in message services

Note to figures: Italicised parameters may be variables, but it is necessary to ensure that the variables have been initialised with the desired values. For example,

```
SET &TXT = &STR(DATA MISSING)
ISPEXEC SETMSG MSG(TSMSG002)
```

for the message definition:

```
┌─ message TSMSG002 ───────────┐
│ TSMSG002 &SMSG .ALARM=NO     │
│ '&TXT ERROR'                 │
└──────────────────────────────┘
```

displays the long message text:

```
DATA MISSING ERROR
```

7.6 INVOCATION OF MESSAGES

Messages can be invoked explicitly be means of one of these previously described services or in conjunction with a number of services and statements. Table 7.1 shows where messages may be used.

Table 7.1 — Setting messages

```
GETMSG      MSG(messageid)
SETMSG      MSG(messageid)
LOG         MSG(messageid)
DISPLAY     MSG(messageid)
TBDISPL     MSG(messageid)
TRANS       MSG = messageid
VER         MSG = messageid
panel       .MSG = messageid
```

8

Panel Processing

8.1 INTRODUCTION

The Display Service Functions are concerned with the processing of panels. **Panels** describe the layout of the terminal display, processing to be performed on variables before and after display, and field attributes. Each panel definition consists of **sections**. The facilities offered by the Display Service Functions are to a large extent limited by the hardware characteristics of the display terminals.

8.2 HARDWARE CHARACTERISTICS

A basic understanding of the hardware characteristics of the display terminals is necessary for appreciation of the facilities offered by ISPF. Most display terminals used on IBM mainframe computer systems operate in alphanumeric mode and so offer relatively limited features. A typical representative of this class of computer terminal is the IBM 3278 unit (or compatible). This terminal has 24 (or 32) lines each having 80 characters giving a maximum screen capacity of 1920 (or 2560) characters. The screen is divided into fields, each field being prefixed by an **attribute byte** which specifies the attributes for the following field (display intensity, protected (non-input), etc.). The attribute byte occupies a screen location but is not displayed. The screen content is buffered and may only be processed when one of the transmit keys (ENTER, END, PF-key) has been pressed. This means that the form of the display cannot be dynamically changed because of input made in the same screen (although this may, to some extent, be simulated). Hardware features of more advanced display terminals, such as the IBM 3297 (character-oriented attributes, etc.), are not supported by ISPF. The lower level IBM GDDM package must be used here, although GDDM graphics can be included in panels.

ISPF 4.1 has an optional GUI (Graphical User Interface) that permits ISPF application panel displays to be shown on an OS/2 terminal. This GUI enables existing mainframe applications to be easily ported to workplace computers, although there it provides limited workstation-like support (e.g. use of the mouse, push-buttons).

Data is represented in the screen buffer as below:

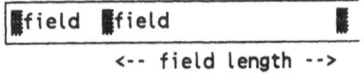

The symbol ▌ is used to represent the attribute byte. The interpretation and meaning of the field contents depends on the characteristics of the attribute byte. The attribute byte specifies the characteristics of the following field and occupies one position in the display. It is protected and displayed as blank. The characteristics of an attribute remain in effect until the next attribute byte is specified. This also applies across lines. The distance between successive attribute bytes determines the length of the field. A field may exist across lines. There are two classes of fields: **text** and **data**. Data fields are subdivided into **input** and **output** fields. Text fields are displayed in the same form as they are defined, symbolic variables (an ISPF variable prefixed by &) being replaced by their current value. Data fields are the names of ISPF variables and replaced by the current value and length from the dialogue variable pool. Output means that the field may only used for output, i.e. is **protected** against being altered by the user. Input fields may be used for both input and output, i.e. are **non-protected**. The names of data fields have a maximum length of 8 characters - the ISPF restriction for the maximum length of a variable name. Should the field length be less than the length of the variable name, a placeholder (the system variable Z) may be assigned to this field. The .ZVARS system variable is used to contain the assignment of variable names to placeholders.

Example:
Assume that the variable BETA has the contents gamma
▒ represents an attribute byte for text fields
▌ represents an attribute byte for input fields,

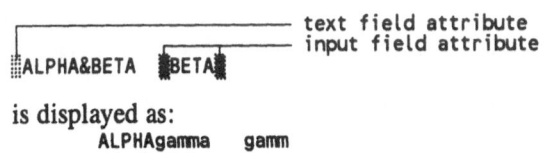

is displayed as:
            ALPHAgamma   gamm

8.3 FORM OF A PANEL

A panel is a member of the ISPPLIB library and consists of a number of sections, some of which are mandatory while others are optional. Sections are identified by a section header in column 1 of the panel definition. The **panel section**,)PANEL, indicates that the panel is to be displayed in CUA mode and specifies the associated keylist. The **attribute section**,)ATTR, specifies field attributes. The **action bar choice** section,)ABC, specifies the entries that appear in the action bar. The **action bar choice initialisation** section,)ABCINIT, specifies initialisation to be performed for the action bar choice entries. The **action bar choice processing** section,)ABCPROC, specifies the processing to be performed on the selected action bar entry. The **body section**,)BODY, defines the form of the panel as it will be displayed. The **scrollable area** section,)AREA, specifies a scrollable area. The **initialisation section**,)INIT, specifies processing which is to be performed before the panel is displayed. The **reinitialisation section**,)REINIT, specifies processing which is to be performed before the panel is redisplayed because of a message being set. The **processing section**,)PROC, specifies processing which is to be performed after the panel is displayed. The **model section**,)MODEL, specifies the display form of a logical line from an ISPF table, this special section is only used for table display processing. The **point-and-shoot section** ,)PNTS, specifies the point-and-shoot fields. The **help section** ,)HELP, specifies the help panels and reference phrases associated with fields. The **end section**,)END, terminates the panel definition.

Each section consists of a mandatory **section header** and a variable number of **detail lines**.

8.3.1 Panel Section ( )PANEL) (Optional)

If present, the panel section indicates that the panel is to be displayed in CUA mode. If can also specify the associated keylist. The keylist defines the function keys and their corresponding actions as they apply to this panel.

Header:
```
)PANEL [KEYLIST(keylistname[,keylistid])]
```

keylistname
> The name of the associated keylist. **Keylistname** is contains 1-8 alphanumeric characters (the first character must be alphabetic). Lowercase characters are converted to uppercase.

keylistid
> The optional application-id used to locate the keylist. The keylist has the name keylistidKEYS.
> If no **keylistid** is specified, ISPKYLST is used.

Example:
```
)PANEL KEYLIST(DEMO)
```
The DEMO keylist is associated with this panel.

8.3.2 Attribute Section ( )ATTR) (Optional)

The attribute section defines the attributes of fields used in the panel display. The **attribute character** defined in the attribute section is converted to the appropriate **hardware attribute byte** as used in the panel definition.

Header:
)ATTR [DEFAULT(abc)]

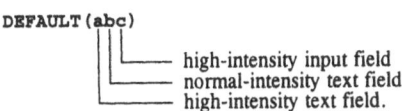

DEFAULT defines the default attribute characters. ISPF has the following default attribute characters (DEFAULT(%+_)):

%	high-intensity text field
+	normal-intensity text field
_	high-intensity input field.

If the user defines his own default characters, all three default attribute characters must be defined (the original default characters may be retained or redefined).

Example:
       DEFAULT($/+)
defines

$	high-intensity text field
/	normal-intensity text field
+	high-intensity input field.

Tip
No default attribute character exists for output fields. However, output fields can in most circumstances be represented as text fields. Assume that the following attribute characters exist:

ә	output field
%	text field

Then the following two entries are equivalent (ALPHA is a variable):
        әALPHA
       %&ALPHA

Note: An output field has a fixed length whereas the length of a text field is variable.

Detail line:
A detail line assigns field attributes to the specified special-character (non-alphanumeric). As many detail lines as necessary may be specified, provided that the number of lines does not exceed the physical screen size.

```
attributecharacter
        [TYPE(TEXT | INPUT | OUTPUT | DATAIN | DATAOUT | type)]
        [AREA(DYNAMIC | GRAPHIC | SCRL)]
        [ATTN(ON | OFF)]
        [CAPS(ON | OFF | IN | OUT)]
        [CKBOX(ON | OFF)]
        [COLOR(WHITE | RED | BLUE | GREEN | PINK | YELLOW | TURQ)]
        [DATAMOD(code)]
        [EXTEND(ON | OFF)]
        [HILITE(USCORE | BLINK | REVERSE)]
        [INTENS(HIGH | LOW | NON)]
        [JUST(LEFT | RIGHT | ASIS)]
        [NUMERIC(ON | OFF)]
        [OUTLINE( [L] [R] [O] [U] | BOX | NONE)]
        [PAD(NULLS | USER | character)]
        [PADC(NULLS | USER | character)]
        [PAS(ON | OFF)]
        [REP(character)]
        [SKIP(ON | OFF)]
        [SCROLL(ON | OFF)]
```

The following parameters are only applicable for Double-Byte Character Set (DBCS) terminals which are not discussed here:

```
[GE(ON | OFF)]
[FORMAT(EBCDIC | DBCS | MIX)]
```

attributecharacter

The **attributecharacter** is a single character or a byte with the specified hexadecimal digit-pair representation (e.g. 01 represents the byte X'01') which is to be assigned the following field attributes and is used in the panel definition ( )BODY section) as hardware attribute byte to identify the start of a field. Those characters used as attribute characters must be chosen not to conflict with characters required in the panel display; in general, non-alphabetic, non-numeric characters (e.g. $, %) should be used.

The following characters may not be used:
> null (X'00')
> blank (X'40')
> & (ampersand).

TYPE(TEXT)
A text field (protected).

TYPE(INPUT)
An input field (non-protected). Default.

TYPE(OUTPUT)
An output field (protected).

TYPE(DATAIN)
An input (non-protected) sub-field within dynamic field.

TYPE(DATAOUT)

An output (protected) sub-field within dynamic field.

TYPE(type)

Type is one of the following CUA attributes:

AB	Action bar unselected choices. Mandatory. [COLOR(WHITE), INTENS(HIGH)].
ABSL	Action bar separator line. Mandatory. [COLOR(BLUE), INTENS(LOW)].
CEF	Choice entry field. [COLOR(TURQ), INTENS(LOW), HILITE(USCORE), CAPS(OFF), JUST(LEFT)].
CH	Column heading. [COLOR(BLUE), INTENS(HIGH)].
CHAR*	Character attributes in a dynamic area.
CT	Caution text. [COLOR(YELLOW), INTENS(HIGH)].
DATAIN*	Input field in a dynamic area. [CAPS(OFF), JUST(LEFT)].
DATAOUT*	Output field in a dynamic area. [CAPS(OFF), JUST(LEFT)].
DT	Descriptive text. [COLOR(GREEN), INTENS(LOW)].
EE	Error emphasis. [COLOR(YELLOW), INTENS(HIGH), HILITE(RVERSE), CAPS(OFF), JUST(LEFT)].
ET	Emphasized text. [COLOR(TURQ), INTENS(HIGH)].
FP	Field prompt. [COLOR(GREEN), INTENS(LOW)].
INPUT*	Input field. [CAPS(ON), JUST(LEFT)].
LEF	List entry field (e.g. table input field). [COLOR(TURQ), INTENS(LOW), HILITE(USCORE), CAPS(OFF), JUST(ASIS)].
LI	List items (e.g. table output field). [COLOR(WHITE), INTENS(LOW), CAPS(OFF), JUST(ASIS)].
LID	List item description. [COLOR(GREEN), INTENS(LOW), CAPS(OFF), JUST(ASIS)].
NEF	Normal entry field. [COLOR(TURQ), INTENS(LOW), HILITE(USCORE), CAPS(OFF), JUST(LEFT)].
NT	Normal text. [COLOR(GREEN), INTENS(LOW)].
OUTPUT*	Output field. [CAPS(ON), JUST(LEFT)].
PIN	Panel instruction. [COLOR(TURQ), INTENS(LOW)].
PS	Point-and-shoot. This type must be used for point-and-shoot text fields. [COLOR(TURQ), INTENS(HIGH), JUST(LEFT)].
PT	Panel title. [COLOR(BLUE), INTENS(LOW)].
RP	Reference phrase. Mandatory. [COLOR(TURQ), INTENS(HIGH)].
SAC	Select available choices. [COLOR(WHITE), INTENS(LOW)].
SI	Scroll information. [COLOR(WHITE), INTENS(HIGH)].
SUC	Select unavailable choices. [COLOR(BLUE), INTENS(LOW)].
TEXT*	Text field.
VOI	Variable output information. [COLOR(TURQ), INTENS(LOW), CAPS(OFF), JUST(LEFT)].
WASL	Work area separator line. [COLOR(BLUE), INTENS(LOW)].

WT   Warning text. [COLOR(WHITE), INTENS(HIGH)].

Those attributes marked with mandatory must be used for the indicated attribute. Many types (for example, the various text attributes) can be used at the developer's discretion. Those entries marked with an asterisk (*) are not CUA attributes, but are included for completeness.

Protected means that the contents of that field are protected against being changed, i.e. the field cannot be used for input. Text means that the contents of that field are interpreted as being text data, variable data must be specified as a symbolic variable (&variablename). Input and output mean that the following field is interpreted as being the name of a variable, the contents of which are placed at this location in the panel display. Output has only the significance that the displayed field contents cannot be altered, i.e. the field is only used for output. The use of DATAIN and DATAOUT fields is explained in the dynamic field section.

Example 1:
       ə TYPE(OUTPUT)
The ə character is used as field attribute for output fields.

Example 2:
       01 TYPE(INPUT)
The hexadecimal code X'01' is used as field attribute for input fields.

Tip
Attribute characters must be chosen carefully, as such characters cannot then appear in text fields. However, such attribute characters may appear as data in non-text fields.

AREA(DYNAMIC)
        The data area is dynamic.

AREA(GRAPHIC)
        The data area is graphic, i.e. is to contain a GDDM diagram.

AREA(SCRL)
        The data area is scrollable.

INTENS(HIGH)
        Display the field contents with high-intensity. Default.

INTENS(LOW)
        Display the field contents with low-intensity (normal).

INTENS(NON)
        Do not display the field contents.

Tip
The INTENS(NON) attribute is primarily used for the input of passwords, which should not be visible.

CAPS(ON)
Convert the field contents to uppercase before being displayed (input data are converted to uppercase before being stored). Default.

CAPS(OFF)
The field contents remain as defined (no data conversions are performed).

JUST(LEFT)
Store the field contents left-justified in the field before being displayed. Leading blanks are removed before the field data are stored. Default.

JUST(RIGHT)
Store the field contents right-justified in the field before being displayed. Trailing blanks are removed before the field data are stored. Right-justification is well suited for output numeric fields.

JUST(ASIS)
Do not alter the field alignment of the field contents before being stored before display. Leading blanks are not removed before the field data are stored.

Example:
The field having content " alpha beta " is stored in 16 byte field as follows:

```
................
alpha beta         JUST(LEFT)
      alpha beta   JUST(RIGHT)
   alpha  beta     JUST(ASIS)
```

PAD(NULLS)
Pad the field contents with the null-character (X'00') before being stored.

PAD(USER)
Pad using the padding character specified for ISPF/PDF (option 0.1).

PAD(character)
Pad using the specified **character**. Apostrophes must enclose the following characters:

blank < > ( ) : ; , ¬ + =

For example, '<'. In other cases the enclosing apostrophes are optional (i.e. PAD(0) and PAD('0') are both valid). The apostrophe character itself must be defined as paired apostrophes within apostrophes, i.e. PAD(''''). The specified padding character is appended to the field content before it is displayed, and removed before it is stored. The field alignment (JUST parameter) determines whether the padding is at the start or end of the field.

Example:
The field having content "1" is stored in a 5 byte field as follows:

```
.....
10000  JUST(LEFT)  PAD('0')
00001  JUST(RIGHT) PAD('0')
```

Justification is performed before padding. For an input field the following processing is performed:

RIGHT leading pad characters removed
LEFT   leading and trailing pad characters removed
ASIS   trailing pad characters removed

PADC(character)

Conditional padding. The specified pad **character** is used as filed filled only when the field is initially blank. Otherwise PADC is processed as PAD.

SKIP(ON)

Skip the field. Fields with the skip attribute set are automatically by-passed. SKIP(ON) may only be specified for text or output fields.
Default: SKIP(OFF).

Tip

Unfortunately, for reasons of compatibility with the original SPF version, the default is SKIP(OFF). The input of data is greatly simplified if non-input fields are by-passed, i.e. SKIP(ON) explicitly specified for such fields. As always, it is important to be consistent with the convention adopted.

ATTN(ON)

The field can be selected using the light pen or cursor select key. Three blanks, as required by 3270 hardware, must be placed around the attention attribute character.
Default: ATTN(OFF).

REP(character)

The REP parameter defines a character which is to be replaced by the hex-pair specified as attribute character.

The number of special characters on an alphanumeric terminal is limited. From this limited number of characters several characters must be reserved for attribute characters. The majority of the 256 possible ECBDIC characters (X'01', X'FF' etc.) have no representation on a normal display. These characters may, however, be used for attribute characters. Rather than entering the hexadecimal coding into the panel definition, the required hexadecimal coding can be defined in the)ATTR section as an attribute character and a displayable character used to represent this attribute character in the)BODY section (this displayable character is not an attribute character and so may be used as a normal text character).

If no REP character is specified, the hexadecimal code can be entered directly in the panel definition (see Example 2).

Tip
This feature allows a far wider range of attribute characters to be used without the complexity of entering the hexadecimal codes in the panel definition. However, this simplification is paid for by a more complex panel definition.

Example 1:
```
)ATTR
01 TYPE(TEXT) INTENS(HIGH) REP($)
02 TYPE(INPUT) INTENS(LOW) REP(%)
```
Attribute character code X'01' is represented by $ and X'02' by %; this representation is made in the following line in the)BODY definition, $ and % in the second line signify where the attribute character is to be placed, this second line only occurs in the definition and is not displayed.

```
)BODY
 ALPHA    BETA GAMMA
 $      %    $
```
ALPHA and GAMMA% are text fields and will be assigned the attribute character X'01', BETA is an input field and will be assigned the attribute character X'02', the actual assignment of the specified hexadecimal code is made just before the panel is processed.

Example 2:
```
)ATTR
5B TYPE(TEXT) INTENS(HIGH)
5C TYPE(INPUT) INTENS(LOW)
```
The attribute section defines two attribute characters code X'5B' (the $ character) and X'5C' (the * character) are defined.

```
)BODY
$ALPHA  *BETA$GAMMA
```

COLOR(WHITE|RED|BLUE|GREEN|PINK|YELLOW|TURQ)
The colour in which the field is displayed (TURQ represents turquoise). This parameter only applies to 7-colour display terminals. If no COLOR attribute is explicitly specified, the following defaults apply:

```
TEXT      HIGH    WHITE
OUTPUT    HIGH    WHITE
TEXT      LOW     BLUE
OUTPUT    LOW     BLUE
INPUT     HIGH    RED
INPUT     LOW     GREEN
```

HILITE(USCORE)
Underscore the field.

HILITE(BLINK)
Make the field blink.

HILITE(REVERSE)

Display the field in reverse video.

Note: The HILITE attribute applies to display terminals which support extended highlighting. Extended highlighting specified for display terminals which do not support it is ignored.

CKBOX(ON)

Allow a one-byte input field that is followed by an output field to be processed in GUI-mode as a checkbox.

Example:
```
)ATTR
@ TYPE(CEF) CKBOX(ON)
# TYPE(SAC)
)BODY
@Z#Check box description+
)INIT
.ZVARS = 'CHKBOX1'
```

NUMERIC(ON)

Activate the Numeric Lock feature. If activated, the keyboard locks if non-numeric input (the digits 0 through 9, - (minus), . (period) and DUP) is input.

OUTLINE([L][R][O][U] | BOX | NONE)

The default value for TYPE(INPUT) and TYPE(DATAIN) fields. The default also can be defined in the)BODY header.

L   left-hand vertical bar
R   right-hand vertical bar
O   horizontal bar over (above) field
U   horizontal bar under (below) field
BOX   field boxed
NONE   field not outlined (default.

PAS(ON)

PAS(ON) specifies a point-and-shoot field. If the cursor is positioned on a point-and-shoot field and the ENTER key is pressed, the action associated with the field (defined in the)PNTS section) is performed.

The PAS attribute is valid for input and output fields. In GUI-mode, a point-and-shoot field is displayed as a button.

Example:
```
)ATTR
@ TYPE(OUTPUT) PAS(ON)
)BODY
@CANCEL+
@OK+
)PNTS
FIELD(CANCEL) VAR(OPT) VALUE(1)
FIELD(OK) VAR(OPT) VALUE(2)
```

Example:
```
)ATTR DEFAULT(%?/)
* TYPE(INPUT) INTENS(NON)
@ TYPE(TEXT) INTENS(LOW) COLOR(BLUE) HILITE(REVERSE)
```

The DEFAULT parameter redefines the default attribute characters:

%   text field, high intensity (standard definition);

?   text field, low (normal) intensity;

/   input field, high intensity

The following attribute assignments define the following attribute characters:

*   input field, no display;

@   text field, low intensity, reverse video blue.

Note: The same attribute character may appear as DEFAULT parameter and as explicit assignment. Example:
```
)ATTR DEFAULT(*?/)
/ TYPE(INPUT) INTENS(NON)
```
The default attribute character for input fields (_) is replaced by "/" which has been given the additional attribute of non-display.

8.3.3 Action Bar Choice Section ( )ABC)

The action bar choice section specifies the text to be used in the pull-down windows (PDC operation) together with any processing to be performed (ACTION operation). One)ABC entry must be present for each pull-down menu selection. In non-GUI mode, each entry is automatically numbered.

Header:
```
)ABC DESC(choicetext)
     [MNEM(number)]
```

choicetext
> The **choicetext** is the text that appears in the action bar choice. Each ABC entry has one or more PDC entries that defines the pull-down choice items for the action bar selection. **Choicetext** must be written within quotes if it contains special characters (including blanks)
>
> The **choicetext** must correspond (case-sensitive, but without the enclosing quotes) with the associated entry in the action bar.

Example:
```
)ABC DESC('file')
```

number

The position in the **choicetext** that is used as mnemonic in GUI-mode — the corresponding character is displayed underscored.

Example:
```
)ABC DESC(file) MNEM(1)
```
f is used as mnemonic.

Pull-down choice item:
```
PDC DESC(itemchoicetext)
        [UNAVAIL(varname)]
        [MNEM(number)]
```

itemchoicetext

The **itemchoicetext** specifies the (pull-down choice) text which is to appear in the pull-down window. The individual PDC items are automatically numbered, starting with 1. Each PDC entry has one or more ACTION entries that specify the processing to be performed when the choice is selected.

Example:
```
)ABC DESC('file')
 PDC DESC(open)
 PDC DESC(save)
 PDC DESC('save as')
 PDC DESC(close)
```

varname

The name of a variable that indicates whether the choice is available (0 = false) or not (1 = true).

Example:
```
SET &FLAGVAR = 1 /* CLIST - set SAVE unavailable */
...
)ABC DESC(file)
 PDC DESC(open)
 PDC DESC(save) UNAVAIL(FLAGVAR)
 PDC DESC(close)
```
Set SAVE unavailable.

number

The position in the **itemchoicetext** that is used as mnemonic in GUI-mode — the corresponding character is displayed underscored.

Example:
```
)ABC DESC(file)
 PDC DESC('save as ...') MNEM(2)
```
a is used as mnemonic.

The relationship between action bar choices and pull-down items is illustrated in the following diagram. The ə represents the action bar attribute.

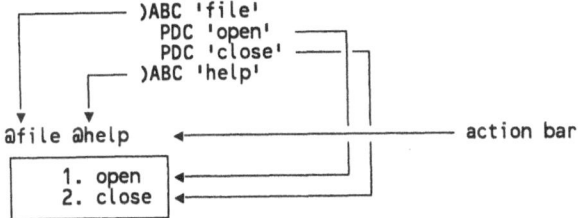

ACTION operation

The ACTION operation specifies the processing to be performed on the selected pull-down choice.

The following entry may be specified:
· RUN — invoke a command.

Format:
```
ACTION RUN(commandname) [PARM(parm [parm]...) | PARM(&varname
[&varname]...)]
```

commandname

The **commandname** is the name of the command table entry that is to be performed.
The START command invokes a command in the second screen. Note: The ISPSTRT program also can be used to invoke the START command.

parm | varname

A parameter or value of a variable that is to be passed to the command.

Example:
```
)ABC DESC('file')
  PDC DESC('open')
   ACTION RUN(CMD01) PARM('OMEGA')
  PDC DESC('save')
  PDC DESC('save as...')
  PDC DESC('close')
   ACTION RUN(EXIT)
)ABC DESC('help')
   ...
```

This example defines two action bar choices (file and help). The file action bar choice has four choices (open, save, save as, and close) in the pull-down menu. The choice open invokes the command CMD01 with parameter OMEGA; the choice close invokes the command EXIT; no command is associated with the save and save as choices.

8.3.4 Action Bar Choice Initialisation Section ( )ABCINIT)

The action bar choice initialisation section specifies the initialisation to be performed when the action bar choice is selected. The)ABCINIT section follows the corresponding)ABC section.

The .ZVARS control variable is used to associate the action bar choice selection with a variable, for example,

```
.ZVARS=USERPDC
&USERPDC='' /* clear selection */
```

Note: The .ZVARS placeholder specified here is independent of any placeholders specified in the panel body and model sections.

Example:
```
)ABC DESC('file')
 PDC DESC('open')
  ACTION RUN(CMD01) PARM('OMEGA')
 PDC DESC('view')
 PDC DESC('close')
  ACTION RUN(EXIT)
)ABCINIT
 .ZVARS=USERPDC
 &USERPDC=2 /* set 2 as default selection */
```

8.3.5 Action Bar Choice Processing Section ( )ABCPROC)

The action bar choice processing section specifies the processing to be performed on the selected pull-down entry. The)ABCPROC section follows the corresponding)ABCINIT section. ISPF validates the selected action bar choice.

Example:
```
)ABC DESC('file')
 PDC DESC('open')
  ACTION RUN(CMD01) PARM('OMEGA')
 PDC DESC('view')
 PDC DESC('close')
  ACTION RUN(EXIT)
)ABCINIT
 .ZVARS = UPDC
)ABCPROC
 IF (&UPDC=2)
   &DELTA='123' /* View selected */
```

8.3.6 Body Section ( )BODY) (Mandatory)

The body section defines the form of the display as it will appear on the display terminal. Each line in the body section corresponds to a line on the display screen. The first line in the body section corresponds to the top line of the display, the first column in the first line being the first position on the top line of the display. The number of lines in the body section may not exceed the number of physical lines on the screen (normally 24). Likewise the line width in the body section (record length of the library) may not exceed the physical line size of the terminal display (normally 80). Figure 8.1 shows the mapping on to the display screen.

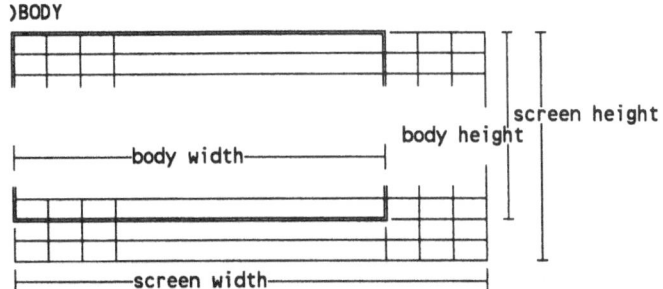

Figure 8.1 - Mapping of)BODY section on terminal display screen

The body section is comprised of fields, each field having the appropriate attribute character. Variable-names appearing in INPUT or OUTPUT fields must be unique. An output field which is to appear more than once must be defined as a text field.

Header:

```
)BODY
        [CMD(fieldname)]
        [SMSG(fieldname)]
        [LMSG(fieldname)]
        [ASIS]
        [WIDTH(width)]
        [EXPAND(delimiter1 delimiter2)]
        [WINDOW(width,depth)]
        [DEFAULT(abc)]
        [OUTLINE( [L] [R] [O] [U] |BOX|NONE)]
```

CMD(fieldname)

Fieldname specifies the variable which is to be interpreted as being the command field. This field must have the attribute TYPE(INPUT). If no fieldname is specified (i.e. CMD()), the panel does not have a command field.

Default: The first input field.

It is recommended that the ZCMD system variable for reasons of consistency be used as command field name.

SMSG(fieldname)

Fieldname specifies the variable which is to contain short messages in the display. This field must have the attribute TYPE(OUTPUT).

Default: the last 24 characters on the top line of the display.

LMSG(fieldname)

Fieldname specifies the variable which is to contain long messages in the display; this field must have the attribute TYPE(OUTPUT).

Default: line 3 of the display.

ASIS

Display the command and long message fields as defined in the panel definition. ASIS overrides any placement specified in the PARM option 0.4 or using the system variable ZPLACE.

WIDTH(width)

Width specifies the number of columns to be used in formatting the panel display. The specified width may not be less than 80 or exceed the physical screen width.

The default width is 80.

EXPAND(delimiter1 delimiter2)

Delimiter1 and **delimiter1** specify the delimiter characters used to enclose a single character which is to be expanded in the line to the specified width. The two delimiter characters may be the same character and must be specified as direct values (i.e. not as a variable). The number of characters to be inserted is determined before any substitutions are made in the line. Note: EXPAND precludes the preprocessing of panels; preprocessing minimises the run-time processing required for the panel.

WINDOW(width,depth)

The WINDOW keyword specifies size of the panel when it is displayed as a pop-up display (window).

Width specifies the number of columns to be used in formatting the panel display. **Depth** specifies the number of rows to be used in formatting the panel display.

DEFAULT(abc)

The DEFAULT defines the default attribute characters. The default characters also can be defined in the)ATTR header. ISPF has the following default attribute characters (DEFAULT(%+_)):

%	high-intensity text field
+	normal-intensity text field
_	high-intensity input field.

OUTLINE([L][R][O][U]|BOX|NONE)

The default value for TYPE(INPUT) and TYPE(DATAIN) fields. The default also can be defined as a)ATTR detail line.

Example:
```
)BODY EXPAND(//)
+1.1 &TITLE /-/
```
This example performs the substitution for the variable TITLE and fills the line on the right with "-"s, e.g. assuming the variable TITLE contained ALPHA, the following line would be displayed:

```
+1.1 ALPHA  ------------------------------------------
```

Tip
The EXPAND facility is normally used to centralise headings and text elements. This is achieved by specifying expansion strings on both sides of the text element, an equal number of fill characters is set into each expansion string.

Detail line:
Each detail line in the)BODY section represents a line on the screen, a line consists of fields. Each field is prefixed by the appropriate attribute character which determines the attributes of the following field (INPUT, OUTPUT or TEXT). Attribute characters remain in effect until the next attribute character is specified and a field (but not the field name) can extend onto the next line. Attribute characters are either the default characters or those characters defined in the)ATTR section.

Example:
```
)BODY
%---------------- Employee Record --------------------
%COMMAND ===>_ZCMD
%
%Employee number: &PNO
%
%     Surname ===>_NAME          +
```

This simple panel uses the default attribute characters and contains three fields:

Two input fields:
  ZCMD command field

  NAME surname
      The "+" attribute character following the NAME field serves as delimiter and
      limits the input in this field to a maximum of 12 characters;

One text field:
  PNO personnel number.
      This text field could also have been defined as an output field (an attribute
      character would need to be defined, as there is no default attribute character
      for output fields).

Assuming the variable PNO contained 1234, the following panel would be displayed:
```
-------------- Employee Record ---------------
  COMMAND ===>

  Employee number: 1234

      Surname ===>
```

Tip
Panels should have a uniform layout. The following general layout is based on the form of panels used by IBM in the PDF application. The position of fields be may changed. However, the developer should have good reasons for doing this. In particular, it is desirable to distinguish between input and output fields (for example, prefix input fields with ===> and output fields with :). Similarly,

mandatory input fields can be distinguished by highlighting the arrow preceding the field. This all results in simplifying data input.

ISPF applications evolve and, as such, various versions may be used at any one point in time. The **version** in the panel heading enables the version being used to be identified. To ease maintenance the version should be defined as a variable in the initial function. Likewise, **panelid** (panel identification) and **title** serve to identify in which panel the user currently is, and so simplify troubleshooting. A **command field** should usually be present, even if the panel itself does not use commands, as this enables TSO/ISPF commands to be invoked without exiting from the current application. Such commands can be considered as being extended help information. However, for applications being used by novices it may be advantageous to inhibit the use of commands to save the user from himself (Chapter 13 discusses how this can be achieved using command tables). The **PF-key usage** should reflect the usage of PF-keys in the current panel.

8.3.7 Model Section( )MODEL)

The)MODEL section specifies the display format of a logical line (row) of an ISPF table and is only used in conjunction with the table display (TBDISPL) service.

Header:
```
)MODEL [CLEAR(variablename [,variablename]...)] [ROWS(ALL|SCAN)]
```

CLEAR(variablename [,variablename)]...
> Clear the specified dialogue variables (**variablename**) from the model lines before reading a table line.
> **Tip**
> This option should be used to clear references in the model line to non-table variables and extension variables.

ROWS(SCAN)
> Display only those table lines identified by the preceding TBSARG service.
> Default: ROWS(ALL).

Detail lines:
The)MODEL section contains a minimum of one line and a maximum of eight lines. The)MODEL detail lines represent one table line. The)MODEL section may contain neither dynamic areas nor graphic areas, similarly, variables within text fields may not be used.

A variable line may be used to define a model detail line. This variable line must contain a single variable (starting in position 1) and have been initialised before the panel is displayed (an initialisation in the)INIT section is too late), e.g. the panel definition:

```
)ATTR
ã TYPE(OUTPUT)
)MODEL
_OP _PNO    ãNAME
```

and the CLIST statement:
```
SET &LINE = &STR(_OP _PNO    ãNAME)
```

with panel definition:

```
)ATTR
@ TYPE(OUTPUT)
)MODEL
&LINE
```

are equivalent.

8.3.8 Area Section( )AREA)

The optional)AREA section specifies a scrollable area. The name specified on the)AREA header is associated with the same name in the panel body definition. The attribute character for the associated scrollable area in the panel body definition must have AREA(SCRL). A panel can have more than one scrollable area, each of which is defined in its own)AREA section. All scrollable areas scroll in synchronisation.

To allow for the scroll line that appears as the first line of the display, scrollable areas in the body section must be defined with at least two lines. Similarly, the scrollable areas must have a width of at least 20 characters.

An area section cannot contain the following items:

· action bar lines
· graphics area
· model section
· command line
· alternate message locations
· another scrollable area
· dynamic area with EXTEND(ON) or SCROLL(ON).

Header:
)AREA name [DEPTH(depth)]

name
          The name of the scrollable area.

depth
          The minimum line depth of an extendible scroll area.

Example:
```
)ATTR
# AREA(SCRL)
)BODY
#SAREA                    #
#                         #
#                         #
)AREA SAREA
+     Surname:_SNAME      +
+ First Name:_FNAME       +
+Dialing Code:_DCODE+
+Telephone No:_TNUM       +
)END
```

Sample display (scrolled down one line):
```
              More:    - +
      First Name: John
      Dialing Code:
```

8.3.9 Initialisation Section ( )INIT)

The)INIT section specifies the processing which is to be performed before the panel is displayed. The statements which may be used in the)INIT section are described in the)PROC section.

8.3.10 Reinitialisation Section ( )REINIT)

The)REINIT section specifies the processing which is to be performed before the panel is redisplayed, the redisplay being under control of the panel display service. A redisplay is invoked under the following circumstances:

· The .MSG control variable is non-blank, i.e. a statement in the)PROC section has implicitly (using a VER or TRANS statement) or explicitly (by assignment) set a message.
· The DISPLAY or TBDISPL service is used without a panel name being specified.

The statements which may be used in the)REINIT section are described in the)PROC section.

8.3.11 Processing Section ( )PROC)

The)PROC section specifies the processing which is to be performed after the panel is displayed and before control is returned to the point of invocation. The)PROC section typically is used to validate the input.

In general, the same statements may be used in the)INIT,)REINIT and)PROC sections. Any restrictions to this general rule will be stated.

Within statements, three types of data item may be used, although not always interchangeably:

· Dialog variables - a name preceded by an ampersand (&). Section 6.6 contains a list of the system variables.

· Control variables - a special name preceded by a period (.). Section 8.6 contains a description of the control variables.

· Literal - a character or numeric string, a literal may be enclosed within apostrophes (').
A literal value containing one of the following special characters:

    blank < > ( ) + - | ¬ = : ; , . &

must be enclosed within apostrophes:

A literal value may contain a dialog variable (a name preceded by an ampersand). This variable is replaced by the current value of the variable. If an ampersand itself is to appear, two ampersands must be used, e.g.

if the variable ALPHA contains BETA then

'&ALPHA' results in BETA
'&&ALPHA' results in &ALPHA

If the literal is to contain an embedded apostrophe, paired apostrophes must be used, e.g.

'USER'S' is invalid (non-paired apostrophes)
'USER''S' results in USER'S.

Blank characters at the end of a literal are ignored. If, however, the literal contains only a single blank character, this one blank is retained. Imbedded blank characters are retained, e.g.

' ', ' ' and '' represent the same value, namely a single blank character;
'ALPHA   ' and 'ALPHA' represent the same value, namely the character string containing the five characters: "ALPHA";
'ALPHA   BETA' represents   the character string containing the eleven characters: "ALPHA   BETA".

A literal defined within apostrophes can be continued on the following line by setting "+" at the end of the line to be continued, the literal continues at the first non-blank character on the following line (blanks up to the "+" on the continued line are retained), e.g.

'alpha +
        beta'

is equivalent to 'alpha   beta'.

8.3.12 Point-And-Shoot Section ( )PNTS)

The)PNTS section specifies the point-and-shoot fields. If the cursor is placed in a point-and-shoot field and the ENTER key is pressed, the action associated with the field is performed. This action assigns the specified value to the named variable.

Point-and-shoot fields can be associated with both variables (input and output fields) and with text fields. In both cases the appropriate attribute must have been assigned (PS(ON) (for input and output fields) or TYPE(PS) (for text field)).

The panel processing can use this set variable to perform additional processing, for example, to change the colour of the activated field.

Note: Because point-and-shoot fields are processed internally as non-modifiable input fields, a command field should be specified explicitly. The (optional) CMD operand in the)BODY section header specifies the name of the command field. CMD()

can be used to specify that there is no command field. If no CMD operand is present, the first input field is assumed to be the command field.

Format:
```
FIELD(fieldname) VAR(varname) VAL(value)
```

fieldname

The name of the associated point-and-shoot field. Text point-and-shoot fields are assigned a pseudo-name (ZPSmmnnn: mm = the number of the scrollable area (01,...,99; 00 = normal text field), nnn = number of the point-and-shoot field within the scrollable area or body section (for normal text fields)).

varname

The name of the variable that is to be set.

value

The value to be assigned to the variable.

Example 1:
```
)ATTR
ə TYPE(OUTPUT) PAS(ON)
)BODY
əCANCEL+
əOK+
)INIT
&CANCEL = CANCEL
&OK = OK
)PNTS
FIELD(CANCEL) VAR(OPT) VALUE(1)
FIELD(OK) VAR(OPT) VALUE(2)
```
If the cursor is placed on the CANCEL or OK field and ENTER is pressed, the OPT variable is set to 1 or 2, respectively.

Example 2:
```
)ATTR
ə TYPE(PS)
)BODY
əCancel+
əOK+
)PNTS
FIELD(ZPS00001) VAR(OPT) VALUE(1)
FIELD(ZPS00002) VAR(OPT) VALUE(2)
```
If the cursor is placed in the Cancel or OK text field and ENTER is pressed, the OPT variable is set to 1 or 2, respectively.

8.3.13 Field-Level Help Section ( )HELP)

The help section specifies the associated help panels for those fields which have field-level help or reference phrase. If the cursor is placed in a field that has field-level help or is a reference phrase and the HELP PF-key is pressed, the help panel associated with the field is displayed.

Format:
```
FIELD(varname) PANEL(panname)
```

varname
> The name of the field that is to have an associated help panel.

panname
> The name of the panel field associated with the field.

Example:
```
)HELP
FIELD(DAY) PANEL(PDTLH01)
FIELD(WEEK) PANEL(PDTLH02)
```
This example defines two field-level helps; help panels PDTLH01 and PDTLH02 are associated with the fields DAY and WEEK, respectively.

8.3.13.1 Reference Phrase. A reference phrase is similar to a field-help. Whereas a field-help is associated with a named field, a reference phrase is a text field that has the RP attribute. Reference phrases are assigned a pseudo-name (ZRPmmnnn: mm = the number of the scrollable area (01,...,99; 00 = normal text field), nnn = number of the reference phrase within the scrollable area or body section (for normal text fields)). Reference phrases and scrollable areas are numbered left to right, top to bottom.

Example 1:
```
)ATTR
# TYPE(RP) /* reference phrase
)BODY
+
#    vowel:_VOWEL+
#consonant:_CONS +
+  number:_NUM  +
)HELP
 FIELD(ZRP00001) PANEL(RPH001)
 FIELD(ZRP00002) PANEL(RPH002)
 )END
```
This panel has two reference phrases (shown italicised).

Example 2:
```
)ATTR
# TYPE(RP) /* reference phrase
a TYPE(SCRL) /* reference phrase
)BODY
+
+         vowel:_VOWEL+
+#special char:_SPECL+
+aSAREA                a+
+a                     a+
)AREA SAREA
+  consonant:_CONS + +
+#    number:_NUM  + +
+#alphabetic:_ALPHA+ +
```

```
)HELP
 FIELD(ZRP00001) PANEL(RPH001) /* special char
 FIELD(ZRP01001) PANEL(RPH002) /* number
 FIELD(ZRP01002) PANEL(RPH003) /* alphabetic
)END
```

This panel has three reference phrases (shown italicised). The second and third reference phrases are in the SAREA scrollable area.

8.3.14 End ( )END) (Mandatory)

The)END section terminates the panel definition.

Example:
```
)PANEL
)BODY
 ...
)PROC
 ...
)END
```

8.4 PANEL STATEMENTS

Subject to a few restrictions, the following statements may be used in detail lines in the initialisation ( )ABCINIT,)INIT,)REINIT) and processing ( )ABCPROC,)PROC) sections:

- Assignment (=)
- EXIT
- GOTO
- IF (ELSE)
- PANEXIT (panel exit)
- REFRESH
- TOG (toggle)
- VEDIT (variable edit)
- VER (verify)
- VGET
- VPUT.

A detail line may contain multiple statements.

8.4.1 Assignment Statement (=)

The assignment statement assigns a value to the specified variable. The variable may be a user defined variable, modifiable system variable or modifiable control variable. Value may be a literal, user variable, system variable or control variable.

Syntax:
```
variable = value
```

Example:
```
&ALPHA = ' '
&ALPHA = &ZTIME
&ALPHA = .CURSOR
&ALPHA = 123
.CURSOR = ALPHA
```

Note: The literals '' and ' ' both represent a single blank. The system variable &Z must be used to set the null variable (X'0').

8.4.2 EXIT Statement

The EXIT statement terminates processing in the section. The EXIT statement can be used to avoid complex nested IF-statements.

Syntax:
```
EXIT
```

Example 1:
```
IF (.RESP = END) EXIT
```

Example 2:
```
&RESULT = ''
&C = TRUNC(&OPTS,',')
&OPTS = .TRAIL
IF (&OPTS EQ '') EXIT
&RESULT = '&RESULT.&C'
&C = TRUNC(&OPTS,',')
&OPTS = .TRAIL
IF (&OPTS EQ '') EXIT
&RESULT = '&RESULT.&C'
&C = TRUNC(&OPTS,',')
&OPTS = .TRAIL
IF (&OPTS EQ '') EXIT
&RESULT = '&RESULT.&C'
```
These statements separate the individual operands (each delimited with a comma) from the OPTS variable. The operands (without delimiter) are set into the RESULT variable.

8.4.3 GOTO Statement

The GOTO statement passes control to a subsequent label.
A label has the format: label:. **Label** is 1-8 alphanumeric characters, the first character of which must be alphabetic. Lowercase characters are translated to uppercase.

Syntax:
```
GOTO label
```

Example:

```
&RESULT = ''
&C = TRUNC(&OPTS,',')
&OPTS = .TRAIL
IF (&OPTS EQ '') GOTO PARSEND
&RESULT = '&RESULT.&C'
&C = TRUNC(&OPTS,',')
&OPTS = .TRAIL
IF (&OPTS EQ '') GOTO PARSEND
&RESULT = '&RESULT.&C'
&C = TRUNC(&OPTS,',')
&OPTS = .TRAIL
IF (&OPTS EQ '') GOTO PARSEND
&RESULT = '&RESULT.&C'
PARSEND:
```

These statements separate the individual operands (each delimited with a comma) from the OPTS variable. The operands (without delimiter) are set into the RESULT variable.

8.4.4 IF Statement

The IF statement compares the contents of the specified variable with a value. This comparison yields the result: equal or unequal. Should this result correspond to the logical operator set in the IF statement (= represents equal, ¬= represents not equal), the following statements up to the end of the IF group are executed. An IF group is column-sensitive and is terminated by the first statement which starts in the same column or column further to the left.

The ELSE substatement introduces a group of statements that is executed should the previous IF statement not be satisfied. The ELSE group is column-sensitive and is terminated by the first statement which starts in the same column or column further to the left.

Nesting of IF statements is permitted. These nested IF statements are connected through the AND relationship.

Syntax:

```
IF (expression [boolop expression] ...])
[ELSE]
```

expression

> **Expression** is either a basic value test expression: variable relop value
> [,value ...]
> or a VER statement without a MSG= parameter:
> VER (variable[,NONBLANK],keyword[,value...])

boolop

> **Boolop** is a Boolean operator:
>
> | | |
> |---|---|
> | &, AND | AND Boolean operator. All the specified conditional expressions must be satisfied for the IF condition to be true. |
> | \|, OR | OR Boolean operator. At least one of the specified conditional expressions must be satisfied for the IF condition to be true. |

relop

> **Relop** is a relational operator:
>
> | | |
> |---|---|
> | EQ, = | equal |
> | NE, ¬= | not equal |
> | GT, > | greater than |
> | GE, >= | greater than or equal |
> | LT, < | less than |
> | LE, <= | less than or equal |
> | NG, ¬> | not greater than |
> | NL, ¬< | not less than. |
>
> A series of values (maximum 255) can be specified for the EQ and NE operators. The condition is satisfied if one of these values is true (OR relationship).

ELSE

> The optional ELSE keyword introduces the statements that are processed if the condition is not satisfied.

Example 1:
```
&ALPHA = 1
IF (&ALPHA ¬= 0)
  &BETA = 2
  &GAMMA = 3
&DELTA = 4
```
This IF-group is terminated by the statement &DELTA = 4.

Example 2:
```
&ALPHA = 1
IF (&ALPHA = 0,1,2)
  &BETA = 2
```
These statements assign 2 to BETA as the current value of ALPHA satisfies one of the values in the list.

Example 3:
```
&ALPHA = 1
&BETA = 2
IF (&ALPHA = 1)
  IF (&BETA = 2)
    &GAMMA = 3
  ELSE
    &GAMMA = 4
```
These statements assign 3 to GAMMA as the conditional statement &ALPHA = 1 and the conditional statement &BETA = 2 are both satisfied.

Example 4:
```
IF (VER (&PARM,NB,DSNAME))
  &Q1 = TRUNC(&PARM,'.')
```
These statements separate the first qualifier from PARM (into Q1) if it is a valid dataset-name.

Example 5:
```
IF (&A = 1 AND &B = 2)
    ...
```
The IF statement is true if both conditions are satisfied.

Example 6:
```
IF (&A = 1 OR VER(&B,NB,NAME))
    ...
```
The IF statement is true if either A is 1 or B is a valid (non-blank) name.

Tip

A statement with ¬= as operator and a list having more than one value, e.g.
```
IF (&ALPHA ¬= 0,1,2)
```
should not be used, because one of the conditions is always met. In the example, if ALPHA is 0, ALPHA is not 1, and if ALPHA is 1, ALPHA is not 0, etc.

However, a statement with ¬= as operator and a list having a single value, e.g.
```
IF (&ALPHA ¬= 0)
```
is perfectly legitimate.

8.4.5 PANEXIT (Panel Exit) Statement

The PANEXIT statement temporarily passes control to a program. This (panel exit) program receives parameters from the PANEXIT statement. Processing is resumed where it left off. Sections 14.10 and 14.12 contain a detailed description of the PANEXIT interface.

Tip

The use of panel exits in their current form cannot be recommended. Section 8.13.8 describes a method for extended processing which in most cases is simpler than using panel exits.

Syntax:
```
PANEXIT (variablename [,variablename]... ),PGM,exitaddr
        [,exitparm]
        [,MSG=messageid]
```

variablename

    The name of the variable to be passed to the exit routine. The exit routine receives the name of the variable and its content. The exit routine can modify the variable's content but not its length.

PGM

    Invoke a **program** exit. Only a program exit is currently supported. Section 14.12.2 describes a panel exit program that can be used to invoke a REXX procedure.

exitaddr

    The variable which contains the entry point address of the exit routine. This variable must have FIXED format and length 4 bytes (see Chapter 14 for a description of program variables).

exitparm
>The optional variable which contains the address of the parameter which is to be passed to the exit routine. This variable must have FIXED format and length 4 bytes.

MSG=messageid
>Display the **messageid** message if the exit routine returns with code 8.

Example:
```
PANEXIT ((ALPHA,BETA),PGM,&GAMMA,&DELTA
```
invokes the panel exit whose entry point address is contained in the variable GAMMA. The panel exit receives two variables ALPHA and BETA, and the parameter whose address is contained in the variable DELTA.

8.4.6 REFRESH Statement

The REFRESH statement forces the specified variables in the panel body to be updated before redisplay. Normally the panel fields are not updated when the panel is redisplayed, i.e. the fields have the same values as when the user last saw them. A redisplay occurs when a message is set (explicitly or implicitly) in the processing section or a panel display is made without a panel name being specified.

Tip
REFRESH is only necessary if the panel is to be redisplayed after variables have been modified as a result of processing.

Syntax:
```
REFRESH (variablename [,variablename]...)
```

The pseudo-variablename asterisk (*) indicates that all panel fields having the attribute input or output will be refreshed.
>The parentheses may be omitted if only a single field is specified.

Example:
```
REFRESH (ALPHA, BETA)
```
Refresh the two panel fields ALPHA and BETA;

```
REFRESH (*)
```
Refresh all panel fields having the attribute INPUT or OUTPUT.

8.4.7 TOG (Toggle) Statement

The TOG statement alternates the value of a variable between two values.

Syntax:
```
TOG (mode,panelfield,&variable[,value1,value2])
```

mode

The processing mode:

S   Single. The mode used for pull-downs and single choice selection fields.

M   Multiple. The mode used for multiple choice selection fields.

panelfield

The panel field that controls whether **variable** alternates.

In single mode: if the field has been changed.

In multiple mode: if the field previously contained a non-blank and has not been changed to a blank, or was blank and now contains a non-blank.

variable

The name of a dialogue variable whose value alternates between **value1** and **value2**.

value1

The value that **variable** receives if **variable** does not equal **value1**. Default: 0.

value2

The value that **variable** receives if **variable** does not equal **value2**. Default: 1.

Example:
```
)BODY
+Field1:_FLD1
+Field2:_FLD2
+Field3:_FLD3
)INIT
)PROC
TOG(S,FLD1,&FLD3,1,2)
TOG(S,FLD2,&FLD3,1,2)
)END
```

8.4.8 VEDIT (Variable Edit) Statement

The VEDIT statement specifies the variables that are used for mask validation. The VMASK program service associates masked variables with program variables and performs the specified validation (various date and time formats, or user specified mask) when a value is entered into the variable.

In a panel, masked variables should be identified with VEDIT statement before they are used for any other processing.

Syntax:
```
VEDIT (variablename)
      [,MSG=messageid]
```

variablename

The name of a dialogue variable that is to be checked for mask validation.

MSG = messageid

Display the message identified by **messageid** should the validation fail. A standard message, dependent on the verification form, is displayed if no explicit message is specified.

Example:
```
)BODY
+ Date:_UDATE    +
+Value:_UVAL          +
)INIT
 &UDATE= '98/12/31'
 &UVAL= '-123,456.78'
)PROC
 VEDIT (UDATE)
 VEDIT (UVAL)
)END
```

Associated program:
```
IDENTIFICATION DIVISION.
PROGRAM-ID. TVMASK.
ENVIRONMENT DIVISION.
DATA DIVISION.
WORKING-STORAGE SECTION.
01 C-DISPLAY PIC X(8) VALUE 'DISPLAY'.
01 C-VGET PIC X(8) VALUE 'VGET'.
01 C-VDEFINE PIC X(8) VALUE 'VDEFINE'.
01 C-VMASK PIC X(8) VALUE 'VMASK'.
01 C-FORMAT PIC X(8) VALUE 'FORMAT'.
01 C-MASK PIC X(8) VALUE 'MASK'.
01 C-USER PIC X(8) VALUE 'USER'.
01 C-CHAR PIC X(8) VALUE 'CHAR'.
01 C-FIXED PIC X(8) VALUE 'FIXED'.
01 C-IDATE PIC X(8) VALUE 'IDATE'.
01 P-UDATE PIC X(8) VALUE 'UDATE'.
01 P-UVAL PIC X(8) VALUE 'UVAL'.
01 V-UDATE PIC X(6).
01 V-UVAL PIC S9(9) BINARY.
01 V-MASK PIC X(11) VALUE 'S999,999.99'.
01 PN PIC X(8).
01 VL PIC 9(9) BINARY.
PROCEDURE DIVISION.
    MOVE 6 TO VL
    CALL 'ISPLINK' USING C-VDEFINE P-UDATE V-UDATE C-CHAR VL
    MOVE 4 TO VL
    CALL 'ISPLINK' USING C-VDEFINE P-UVAL V-UVAL C-FIXED VL
    CALL 'ISPLINK' USING C-VMASK P-UDATE C-FORMAT C-IDATE
    MOVE 11 TO VL
    CALL 'ISPLINK' USING C-VMASK P-UVAL C-USER V-MASK VL
    MOVE 'XVEDIT' TO PN
    CALL 'ISPLINK' USING C-DISPLAY PN
* 98/12/31 -> 981231
    DISPLAY 'VUDATE:' V-UDATE
    DISPLAY 'VUVAL:' V-UVAL
    STOP RUN.
```

8.4.9 VER (Verification) Statement

The VER statement verifies that the contents of a specified variable conform with the specified field type or is one of the list of values, as appropriate.

Syntax:
```
VER (variable
  [,{NONBLANK | NB}]
  [,class
  [[,value]...]]
  [,MSG=messageid])
```

variable
> The dialogue variable that is to be verified.

NONBLANK
> The field must be non-blank, i.e. a blank field is invalid. NONBLANK may be abbreviated to NB.
>
> Example:
> VER(&ALPHA,NB)
> This statement makes ALPHA a mandatory field.
>
> **Tip**
> Although the NONBLANK test can be combined with other verifications, it may be preferable to make a separate test and so produce a more explicit message.

class
> The keyword that specifies the class test to be performed. No test is performed if NONBLANK is not specified and the variable is blank.
>
> The following verification classes can be specified:

ALPHA	Alphabetic or national character
ALPHAB	Strictly alphabetic
BIT	Bit
DSNAME	Dataset-name
ENUM	Extended numeric
FILEID	CMS Fileid
HEX	Hexadecimal
INCLUDE	List of parameters that specify the allowed character types
LEN	Length
LIST	List of values
LISTV	List of values specified in a variable
NAME	Name
NUM	Numeric
PICT	Picture
RANGE	Numeric range.

Important

No formal verification is performed on a blank field, although the NONBLANK
parameter may be used to force input to be made to the field in question.

ALPHA

The variable may only contain the following characters:
a,...,z A,...,Z # $ a

The INCLUDE,IMBLK,ALPHA verification can be used to allow embedded
blanks.

ALPHAB

The variable may only contain strictly alphabetic characters:
a,...,z A,...,Z

The INCLUDE,IMBLK,ALPHAB verification can be used to allow embedded
blanks.

BIT

The variable may only contain the following characters:
blank 0 1
Embedded blanks are not valid.

The INCLUDE,IMBLK,BIT verification can be used to allow embedded blanks.

DSNAME

The variable may only contain a valid TSO data set name. A data set name
has a maximum length of 44 characters. A data set name consists of one or
more qualifiers separated by periods (.). Each qualifier has a maximum
length of 8 characters, the first character of which must be alphabetic. A
data set name may be enclosed within apostrophes, in which case the
maximum length does not include these apostrophes.

Example:
ALPHA.BETA   valid
'ALPHA.BETA' valid
ALPHA.1234   invalid, first character of qualifier non-alphabetic
A12345678   invalid, qualifier longer than 8 characters.

Note: If the data set name is entered without apostrophes no check is made
to ensure that the length of the data set name, including the implicitly
prefixed first qualifier, exceeds 44 characters.

Example:
AAAAAAAA.AAAAAAAA.AAAAAAAA.AAAAAAAA.AAAAAAAA is 44 characters long and
will be accepted as being a valid data set name, although, if so used without
enclosing apostrophes a run-time error will result, because the current TSO
userid will be prefixed.

Tip
Display data set names in the form they will be used. The input data set
field should be normalised to this form. For example, if the data set name is
to be used as a fully qualified data set, a data set name entered without
enclosing apostrophes should be prefixed with the current TSO userid and
set within apostrophes before it is displayed.

Example:
```
&C = TRUNC(&DSN,1)
IF (&C ¬= '''')
  &DSN = '''&ZUSER..&DSN'''
```

ENUM

Validate that the variable contains data in extended numeric format.
Extended numeric data consists of the digits 0-9 and the following
characters:
plus sign (+)
minus sign (-) or number enclosed within parentheses
decimal symbol (, or . , as appropriate for the language)
thousands separator (, or . , as appropriate for the language)
leading blanks.

Example:
```
VER(&ALPHA,ENUM)
```
This statement would accept ALPHA containing the value +1234.

FILEID

The variable may only contain a valid CMS fileid.
A fileid has the format: filename [filetype [filemode]]

Filename and **filetype** are 1-8 alphanumeric characters, $, #, @, +, -, :,
and _.
The **filemode** is a single alphabetic character that can be suffixed with a
single digit.
One or more fields in the fileid can be a single asterisk or a string of
characters suffixed with an asterisk.

HEX

The variable may only contain the following hexadecimal characters:
blank 0,...,9 a,...,f A,...,F
Embedded blanks are not valid.

The INCLUDE,IMBLK,HEX verification can be used to allow embedded blanks.

INCLUDE

The INCLUDE keyword is followed by a list of character types (classes) that
the variable may have. Not more than two classes can be specified. If the
IMBLK positional parameter precedes the first entry, the variable can contain
embedded blanks.

Example:
```
VER (&VN,INCLUDE,IMBLK,ALPHAB)
VER (&VN,INCLUDE,NUM,ALPHAB)
```

LEN,operator,length

Validate that the length of data in the variable satisfies the specified condition.

Operator may have one of the following values:

EQ, =	equal
NE, ¬=	not equal
GT, >	greater than
GE, >=	greater than or equal
LT, <	less than
LE, <=	less than or equal
NG, ¬>	not greater than
NL, ¬<	not less than

Example:
```
VER(&ALPHA,LEN,'=',6)
```
validates that variable ALPHA contains exactly 6 bytes of data.

LIST,value[,value...]

A list of values, one of which the variable must have. Example:
```
VER(&ALPHA,LIST,alpha,beta,gamma)
```
validates that the variable ALPHA, if non-blank, contains either alpha, beta or gamma.

There are two special forms of the LIST keyword. The first, where the list entry is omitted:
```
VER(&varname,LIST,)
```
validates that the specified variable is blank, i.e. the reverse of VER(&varname,NB). This test can be useful where certain combinations of fields are not allowed.

The second, where the variable and the list entry are identical:
```
VER(&varname,LIST,&varname)
```
is always true. An important use for this apparently trivial validation is for implicit cursor positioning.

Tip

The standard message text associated with the LIST keyword is not very useful; the long message merely states ENTER ONE OF THE LISTED VALUES without explaining what the listed values are. Here it is better for the developer to issue his own message which contains a list of the valid operands. the next LISTV verification uses a variable that contains the verification values.

Example:
```
┌─ message ──────────────────┐
│  TSMSG000 'invalid input'  │
│  'valid input: &LIST'      │
└────────────────────────────┘
```

with panel statements:
```
&LIST = 'alpha,beta'
VER(&ALPHA,LIST,alpha,beta,MSG=TSMSG000)
```

LISTV,&varlist

The **&varlist** variable contains a list of values. The verification is made that the variable matches one of these values in the list. Each entry in the list is separated by a blank or a comma. A list value that contains one of the following special values must be enclosed within paired quotes:

Blank < (+ |) ; ¬ - , > : =

Ampersands (&) in the variable list must be paired to represent a single ampersand. A single ampersand prefixed to a name specifies a variable that is replaced by the current value for that variable.

Example:
```
&A = n
&XVL = 'N &A &&A'
&VL = 'Y y '';'' O''BRIEN ''D''''ell Orto'' &XVL'
VER(&VAR,LISTV,&VL,MSG=XXMSG003)
```
This example validates that the variable VAR, if non-blank, contains one of the following values:

Y, y, ;, O'BRIEN, D'ell Orto, N, n, &A

If the LISTV verification issues a message that uses the name of the variable list, a tailored display message appears. For example (TSMSG000 is defined as above):
```
&LIST = 'alpha,beta'
VER(&ALPHA,LISTV,&LIST,MSG=TSMSG000)
```

Tip
Many applications have general code values that need to be validated, e.g. department codes. To simplify the maintenance of such codes, rather than hard-coding them in panels, it is better to define them centrally and to use them as global variables.

NUM

The variable may only contain the following characters:
blank 0,...,9
Embedded blanks are not valid.

PICT,'mask'

The mask specifies the picture mask, which defines the form of the variable contents.

The picture mask may contain the following characters:

C   any character

A   an alphabetic character (a,...,z A,...,Z # $ a)

N   a numeric digit (0,...,9)

X   a hexadecimal character (0,...,9 a,...,f A,...,F)

9   same as N.

The picture mask may also contain special characters (except # $ and a) which adopt their own value.

Example:

PICT,'A/NNN'

This statement requires that the variable contains 5 characters, the first of which is alphabetic, the second character must be "/" and the last three characters numeric.

a/123   valid

ab123   invalid, the second character is not "/"

a/12   invalid, the fifth character is non-numeric.

Note: The PICT and NUM keywords are not equivalent. Consider the 5 character input field ALPHA, the input "123 " will satisfy the NUM validation but fail PICT,'99999'.

NAME

The variable may only contain a valid member name. A member name (of a partitioned data set or library) has a maximum length of 8 characters, the first character of which must be alphabetic. Example:

ALPHA   valid

1234   invalid, first character non-alphabetic

A12345678   invalid, variable longer than 8 characters.

RANGE,lowerlimit,upperlimit

Lowerlimit and **upperlimit** specify the inclusive limits within which the numeric value of the variable must lie. The specified range includes the limit values.

Example:

RANGE,100,199

This statement validates that the variable contains numeric values in the range 100 through 199.

RANGE,100,100

This statement requires that the variable has the single numeric value 100.

MSG=messageid

Display the message identified by **messageid** should the validation fail. A standard message, dependent on the verification form, is displayed if no explicit message is specified.

Example:
```
VER(&ALPHA,LIST,alpha,beta,MSG=TSMSG000)
```
The TSMSG000 message is displayed, should the variable ALPHA not contain one of the entries in the list, namely alpha or beta.

8.4.10 VGET Statement

The VGET statement explicitly fetches the specified variables from the specified variable pool into the function pool.

ISPF variables used in a panel are implicitly fetched from a variable pool. The pools are searched in the sequence: function pool, shared pool, profile pool.

Syntax:
```
VGET (variablename [,variablename]...)
      [ASIS|SHARED|PROFILE])
```

variablename
>   The name of a dialogue variable that is to be fetched.

ASIS
>   The variable is obtained from the shared or, if not present, from the profile pool. Default.

SHARED
>   The variable is fetched from the shared pool.

PROFILE
>   The variable is fetched from the profile pool. Should a variable having the same name exist in the shared pool, it will be deleted from the shared pool.

Example:
```
VGET (ALPHA,BETA) PROFILE
```
This example transfers the two variables ALPHA and BETA from the profile pool to the function pool.

8.4.11 VPUT Statement

The VPUT statement copies the specified variables from the function pool to the specified variable pool.

Syntax:
```
VPUT (variablename [,variablename]...)
      [ASIS|SHARED|PROFILE])
```

variablename
>   The name of a dialogue variable that is to be stored.

ASIS

The variable is returned to the pool where it is currently stored. If the variable is not found in either the shared or profile pool, it is stored in the shared pool. Default.

SHARED

The variable is stored in the shared pool.

PROFILE

The variable is stored in the profile pool. Should a variable having the same name exist in the shared pool, it will be deleted from the shared pool.

Example:
```
VPUT (ALPHA,BETA) SHARED
```
Transfer the two variables ALPHA and BETA from the function pool to the shared pool.

8.5 PANEL FUNCTIONS

One of the following four functions may be used in place of a source variable:

· LVLINE   Last visible line
· PFK   PK key assignment
· TRANS   Translate
· TRUNC   Truncate.

8.5.1 LVLINE Function

The LVLINE function returns the last visible line for a dynamic or graphic area; this represents the height of such an area. The LVLINE function makes allowance for split screen mode.

Syntax:
```
LVLINE(areaname)
```

areaname

The name of the dynamic or graphic area whose current height is to be obtained.

Example:

```
)ATTR
* AREA(DYNAMIC)
)BODY
...
*ALPHA                    *+
*                         *+
*                         *+
)PROC
&A = LVLINE(ALPHA)
)END
```

This example assigns 3 to A.

8.5.2 PFK Function

The PFK function returns either the name of the PF-key (PF01,...,PF24) which has been assigned the specified value or the value which has been assigned to the specified PF-key (1,...,24). The null value is returned if no PF-key has been assigned this value. If 24 PF-keys have been defined, the set PF13 through PF24 is checked first.

Syntax:
```
PFK(value)
```

value

Either the number of the PF-key (1,...,24) whose value is to be returned or, if non-numeric, the value that is associated with a PF-key.

Example: Assume PF2 has been assigned the value alpha.
```
PFK(2)        returns alpha
PFK(alpha)    returns PF02.
```

8.5.3 TRANS Function

The TRANS function uses a list of paired values, the first value is the input value (**value-in**) and the second value is the output (translated) value (**value-out**). The value-out associated with the value-in corresponding to the value of the specified variable is returned.

Should the contents of the variable not correspond to any of the input values:

· If a message is explicitly specified, it will be issued.
· If the last value-in is asterisk (*), the value-out replaces any values which do not occur in the preceding list, asterisk (*) as value-out here has the special meaning that the input value is retained.
· Otherwise blank is returned.

Syntax:
```
TRANS(variable [value-in,value-out]... [MSG=message-id])
```

Example:
```
TRANS(&ALPHA 1,OLD 2,NEW MSG=TSMSG002)
```
returns

    OLD   if ALPHA contains 1

    NEW   if ALPHA contains 2

otherwise the message TSMSG002 will be issued.

```
TRANS(&ALPHA 1,OLD 2,NEW *,NONE)
```
returns

    OLD   if ALPHA contains 1

    NEW   if ALPHA contains 2

otherwise NONE

```
TRANS(&ALPHA 1,OLD 2,NEW)
```
returns

    OLD   if ALPHA contains 1

    NEW   if ALPHA contains 2

otherwise blank.

```
TRANS(&ALPHA 1,OLD 2,NEW *,*)
```
returns

    OLD   if ALPHA contains 1

    NEW   if ALPHA contains 2

otherwise ALPHA remains unchanged.

```
TRANS(&ALPHA 1,OLD 2,NEW *.* *,*)
```
returns

    OLD   if ALPHA contains 1

    NEW   if ALPHA contains 2

    *   if ALPHA contains *

otherwise ALPHA remains unchanged.

Tip 1
If a field is to be both translated and validated, the TRANS function optimises this processing by combining these two operations in a single statement.

Tip 2
The TRANS function can be used to define synonyms. Example:
```
&FLD = TRANS(&FLD y,Y Y,Y yes,Y YES,Y)
```
defines 4 synonyms (y, Y, yes and YES) for the field FLD.

8.5.4 TRUNC Function

The TRUNC function truncates the contents of variable using either the specified delimiter character or the length of the result. If **delimiter** is numeric, this number specifies the number of characters to be assigned to the target variable. Those residual characters remaining are assigned to the control variable .TRAIL. If **delimiter** is non-numeric, all characters in the input variable up to this delimiter are assigned to the target variable. Those characters remaining after the delimiter

are assigned to the control variable .TRAIL (the delimiter character in the input
string is not transferred to either of these fields).

Syntax:
```
TRUNC(variable,[length | 'delimitercharacter'])
```

variable
> The variable to be processed.

length
> The length of the string to be extracted.

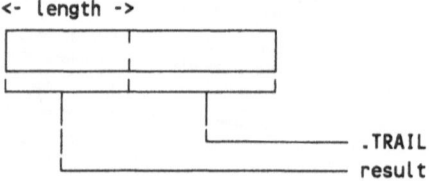

'delimitercharacter'
> The character used to delimiter the string to be extracted.

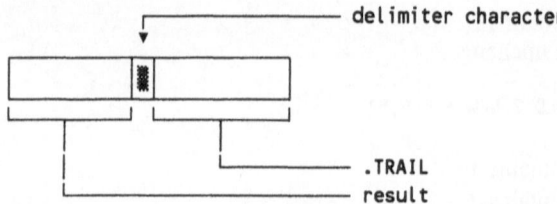

Example:
```
      &A = '1.2.3'
      &B = TRUNC(&A,3)
```
B contains 1.2
.TRAIL contains .3

```
      &B = TRUNC(&A,'.')
```
B contains 1
.TRAIL contains 2.3

8.6 PANEL CONTROL VARIABLES

Control variables are used to control the panel processing. Control variables may
generally be used where variables are used. Certain control variables (.CSRPOS,
.CURSOR, .MSG and .RESP) may only be set once, any subsequent assignment to such
a variable is ignored, this restriction is reset by the next panel display.

8.6.1 .ALARM - Acoustic Signal Setting

The .ALARM control variable is used to set the status of the acoustic signal to be used when the next panel is displayed.

Syntax:
```
.ALARM = [YES|NO|' ']
```

.ALARM = YES
Sound the acoustic signal when the next panel is displayed.

.ALARM = NO
.ALARM = ' '
Do not sound the acoustic signal when the next panel is displayed. .ALARM=YES specified for the message to be displayed takes precedence.

8.6.2 .ATTR - Field Attributes

.ATTR is used to override the standard attribute characteristics for a field. Attribute characters set in the)INIT section remain in effect should the panel be redisplayed, unless the attribute characters have been further changed in the)REINIT or)PROC section.

Tip
.ATTR can be used to accentuate a field for error processing.

Syntax:
```
.ATTR(field) = 'keyword(value) [,keyword(value)...]'
```

field
> **field** is either the name of a panel field in the)BODY section or the .CURSOR control variable which currently contains the name of the panel field whose attributes are to be changed or the name of a dialog variable (preceded by ampersand) which currently contains the name of the panel field whose attributes are to be changed.

keyword(value)
> **Keywords** and their **values** are as specified in the)ATTR section.

Field attributes set in the)INIT section remain in effect should the panel be redisplayed, unless the attribute characters have been further changed in the)REINIT or)PROC section.

Example:
```
.ATTR(PNO) = 'INTENS(HIGH) COLOR(YELLOW)'
```
Change the attributes of the panel field PNO to high intensity and set the colour to yellow. Should the cursor currently be positioned at this field, the following statement has the same effect:
```
.ATTR(.CURSOR) = 'INTENS(HIGH) COLOR(YELLOW)'
```

Similarly, the following two statements serve the same function:

```
&FIELD = PNO
.ATTR(&PNO) = 'INTENS(HIGH) COLOR(YELLOW)'
```

8.6.3 .ATTRCHAR - Attribute Characteristics

.ATTRCHAR is used to override the standard attribute characteristics assigned to an attribute character.

Syntax:

```
.ATTRCHAR(character) = 'keyword(value) [,keyword(value)...]'
```

character
>   **Character** is either an attribute character or pair of hexadecimal characters, as defined (implicitly or explicitly) in the)ATTR section

keyword(value)
>   **Keywords** and their **values** are as specified in the)ATTR section.

Attribute characters set in the)INIT section remain in effect should the panel be redisplayed, unless the attribute characters have been further changed in the)REINIT or)PROC section.

Example:

```
.ATTRCHAR(+) = 'INTENS(HIGH) COLOR(YELLOW)'
```
Change the intensity of the default attribute character "+" from low to high and set the colour to yellow.

```
.ATTRCHAR(01) = 'INTENS(HIGH) COLOR(RED)'
```
Change the intensity of the pair of hexadecimal attribute characters "01" from low to high and set the colour to red.

8.6.4 .AUTOSEL - Auto-Select Option

.AUTOSEL is used in conjunction with table display panels. It is used to indicate whether the line at which the cursor has been explicitly positioned is to be interpreted as having been selected. The use of this control variable is described in Section 9.4.6.

8.6.5 .CSRPOS - Cursor Position Within Field

.CSRPOS is used to specify the position of the cursor within a panel field (the .CURSOR control variable is used to specify the panel field name). Initially .CSRPOS contains the current position of the cursor.

8.6.6 .CSRROW - Cursor Row

.CSRROW is used in conjunction with table display panels. It is used to set the cursor line at the corresponding row in the table. The use of this control variable is described in Section 9.4.6.

8.6.7 .CURSOR - Cursor Field

.CURSOR is used to specify the name of the variable where the cursor is to be initially placed for the panel display. This variable name must be the name of a panel field. If the cursor is not explicitly positioned, the cursor is placed at the start of the first empty input field. Initially .CURSOR contains the name of the field where the cursor is currently positioned.

.CURSOR may only be explicitly set once, any subsequent assignments are ignored.

Example: The two statements:
```
.CURSOR = ALPHA
.CURSOR = BETA
```
position the cursor at the start of the panel field ALPHA; the second assignment to panel field BETA is ignored.

8.6.8 .HELP - Name of Help Panel

.HELP is used to specify the name of the panel which is to be displayed in response to pressing the HELP key, e.g.
```
.HELP = 'TSSPF001'
```
is used to specify that the TSSPF001 panel is to be displayed in response to pressing the HELP key.

Tip

If .HELP has not been set, the invocation of the help command will cause the last set help panel to be displayed. This panel is most probably unrelated to the current application and could confuse the user. It is recommended that every panel sets .HELP to be the name of some appropriate help panel for the application (see Chapter 15 for a comprehensive discussion of the help environment). It is better to display a dummy help panel saying that there is (currently) no help panel available rather than a non-appropriate help panel.

8.6.9 .MSG - Message-identifier

.MSG can be explicitly assigned the message-id of the message to be displayed with the next panel display, e.g.
```
.MSG = 'TSMSG001'
```
causes the message TSMSG001 to be displayed at the next panel display.

.MSG is implicitly set should a TRANS or VER statement cause the error condition to be set. If a message has been explicitly specified, .MSG contains this message-id, otherwise the standard message appropriate for this operation.

Tip

.MSG cannot be changed once it has been set during the current panel display. This problem can be solved by using an intermediate variable.

Examples:

```
VER(&ALPHA,NB)
```

Assign the standard message to .MSG should ALPHA be non-blank.

```
VER(&ALPHA,NB,MSG=TSMSG002)
```

Assign TSMSG002 to .MSG should ALPHA be non-blank.

8.6.10 .PFK - PF-Key

.PFK is set to contain a value indicating which PF key has been pressed
(PF01,...,PF24). Should no PF key have been pressed, .PFK contains blanks.
Similarly, .PFK is blank during processing of the)INIT and)REINIT sections.

8.6.11 .RESP - Input Response

.RESP contains the operator's response, either ENTER or END. END is only set if the
operator terminated the panel display with the END key (normally PF3 or PF15),
ENTER is set for all other responses. If .RESP is set in the)INIT section, the panel is
not displayed.

Example:

```
)BODY
IF (.RESP = ENTER)
  &ALPHA = 1
```

Set variable ALPHA only if the operator has not terminated the display with the END
key.

Tip

ISPF applications usually adopt the convention that the END key terminates the
panel display without any input being processed. Hence, processing in the)PROC
section should only be performed if the operator has used the ENTER key (or
equivalent) to terminate the panel display, i.e. all processing in the)PROC section
should be inside the IF-group (.RESP = ENTER).

Example 1:

```
...
)PROC
IF (.RESP = ENTER)
   processing
```

Example 2:

```
)PROC
IF (.RESP = END) EXIT
```

8.6.12 .TRAIL - Residual TRUNC String

.TRAIL contains the string which remains after a variable has been processed with
the TRUNC function. Example:

```
&ALPHA = 'GAMMA'
&BETA = TRUNC(&ALPHA,2)
```

then BETA contains GA and .TRAIL contains MMA.

.TRAIL cannot itself be used as the variable in the TRUNC function. Example:
```
&ALPHA = 'GAMMA'
&BETA = TRUNC(&ALPHA,2)
&DELTA = TRUNC(.TRAIL,1)
```
assigns a null string to DELTA, and not MM, as would have been expected.

If a further truncation of this residual field is to be made, this field must be assigned to an intermediate field, which is then used as a variable in the TRUNC function. Continuing this previous example:
```
&X = .TRAIL
&DELTA = TRUNC(&X,2)
```
DELTA contains MM and .TRAIL contains A.

8.6.13 .ZVARS - Placeholder

.ZVARS is used in the)INIT section to contain the names which are to be assigned to placeholders in the)BODY or)MODEL section. The z system variable is used as placeholder. The sequence of the variable-names specified in the .ZVARS operand list determines which variable-name is to be assigned to which placeholder, the first variable-name replaces the first placeholder, the second variable-name replaces the second placeholder, etc. The number of variable-names and placeholders must be identical.

Syntax:
```
.ZVARS = '(variablename [,variablename]...)'
```
Note: The parentheses may be omitted for a single variable-name.

variablename
>   The name of a variable which is represented by a placeholder (z) in the body section of the panel definition.

Example:
The following panel performs the processing:
- assign ZCMD to the COMMAND variable;
- assign PNO to the Employee number variable;
- assign NAME to the Surname variable.

```
)BODY
+
%COMMAND ===>_Z
+
%Employee number ===>_Z   +
%Surname         ===>_Z              +
)INIT
.ZVARS = '(ZCMD,PNO,NAME)'
)END
```

This panel definition is identical with the following definition:

```
)BODY
+
%COMMAND ===>_ZCMD
+
%Employee number ===>_PNO +
%Surname         ===>_NAME            +
)END
```

Tip
The excessive use of placeholders results in panels which are difficult to maintain. Placeholders should only be used where they are necessary, namely where the variable name associated with a field is longer than the data it contains.

8.7 DYNAMIC AREA

Previously only static panel definitions have been made, i.e. each field had a fixed location in the panel. Dynamic areas enable the form of panel fields to be defined at the time of processing, and so offer greater flexibility in the construction of panels. For example, a single field can be divided into a number of individual fields, each with its own attributes, whereas, the setting of the attribute character using the .ATTRCHAR or .ATTR control variable) applies to the field as a whole. A **shadow** variable that specifies attribute characters for the corresponding position can be associated with a dynamic area.

8.7.1 Format of a Dynamic Area

The bounds of a dynamic area are defined by the attribute character associated with it. This attribute character must have the parameter AREA(DYNAMIC). A dynamic area may occupy one or more lines, and, depending on the parameter specified for the attribute character, may be extendable in the vertical direction. The definition of a dynamic area must satisfy a number of conditions:

· Dynamic areas must be rectangular.
· The name associated with a dynamic area must immediately follow the first bounding attribute character, the name may only occupy the first line of the dynamic area and must be delimited by at least one blank. This name defines a normal dialogue variable.
· Left-hand bounding attributes on the following lines must be followed by a blank.

Figure 8.2 illustrates the definition of a dynamic area; "name" is the name of the dynamic area, the contents of the dynamic area are contained in the NAME variable. "*" is the attribute character defined for the dynamic area. Figure 8.3 shows examples of invalid dynamic areas; the name of the dynamic area (ALPHA) does not immediately follow the first attribute character, the dynamic area (BETA) is rectangular.

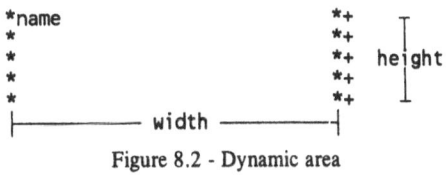

Figure 8.2 - Dynamic area

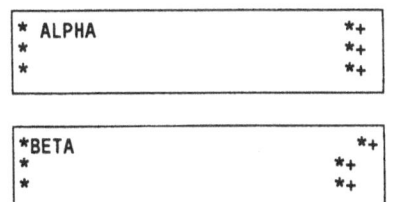

Figure 8.3 - Examples of invalid dynamic area definitions

Placement of dynamic areas in the panel definition is subject to a number of restrictions:

·   A dynamic area may only follow a text field.
·   Normal fields may not overlap dynamic areas.
·   The attribute characters used to define a dynamic area are not field delimiters in the usual sense, an input field within a dynamic area should be delimited by a DATAOUT or TEXT attribute character. This is why in Figure 8.2 a text attribute character ("+") follows the terminating attribute character for the dynamic area ("*") in each line to avoid any data entered from overflowing outside the dynamic area.

Information is entered into the dynamic area using standard statements (assignment, etc.). Similarly, information is retrieved from a dynamic area by using the name of the dynamic area as source variable.

If the dynamic area occupies more than one line, the data assigned to the dynamic area is continued onto the following line when one line is full, e.g.

```
    *ALPHA *+
    *      *+
```

The dynamic area named ALPHA occupies 2 lines each of 8 characters, if the string "1234567890" is assigned to the variable ALPHA, the dynamic area contains the following data:

```
12345678
9
```

Data in a dynamic area comprise one or more fields, each field being prefixed with a special attribute character (DATAIN or DATAOUT).

8.7.2 Dynamic Area Definition

The use of dynamic areas requires two sets of definitions to be made:
· An attribute character is used to define the horizontal bounds of the dynamic area.
· Attribute characters are used to define the input (DATAIN) and output (DATAOUT) sub-fields of a dynamic area. These attribute characters are not related to the standard attribute characters.

These definitions are made in the)ATTR section.

The attribute character used to define the bounds of a dynamic area has the following syntax:
```
attributecharacter AREA(DYNAMIC)
        [EXTEND(ON |OFF)]
        [SCROLL(ON |OFF)]
        [USERMOD(character)]
        [DATAMOD(character)]
```

attributecharacter
> The attribute character or pair of hexadecimal characters used to define the horizontal bounds of a dynamic area in the)BODY section of the panel definition. The name of the dynamic area immediately follows the first attribute character for the dynamic area.

AREA(DYNAMIC)
> Identify this attribute character as defining a dynamic area, e.g.

```
)ATTR
* AREA(DYNAMIC)
)BODY
*ALPHA                          *+
*                               *+
```

> This example defines a dynamic area occupying two lines and having the name ALPHA.

EXTEND(ON)
> The number of vertical lines in the dynamic area can, if necessary, be automatically increased to fill the whole display screen. Only one extendable area may be defined for a particular screen display.
> Default: EXTEND(OFF).

SCROLL(ON)
> The dynamic area is scrollable. This means that the scroll commands (UP, DOWN, etc.) are enabled. Only one scrollable dynamic area may be defined for a particular screen display. A scrollable dynamic area may be defined in conjunction with an extendable dynamic area for a particular screen display.
> Default: SCROLL(OFF).

> Note: The panel display service does not perform scrolling but does process the scroll command, i.e. the scroll direction, number of lines to be scrolled, etc. are available in the appropriate system variable.

The following system variables contain pertinent scrolling information:

```
Name        pool   type len  description
```

Name	pool	type	len	description
ZVERB	shr	out	8	scrolling command: UP, DOWN, etc.
ZSCROLLN	shr	out	4	number of lines to be scrolled

The following sample code can be used to perform explicit vertical scrolling:

```
SET &Y = 0
ISPEXEC VGET (ZVERB ZSCROLLN) SHARED
IF (&ZSCROLLN EQ &STR()) THEN SET &ZSCROLLN = 0
SELECT
  WHEN (&ZVERB EQ UP) SET &Y = &Y - &ZSCROLLN
  WHEN (&ZVERB EQ DOWN) SET &Y = &Y + &ZSCROLLN
END
    process
```

USERMOD(usermod-code)

DATAMOD(datamod-code)

These codes are either a character or two hexadecimal characters used to replace the specified attribute character after user input has been made. This code designates the start of a sub-field within the dynamic area. USERMOD(usermod-code) and DATAMOD(datamod-code) may be used alone, in combination or omitted. The interpretation of these codes depends on which combination has been specified. Table 8.1 summarises the various combinations (x = present, - = absent).

Table 8.1 - USERMOD and DATAMOD processing

USERMOD	DATAMOD	input field	attribute character
x x	x x	changed unchanged	datamod usermod
x	-	x	usermod
-	x	changed	datamod
-	-	x	unchanged

Example:

```
)ATTR
@ AREA(DYNAMIC) USERMOD(01)
```

The hexadecimal character X'01' replaces the attribute character for each field in the dynamic area.

```
)ATTR
@ AREA(DYNAMIC) DATAMOD(02)
```

The hexadecimal character X'02' replaces the attribute character for those fields in the dynamic area which have been changed in value.

8.7.3 Shadow Variable

A shadow variable can be associated with a dynamic area. Such a shadow variable specifes the attribute character for the corresponding position in the dynamic area. The name of the shadow variable is specified after the name of the dynamic area. Shadow variables are ignored in GUI mode,

Example:
```
)ATTR
} TYPE(DATAOUT) CAPS(OFF) COLOR(BLUE)
{ TYPE(DATAIN) CAPS(ON) COLOR(GREEN)
% TYPE(TEXT)
? TYPE(CHAR) COLOR(WHITE)
# TYPE(CHAR) COLOR(YELLOW)
| TYPE(CHAR) COLOR(RED) HILITE(BLINK)
@ AREA(DYNAMIC)
)BODY CMD()
@DAREA,SVAR          @%
@                    @%
)INIT
&SVAR  = ' ?  |#'
&DAREA = '{_}Select'
)END
```

Displayed dynamic area:

```
 ┌ Select
 │ │ └──────► yellow
 │ └─────────► red blinking
 └────────────► white
```

8.8 USE OF DYNAMIC AREAS

Fields within a dynamic area are defined by means of the attribute character specified with the DATAIN or DATAOUT parameter. These two attribute characters mean that the following field is either an input field (unprotected) or non-input field (protected), respectively. Text fields, as such, do not exist, because dynamic areas contain only text. The data following the attribute characters are not variable names but fixed text. Example, the panel definition shown in Figure 8.4 results in the same display as the panel definition in Figure 8.5.

```
)ATTR
* AREA(DYNAMIC) EXTEND(ON)
{ TYPE(DATAIN)
} TYPE(DATAOUT)
)INIT
&ALPHA = '+
)Employee number: &PNO              +
}      Surname ===>{&NAME          }'
)BODY
%--------------- Employee Record --------------------
%COMMAND ===>_ZCMD
! %
 *ALPHA                             *+
 *                                  *+
```

Figure 8.4 - Panel definition illustrating the use of dynamic areas

```
)BODY
%--------------- Employee Record --------------------
%COMMAND ===>_ZCMD
%
%Employee number: &PNO
%     Surname ===>_NAME         +
```

Figure 8.5 - Panel definition using static fields

Explanation:

The dynamic area ALPHA has been assigned the 2 line literal in the)INIT section. The two variables (PNO and NAME) are defined as text variables (&PNO and &NAME, respectively) in order that the current value for these variables is substituted. The field corresponding to NAME is an input field, hence a DATAIN attribute character must be specified at this position. Assuming that the variables PNO and NAME contain 1234 and BETA, respectively, the variable ALPHA contains the following string before display:

```
")Employee number: 1234          }    Surname ===>{BETA     }"
```

If the surname has been changed through input to GAMMA, the variable ALPHA contains the following string after display:

```
")Employee number: 1234          }    Surname ===>{GAMMA     }"
```

The new field contents (GAMMA) can be obtained by extracting the appropriate substring from the variable ALPHA, example:

```
)PROC
&X=TRUNC(&ALPHA,'{')
&NAME=.TRAIL
```

These statements assign the new surname to the variable NAME.

This example makes the drawbacks of dynamic areas apparent, namely, the flexibility in panel formatting is bought at the cost of inflexibility in the processing. For example, if an additional input field was set into the dynamic area before the surname field, this method would return the wrong value for NAME.

8.8.1 Scrolling

As will be shown later, the TBDISPL (table display) service can be used to vertically scroll through a display of rows. However, all screen displays in the horizontal direction are restricted to the physical screen width; dynamic areas can be used to simulate **horizontal** (and **vertical**) scrolling of a single data field. A single dynamic area may contain a virtually unlimited number of sub-fields.

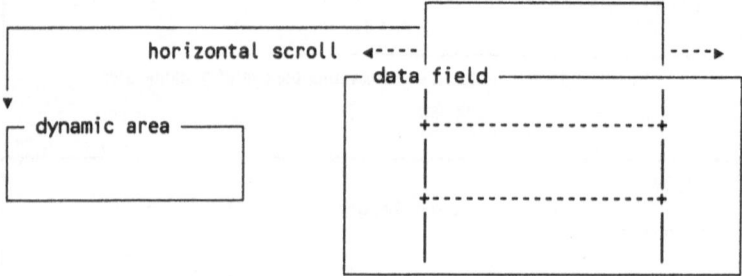

Figure 8.6 - Horizontal scrolling with dynamic areas

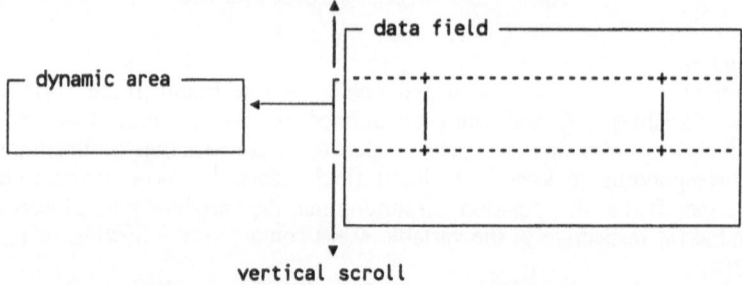

Figure 8.7 - Vertical scrolling with dynamic areas

Sample REXX procedure to perform scrolling:

```
/* REXX */
/* set sample data into R. stem variables */
r.1 = 'aaaaaaaaaaaaaaaaaaaaaaaaaaaaaaaa'
r.2 = 'bbbbbbbbbbbbbbbbbbbbbbbbbbbbbbbb'
r.3 = 'cccccccccccccccccccccccccccccccc'
r.4 = 'dddddddddddddddddddddddddddddddd'
r.5 = 'eeeeeeeeeeeeeeeeeeeeeeeeeeeeeeee'
r.6 = 'ffffffffffffffffffffffffffffffff'
r.0 = 6 /* number of stem variables */

ADDRESS ISPEXEC
x = 1 /* initial X-coordinate */
y = 1 /* initial Y-coordinate */
width = 20 /* width of dynamic area in panel */
```

```
DO FOREVER
  darea = '' /* initialise dynamic area */
  DO i = x TO r.0
    darea = darea || SUBSTR(r.i,y,width)
  END
  "DISPLAY PANEL(XDA)"
  IF RC > 0 THEN LEAVE
  "VGET (zverb zscrolln) SHARED"
  SELECT
    WHEN zverb = 'UP' THEN DO
      x = MAX(x-zscrolln,1)
    END
    WHEN zverb = 'DOWN' THEN DO
      x = MIN(x+zscrolln,r.0)
    END
    WHEN zverb = 'LEFT' THEN DO
      y = MAX(y-zscrolln,1)
    END
    WHEN zverb = 'RIGHT' THEN DO
      y = y+zscrolln
    END
    OTHERWISE
      /* other command processing, e.g. ENTER */
  END
END
```

Note: For simplicity, no check is made on the right-hand scrolling limit.
Similarly, no processing is performed on the returned data.

Associated XDA panel:

```
)ATTR
% TYPE(TEXT)
_ TYPE(INPUT)
a AREA(DYNAMIC) EXTEND(OFF) SCROLL(ON)
)BODY CMD()
%                 +SCROLL ===>_SAMT+
aDAREA                a%
a                     a%
a                     a%
a                     a%

)INIT
IF (&SAMT = &Z) &SAMT = 'HALF'
)END
```

8.9 GRAPHIC AREAS

ISPF panels can incorporate pictures or graphs generated by the IBM Graphical Data
Display Manager (GDDM) licensed program or the licensed application program
GDDM Presentation Graphics Feature (PGF), by defining a **graphic area**. A panel
may only contain a single graphic area.

8.9.1 Format of a Graphic Area

The bounds of a rectangular graphic area are defined by the attribute character associated with it. This attribute character must have the parameter AREA(GRAPHIC). A graphic area may occupy one or more lines, and, depending on the parameter specified for the attribute character, may be extendable in the vertical direction. The name associated with the graphic area must immediately follow the first bounding attribute character. This name defines a normal dialogue variable and must be present although it is not explicitly used. Figure 8.8 illustrates the definition of a graphic area; "name" is the name of the graphic area — "*" is the attribute character defined for the graphic area.

Figure 8.8 - Graphic area

8.9.2 Graphic Area Definition

The use of graphic areas requires that an attribute character used to specify the horizontal bounds of the graphic area be defined. This definition is made in the)ATTR section. Normal ISPF fields may be used in conjunction with graphic areas, these fields may partially overlap the graphic area. The attribute character used to define the bounds of a graphic area has the following syntax:

```
attributecharacter AREA(GRAPHIC) [EXTEND(ON|OFF)]
```

attributecharacter

> The attribute character or pair of hexadecimal characters used to define the horizontal bounds of a graphic area in the)BODY section of the panel definition.
>
> The name of the graphic area immediately follows the first attribute character for the graphic area.

AREA(GRAPHIC)

> This attribute character defines the horizontal bounds of a graphic area. Example:

```
)ATTR
* AREA(GRAPHIC)
)BODY
*ALPHA              *+
*                   *+
*                   *+
```

This example defines a graphic area occupying 3 lines and having the name ALPHA.

EXTEND(ON)
The number of vertical lines in the graphic area can, if necessary, be automatically increased to fill the whole display screen. Only one extendable area may be defined for a particular screen display.
Default: EXTEND(OFF)

8.10 USE OF GRAPHIC AREAS

A graphic area can only be utilised from a program using GDDM routines. This program must satisfy a number of conventions:

· An **anchor application block** (AAB), an 8-byte area aligned on a full-word boundary, must be supplied to the GRINIT call. This AAB must be used for all GDDM calls from the program.
· The name of the panel to be displayed is passed to the GRINIT function.
· The GDDM processing is terminated by calling the GRTERM function.

A sample PL/I program torso follows:

```
pgmname: PROC OPTIONS(MAIN);
DCL panel CHAR(8) INIT('panelname');
DCL aab INIT(0,0) FIXED BIN(31);
DCL ISPLINK ENTRY EXTERNAL OPTIONS(ASM,INTER,RETCODE);
DCL FSINR ENTRY EXTERNAL OPTIONS(ASM,INTER,RETCODE);
CALL ISPLINK('GRINIT',aab,panel);
  ...
  GDDM function calls
  ...
CALL ISPLINK('DISPLAY',panel);
CALL ISPLINK('GRTERM',aab);
%INCLUDE SYSLIB(ADMUPIRG);
END pgmname;
```

The dialogue program may not use any of the following GDDM calls:

FSEXIT	FSINIT	FSRNIT	FSTERM	SPINIT
ASREAD	FSSHOW	FSSHOR	GSREAD	MSREAD
MSPCRT	PTNCRT	PTNDEL	PTNMOD	PTNSEL
PTSCRT	PTSDEL	PTSSEL	MSCPOS	MSDFLD
MSGET	MSPCRT	MSPUT	MSREAD	MSPQRY
MSQADS	MSQGRP	MSQMAP	MSQMOD	MSQPOS
DSCLS	DSDROP	DSOPEN	DSRNIT	DSUSE

Alphanumeric fields may only be displayed using GDDM calls when there are no fields in the)BODY section of the panel definition.

8.11 SCROLLABLE AREA

A scrollable area is a mapping of field definitions into a vertically scrollable area. Unlike a dynamic area, ISPF performs the scrolling for a scrollable area. If a panel has more than one scrollable area, the same scrolling is performed on all these scrollable areas.

8.11.1 Format of a Scrollable Area

The bounds of a rectangular scrollable area are defined by the attribute character associated with it. This attribute character must have the parameter AREA(SCRL). A scrollable area occupies at least two lines; the first line contains scrolling information (MORE + -, etc.). The name associated with the scrollable area must immediately follow the first bounding attribute character. This name corresponds to the name used in the)AREA definition. Figure 8.9 illustrates the definition of a scrollable area; ALPHA is the name of the scrollable area — "*" is the attribute character defined for the scrollable area.

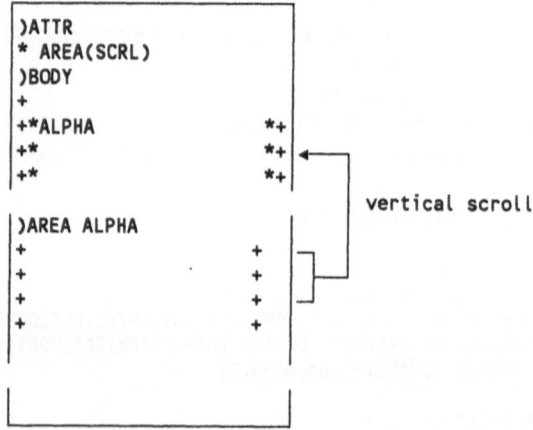

Figure 8.9 - Scrollable area

8.11.2 Definition of a Scrollable Area

The use of scrollable areas requires two sets of definitions to be made:
· The attribute character used to define the horizontal bounds of the scrollable area. The scrollable area specified in the body section is assigned a name.
· An)AREA section for the above specified name that contains the field definitions for this scrollable area.

The attribute character used to define the bounds of a dynamic area has the following syntax:
```
attributecharacter AREA(SCRL)
    [EXTEND(ON|OFF)]
```

attributecharacter
> The attribute character or pair of hexadecimal characters used to define the horizontal bounds of a scrollable area in the)BODY section of the panel definition. The name of the scrollable area immediately follows the first attribute character for the scrollable area.

AREA(SCRL)
> Identify this attribute character as defining a scrollable area, e.g.

```
)ATTR
* AREA(SCRL)
)BODY
+*ALPHA                    *+
+*                         *+
)AREA ALPHA
+                      +
+                      +  .
+                      +
```

This example defines a scrollable area occupying 2 lines and having the name ALPHA.

EXTEND(ON)

The number of vertical lines in the scrollable area can, if necessary, be automatically increased to fill the whole display screen. Only one extendable area may be defined for a particular screen display.
Default: EXTEND(OFF).

The associated named)AREA section defines the individual fields in the scrollable area. Each line in the)AREA section has the same width as each line in the associated scrollable area. The usual attribute characters (input, output, text, etc.), variables and text are used in the)AREA section definition.area.

8.12 USE OF SCROLLABLE AREAS

Scrollable areas are suitable to be used where a panel is to contain more information than can fit onto a single screen. Whereas a dynamic area is better suited to be used for information that has a variable format, scrollable areas can be used where the display has a fixed format (scrollable areas also are scrolled automatically) - if only fixed-format data are to be displayed, a table display is an alternative.

Example:
```
)ATTR
# AREA(SCRL)
)BODY
#SAREA                 #
#                      #
#                      #
)AREA SAREA
+     Surname_SNAME     +
+ First Name_FNAME      +
+Dialing Code_DCODE+
+Telephone No_TNUM     +
)PROC
)END
```

Associated panel display (after being scrolled down):

```
                     More:    - +
        First Name VV
        Dialing Code
```

8.13 PANEL AREA INFORMATION

The size and other characteristics of a DYNAMIC or GRAPHIC area may be obtained with the PQUERY service.

Syntax:
```
ISPEXEC PQUERY PANEL(panel-name) AREA(area-name)
        [AREATYPE(area-type-varname)]
        [WIDTH(area-width-varname)]
        [DEPTH(area-depth-varname)]
        [ROW(row-number-varname)]
        [COLUMN(column-number-varname)]
```

PANEL(panelname)
> **Panelname** is the name of the panel for which the information is to be retrieved.

AREA(areaname)
> **Areaname** is the name of the panel field for which the information is to be retrieved.

AREATYPE(areatypevarname)
> **Areatypevarname** is the name of the variable in which the area type is to be stored:

> DYNAMIC   dynamic area
> GRAPHIC   graphic area.

WIDTH(areawidthvarname)
> **Areawidthvarname** is the name of the variable in which the area width (number of columns) is to be stored.

DEPTH(areadepthvarname)
> **Areadepthvarname** is the name of the variable in which the area depth (number of rows) is to be stored.

ROW(row-number-varname)
> **Rownumbervarname** is the name of the variable in which the row number for the top row of the area is to be stored.

COLUMN(columnnumbervarname)
> **Columnnumbervarname** is the name of the variable in which the column number for the leftmost column of the area is to be stored.

The service issues one of the following return codes:

    0   Normal termination.

    8   The panel does not contain the specified area.

  12   The specified panel could not be found.

  16   Truncation error, not all data values have been returned.

  20   Severe error.

Example:
```
ISPEXEC PQUERY PANEL(TSPANO29) AREANAME(ALPHA) +
AREATYPE(TYPE) HEIGHT(AHEIGHT) COLUMN(ACOL)
```

These statements return the values:
```
TYPE     GRAPHIC
AHEIGHT  5
ACOL     1
```
for the following panel:

```
)ATTR
* AREA(GRAPHIC)
)BODY
%
%COMMAND ===>_ZCMD
+
+Persno. ===>_PNO +
+Name    ===>_NAME
+
+
*ALPHA                    *+
*                         *+
*                         *+
*                         *+
*                         *+
+
)PROC
)END
```

8.14 KEYLISTS

A keylist specifies the function keys and their corresponding action as they apply to the associated panel. The)PANEL section header can specify a keylist-name and (optionally) the application-id used to locate the keylist (default: ISPKYLST).

    Although the use of different keylists for various panels permits the use of function keys to be tailored to the type of panel being displayed (e.g. scrolling keys disabled for a non-scrollable panel), it is desirable to have a consistent function key usage in an application.

    Section 13.5.1 contains a detailed description of keylists.

8.15 PROCESSING SEQUENCE IN PANELS

A detailed understanding of how ISPF performs panel processing is essential for the development of advanced applications.

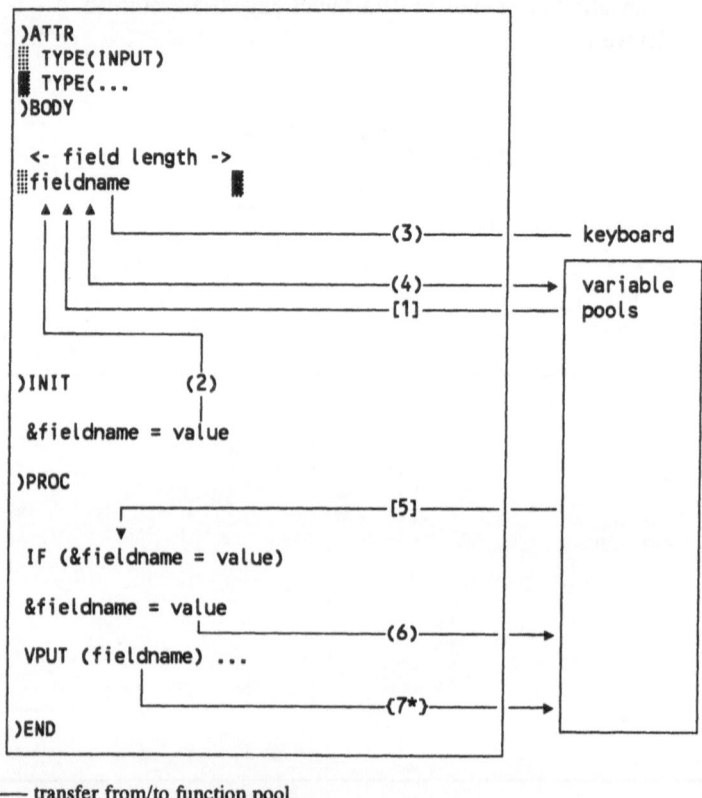

—( )— transfer from/to function pool
—[ ]— transfer from/to pool (function, shared, profile)
—( )— transfer to shared or profile pool
n = sequence
*   value associated with field name

Figure 8.10 - Data flow during panel processing

Explanation of the processing shown in Figure 8.10:

·   (1) data value obtained from pool (function, shared or profile).
·   (2) data value obtained from initialisation section.
·   (3) data value obtained from keyboard.
·   (4) current data value stored in function pool.
·   (5) current data value obtained from pool (function, shared or profile).
·   (6) current data value stored in function pool.
·   (7) current data value stored in pool (shared or profile).

Note: If an action bar selection is made, the associated processing is performed before the other panel processing.

ISPF performs the following processing in panel sections ()INIT,)REINIT and)PROC):
· All statements are analysed for syntactical errors. Such errors result in an ISPF run-time error message and the immediate termination of the processing. For example, the following statements would cause syntax errors:
```
SET &PNO = 10
VER (&PNO,XXX)
VER (&PNO,RANGE,1)
```

SET is not a valid ISPF function, XXX is not a valid verification class, the upper range is missing, respectively.

· Statements are processed sequentially. Conditional statements are only processed if the condition (IF) is satisfied. If the END (or RETURN) key has been pressed, VER statements are not processed. This means that unexpected situations can occur if .RESP is not checked.

· If an error has been detected, the .MSG variable is set, provided it has not previously been set, and the section processing continues.

These processing rules have consequences when statements use variables as comparands, e.g.
```
VER(&PNO,RANGE,1,&HIGH)
```
rather than
```
VER(&PNO,RANGE,1000,1999)
```
If the comparand, here HIGH, is undefined, a run-time syntax error will result.

The statements:
```
VER(&HIGH,NB,NUM)
VER(&PNO,RANGE,1,&HIGH)
```
do not help, as the first VER statement detects an error but does not terminate processing. The following statements provide a solution for this problem:
```
VER(&HIGH,NB,NUM)
IF (.MSG = &Z) VER(&PNO,RANGE,1,&HIGH)
```
Here the RANGE verification is only performed when no error has occurred (i.e. the .MSG control variable has not been set).

8.16 SPECIAL PANEL PROCESSING

The standard statements and functions previously discussed fulfill the basic processing requirements. However, much common panel processing may only be accomplished by using these statements and functions in combination. This section describes how such processing can be performed.

8.16.1 Panel Error Processing

One of the major advantages of a dialogue system compared with a batch system is the ability to detect errors at their source. Error detection is usually accomplished using VER statements. Error correction is facilitated by meaningful messages and cursor positioning at the field in question, and, if necessary, at the particular erroneous character within the field. The use of ISPF statements for basic field validation has been described in section 8.4.5, this section describes advanced error processing together with the necessary cursor positioning.

8.16.2 Extended Alphabetic Validation

The alphabetic class validation (VER(variable,ALPHA)) checks only for the standard alphabetic characters and the three national characters (a,...,z A,...,Z $ # @ blank), however, fields which are used for people's names may well contain special characters (e.g. "-" in hyphenated names). The following statements can be used to validate such compound names:

```
&A = TRUNC(&NAME,'-')
&B = .TRAIL
VER (&A,NB,ALPHA)
VER (&B,ALPHA)
```

These statements check that NAME is non-blank and only contains valid alphabetic characters (which may include a single hyphen).

8.16.3 Fields Containing Mixed Data

Often the data contained in a field is of a mixed format (e.g. alphabetic and numeric). When the length of data in the field is variable, the picture class cannot be used for verification. Such fields must be processed by splitting the field into its components, and then checking each component individually. In the following example the first character of DCODE is alphabetic, the rest of the field is numeric and must contain at least one digit:

```
)BODY
%
%Department code ===> _DCODE+
%
)PROC
&D1=TRUNC(&DCODE,1)
&D2=.TRAIL
VER(&D1,NB,ALPHA)
VER(&D2,NB,NUM)
```

The statement:

```
VER(&DCODE,NB,PICT'A9999')
```

cannot be used, because this statement requires that the DCODE field always contains 5 characters, one alphabetic character followed by four numeric digits, e.g.

A0123   valid

A0   invalid.

However, if the specification requires that second entry (A0) be accepted, the
following statements perform the required processing:

```
&D1=TRUNC(&DCODE,1)
&D2=.TRAIL
VER(&D1,NB,ALPHA)
VER(&D2,NB,NUM)
```

8.16.4 Date Validation

Dates in commercial data processing form a significant part of the data input. ISPF
does not have any explicit functions for date validation, although the VMASK program service can be used for this purpose. However, the standard functions and
statements can be used in combination to perform the required processing. The
following statements formally validate the employee's date of entry (ED = day, EM
= month, EY = year) in our personnel information system application:

```
)BODY
+Entry Date ===>_ED+(day) _EM+(month) _EY+(year)
+
)PROC
IF (.RESP = ENTER)
  &EDATE='&EY&EM&ED'
  IF (&EDATE ¬= &Z)              /* process if date field non-blank
    VER (&EY,NB,PICT,'99')       /* year 00,...,99
    IF (.MSG = &Z)               /* process if no error
      VER (&EM,NB,PICT,'99')
      VER (&EM,NB,RANGE,01,12)   /* month 01,...,12
      IF (.MSG = &Z)             /* process if no error
        &FEB = '28'              /* default, no leap year
        IF (&EY = '00','04','08','12','16','20','24','28','32','36',
                  '40','44','48','52','56','60','64','68','72','76',
                  '80','84','88','92','96')
          &FEB = '29'            /* leap year
        &MONTHDAY = TRANS(&EM 01,'31' 02,&FEB 03,'31' 04,'30'
                               05,'31' 06,'30' 07,'32' 08,'31'
                               09,'30' 10,'31' 11,'30' 12,'31')
        VER (&ED,NB,RANGE,01,&MONTHDAY)
)END
```

The three parts of the input date (ED, EM and EY) are transferred to the compound
field EDATE. If this field is non-blank, at least one of the input fields has been
defined. EY is verified as being numeric (with leading zero). EM is verified as being
numeric (with leading zero) and in the range 01 through 12. The intermediate
variable FEB is set initially to 28, should EY be a leap year, FEB is set to 29. The
number of days on the month is set into MONTHDAY, ED is checked that it lies within
the range 01 through MONTHDAY.

8.16.5 Validation of the Number of Data Fields

Should the number of fields which actually contain data be required, the following statements can be used to obtain this information:

```
)ATTR
)BODY
%
%COMMAND ===>_ZCMD
+
+No. of lines ===>_N+
+
+       Line 1 ===>_LINE1
+       Line 2 ===>_LINE2
+       Line 3 ===>_LINE3
+
)INIT
)PROC
IF (.RESP = ENTER)
  &X1 = TRANS(&LINE1 &Z,0 *,1)
  &X2 = TRANS(&LINE2 &Z,0 *,1)
  &X3 = TRANS(&LINE3 &Z,0 *,1)
  &X = '&X1&X2&X3'
  &M = TRANS(&X 000,0 100,1 110,2 111,3)
  VER(&N,NB,NUM)
  VER(&N,LIST,&M)
```

Explanation of the processing:

- &Xn = 0 if LINEn contains data, otherwise 1.
- &X is the active vector for LINE1 ... LINE3
  000 = no LINE contains data
  100 = LINE1 contains data
  110 = LINE1 and LINE2 contain data, etc.
- &M = number of LINEs which contain data, not only is the number of lines which contain data checked but also the sequence, e.g. LINE2 may only contain data when LINE1 also contains data.
- M (the actual number of lines) and N (the number expected lines) must be identical.

This example, in itself, is fairly trivial. However, the technique used here to check which combination of fields contains data is often required for practical applications.

8.16.6 Arithmetic Processing

ISPF panel processing statements do not include any arithmetic operations (e.g. &N = &N + 1). Simple arithmetic operations can be performed by breaking the operation into elementary steps. A panel exit may be more appropriate for more extensive processing.

Example:
The following statement adds 2 to a single digit (variable N):
```
&N = TRANS(&N 0,2 1,3 2,4 3,5 4,6 5,7 6,8 7,9 8,10 9,11)
```

For a number with more than one digit the processing is more extensive, each digit must be handled separately. The following statements add 2 to a 2-digit number (variable N):
```
&N1 = TRUNC(&N,1) /* high-order digit
&N2 = .TRAIL /* low-order digit
/* increment low-order digit by 2, result in X
&X = TRANS(&N2 0,02 1,03 2,04 3,05 4,06 5,07 6,08 7,09 8,10 9,11)
&CY = TRUNC(&X,1) /* extract carry
&N2 = .TRAIL /* low-order result
/* if carry (CY=1), increment high-order digit by 1
IF (&CY = 1) &N1 = TRANS(&N1 0,1 1,2 2,3 3,4 4,5 5,6 6,7 7,8 8,9 9,10)
/* transfer result into N
&N = '&N1&N2'
```
Such processing is only practicable for short fields as ISPF does not support loops, either explicitly or implicitly, in panel sections. Similar processing can be used for subtraction.

8.16.7 Extended Processing

Although the processing facilities offered in panels are extensive, there are some cases where the more general processing permitted in a procedure or program is required. Unfortunately there is no provision for a display panel to use a procedure. Although a panel exit (PANEXIT statement) can be used to invoke a program, this interface is not particularly easy to use. The technique of reversing the logic by using a procedure (or program) to display the panel is in most cases a better solution.

Example:
The panel field (PNO) is required to be a multiple of 2, such a validation can be performed far easier in a procedure. The following CLIST validates PNO and, if invalid, sets an ISPF message (messageid must be set appropriately) and forces a panel redisplay.
```
PROC 0
SET &PAN = panelname
SET &RC = 4
```

```
DO WHILE &RC EQ 4
  ISPEXEC DISPLAY PANEL(&PAN)
  SET &RC = &LASTCC
  IF &RC LT 8 THEN DO
    SET &PAN = &STR()
    IF &PNO//2 NE 0 THEN DO
      SET &RC = 4
      ISPEXEC SETMSG MSG(messageid)
    END
  END
END
```

8.16.8 Cursor Positioning

Cursor positioning is closely, but not exclusively, related to error processing. In general, the cursor should be positioned at the field where the next input is to be made. In the case of error processing, this is the field in error.

The cursor can be positioned at a panel field either explicitly (by setting the .CURSOR control variable) or implicitly (as a result of a VER or TRANS function). The .CURSOR control variable (or ZCURSOR system variables) contains the name of the last referenced panel field as transient value, provided that it has not been set. The cursor, once it has been set, cannot be changed during the current panel processing.

The setting of the cursor is best illustrated with an example:

```
)BODY
%
%COMMAND ===>_ZCMD
%
%Employee number ===>_PNO +
%Department code ===>_DCODE+
%
)PROC
VER(&PNO,NB)                           PNO
VER(&DCODE,NB)                         DCODE
VER(&PNO,NUM)                          PNO
&D1=TRUNC(&DCODE,1)                    DCODE
&D2=.TRAIL                             DCODE
VER(&D1,LIST,A,B,C)                    DCODE
VER(&D2,NB,NUM)                        DCODE
```

The panel field name currently contained in .CURSOR is shown in italics. D1 and D2 do not alter .CURSOR because they are not panel fields.

8.16.9 Comprehensive Verification

Sometimes verification must be made on fields whose content can have various formats. In this case verification may need to be performed in stages. The following example illustrates this technique.

Example:

The SIZE input field is to be checked that it is a valid specification for the Binder. SIZE contains two parameters of the form: size1,size2 . Each size parameter can be specified as a decimal number (e.g. 16384) or as its K-equivalent (e.g. 16K).

```
IF (&SIZE NE '')
  &SIZE1K = TRUNC(&SIZE,',')
  &SIZE2K = .TRAIL

  &SIZE1 = TRUNC(&SIZE1K,'K')
  IF (&SIZE1 = &SIZE1K) /* nnnn */
    VER (&SIZE1,NB,RANGE,16384,16192000)
  ELSE /* nnnnK */
    &C = '&SIZE1.K'
    VER (&SIZE1K,LIST,&C) /* format: nnnnK ? */
    VER (&SIZE1,NB,RANGE,16,16000)

  &SIZE2 = TRUNC(&SIZE2K,'K')
  IF (&SIZE2 = &SIZE2K) /* nnnn */
    VER (&SIZE2,NB,RANGE,512,65520)
  ELSE /* nnnnK */
    &C = '&SIZE2.K'
    VER (&SIZE2K,LIST,&C) /* format: nnnnK ? */
    VER (&SIZE2,NB,RANGE,1,64)
```

8.16.10 Dynamic Area Scrolling

The following example illustrates the use of scrollable dynamic areas. The dynamic area in the panel (FLD) has space for two lines. Each line in the dynamic area has the same format: a one-byte input field and a 17-byte output (message) field. The appropriate attribute (< for input, > for output) precedes each field. The REXX exec maintains the internal area as stem variables (LINE.1,...,LINE.5). The exec creates the displayed dynamic area (FLD) from these stem variables (the current position is scrolled appropriately; UP or DOWN command returned in the ZVERB system variable — the ZSCROLLN system variable contains the scroll amount in lines).

Sample REXX exec to perform vertical scrolling:

```
/* REXX */
ADDRESS ISPEXEC
/* define FLD data */
line.1 = "<_>"LEFT("selection 1",17)
line.2 = "<_>"LEFT("selection 2",17)
line.3 = "<_>"LEFT("selection 3",17)
line.4 = "<_>"LEFT("selection 4",17)
line.5 = "<_>"LEFT("selection 5",17)
i1 = 1 /* initialise: first entry */
i2 = 5 /* initialise: last entry */
DO FOREVER
  fld = '' /* initialise panel dynamic area */
  DO i = i1 TO i2
    fld = fld||line.i
  END
  "DISPLAY PANEL(SAPAN)"
  IF RC > 0 THEN EXIT
```

```
          "VGET (zverb zscrolln)"
          SELECT
            WHEN zverb = 'DOWN' THEN DO
              i1 = i1+zscrolln
              i1 = MIN(i1,i2) /* upper limit */
            END
            WHEN zverb = 'UP' THEN DO
              i1 = i1-zscrolln
              i1 = MAX(i1,1) /* lower limit */
            END
            OTHERWISE /* selection */
              DO i =  i1 TO 9999
                PARSE VAR fld . '<' op '>' fld
                IF op = 'S' THEN SAY "Line" i "selected"
              END
          END
        END
```

Associated panel (SAPAN):

```
)ATTR
> TYPE(DATAOUT)
< TYPE(DATAIN) CAPS(ON)
+ TYPE(TEXT)
@ AREA(DYNAMIC) SCROLL(ON)
)BODY
%COMMAND ===>_ZCMD                                        SCROLL+===>_SAMT+
@FLD                   @+
@                      @+
)INIT
IF (&SAMT = &Z) &SAMT = 'HALF'
)PROC
)END
```

8.16.11 Conditional Setting of Message Variables

In panel processing, if an error occurs, the first error message is not replaced by any subsequent error messages. However, this does not apply to setting of variables. In particular, if the first error message uses variables, these variables can be overwritten by a subsequent process, with the effect that the displayed message is not appropriate for the error. To avoid this, the .MSG variable can be checked, and no variables are set if it is not null.

Example:

```
...
)PROC
...
&LIST = 'Y N'
VER (&VA,LISTV,&LIST,MSG=XXXX001)
IF (.MSG NE '')
  &LIST = '1 2 3'
  VER (&VB,LISTV,&LIST,MSG=XXXX001)
```
The second verification is made only if no message has been set.

The xxxx001 message could typically have the form:
```
XXXX001 'Invalid input'
'Valid input: &LIST'
```

8.16.12 Mixed Panel Processing Elements

This example illustrates the interrelationship between action bar processing and normal panel processing elements, and the associated commands and keylists.

For simplicity, the panel has a single push-down menu. The CMD command that is assigned to the Open selection invokes the XCMD procedure, which returns the number of members in the previously specified dataset name. The PROMPT command (assigned to the PF4 key) is processed directly in the panel and invocating procedure. Depending on the position of the cursor when the PROMPT is invoked, either the DSN or MEM field is validated that the dataset name or member name, respectively, is present; the MSG field in the panel is set with the verification result for the entry. Figure 8.11 illustrates the schematic flow.

The command table and keylist must be assigned to the application, in this case DEMOCMDS and DEMOKEYS.

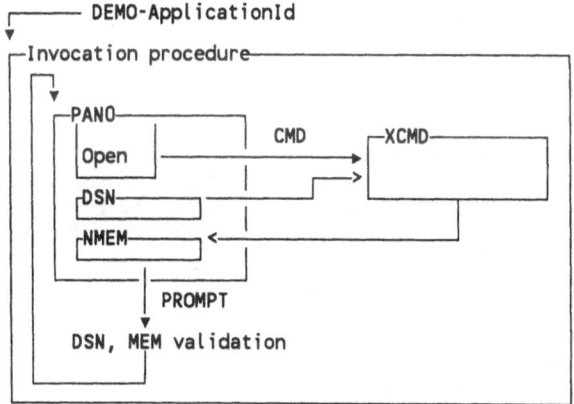

Figure 8.11 - Schematic flow

Panel definition:
```
)PANEL KEYLIST(DISPLAY,DEMO)
)ATTR
? TYPE(OUTPUT) INTENS(HIGH) SKIP(ON) CAPS(OFF)
a TYPE(AB)
_ TYPE(INPUT) CAPS(ON)
)ABC DESC(File)
 PDC DESC('New')
  ACTION RUN(PROMPT)
 PDC DESC('Open')
  ACTION RUN(CMD)
)ABCINIT
 .ZVARS = PDCHOICE
 &PDCHOICE = ' '
)BODY
 a File
%
```

```
%COMMAND ===>_ZCMD                                        +
% ?MSG
%Dataset name . ._DSN                                     +
% Member name . ._MEM        +
%Member count . .?NMEM
)INIT
&ZCMD = ''
)REINIT
&ZCMD = ''
)PROC
VGET (NMEM)
IF (&ZCMD = 'PROMPT')
  &CURFLD = .CURSOR
  IF (&CURFLD = 'DSN')
    VER (&DSN,NB,DSNAME)
  IF (&CURFLD = 'MEM')
    VER (&MEM,NB,NAME)
  VPUT (CURFLD)
  EXIT
)END
```

Invocation procedure:

```
/* REXX */
ADDRESS ISPEXEC
DO FOREVER
  "DISPLAY PANEL(PAN0)"
  IF RC > 0 THEN LEAVE
  IF (zcmd = 'PROMPT') THEN DO
    /* test presence of dataset name or member, depending cursor posn */
    IF (zcurfld = 'DSN') THEN msg = SYSDSN("'"dsn"'")
    IF (zcurfld = 'MEM') THEN msg = SYSDSN("'"dsn"("mem")'")
    "VPUT (dsn)"
  END
END
```

Command definition:

ZCTVERB	ZCTTRUNC	ZCTACT
PROMPT	0	PASSTHRU
CMD	0	SELECT CMD(%XCMD)

The PROMPT command is passed through to the application without being processed.
The CMD command invokes the XCMD procedure.

DISPLAY keylist definition:

```
KEY4DEF = PROMPT
```

That is, the PROMPT command is assigned to the PF4 key.

XCMD procedure:

```
/* REXX */
ADDRESS ISPEXEC
"VGET (dsn)" /* get dsn from pool */
rc = LISTDSI("'"dsn"' DIRECTORY")
nmem = sysmembers
"VPUT (nmem)" /* set value into shared pool */
"CONTROL NONDISPL" /* redisplay */
```

9

Table Services

9.1 GENERAL FORM OF TABLE

A table is a two dimensional array. Each table column is assigned the name of the associated variable. Each table row contains a value for that variable. Two kinds of column variables exist: **keys** and **names**. Keyed tables are accessed by key value, nonkeyed tables are accessed by row number. Of course, this is the general form of a relational data base; many of the elementary operations used for relational data bases are available for ISPF tables. Two forms of table exist: **temporary tables** in main storage and **permanent tables** stored in a table library. Permanent tables are loaded into main storage before being processed and saved at the end of the processing. The structure is determined when the table is created and can only be changed by recreating the table. Figure 9.1 illustrates the basic table structure.

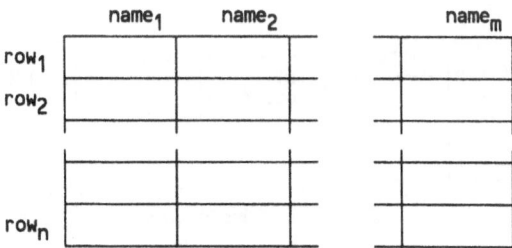

Figure 9.1 - Table structure

However, each row may be assigned additional variables (called **extension variables**). Figure 9.2 illustrates the structure of a table having extension variables.

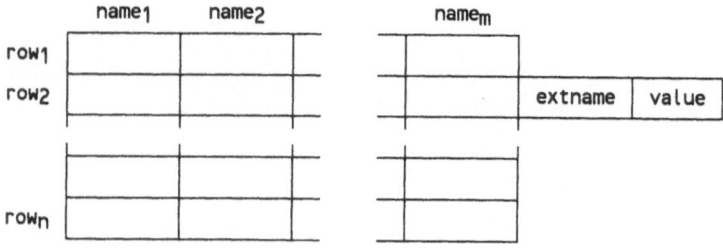

Figure 9.2 - Structure of table having extension variables

9.2 TABLE INPUT/OUTPUT

A table is a member of the table library. Because a table can be used for input and output, two separate library definitions (DD statements) are necessary: ISPTLIB for input and ISPTABL for output. However, other DDNAMEs may be specified. Although two separate library definitions are required, it is important that these refer to the same physical library. Should this not be the case, then the table being updated is not the input table (this is a common cause of error). The input library definition (ISPTLIB) may specify a concatenation of libraries, whereas the output library definition (ISPTABL) may only specify a single library. ISPTABL is not required for temporary tables.

The table libraries are either allocated before ISPF is invoked or dynamically allocated using the LIBDEF service. Each application should allocate ISPTABL when it is required. Services which use the output table library can also specify a file name other than ISPTABL.

For reasons of data consistency a table which is used for output can only be used (opened) by one user. The mechanism of ENQ (lock) and DEQ (unlock) is used to control table access. There is no restriction on the number of users for tables which are opened for input (read). A table being used concurrently by more than one application in the user's session (e.g. split screen) is said to be **shared**.

A table usually rewritten at the end of the output library. However, there is the option to enable it to physically replace the current table, provided space is available; this is known as **updating in place**. Figure 9.3 illustrates the use of table libraries.

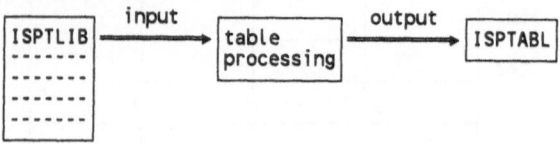

Figure 9.3 - Table libraries

Example: The following CLIST statements are two examples of table library definitions.

```
ALLOC DD(ISPTLIB) DSN(USER.ISPTLIB 'ISPF.ISPTLIB') SHR
ALLOC DD(ISPTABL) DSN(USER.ISPTLIB) SHR

ALLOC DD(ISPTLIB) DSN(USER.ISPTLIB 'ISPF.ISPTLIB') SHR
ALLOC DD(ISPTABL) DSN(TEST.ISPTLIB) SHR
```

The second example is possibly incorrect, because the output library (TEST.ISPTLIB) is not contained in the concatenation of input libraries, i.e. the table being updated is not the same as the table being read.

9.3 USE OF TABLES

Tables can be used in three ways:
- directly processed using table services
- displayed using the TBDISPL service
- data input for file tailoring services.

This chapter describes only the table services. The use of tables with file tailoring services is described in Chapter 11.

9.4 TABLE OPERATIONS

There are two forms of table operations:
- operations involving the table as a whole
- row operations.

All table operations, except TBCREATE, TBERASE, TBOPEN and TBSTATS, require that the table be open.

Row operations, except TBADD, either position the **current row pointer** (CRP) at a specific row or process the row where the CRP is positioned. The CRP can be positioned at the top of the table (before the first row), at the bottom of the table (the last row) or at a specific row. Figure 9.4 illustrates row names.

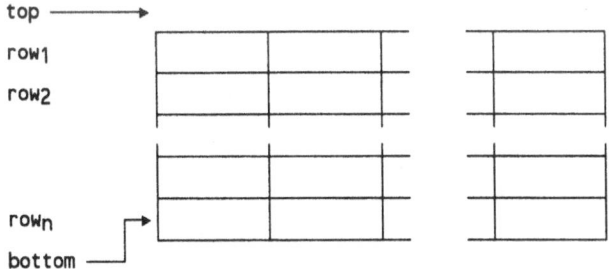

Figure 9.4 - Row names

The table operations are listed in alphabetic order:

- TBADD   Add a line (row) to the table
- TBBOTTOM   Set row pointer at bottom of table
- TBCLOSE   Close table
- TBCREATE   Create table
- TBDELETE   Delete a line (row) from the table
- TBDISPL   Display table contents
- TBEND   Terminate table processing
- TBERASE   Delete table
- TBEXIST   Determine whether a row exists
- TBGET   Get a line (row) from the table
- TBMOD   Unconditional update of a line (row) of the table
- TBOPEN   Open table for processing
- TBPUT   Conditionally update a line (row) in the table
- TBQUERY   Obtain table status (structure)
- TBSARG   Set search argument
- TBSAVE   Save table contents
- TBSCAN   Search table for specified argument
- TBSKIP   Move row pointer
- TBSORT   Sort table
- TBSTATS   Retrieve table statistics
- TBTOP   Set row pointer at top of table
- TBVCLEAR   Clear table variables.

Figure 9.5 shows an overview of table operations. Note: TBDISPL, TBSARG, TBSCAN, TBSORT, and TBVCLEAR are not included.

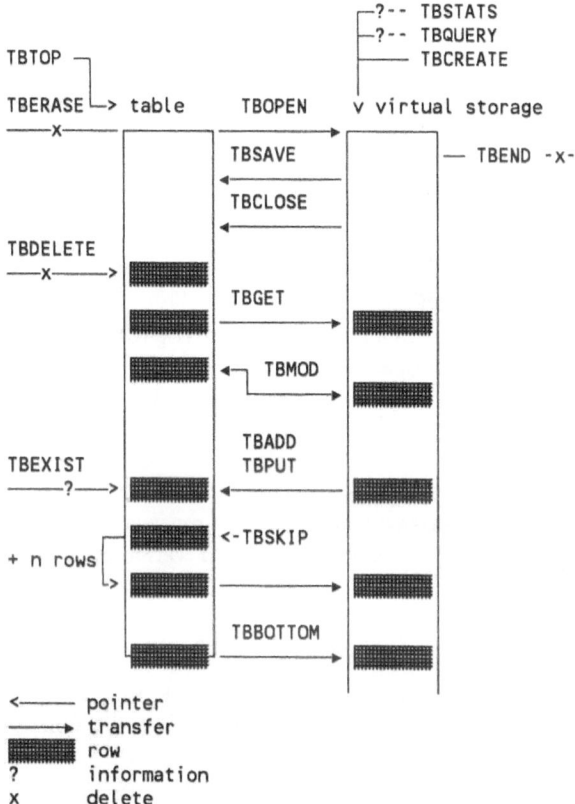

Figure 9.5 - Overview of table operations

9.4.1 TBADD - Add a Row to a Table

The TBADD service adds a new row to a table. The row contains the variables (keys and names) defined by the TBCREATE plus any extension variables specified. The row is added either after the row pointed to by the current row pointer (CRP) or at the row necessary to maintain sequence (if the table has been sorted using TBSORT and ORDER has been specified). The CRP is set to point to the added row.

Note: For keyed tables, the table is searched to ensure that the key is unique.

Syntax:
```
ISPEXEC TBADD tablename
        [SAVE(variablename [,variablename] ...)]
        [ORDER]
```

tablename
        The name of the table to be processed.

variablename
> The name of an extension variable which is to be appended to the table row.

ORDER
> The sequence specified by a previous TBSORT operation is to be maintained. This keyword is ignored if the table has not been sorted or updated without sequence being maintained (e.g. TBADD or other row operation has been performed without ORDER keyword).

The service sets one of the following return codes:

0	Normal completion.
8	The row exists already; CRP is set to TOP (0).
12	The table is not open.
16	Conversion error while processing sorted tables.
20	Severe error.

Example:
```
ISPEXEC TBADD PERSTAB SAVE(EDATE,SALARY) ORDER
```
Add (in sequence) a row to PERSTAB using two variables EDATE and SALARY in addition to the variables specified when the table was created.

9.4.2 TBBOTTOM - Set Row Pointer at End of Table

The TBBOTTOM service sets the current row pointer (CRP) to the last row in the table. The variables associated with this row are retrieved into the function pool, unless NOREAD has been specified.

Syntax:
```
ISPEXEC TBBOTTOM tablename
        [SAVENAME(variablename)]
        [ROWID(rowid-variablename)]
        [NOREAD]
        [POSITION(crp-variablename)]
```

tablename
> The name of the table to be processed.

SAVENAME(variablename)
> **Variablename** is the name of the variable which is to contain a list of the names of any extension variables present for the row. The list has the following format:
> (variablename[,variablename]...).

ROWID(rowid-variablename)
> **Rowidvariablename** is the name of the variable which is to contain a numeric value identifying the row being retrieved.

NOREAD
>   Row variables are not to be stored in the function pool.

POSITION(crp-variablename)
>   **Crp-variablename** is the name of the variable which is to contain the
>   current value of the CRP. 0 is returned for a table positioned at TOP.

The service sets one of the following return codes:

>   0   Normal completion.
>   8   The table is empty; CRP is set to TOP (0).
>   12   The table is not open.
>   16   Truncation error or insufficient space to retrieve all extension
>   variables.
>   20   Severe error.

Example:
```
ISPEXEC TBBOTTOM PERSTAB SAVENAME(ALPHA) POSITION(CRPNAME)
```
This example
·   positions the CRP at the last row of PERSTAB;
·   stores the variables associated with this row in function pool;
·   sets the current value of the CRP into the variable CRPNAME;
·   sets the names of any extension variables into the variable ALPHA - if the two
     variables EDATE and SALARY had been saved as extension variables, the variable
     ALPHA would contain "(EDATE,SALARY)".

9.4.3 TBCLOSE - Close and Save Table

The TBCLOSE service saves and terminates processing of the specified table
currently in main storage. If the table was opened in WRITE mode (TBCREATE ...
WRITE or TBOPEN ... WRITE), TBCLOSE writes the table into the output table library.
TBCLOSE deletes the main storage copy of the table.

A use count is maintained for shared tables; this counter is decremented by one
for each TBCLOSE issued. An actual TBCLOSE is only performed when the use count is
zero, in all other cases a TBSAVE is performed.

Note: If the function using temporary output tables terminates without closing the
table, a re-invocation of this function uses the table in main storage. This can lead
to duplicated rows, etc.

Syntax:
```
ISPEXEC TBCLOSE tablename
        [NEWCOPY|REPLCOPY]
        [NAME(output-tablename)]
        [PAD(percentage|0)]
        [LIBRARY(library-filename|ISPTABL)]
```

tablename
>   The name of the table to be processed.

NEWCOPY

The table is to be written at the current end of the output table library. The original table is only deleted when the new copy has been successfully written into the library.

REPLCOPY

The new copy of the table is to replace the original copy in the output table library. This replacement is only performed when there is sufficient space, otherwise the new copy is written at the current end of the output table library. Default.

NAME(output-tablename)

Output-tablename is the name under which the table is to be stored in the output table library. If a member with this name already exists in the output table library, that member will be replaced.

PAD(percentage)

Percentage is the percentage by which the current table size will be increased to give the total size to be used when the table is stored in the output table library. PAD is not used for updating in place (REPLCOPY). Default: PAD(0).

Tip

A large PAD percentage facilitates future updating in place, even when the size of the table has increased.

LIBRARY(library-filename)

Library-filename is the name of the file (DD statement) which specifies the output table library.
Default: LIBRARY(ISPTABL).

The service sets one of the following return codes:

0	Normal completion.
12	The table is not open.
16	Table output library not allocated.
20	Severe error.

Example:
```
ISPEXEC TBCLOSE PERSTAB PAD(40)
```
Close PERSTAB by writing it into the output library defined by the ISPTABL DD statement, the current table size is increased by 40%.

9.4.4 TBCREATE - Create a New Table

The TBCREATE service creates a new table in main storage, and makes that table open for processing. Creation of a table involves defining the columns (keys and names) of the basic structure. Additional name fields for a particular row can be later appended as extension variables.

Syntax:

```
ISPEXEC TBCREATE tablename
        [KEYS(key-variablename [,key-variablename]...)]
        [NAMES(name-variablename [,name-variablename]...)]
        [NOWRITE|WRITE]
        [REPLACE]
        [LIBRARY(library-filename|ISPTLIB)]
        [SHARE]
```

tablename

> The name of the table to be created.

KEYS(key-variablename[,key-variablename]...)

> **Key-variablename** is the name of a variable in the table which is to be used for keyed access.

NAMES(name-variablename[,name-variablename]...)

> **Name-variablename** is the name of a non-key variable in the table.

NOWRITE

> A temporary table is to be created. This table cannot be saved later in the output table library.

WRITE

> A permanent table is to be created. This table will be saved in the output table library at the end of processing (unless table processing terminated using the TBEND service). Default: WRITE.

REPLACE

> An existing table with the same name will be replaced. A warning is issued if the table does not exist.

LIBRARY(library-filename)

> **Library-filename** is the name of the file (DD statement) which specifies the input table library.
> Default: LIBRARY(ISPTLIB).

SHARE

> The table may be shared between logical screens when the user is in split screen mode. The table may only be created from one logical screen.
>   A use count is maintained for each implicit (TBCREATE) or explicit (TBOPEN) open for the table, this count is decremented by one for each TBEND or TBCLOSE request.

The service sets one of the following return codes:

0	Normal completion.
4	Normal completion; a table having the same name exists and has been replaced (REPLACE was specified).
8	A table having this name exists already (REPLACE was not specified.)

12   The table is in use (SHARED not specified).

16   WRITE parameter specified but no table input library has been
      allocated.

20   Severe error.

Example:
```
ISPEXEC TBCREATE PERSTAB KEYS(PNO) NAMES(NAME) REPLACE
```
Create PERSTAB with two columns, key PNO and non-key NAME. This table is to
replace an existing table having the same name, should one be present.

9.4.5 TBDELETE - Delete a Row from a Table

The TBDELETE service deletes a row from a table. For keyed tables, the current
value of the key variables identifies the row to be deleted. For non-keyed tables,
the value of the current row pointer (CRP) identifies the row to be deleted. After
deletion, the CRP is set to point to the row before that which has been deleted.

Syntax:
```
ISPEXEC TBDELETE tablename
```

tablename
      The name of the table to be processed.

The service sets one of the following return codes:

0   Normal completion

8   The row does not exist (keyed tables) or table is at top; CRP is set to
      TOP.

12   The table is not open.

20   Severe error.

Example:
```
ISPEXEC TBDELETE PERSTAB
```
Delete the current row from PERSTAB table.

9.4.6 TBDISPL - Display Table Contents

The TBDISPL service displays the table contents using a panel definition and either
the whole table or selected rows from the table can be displayed. The information
which is displayed in not restricted to what can fit on a single screen, but may be
scrolled vertically.

To select specific rows, two conditions must have been met:

·   TBSARG service invoked, to set the search argument for the specified rows;
·   ROWS(SCAN) specified in the)MODEL header for the panel definition.

ISPF table

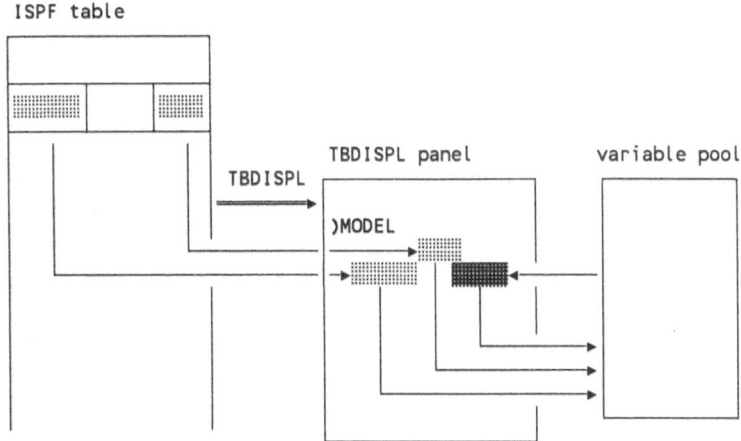

Figure 9.6 - Source of variables used in the TBDISPL display

Figure 9.6 illustrates the source of variables used in the TBDISPL display. Variables in the model line can come from either or both the table and the variable pools; the table variable has priority over the pool variable. The user can update the displayed variables. All the variables from the first changed row in the display are transferred to the function pool. The variables from the subsequent changed rows are retrieved line by line using the TBDISPL service without panel name. Updates to variables in the table must be made explicitly, e.g. by using the TBMOD service.

Syntax:
```
ISPEXEC TBDISPL tablename
        [PANEL(panelname)]
        [MSG(messageid)]
        [CURSOR(panel-fieldname)]
        [CSRROW(table-rownumber)]
        [CSRPOS(cursor-position)]
        [AUTOSEL(YES|NO)]
        [POSITION(crp-name)]
        [ROWID(rowid-name)]
```

tablename
   The name of the table to be processed.

PANEL(panelname)
   Panelname is the name of the panel to be displayed. If no panelname is specified, the current (TBDISPL) panel is redisplayed.
   The redisplay takes one of two forms, depending on whether selections are pending. If selections are pending, the data for the selected row are returned in the corresponding function pool variables and no physical display takes place. If no selections are pending, no data are returned but any outstanding scroll request is processed and a physical display takes place.

MSG(messageid)

Messageid identifies the message to be displayed with the panel. It overrides any pending messages set by the SETMSG service. .MSG in the panel definition takes precedence over this parameter.

CURSOR(panel-fieldname)

Panel-fieldname is the name of a field in the specified panel where the cursor is to be initially positioned. .CURSOR in the panel definition takes precedence over this parameter. If no cursor positioning is specified, the cursor is placed at the first input field.

CSRROW(table-rownumber)

The cursor is positioned at the row in the display corresponding to table-rownumber in the table. This row is automatically selected (retrieved), unless AUTOSEL(NO) was specified. If this row is not on the current screen, the cursor is positioned at the first input field in the panel. .CSRROW in the panel definition takes precedence over this parameter.

CSRPOS(cursor-position)

Cursor-position is the position within the cursor field where the cursor is to be positioned, position 1 is the first position in the field. .CSRPOS in the panel definition takes precedence over this parameter.
Default: CSRPOS(1).

AUTOSEL(YES)

The row identified by CSRROW(table-row-number) or the .CSRROW control variable is to be retrieved, even if it has not been explicitly selected. .AUTOSEL in the panel definition takes precedence over this parameter.
Default: AUTOSEL(YES).

POSITION(crp-name)

Crp-name specifies the name of the variable in which the current row number is to be returned.

ROWID(rowid-name)

Rowid-name specifies the name of the variable in which the number of the row currently being accessed is to be returned.

The TBDISPL service performs two kinds of processing:

·   processing which is performed without returning control (i.e. scrolling or pressing the ENTER key without any lines having been selected);
·   processing which returns control.

When control is returned, either one or more lines have been selected or the END (RETURN) key has been pressed. The)MODEL section defines a logical table row and if any data in this logical row (on the screen) has been altered, this row is said to be **selected**. The values of this row are automatically set into the function pool. If more than one row has been selected, these subsequent rows are said to be

pending. The values of the next of these rows are set into the function pool by invoking the TBDISPL service without specifying a panel name or message-id. Each TBDISPL request returns the values for a single logical table row and decrements the number of selected rows. The CRP is set to point to the row number of the selected row. The row returned in function pool contains the values from the table row together with any values updated in the display. Updates to values in the table itself must be made using explicit table update services (e.g. TBMOD). Updates to values in the display as a result of processing are made using the REFRESH function for those variables in the)REINIT section. The statements in the)PROC section are processed for each selected row and the values apply to that selected row. Chapter 11 "Table Applications" explains table display processing in detail.

Scrolling is an integral part of the TBDISPL service. Two levels of scrolling take place:

· Scrolling without any displayed data being changed, this form of scrolling is administered by ISPF.
· Scrolling in conjunction with data alteration, the changed (selected) rows are passed one by one to the point of invocation. The next physical TBDISPL display without panel name performs any outstanding scroll request. This implicit positioning can be explicitly overridden by using the actual scroll amount as positioning parameter for the TBDISPL service.

The following sample code can be used to perform implicit scrolling in conjunction with the TBDISPL service:

```
ISPEXEC TBTOP tablename
SET &PAN = &STR(PANEL(panelname))
SET &RC = 0
DO WHILE &RC LT 8
  ISPEXEC TBDISPL tablename &PAN
  SET &RC = &LASTCC
  SET &PAN = &STR()
  IF &RC LT 8 THEN DO
     process selected row
  END
END
```

Should the application developer wish to perform his own scroll processing, Section 9.4.6.1 contains system variables with pertinent scrolling information.

The following sample code can be used to perform explicit scrolling in conjunction with the TBDISPL service:

```
SET &N = 0
SET &RC = 4
DO WHILE &RC LT 8
  ISPEXEC TBTOP tablename
  ISPEXEC TBSKIP tablename NUMBER(&N)
  SET &PAN = &STR(PANEL(panelname))
  SET &RC = 4
  DO WHILE &RC EQ 4
    ISPEXEC TBDISPL tablename &PAN
    SET &RC = &LASTCC
    IF &RC LT 8 THEN DO
      SET &PAN = &STR()
      ISPEXEC VGET (ZVERB ZSCROLLN) SHARED
      IF (&ZSCROLLN EQ &STR()) THEN SET &ZSCROLLN = 0
      SELECT
        WHEN (&ZVERB EQ UP) SET &N = &ZTDTOP - &ZSCROLLN
        WHEN (&ZVERB EQ DOWN) SET &N = &ZTDTOP + &ZSCROLLN
      END
      process selected row
    END
  END
END
```

If other display services are requested between retrieval of the pending selected rows, the CONTROL service must be invoked to SAVE and subsequently RESTORE the TBDISPL status. Example:

```
ISPEXEC TBDISPL tabname PANEL(panname1)
ISPEXEC CONTROL DISPLAY SAVE
ISPEXEC DISPLAY PANEL(panname2)
ISPEXEC CONTROL DISPLAY RESTORE
ISPEXEC TBDISPL tabname
```

Table 9.1 shows a decision table that defines the TBDISPL processing (y=condition met or processing performed; n=condition not met or processing not performed).

Table 9.1 - Decision table showing TBDISPL processing

panelname	y	n	n
ZTDSELS	-	>0	0
panel display	y	n	y
)INIT	y	n	n
)REINIT	n	y	y
)PROC	y	y	y

The service sets one of the following return codes:

 0   Normal completion; last row selected.
 4   Normal completion; selected rows are pending.
 8   The user entered END or RETURN command.
12   The specified panel or message could not be found, or the table was not open.
20   Severe error.

Example 1:
```
ISPEXEC TBDISPL PERSTAB PANEL(TSPAN001)
```
Display PERSTAB using panel TSPAN001; the values for the first selected row are set into function pool.

Example 2:
```
ISPEXEC TBDISPL PERSTAB
```
Retrieve the values for the next selected row.

Example 3:
```
SET &PN = TSPAN001
SET &DRC = 4 /* initialise loop condition */
DO UNTIL &DRC NE 4
  ISPEXEC TBDISPL PERSTAB PANEL(&PN)
  SET &DRC = &LASTCC /* display return code */
  IF &DRC < 8 THEN DO
    SET &PN = &STR() /* clear panel name */
    /* process row */
  END
END
```
Example 3 shows general code that can be used to process all table rows.

9.4.6.1 TBDISPL System Variables. The following system variables are used in conjunction with the TBDISPL service

ZSCROLLN
The number of lines to be scrolled [out, 4].

ZTDADD
Indicator (YES, NO) whether the function needs to add rows to the table [out, 3]

ZTDAMT
If ZTADD contains YES, ZTDAMT contains the estimated number of rows necessary to satisfy the scroll request [out, 4]

ZTDMARK
"Bottom-of-Data" text [in, n].

ZTDLROWS
The logical number of rows in the display table [in, 6]. The n in "ROW m OF n" message.

ZTDLTOP
The (top-row-displayed) number [in, 6]. The m in "ROW m OF n" message.

ZTDMSG
Message-id for first row displayed [in, 8].

ZTDRET
Indicator (DOWN, UP, VERTICAL) when control is to be returned to the function [func, in, 8]. UP: Control is returned at the top of the scrollable data. DOWN: Control is returned at the bottom of the scrollable data. VERTICAL: Control is returned at either top or bottom of the scrollable data.

ZTDROWS
Number of table display rows [out, 6].

ZTDSCRP
The number of the row relative to the top of the table that is to be at the top of the panel's scrollable are [func, in/out, 6].

ZTDSELS
Number of rows selected [out, 4]. ZTDSELS includes the currently selected row (if any) and any pending rows.

ZTDSIZE
The number of rows that fill the panel's scrollable area [out, 4].

ZTDSRID
The row-id of the row to which ZTDSCRP points [out, 6].

ZTDTOP
CRP of top row displayed [out, 6].

ZVERB
Scroll command (UP, DOWN) [out, 8].

The ZTDRET, ZTDADD, ZTDSCRP, ZTDLTOP, ZTDLROWS, ZTDSRID, ZTDAMT, and ZTDSIZE system variables are used only for dynamically created tables.

9.4.7 TBEND - Close table without saving

The TBEND service deletes the specified table from main storage. A use count is maintained for shared tables. This counter is decremented by one for each TBEND issued. An actual TBEND is only performed when the use count is zero, in all other cases the TBEND is ignored.

Syntax:
```
ISPEXEC TBEND tablename
```

tablename
>   The name of the table to be processed.

The service sets one of the following return codes:

>   0   Normal completion.
>   12 The table is not open.
>   20 Severe error.

Example:
```
ISPEXEC TBEND PERSTAB
```
Terminate processing of PERSTAB table.

9.4.8 TBERASE - Delete a Table

The TBERASE service deletes the specified table from the output table library.

Note: The TBERASE service is not restricted to processing ISPF tables. It also can be used to delete a member from any partitioned data set.

Syntax:
```
ISPEXEC TBERASE tablename
        [LIBRARY(library-filename|ISPTABL)]
```

tablename
>   The name of the table to be deleted.

LIBRARY(library-filename)
>   **Library-filename** is the name of the file (DD statement) which specifies the
>   output table library.
>   Default: LIBRARY(ISPTABL).

The service sets one of the following return codes:

>   0   Normal completion.
>   8   The table does not exist in the output table library.
>   12 The table is in use.
>   16 no table output library allocated.
>   20 Severe error.

Example:
```
ISPEXEC TBERASE PERSTAB LIBRARY(TABLIB)
```
Delete PERSTAB table from the library defined by the TABLIB DD statement.

9.4.9 TBEXIST - Determine Whether a Table Row Exists

The TBEXIST service determines whether the specified key exists in the table. The current values of the key variables are used as search arguments.

Syntax:
```
ISPEXEC TBEXIST tablename
```

tablename
　　　The name of the table to be processed.

Tip
The complete key is used as search argument, the TBSCAN service can be used for generic or partial keys. TBSCAN may also be used to search for specified rows in non-keyed tables.

The service sets one of the following return codes:

　　0　　Normal completion; CRP is set to the located row.
　　8　　Keyed tables: the row does not exist.
　　　　Non-keyed tables: this service is not available.
　12　　The table is not open.
　20　　Severe error.

Example:
```
SET &PNO = 1111
ISPEXEC TBEXIST PERSTAB
```
Check for the existence of the row with PNO=1111 in PERSTAB table (it is assumed that PERSTAB table has PNO as key).

9.4.10 TBGET - Retrieve a Row From a Table

The TBGET service retrieves the identified row from a table. The row values are stored in function pool unless the NOREAD parameter has been specified. The CRP is set to point to the retrieved row.

　　Keyed tables: the current values of the key variables are used as search argument.

　　Non-keyed tables: the current values of the CRP identifies the row to be retrieved.

Syntax:
```
ISPEXEC TBGET tablename
        [SAVENAME(variablename)]
        [ROWID(rowid-variablename)]
        [NOREAD]
        [POSITION(crp-variablename)]
```

tablename
　　　The name of the table to be processed.

SAVENAME(variablename)

> **Variable-name** is the name of the variable in which the list of extension variable names is to be placed. The list of extension variables has the following form:
> (variablename[variablename]...)

ROWID(rowid-variablename)

> **Rowid-variablename** is the name of the variable in which the number of the located row is to be placed.

NOREAD

> The row values are not to be transferred to the function pool, i.e. the current values are retained.

POSITION(crp-variablename)

> **Crp-variablename** is the name of the variable in which the CRP is to be placed.

The service sets one of the following return codes:

> 0   Normal completion.
>
> 8   The specified row does not exist.
>
> 12   The table is not open.
>
> 16   Variable value has been truncated.
>
> 20   Severe error.

Example:

```
SET &PNO = 1111
ISPEXEC TBGET PERSTAB SAVENAME(VNL) NOREAD
```

Retrieve the names of the extension variables, if any, for the row identified by PNO=1111. The names of the extension variables are stored in the VNL variable and the NOREAD parameter specifies that the data values for the row are not to be returned.

9.4.11 TBMOD - Unconditional Update of a Row in a Table

The TBMOD service updates a row in a table. The row contains the variables (keys and names) defined by the TBCREATE plus any extension variables specified.

If for keyed tables the row identified by the key variables is present, it is updated, otherwise a new row is added. The row is added at the end of the table or at such a position so as to maintain sequence (if ORDER has been specified, and the table is in the sequence as specified by TBSORT). The CRP is set to point at the row which has been processed.

For non-keyed tables the row is added after the row pointed to by the CRP or at such a position so as to maintain sequence (if ORDER has been specified and the table is in the sequence as specified by TBSORT).

Syntax:
```
ISPEXEC TBMOD tablename
        [SAVE(variablename[,variablename]...)]
        [ORDER]
```

tablename

The name of the table to be processed.

variablename

The name of an extension variable which is to be appended to the table row.

ORDER

The sequence specified by a previous TBSORT operation is to be maintained. This keyword is ignored if the table has not been sorted or updated without sequence being maintained (e.g. TBMOD or other row operation has been performed without ORDER keyword).

The service sets one of the following return codes:

   0   Normal completion.
   8   The row did not exist and has been added.
  12   The table is not open.
  16   Conversion error while processing sorted tables.
  20   Severe error.

Example:
```
ISPEXEC TBMOD PERSTAB SAVE(EDATE,SALARY) ORDER
```
Update or add, as appropriate, a row in PERSTAB using two variables EDATE and SALARY in addition to the variables specified when the table was created; the row is to maintain sequence.

Tip

A row of a non-keyed table cannot be directly updated using TBMOD. The following series of operations are required to perform an update:
```
ISPEXEC TBADD table-name
ISPEXEC TBSKIP table-name NUMBER(-1)
ISPEXEC TBDELETE table-name
```
The TBADD must be performed first in order to avoid problems when the first row of the table is logically updated.

9.4.12 TBOPEN - Open Table for Processing

The TBOPEN service loads the specified table from the input table library into main storage. The table is ENQued to ensure it is not being used by another user. For option NOWRITE (the table will not be rewritten to the output table library), the ENQ is for the time the table is being read into main storage. For option WRITE, the ENQ is maintained until the table is closed (using TBCLOSE or TBEND).

Syntax:
```
ISPEXEC TBOPEN tablename
       [NOWRITE|WRITE]
       [LIBRARY(library-filename|ISPTLIB)]
       [SHARE]
```

tablename
> The name of the table to be opened.

NOWRITE
> The table is not to be rewritten to the output table library when the table is closed. Any modifications made to the table apply only to the current session.

WRITE
> The table is to be updated. The table will be rewritten to the output table library when it is closed. Default: WRITE.

LIBRARY(library-filename)
> **Library-filename** is the name of the file (DD statement) which specifies the input table library. Default: LIBRARY(ISPTLIB).

SHARE
> The table may be shared between logical screens when the user is in split screen mode. The table may only be created from one logical screen.
>
> A use count is maintained for each implicit (TBCREATE) or explicit (TBOPEN) open for the table. This count is decremented by one for each TBEND or TBCLOSE request.

Tip
The simplest means of determining whether a table is present is to use the TBOPEN service and test its return code (0 = table present, 8 = table not present).

Note: ISPEXEC CONTROL ERRORS RETURN must have been previously specified, this ensures that control is returned to the application should the table not be present.

The service sets one of the following return codes:

0	Normal completion.
8	The table does not exist.
12	The table is in use (SHARED not specified).
16	No table input library has been allocated.
20	Severe error.

Example:
```
ISPEXEC TBOPEN PERSTAB
```
Make PERSTAB table available for processing by reading it from the input table library into main storage. The table is not to be permanently updated.

Tip

The following CLIST illustrates a technique for checking whether a table can be used for output (opened for write). If the table cannot be opened, a message is issued and the open is retried after the user has entered a response.

```
ISPEXEC CONTROL ERRORS RETURN
SET &RC = 4    /* force first time */
DO WHILE &RC NE 0
  ISPEXEC TBOPEN tablename WRITE
  SET &RC = &LASTCC
  IF &RC NE 0 THEN DO /* display message and wait, if error */
    WRITE TABLE CANNOT BE OPENED, PLEASE WAIT
    READ
  END
END
/* open for write successful */
```

9.4.13 TBPUT - Conditional Update of a Table Row

The TBPUT service updates the current row in a table. The row contains the variables (keys and names) defined by the TBCREATE plus any extension variables specified. The CRP is set to point to the row which has been processed.

For keyed tables the row identified by the key variables must match the key of the record pointed to by the CRP, otherwise no update is performed.

For non-keyed tables the row identified by the CRP is updated.

Syntax:
```
ISPEXEC TBPUT tablename
        [SAVE(variablename [,variablename] ...)]
        [ORDER]
```

tablename
> The name of the table to be processed.

variablename
> The name of an extension variable which is to be appended to the table row.

ORDER
> The sequence specified by a previous TBSORT operation is to be maintained. This keyword is ignored if the table has not been sorted or updated without sequence being maintained (e.g. TBPUT or other row operation has been performed without ORDER keyword).

The service sets one of the following return codes:

0	Normal completion.
8	The key does not match the key of the row pointed to by the CRP; the row is not updated.
12	The table is not open.
16	Conversion error while processing sorted tables.
20	Severe error.

Example:
```
SET &PNO = 1111
ISPEXEC TBPUT PERSTAB SAVE(EDATE,SALARY)
```
Update the row with key 1111 (PNO is assumed to be the key). Two extension variables (EDATE and SALARY) are to be appended to the row.

9.4.14 TBQUERY - Obtain Table Information

The TBQUERY service returns status information for the specified table.

Syntax:
```
ISPEXEC TBQUERY tablename
        [KEYS(key-variablename)]
        [NAMES(name-variablename)]
        [ROWNUM(rownum-variablename)]
        [KEYNUM(keynum-variablename)]
        [NAMENUM(namenum-variablename)]
        [POSITION(crp-variablename)]
```

tablename
> The name of the table to be processed.

KEYS(key-variablename)
> **Key-variablename** is the name of the variable in which the list of key names (TBCREATE KEYS ...) for the table is to be returned. The name list has the form:
> (variablename[variablename]...).

NAMES(name-variablename)
> **Name-variablename** is the name of the·variable in which the list of name variables (TBCREATE NAMES ...) for the table is to be returned. The name list has the following form:
> (variablename[variablename]...).

ROWNUM(rownum-variablename)
> **Rownum-variablename** is the name of the variable which is to contain the number of rows in the table.

KEYNUM(keynum-variablename)
> **Keynum-variablename** is the name of the variable which is to contain the number of key variables in the table.

NAMENUM(namenum-variablename)
> **Namenum-variablename** is the name of the variable which is to contain the number of non-key variables in the table.

POSITION(crp-variablename)
> **Crp-variablename** is the name of the variable which is to contain the value of the CRP.

The service sets one of the following return codes:

     0   Normal completion.
     8   The table is not open.
    12   Insufficient space to return all the names.
    20   Severe error.

Example:
```
ISPEXEC TBQUERY PERSTAB KEYS(VKN) NAMES(VNN) ROWNUM(NR) KEYNUM(NK)
NAMENUM(NN)
```
Return the following information for PERSTAB table (it is assumed that the table currently contains 10 rows):

variable	value
VKN	PNO
VNN	NAME
NR	10
NK	1
NN	1

9.4.15 TBSARG - Set Search Argument

The TBSARG service is used to define the search argument which is subsequently used to search a table with the TBSCAN service or select rows to be displayed using the TBDISPL service.

The parameter list specifies the variables to be used for the search argument, the condition to be met and the direction of the search (forward, backward) relative to the current row pointer (CRP). The specified variables (key variables, name variables or extension variables) from each table row are compared with those in the variable pool, the row is selected if the conditions are satisfied. Those variables not being used should be set to null using the TBVCLEAR service prior to invoking the TBSARG service.

Generic data values are specified with an * (asterisk) at the end of the comparand, e.g. ALP* specifies all values commencing with ALP.

Note: The use of TBSARG in conjunction with the TBDISPL service requires that the)MODEL header in the panel definition specifies ROWS(SCAN).

Syntax:
```
ISPEXEC TBSARG tablename
        [ARGLIST(extension-variablename[,extension-variablename]...)]
        [NEXT|PREVIOUS]
        [NAMECOND(variablename,op[,variablename,op]...)]
```

tablename
    The name of the table to be processed.

ARGLIST(extension-variablename...)
    Extension-variablename is the name of an extension variable to be used as part of the search argument.

NEXT
> The search is to be made in the forward direction. Default: NEXT.

PREVIOUS
> The search is to be made in the backward direction.

NAMECOND(variablename,lop...)
> **Variablename** is the name of a variable which is to be used in the search argument.
>
> **lop** is the logical operator used for comparisons with this variable. The following logical operators may be used:
>
> | | |
> |---|---|
> | EQ | equal (the default) |
> | NE | not equal |
> | LE | less than or equal |
> | LT | less than |
> | GE | greater than or equal |
> | GT | greater than. |
>
> The comparison is made between the values in the table row and in the function pool, e.g.
> ```
> NAMECOND(PNO,LT)
> ```
> specifies that those rows are to be selected where the value of PNO is less than that in the variable pool.

The service sets one of the following return codes:

> 0   Normal completion.
> 8   All column variables are null and no ARGLIST parameter was specified.
> 12   The table is not open.
> 20   Severe error.

Example:
```
ISPEXEC TBVCLEAR PERSTAB
SET &PNO = 1000
SET &NAME = MC*
ISPEXEC TBSARG PERSTAB NAMECOND(PNO,GT,NAME,EQ)
```
Define a search argument to select those rows where the PNO is greater than 100 and the first character of NAME begins with MC.

Tip
When TBSARG is used in a loop, care must be taken to ensure that the search argument values contain the true comparand and not those read from the last table row.

9.4.16 TBSAVE - Save a Table

The TBSAVE service writes the specified table currently in main storage into the output table library. The table must have been opened in WRITE mode (TBCREATE

... WRITE or TBOPEN ... WRITE). The table remains open in main storage and is available for further processing.

Tip

TBSAVE should be regularly used during long running applications to maintain an up-to-date permanent copy of the table as this facilitates recovery should the computer system fail.

Syntax:
```
ISPEXEC TBSAVE tablename
        [NEWCOPY|REPLCOPY]
        [NAME(output-tablename)]
        [PAD(percentage|0)]
        [LIBRARY(library-filename|ISPTABL)]
```

tablename

    The name of the table to be processed.

NEWCOPY

    The table is to be written at the current end of the output table library, the original table is only deleted when the new copy has been successfully written into the library.

REPLCOPY

    The new copy of the table is to replace the original copy in the output table library. This replacement is only performed when there is sufficient space, otherwise the new copy is written at the current end of the output table library. Default: REPLCOPY.

NAME(output-tablename)

    Output-tablename is the name under which the table is to be stored in the output table library. If a member with this name already exists in the output table library, that member will be replaced.

PAD(percentage)

    Percentage is the percentage by which the current table size will be increased to give the total size of the table when it is stored in the output table library. PAD is not used for updating in place (REPLCOPY). Default: PAD(0).

Tip

    A large PAD percentage facilitates future updating in place, even when the size of the table has increased.

LIBRARY(library-filename)

    Library-filename is the name of the file (DD statement) which specifies the output table library. Default: LIBRARY(ISPTABL).

The service sets one of the following return codes:

    0   Normal completion.
  12 The table is not open.
  16 Table output library not allocated.
  20 Severe error.

Example:
```
ISPEXEC TBSAVE PERSTAB PAD(40)
```
Save PERSTAB by writing it into the output library defined by the ISPTABL DD statement, the space is reserved for a table 40% larger than the size of the current table.

9.4.17 TBSCAN - Perform a Table Search

The TBSCAN service is used to scan a table using a search argument. This search argument may be specified as a parameter or previously defined with the TBSARG service.

The parameter list specifies the variables to be used for the search argument, the condition to be met and the direction of the search (forward, backward) relative to the current row pointer (CRP). The specified variables (key variables, name variables or extension variables) from each table row are compared with those in the variable pool and the row is selected if the conditions are satisfied. Those variables not being used should be set to null using the TBVCLEAR service prior to requesting the TBSCAN service.

Generic data values are specified with an * (asterisk) at the end of the comparand, e.g. ALP* specifies all values commencing with ALP.

Tip
When TBSCAN is used in a loop care must be taken to ensure that the search argument values contain the true comparand and not those read from the last table row.

Syntax:
```
ISPEXEC TBSCAN tablename
    [ARGLIST(variablename[,variablename]...)]
    [SAVENAME(variablename)]
    [NEXT|PREVIOUS]
    [NOREAD]
    [POSITION(crp-variablename)]
    [CONDLIST(lop[,lop]...)]
```

tablename
    The name of the table to be processed.

ARGLIST(variablename...)
    Variablename is the name of a variable (key, name or extension) to be used as part of the search argument. This operand, if specified, overrides any search argument set by the TBSARG service.

SAVENAME(variablename)

Variablename is the name of the variable which is to contain a list of the names of any extension variables present for the row. The list has the following format:

(variablename[,variablename]...).

NEXT

The search is to be made in the forward direction. Default: NEXT.

PREVIOUS

The search is to be made in the backward direction.

NOREAD

The row variables are not to be stored in the function pool.

POSITION(crp-variablename)

Crp-variablename is the name of the variable which is to contain the current value of the CRP. Zero is returned for a table positioned at TOP.

CONDLIST(lop...)

Lop is the logical operator used for comparisons with the corresponding variable in the ARGLIST. The following logical operators may be used:

EQ   equal (default)
NE   not equal
LE   less than or equal
LT   less than
GE   greater than or equal
GT   greater than.

The comparison is made between the values in the table row and the function pool, respectively.

If more entries are defined in the ARGLIST than in the CONDLIST, the EQ logical operator is assumed for the missing entries.

Example:
```
ARGLIST(PNO,NAME)
```
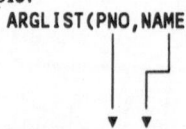
```
CONDLIST(LT,EQ)
```
Those rows are to be selected where the value of PNO is less than (logical operator LT) that in the variable pool and the value of NAME is the same (logical operator EQ) as that in the variable pool.

The service sets one of the following return codes:

0   Normal completion.
8   The row does not exist.

12   The table is not open.

16   Truncation error or insufficient space to retrieve all extension
      variable names.

20   Severe error.

Example:
```
ISPEXEC TBVCLEAR PERSTAB
SET &PNO = 1000
SET &NAME = MC*
ISPEXEC TBSCAN PERSTAB ARGLIST(PNO,NAME) CONDLIST(GT,EQ)
```
Perform a search to select those rows where the PNO is greater than 100 and the
first character of NAME begins with MC.

9.4.18 TBSKIP - Move Row Pointer

The TBSKIP service moves the current row pointer (CRP) either the specified
number of rows forward or backward or sets it to a specific row.

Syntax:
```
ISPEXEC TBSKIP tablename
        [NUMBER([+ | -]number | +1)]
        [SAVENAME(variablename)]
        [ROWID(rowid-variablename)]
        [ROW(row-variablename)]
        [NOREAD]
        [POSITION(crp-variablename)]
```

tablename
  The name of the table to be processed.

NUMBER([+|-]number | +1)
  Number is the rows the current row pointer is to be moved. A positive
  number causes the CRP to be moved towards the bottom of the table and a
  negative number causes the CRP to be moved towards the top of the table.
  Default: NUMBER(+1).

SAVENAMEiablename)
  Variablename is the name of the variable in which the list of extension
  variable names is to be placed. The list of extension variables has the
  following form:
  (variablename[variablename]...)

ROWID(rowid-variablename)
  Rowid-variablename is the name of the variable in which the number of
  the located row is to be placed.

ROW(row-variablename)
  Row-variablename specifies the numeric value which uniquely identifies
  the row at which the CRP is to be positioned.

NOREAD
Do not transfer the row values to the function pool, i.e. the current values are retained.

POSITION(crp-variablename)
Crp-variablename is the name of the variable in which the CRP is to be placed.

The service sets one of the following return codes:

0   Normal completion.
8   The CRP would have been positioned outside the bounds of the table; CRP set to 0 (TOP).
12 The table is not open.
16 Variable value has been truncated, or insufficient space to retrieve all extension variable names.
20 Severe error.

Example:
```
ISPEXEC TBSKIP PERSTAB NUMBER(+2) NOREAD
```
Move the CRP two rows towards the bottom of PERSTAB. The NOREAD parameter specifies that the data values for the row are not to be returned.

9.4.19 TBSORT - Sort Table

The TBSORT service sorts the table using the specified sort criteria. A sorted table (even an empty table) is maintained in this specified sequence, provided all subsequent requests effecting the position of rows (TBADD, etc.) specify the ORDER parameter.

Syntax:
```
ISPEXEC TBSORT tablename
        FIELDS({variablename,{B|C|N},{A|D}}...)
```

tablename
The name of the table to be sorted.

FIELDS({variablename,{B|C|N},{A|D}}...)
Variablename is the name of a variable (key or name) which is to be sorted.

The second parameter specifies the data form:
B   binary
C   character
N   numeric.

The third parameter specifies the sort sequence for this field:
A   ascending
D   descending.

The first variable specified is the major sort field; the last variable specified is the minor sort field. Binary sorts the values into binary (EBCDIC) sequence. Character and numeric values are sorted taking language constraints into consideration. The ZLANG system variable specifies the current language.

Note: ZLANG is defined at the time of ISPF installation.

Example:
In the German language the letters ä, ö, etc. should be collated after a, o, etc. However the equivalent EBCDIC codes for these characters are X'C0' and X'6A', respectively. The c parameter will collate these characters in the required sequence.

   Similarly, the way of writing numeric values is different in various countries. The following table shows the three formats supported by ISPF:

Period	1,234.56
Comma	1.234,56
French	1234,56

A numeric value, in the convention appropriate for the ZLANG parameter, is subject to the following restrictions:

· The field must contain only numeric digits, leading blanks, plus (+) or minus (-) sign and the delimiters as depicted in the previous table.
· The total field length must not exceed 16 characters.
· The maximum absolute value of the field is 2,147,483,647 (2^{31}-1).
· Leading blanks may follow the sign character.

The service sets one of the following return codes:

   0　Normal completion.
　12　The table is not open.
　16　Numeric conversion error.
　20　Severe error.

Example:
```
ISPEXEC TBSORT PERSTAB FIELDS(NAME,C,A,PNO,N,D)
```
PERSTAB is to be sorted, the major sort field NAME is a character field and is to be sorted in ascending sequence. The minor sort field PNO is a numeric field and is to be sorted in descending sequence.

9.4.20 TBSTATS - Retrieve Table Statistics

The TBSTATS service returns statistical information for the table. The table need not be open in order to obtain this information.

Syntax:
```
ISPEXEC TBSTATS tablename
        [CDATE(datecreated-variablename)]
        [CTIME(timecreated-variablename)]
        [UDATE(dateupdated-variablename)]
        [UTIME(timeupdated-variablename)]
        [USER(lastuser-variablename)]
        [ROWCREAT(numbercreatedrows-variablename)]
        [ROWCURR(numbercurrentrows-variablename)]
        [ROWUPD(numberupdatedrows-variablename)]
        [TABLEUPD(numbertableupdates-variablename)]
        [SERVICE(lastservice-variablename)]
        [RETCODE(lastreturncode-variablename)]
        [STATUS1(status1-variablename)]
        [STATUS2(status2-variablename)]
        [STATUS3(status3-variablename)]
        [LIBRARY(tableinputlibrary-variablename)]
```

tablename
> The name of the table to be accessed.

CDATE(datecreated-variablename)
> **Datecreated-variablename** is the name of the variable which is to contain the date (yy/mm/dd) when the table was created.

CTIME(timecreated-variablename)
> **Timecreated-variablename** is the name of the variable which is to contain the time (hh.mm.ss) when the table was created.

UDATE(dateupdated-variablename)
> **Dateupdated-variablename** is the name of the variable which is to contain the date (yy/mm/dd) when the table was last updated.

UTIME(timeupdated-variablename)
> **Timeupdated-variablename** is the name of the variable which is to contain the time (hh.mm.ss) when the table was last updated.

USER(lastuser-variablename)
> **Lastuser-variablename** is the name of the variable which is to contain the userid of the user who last updated the table. The userid of the user who created the table is stored when the table has not yet been updated.

ROWCREAT(numbercreatedrows-variablename)
> **Numbercreatedrows-variablename** is the name of the variable which is to contain the initial number of rows in the table when it was created.

ROWCURR(numbercurrentrows-variablename)
> **Numbercurrentrows-variablename** is the name of the variable which is to contain the current number of rows in the table.

ROWUPD(numberupdatedrows-variablename)

Numberupdatedrows-variablename is the name of the variable which is to contain the number of rows in the table which have been updated. TBMOD and TBPUT requests increment this number, such rows, when deleted, decrement this number.

TABLEUPD(numbertableupdates-variablename)

Numbertableupdates-variablename is the name of the variable which is to contain the count of the number of times the table has been updated.

SERVICE(lastservice-variable-name)

Lastservice-variablename is the name of the variable which is to contain the name of the last service request performed on this table. This value applies only to the current session, and requires that the table be open.

RETCODE(lastreturncode-variablename)

Lastreturncode-variablename is the name of the variable which is to contain the return code issued by the last service request performed on this table. This value applies only to the current session, and requires that the table be open.

STATUS1(status1-variablename)

Status1-variablename is the name of the variable which is to contain the status of the table in the input table library concatenation. The following values can be set:

1   The table exists in the concatenation of input table libraries.
2   The table does not exist in the concatenation of input table libraries.
3   No table input library is allocated.

STATUS2(status2-variablename)

Status2-variablename is the name of the variable which is to contain the status of the table in the logical screen. The following values can be set:

1   Table is not open in this logical screen.
2   Table is open with option NOWRITE in this logical screen.
3   Table is open with option WRITE in this logical screen.
4   Table is open with options SHARED NOWRITE in this logical screen.
5   Table is open with options SHARED WRITE in this logical screen.

STATUS3(status3-variablename)

Status3-variablename is the name of the variable which is to contain the status of the table WRITE availability. The following values can be set:

1   Table is available for WRITE.
2   Table is not available for WRITE.

LIBRARY(tableinputlibrary-variablename)

Tableinputlibrary-variablename is the name of the variable which is to contain the file name (DD name) allocated to the table input library.

The service sets one of the following return codes:

0 Normal completion, even if the table does not exist.
16 A variable has been truncated.
20 Severe error.

Example:
```
ISPEXEC TBSTATS PERSTAB ROWCURR(NR)
```
Return the current number of rows in PERSTAB table. If PERSTAB currently contains 10 rows the variable NR has the value 10.

9.4.21 TBTOP - Set Row Pointer at Top of Table

The TBTOP service sets the current row pointer (CRP) at the top of the table. The top of table is row 0 which is before the first row in the table.

Syntax:
```
ISPEXEC TBTOP tablename
```

tablename
> The name of the table to be processed.

The service sets one of the following return codes:

0 Normal completion
12 The table is not open.
20 Severe error.

Example:
```
ISPEXEC TBTOP PERSTAB
```
Position the CRP at the top of PERSTAB.

9.4.22 TBVCLEAR - Clear table variables

The TBVCLEAR service sets all variables (keys, names) defined for the table to null in the function pool. The table itself is not effected.

Tip
This service is normally used prior to setting a search argument.

Syntax:
```
ISPEXEC TBVCLEAR tablename
```

tablename
> The name of the table which defines the variables to be processed.

The service sets one of the following return codes:

      0   Normal completion.
    12   The table is not open.
    20   Severe error.

Example:
```
ISPEXEC TBVCLEAR PERSTAB
```
Set all variables defined for PERSTAB table in the function pool to null.

10

Table Applications

10.1 INTRODUCTION

This chapter describes application oriented processing using table services.

This worked example can be used in two ways:

· an annotated explanation of the various file tailoring statements;
· the solution with which the reader can compare his own answer.

10.2 EXAMPLE

The table processing example shown here builds a table containing personnel data. This table will be used in the following file tailoring application. The worked example is divided into several processing steps:

· The permanent table PERSTAB is created. The table has two variables: PNO and NAME, PNO is a key variable.
· Data for the table is input, the panel TSPAN000 is used for data acquisition (PNO and NAME fields).
· The table content is displayed using panel TSPAN001. Each table row is displayed in the panel, the field OP may be used for selection.
· Selected table rows are updated. Rows to be updated are selected with "u" in the operation column.
· The cursor is positioned at a specific row, the personnel number at which the cursor is to be positioned is entered in the command field ("L pno").

·   The table is searched for a specific parameter (field NAME), searched for a
    specific parameter (field NAME). The search parameter is entered in the command
    field ("s name").
·   The updated table is written to the table library.

10.3 TABLE CREATION

Two forms of table exist: temporary and permanent. A permanent table is retained
across sessions and is saved in the output table library, a temporary table exists
only for the current session and does not require the allocation of an output table
library.

For a permanent table, the table creation is a once-only task, and, as such,
could be implemented as a separate task. However, it is usually simpler to include
the TBCREATE in the mainline. We shall use this method in our example.

REXX statements for table creation:

```
1       ADDRESS TSO "ALLOC F(ISPTABL) DA(EX.ISPTLIB) SHR REUS"
2       ADDRESS ISPEXEC
3       "CONTROL ERRORS RETURN"
4       "TBOPEN PERSTAB"
5       IF RC <> 0 THEN DO
6         "TBCREATE PERSTAB KEYS(PNO) NAMES(NAME) WRITE"
7         "TBSORT PERSTAB FIELDS(PNO,C,A)"
8       END
```

Explanation:

1   Allocate the "EX.ISPTLIB" dataset as the ISPTABL file (table output library).

2   Set ISPEXEC as the default address environment.

3   The "ISPEXEC CONTROL ERRORS RETURN" statement is required to return control
    to the procedure should an error occur. An error is signalled by a return
    code greater than 4.

4   The "TBOPEN PERSTAB" statement attempts to open the PERSTAB table. The first
    request will result in an error condition (return code (RC) = 8) because the
    table is not present, subsequent requests will set the return code to 0 (=
    open successful).

6   The "TBCREATE PERSTAB KEYS(PNO) NAMES(NAME) WRITE" statement creates a
    permanent (WRITE) table named PERSTAB with key PNO and name variable
    NAME.

7   The "TBSORT PERSTAB FIELDS(PNO,C,A)" statement creates the sort
    information record for the table, which ensures that future additions to the
    table maintain PNO sequence. Additions and modifications to the table
    require the ORDER parameter to maintain sequence.

Only a single statement is required for the creation of a temporary table, an unconditional TBCREATE:

```
ISPEXEC TBCREATE PERSTAB KEYS(PNO) NAMES(NAME) REPLACE
```

The REPLACE parameter (overwrite the table, should the table exist already) is required in case the function is re-invoked from within the session.

The application can be implemented also using a non-keyed table. The only modification is to replace the TBCREATE with the following statement:

```
ISPEXEC TBCREATE PERSTAB NAMES(PNO NAME) WRITE
```

10.4 INPUT OF DATA INTO THE TABLE

The second task is to fill the table with data. In dialogue systems this is usually performed with a data acquisition dialogue function. Our example uses the TSPAN000 panel for data acquisition.

```
┌─ Panel TSPAN000 ─────────────────────────────────
│ )BODY
│ %--------------- Employee Record ------------------
│ %COMMAND ===>_ZCMD
│ %
│ %Employee number ===>_PNO +
│ %
│ %         Surname ===>_NAME        +
│ )END
```

Note: The panel definition is simplified by the omission of validity checks.

The following CLIST statements display the panel and write the input data as a row in the PERSTAB table. Processing is terminated by the user pressing the END key (return code 8 from the ISPEXEC DISPLAY service).

```
1      SET &LRC = 0
2      DO WHILE LRC LT 8
3         ISPEXEC DISPLAY PANEL(TSPAN000)
4         SET &LRC = &LASTCC
5         IF &LRC EQ 0 THEN +
6           ISPEXEC TBADD PERSTAB ORDER
7      END
```

1   LRC is the loop control variable.

2   The loop continues until the display terminates with return code (LASTCC) 8.

6   TBADD adds a record to the table.

This example is overly simple as there is no check whether the personnel record exists already. This example would ignore duplicates (TBADD exits with return code 8).

There are several ways of performing this check. The most direct method is to use the TBEXIST service. The extended CLIST procedure:

```
1      SET &LRC = 0
2      DO WHILE &LRC LT 8
3        ISPEXEC DISPLAY PANEL(TSPAN000)
4        SET &LRC = &LASTCC
5        IF &LRC EQ 0 THEN DO
6          ISPEXEC TBEXIST PERSTAB
7          IF &LASTCC EQ 0 THEN +
             ISPEXEC SETMSG MSG(TSMSG002)
9          ELSE +
             ISPEXEC TBADD PERSTAB ORDER
10       END
11     END
```

6   TBEXIST checks whether the record is present. Return code 0 indicates that the record exists (i.e. the new record is a duplicate).

7   The message TSMSG002 is issued for duplicate records.

```
┌─ Message TSMSG002 ─────────────────────────────┐
│ TSMSG002 'DUPLICATE RECORD' .ALARM=YES          │
│ 'record with Employee Number &PNO exists already'│
└─────────────────────────────────────────────────┘
```

10.5 DISPLAY OF TABLE RECORDS

The display of records in the table is made on completion of the data acquisition dialogue. The TSPAN001 table display panel is used for the display. A line update function is combined with the display, the line operand "**u**" indicates that specified name is to be used to update the table record.

```
┌─ Panel TSPAN001 ──────────────────────────────┐
│ )ATTR                                          │
│   TYPE(INPUT) CAPS(ON)                         │
│ ₮ TYPE(OUTPUT) SKIP(ON)                        │
│ )BODY                                          │
│ %--------------------- Selection Results ----------- │
│ %COMMAND ===>_ZCMD                             │
│ +                                              │
│ + Persno    Name                               │
│ +----------------------------------------------------- │
│ )MODEL CLEAR(OP) ROWS(&ROWS)                   │
│  OP*PNO    _NAME                               │
│ )INIT                                          │
│ IF (&ROWS = &Z) &ROWS=ALL                      │
│ )PROC                                          │
│ VER(&OP,LIST,U)                                │
│ &CMD=TRUNC(&ZCMD,' ')                          │
│ &OPRD=.TRAIL                                   │
│ )END                                           │
└────────────────────────────────────────────────┘
```

The CLIST statements for the display of table records:

```
 1     ISPEXEC TBTOP PERSTAB
 2     SET &PAN = TSPAN001
 3     SET &LRC = 0
 4     DO WHILE &LRC LT 8
 5       ISPEXEC TBDISPL PERSTAB PANEL(&PAN)
 6       SET &LRC = &LASTCC
 7       SET &PAN = &STR()
 8       IF &LRC LT 8 THEN DO
 9         IF &STR(&OP) EQ U THEN DO
10           ISPEXEC TBMOD PERSTAB
11         END
12       END
13     END
```

1   The table display is positioned at the first table line.

3   The loop control variable (LRC) is initialised to 0.

4   The loop continues until the TBDISPL service terminates with return code 8 (END).

5   The first TBDISPL request is with panel name. Subsequent requests are without panel name.

9   The variable OP is the line operation from panel TSPAN001.

10.6 UPDATE OF SELECTED TABLE ROWS

The values of the selected table rows are returned by the TBDISPL service in the function pool. These values are those entered on the screen together with any other non-displayed columns from the table. The table is updated by using one of the table row update services (e.g. TBMOD).

CLIST statements to update selected table rows:

```
1     IF &STR(&OP) EQ U THEN DO
2       ISPEXEC TBMOD PERSTAB
3     END
```

1   The processing is performed when the line operation is "U".

   Note: It is important to explicitly check the line operation. There is no means of explicitly **un-selecting** a line in the TBDISPL display. A line remains selected once it has been selected. If the selection code is invalid it can only be "de-selected" by overwriting the selection code with a blank. This selection, however, is passed to the processing routine. It is the responsibility of the processing routine to ignore such "non-selections".

2   TBMOD can be used to update the row, as the row must exist.

10.7 EXPLICIT ROW POSITIONING

Manual positioning within large tables can be quite time consuming. Our application allows the user to enter a **locate** command with the required employee number in the panel command field. CMD contains the command (here "L") and OPRD contains the parameter (employee number).

CLIST statements for explicit row positioning:

```
1      IF &STR(&CMD) EQ L THEN DO
2        SET &PNO = &STR(&OPRD)
3        ISPEXEC TBTOP PERSTAB
4        ISPEXEC TBEXIST PERSTAB
5        IF &LASTCC NE 0 THEN +
           ISPEXEC SETMSG MSG(TSMSG004)
6        ELSE SET &PAN = TSPAN001
7      END
```

1   The CMD variable is explicitly checked for the "L" command.

3   TBTOP positions the CRP at the table top.

4   TBEXIST sets the return code (LASTCC) to non-zero when the row does not exist, the TSMSG004 error message is set here.

```
┌─ Message TSMSG004 ─────────────────────────────
│ TSMSG004 'ROW DOES NOT EXIST' .ALARM=YES
│ 'record with Employee Number &PNO does not exist'
└──────────────────────────────────────────────
```

6   CRP has been set by TBEXIST to point to the required row. The panel name is set to cause a new panel display (positioned at CRP).

7   END terminates the DO-group.

10.8 SEARCHING ON DATA FIELDS

Selecting table rows based on given search criteria is well suited to being implemented using table services. Our application allows the user to enter a **search** command with the required generic search string in the panel command field. CMD contains the command (here "S") and OPRD contains the parameter (employee surname).

CLIST statements to search table for specified data values:

```
1      IF &STR(&CMD) EQ S THEN DO
2        ISPEXEC TBTOP PERSTAB
3        ISPEXEC TBVCLEAR PERSTAB
4        SET &NAME = &STR(&OPRD*)
5        ISPEXEC TBSARG PERSTAB NAMECOND(NAME,EQ)
6        SET &PAN = TSPAN001
7        SET &ROWS = SCAN
8      END
```

1   The CMD variable is explicitly checked for the "S" command.

2   TBTOP positions the CRP at the table top.

3   TBVCLEAR clears table variables in function pool.

4   The search string is set into the dialogue variable (NAME); the terminating "*" forces a generic search.

5   TBSARG sets the search argument to match rows with the same NAME.

6   The panel name is set to cause a new panel display.

7   The ROWS variable is used in the panel)MODEL header to define whether the complete table (ROWS(ALL)) or only those rows matching the specified search argument (ROWS(SCAN)) are to be displayed.

8   END terminates the DO-group.

10.9 TERMINATION

The updated table must be rewritten at the end of processing.

CLIST statement to terminate table processing:

```
ISPEXEC TBCLOSE PERSTAB
```

10.10 COMPLETE CLIST

```
PROC 0
/* EXAMPLE: KEYED TABLE
ALLOC F(ISPTABL) DA(EX.ISPTLIB) SHR REUS
/* OPEN/CREATE TABLE
ISPEXEC CONTROL ERRORS RETURN
ISPEXEC TBOPEN PERSTAB
IF &LASTCC NE 0 THEN DO
  ISPEXEC TBCREATE PERSTAB KEYS(PNO) NAMES(NAME) +
    WRITE
  ISPEXEC TBSORT PERSTAB FIELDS(PNO,C,A)
END
/* DATA ACQUISITION
SET &LRC = 0
DO WHILE &LRC LT 8
  ISPEXEC DISPLAY PANEL(TSPAN000)
  SET &LRC = &LASTCC                    /* DISPLAY RC
  IF &LRC EQ 0 THEN DO
    ISPEXEC TBEXIST PERSTAB
    IF &LASTCC EQ 0 THEN +
     ISPEXEC SETMSG MSG(TSMSG002)  /*DUPLICATE
    ELSE DO
      ISPEXEC TBADD PERSTAB ORDER
      IF &LASTCC EQ 0 THEN +
       ISPEXEC SETMSG MSG(TSMSG003)  /*OK
    END
  END
END
/* TABLE DISPLAY
ISPEXEC TBTOP PERSTAB
SET &PAN = TSPAN001
SET &LRC = 4                           /*INITIALISE
DO WHILE &LRC LT 8
  ISPEXEC TBDISPL PERSTAB PANEL(&PAN)
  SET &LRC = &LASTCC
  SET &PAN = &STR()
  IF &LRC LT 8 THEN DO
    IF &STR(&CMD) EQ L THEN DO
      /* POSITION AT RECORD
      SET &PNO = &STR(&OPRD)
      ISPEXEC TBTOP PERSTAB
      ISPEXEC TBEXIST PERSTAB
      IF &LASTCC NE 0 THEN +
       ISPEXEC SETMSG MSG(TSMSG004)  /*NOK
      ELSE SET &PAN = TSPAN001
    END
    IF &STR(&CMD) EQ S THEN DO
      /* SEEK GENERIC NAMES
      ISPEXEC TBTOP PERSTAB
      ISPEXEC TBVCLEAR PERSTAB
      SET &NAME = &STR(&OPRD*)
      ISPEXEC TBSARG PERSTAB NAMECOND(NAME,EQ)
      SET &PAN = TSPAN001
      SET &ROWS = SCAN
    END
    IF &STR(&OP) EQ U THEN DO
      /* UPDATE RECORD
      ISPEXEC TBMOD PERSTAB
    END
  END
END
/* REWRITE PERMANENT TABLE
ISPEXEC TBCLOSE PERSTAB
```

Figure 10.1 - Complete CLIST

10.11 EQUIVALENT PROCESSING FOR NON-KEYED TABLES

The previous section illustrated a typical application using tables with keys. Equivalent processing can also be done using tables without keys, although some operations are not quite so simple. Figure 10.2 shows the sample CLIST modified to use non-keyed tables and the changes are italicised. The principal difference is the method used to update a table row. Keyed tables can be directly updated with the TBMOD service, non-keyed tables require that the new row is first added and then the original row deleted (Note: TBADD must precede TBDELETE to avoid problems when the first row of the table is deleted). Figure 10.2 shows the equivalent CLIST using non-keyed table.

```
PROC 0
CONTROL MSG LIST CONLIST
ALLOC F(ISPTABL) DA(EX.ISPTLIB) SHR REUS
/* OPEN/CREATE TABLE
ISPEXEC CONTROL ERRORS RETURN
ISPEXEC TBOPEN PERSTAB
IF &LASTCC NE 0 THEN DO
   ISPEXEC TBCREATE PERSTAB NAMES(PNO NAME) WRITE
   ISPEXEC TBSORT PERSTAB FIELDS(PNO,C,A)
END
/* DATA ACQUISITION
SET &LRC = 0
SET &PAN = TSPAN000
DO WHILE &LRC LT 8
  ISPEXEC DISPLAY PANEL(&PAN)
   SET &LRC = &LASTCC
   SET &PAN = &STR()
  IF &LRC EQ 0 THEN DO
    ISPEXEC TBTOP PERSTAB
    ISPEXEC TBSCAN PERSTAB ARGLIST(PNO) CONDLIST(EQ)
    IF &LASTCC EQ 0 THEN +
     ISPEXEC SETMSG MSG(TSMSG002)   /*DUPLICATE
    ELSE DO
      ISPEXEC TBADD PERSTAB ORDER
      IF &LASTCC EQ 0 THEN +
       ISPEXEC SETMSG MSG(TSMSG003)   /*OK
    END
  END
END
/* TABLE DISPLAY
ISPEXEC TBTOP PERSTAB
SET &PAN = TSPAN001
SET &CRP = &STR()
SET &LRC = 4                        /*INITIALISE
DO WHILE &LRC LT 8
  ISPEXEC TBDISPL PERSTAB PANEL(&PAN) CSRROW(&CRP)
   SET &LRC = &LASTCC
   SET &PAN = &STR()
  IF &LRC LT 8 THEN DO
    IF &STR(&CMD) EQ L THEN DO
      /* POSITION AT RECORD
      ISPEXEC TBTOP PERSTAB
      ISPEXEC TBVCLEAR PERSTAB
      SET &PNO = &STR(&OPRD)
      ISPEXEC TBSARG PERSTAB NAMECOND(PNO,EQ)
      ISPEXEC TBSCAN PERSTAB POSITION(CRP)
      IF &LASTCC NE 0 THEN +
       ISPEXEC SETMSG MSG(TSMSG004)   /*NOK
    ELSE SET &PAN = TSPAN001
    END
```

Figure 10.2 - Equivalent CLIST using non-keyed table (part 1)

```
  IF &STR(&CMD) EQ S THEN DO
    /* SEEK GENERIC NAMES
    ISPEXEC TBTOP PERSTAB
    ISPEXEC TBVCLEAR PERSTAB
    SET &NAME = &STR(&OPRD*)
    ISPEXEC TBSARG PERSTAB NAMECOND(NAME,EQ)
    SET &PAN = TSPAN001
    SET &ROWS = SCAN
  END
  IF &STR(&OP) EQ U THEN DO
    /* UPDATE RECORD
    ISPEXEC TBADD PERSTAB
    ISPEXEC TBSKIP PERSTAB NUMBER(-1)
    ISPEXEC TBDELETE PERSTAB
  END
 END
END
/* REWRITE PERMANENT TABLE
ISPEXEC TBCLOSE PERSTAB
```

Figure 10.2 - Equivalent CLIST using non-keyed table (part 2)

11

File Tailoring (Skeleton) Services

11.1 GENERAL FORM OF SKELETON

A **skeleton** is a member of the **file tailoring library** (ISPSLIB). A skeleton
describes the form of an **output file**. This file may contain fixed data, ISPF
variables and make use of control statements (e.g. conditional operations). File
tailoring was originally conceived for the generation of Job Control Statements,
but is by no means limited to this application.

A skeleton consists of **control statements** and **data records**; a data record is
any record which is not identified as being a control statement. Control statements
are identified by the ")" character in column 1 followed by a non-blank character.
The member of the file tailoring library consists of records having a maximum
record length of 255 bytes, the last 8 characters of the input records are ignored.
In general, one input data record generates one output record. A fixed length input
record may be continued by setting "?" in the last input column.

The input data record may contain both fixed and variable data, and is mapped
column for column into the output record; column oriented output is possible
using the tabulator function. The number of blanks between fields (fixed and
variable) in the data record is preserved in the output record, unless the tabulator
has been used.

A skeleton is invoked using file tailoring services. Figure 11.1 illustrates file
tailoring processing; ▓▓▓▓ represents control statements.

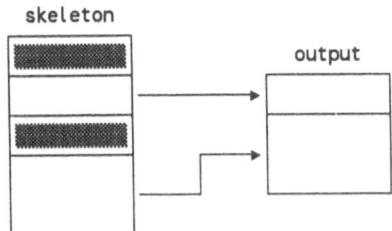

Figure 11.1 - Schematic file tailoring processing

11.2 FILE TAILORING OPERATIONS

The file tailoring operations are listed in alphabetic order:

· FTCLOSE   Terminate file tailoring.
· FTERASE   Delete a member from the output library.
· FTINCL   Make a skeleton available for file tailoring.
· FTOPEN   Initiate the file tailoring process.

11.2.1 FTCLOSE - Terminate file tailoring

The FTCLOSE service terminates the file tailoring process. The processed skeleton is transferred to the output library or file.

Syntax:
```
ISPEXEC FTCLOSE [NAME(member-name)]
        [LIBRARY(library-filename|ISPFILE)]
        [NOREPL]
```

NAME(member-name)
>   **Member-name** is the name with which the processed skeleton is to be stored in the output library. This parameter must be omitted for a sequential output file.

LIBRARY(library-filename)
>   **Library-filename** is the name of the file (DD statement) which specifies the output library (partitioned data set) or output file (sequential data set). Default: LIBRARY(ISPFILE).

NOREPL
>   A member in the output library having the same name will not be replaced.

The service sets one of the following return codes:

    0   Normal completion.

    4   The member exists already in the output library and NOREPL was specified; the processed skeleton is not stored and the original member remains unchanged.

    8   The output library (file) has not been opened; FTOPEN has not been used to open the output file (library).

   12   The output library is in use.

   16   The output library has not been allocated.

   20   Severe error.

Example:
```
ISPEXEC FTCLOSE NAME(TSSKL000) LIBRARY(ISPSKL) NOREPL
```
Store the processed skeleton with member name TSSKL000 in the library defined for file ISPSKL (DD name). A member having the same name in the library is not to be replaced (NOREPL).

11.2.2 FTERASE - Delete Member from Output Library

The FTERASE service deletes the named member from the output library. The file tailoring output library need not be open to use this service.

Tip
Although this service is included in the file tailoring services, the delete function can be used for any output library.

Syntax:
```
ISPEXEC FTERASE [NAME(member-name)]
        [LIBRARY(library-filename|ISPFILE)]
```

NAME(member-name)
Member-name is the name of the member which is to be deleted from the output library.

LIBRARY(library-filename)
Library-filename is the name of the file (DD statement) which specifies the output library (partitioned data set). Default: LIBRARY(ISPFILE).

The service sets one of the following return codes:

    0   Normal completion.

    8   The member does not exist.

   12   The output library is in use.

   16   The output library has not been allocated.

   20   Severe error.

Example:
```
ISPEXEC FTERASE TSSKL000 LIBRARY(ISPSKL)
```
Delete the member with the name TSSKL000 from the library defined for file ISPSKL (DD name).

11.2.3 FTINCL - Include Skeleton for Processing

The FTINCL service reads the named skeleton from the ISPSLIB library into main storage and invokes file tailoring processing on the skeleton. FTINCL invokes the FTOPEN service (with TEMP parameter) if file tailoring services have not been opened.

Syntax:
```
ISPEXEC FTINCL skeleton-name
        [NOFT]
```

skeleton-name
> The name of the member (skeleton) which is to be processed from the ISPSLIB library.

NOFT
> No file tailoring is to be performed on the skeleton, i.e. the skeleton is used as data.

The service sets one of the following return codes:

  0   Normal completion.
  8   The member (skeleton) does not exist.
 12   The member (skeleton) is in use.
 16   Data truncation (skeleton too large) or the input library has not been allocated.
 20   Severe error.

Example 1:
```
ISPEXEC FTINCL TSSKL000
```
The member TSSKL000 is to be read from the ISPSLIB and used for file tailoring processing.

Example 2:
```
ISPEXEC FTINCL TSSKL000 NOFT
```
The member TSSKL000 is to be read from the ISPSLIB and inserted into the skeleton currently being used for file tailoring processing, no additional processing is performed (NOFT).

11.2.4 FTOPEN - Open File Tailoring Processing

The FTOPEN service is used to specify the form of the processed skeleton. The processed skeleton may be either **temporary** or **permanent**. A temporary skeleton is stored in a sequential file which is automatically allocated by the file tailoring service (no explicit output library is required). A permanent skeleton is stored at the end of the file tailoring process in the file or library defined by the user (an explicit output library (file) must have been allocated).

Syntax:
```
ISPEXEC FTOPEN [TEMP]
```

TEMP

A temporary skeleton is to be created. The data set name of the generated file is contained in the ZTEMPF variable. File tailoring which has been opened with the TEMP parameter cannot be stored as a permanent member.

Note: The ZTEMPF variable must be explicitly retrieved from shared pool in order that it can be used, e.g.
```
ISPEXEC VGET (ZTEMPF) SHARED
```

Tip

The content of the generated temporary output file can be most easily displayed using the BROWSE service. Example:
```
ISPEXEC FTOPEN TEMP
ISPEXEC FTINCL ...
ISPEXEC FTCLOSE
ISPEXEC VGET (ZTEMPF) SHARED
ISPEXEC BROWSE DATASET('&ZTEMPF')
```

Tip

The FTOPEN without the TEMP parameter requires that the ISPFILE be allocated, even when the TBCLOSE uses a different file, i.e. a dummy allocation must always have been made for ISPFILE.

The service sets one of the following return codes:

        0   Normal completion.
        8   FTOPEN has already been invoked.
       16   ISPFILE has not been allocated (TEMP not specified).
       20   Severe error.

Example:
```
ISPEXEC FTOPEN
```
File tailoring is to be initiated. The processed skeleton will be later stored in the output library.

11.3 FILE TAILORING CONTROL STATEMENTS

The file tailoring control statements are listed in alphabetic order:

·)BLANK   Generate blank lines in the output file.
·)CM   Define a comment line.

-)DEFAULT   Redefine the standard delimiters used by file tailoring services.
-)DOT   Introduce a block of statements which are to be processed in a loop using data from an ISPF table.
-)ENDDOT   Terminate a block of statements introduced by a)DOT statement.
-)ENDSEL   Terminate a block of statements introduced by a)SEL statement.
-)IM   Include a further file tailoring member in the processing sequence.
-)SEL   Perform conditional processing.
-)SET   Assign a value to an ISPF variable.
-)TB   Define tab stop positions.

The following terms may be used within a skeleton (control statements and data records):

- Numeric literal, e.g. 100.
- Alphanumeric literal, e.g. ALPHA. Note: The literal 'ALPHA' represents 7 characters "'ALPHA'".
- Variable — variable name prefixed by & (ampersand), e.g. &ALPHA.
  Note: The target variable in the)SET statement is the one exception.
- A concatenation of these above terms. Example: If the content of the variable ALPHA is BETA, 1&ALPHA represents "1BETA".

11.3.1)BLANK - Blank Statement

The)BLANK statement generates the specified number of blank lines in the output file. Blank lines in the (input) skeleton definition are not passed to the output record and as such the)BLANK statement is required to generate blank lines.

Syntax:
```
)BLANK [number|1]
```

number
> Place blank lines in the output file.
> Default:)BLANK 1

Example:
```
)BLANK 2
```
Insert 2 blank lines in the output file.

11.3.2)CM - Comment Statement

The)CM Statement specifies that the following data in the input record is to be treated as a comment, i.e. not used for processing.

Syntax:
```
)CM [text data]
```

Example:
```
)CM this is a comment line
```
Define a comment line.

11.3.3)DEFAULT - Default Statement

The)DEFAULT Statement redefines the standard file tailoring delimiters. All seven delimiters must be specified. Redefinition is required when the data records contain one or more of the standard delimiters. Section 11.4 contains a description of the delimiter characters.

Syntax:
```
)DEFAULT [abcdefg | )&?!<|>]
```

abcdefg
>   The string of characters which is to replace the standard delimiters: ")&?!<|>", respectively. Seven characters must be defined and the sequence specifies the new definition, e.g. the first character replaces the ")" character.
>   Default:)DEFAULT)&?!<|>

Example:
```
)DEFAULT )&?!<\>
```
The "⟩" and "\" characters are to adopt the function of the "⟩" and "|" delimiters, respectively, i.e. the)SET control statement is used rather than)SET.

11.3.4)DOT - Do Table Statement

The)DOT statement introduces a DOT-group. The DOT-group specifies that each row of the named table is to be processed by the statements in the group. The DOT-group is terminated by an)ENDDOT statement. The table need not be open. DOT processing is illustrated in Figure 11.2.

A DOT-group can include further DOT-groups. However, the same table may not be used. A maximum of four levels of nesting is allowed.

Note: Temporary tables can be created to produce a variable number of records in the skeleton.

Syntax:
```
)DOT table-name
```

table-name
>   The name of the table to be processed.

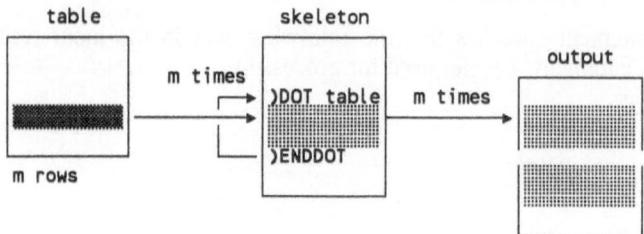

Figure 11.2 - Schematic)DOT processing

Example:
```
)DOT PERSTAB
```
The current content of the PERSTAB table is to be used in the DOT-group.

11.3.5)ENDDOT - End Do Table Statement

The)ENDDOT statement terminates the innermost DOT-group.

Syntax:
```
)ENDDOT
```

Example:
```
1       )DOT PERSTAB
        ...
2       )DOT TEMP
        ...
3       )ENDDOT
```
The)ENDDOT statement terminates the DOT-group defined by statement 2.

11.3.6)ENDSEL - End Selection Statement

The)ENDSEL statement terminates the innermost SEL-group.

Syntax:
```
)ENDSEL
```

Example:
```
1       )SEL &PNO EQ 1111
        ...
2       )SEL &NAME GT A
        ...
3       )ENDSEL
```
The)ENDSEL statement terminates the SEL-group defined by statement 2.

11.3.7)IM - Imbed Statement

The)IM statement includes an external skeleton (contained in the ISPSLIB library) at this point in the processing sequence. A skeleton included with the)IM statement can itself include further skeletons. A maximum of three levels of embedding is allowed.

Syntax:
```
)IM skeleton-name [NT] [OPT]
```

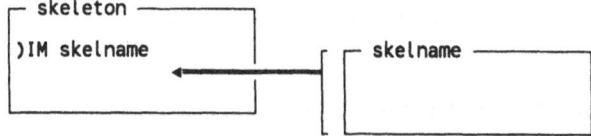

Figure 11.3 - Schematic)IM processing

skeleton-name
> The name of the skeleton to be included. The skeleton is a member of the ISPSLIB library.

NT (no tailoring)
> The skeleton being embedded is to be included as data; i.e. the contents are not to be processed as file tailoring statements.

OPT (optional)
> The presence of the skeleton in the ISPSLIB library is optional, i.e. no error will be signalled should the skeleton not be present.

Example:
```
)IM TSSKL000 OPT
```
The TSSKL000 skeleton is to be included and processed as file tailoring input (NT not specified). Processing will not terminate if the skeleton member is not present.

11.3.8)SEL - Select Statement

The)SEL statement introduces a SEL-group. A SEL-group specifies a group of statements (control statements and data records) which are conditionally processed. The)SEL statement specifies the condition to be satisfied in order that the statements within this SEL-group are processed. Each SEL-group must be terminated by an)ENDSEL statement.

A SEL-group can include further SEL-groups. A maximum of **eight** levels of nesting is allowed.

Syntax:
```
)SEL variable op value [lop variable op value]...
                )SEL condition₁
                   condition₁ satisfied



                )SEL condition₂
                  condition₁ and
                  condition₂ satisfied



                )ENDSEL   end condition₂ satisfied

                )ENDSEL   end condition₁ satisfied
```
Figure 11.4 - Schematic)SEL processing

variable
> The name of a variable, prefixed by & (ampersand).

op

An operator, which can be one of the following:

EQ	equal [=]
NE	not equal [¬=]
GT	greater than [>]
GE	greater than or equal [>=]
LT	less than [<]
LE	less than or equal [<=]
NG	not greater than [¬>]
NL	not less than [¬<].

The symbol shown in brackets may also be used, e.g. EQ and "=" are equivalent.

value

The comparand, either numeric constant (e.g. 100), alphanumeric literal (e.g. ALPHA), or variable (variable-name prefixed with &, e.g. &ALPHA).

lop

A logical operator, which is one of the following:

|	OR
&&	AND

The symbol (e.g. &&) and the operator name (e.g. AND) are equivalent.

A)SEL statement may contain up to **eight** comparisons joined by logical operators; the comparisons are performed from left to right (parentheses are not allowed).

Example:
Assuming A contains 1, B contains 2, C contains 3

```
)SEL &A = 1 AND &B = 3 OR &C = 3
```
is true, whereas

```
)SEL &A = 1 OR &C = 3 AND &B = 3
```
is false.

expression	statement		
&A = 1	true		
		AND	false
&B = 3	false		
		OR	true
&C = 3	true		

expression	statement		
&A = 1	true		
		OR	true
&C = 3	true		
		AND	false
&B = 3	false		

If all conditions specified by the)SEL statement are met, the following statements (control statements and data records) until the next)ENDSEL statement at the same nesting level are processed.

Example:

```
1       )SEL &ALPHA EQ 1 && &BETA EQ &ALPHA
        ...
2       )SEL &GAMMA GT 3 OR &DELTA < D
        ...
3       )ENDSEL
        ...
4       )ENDSEL
```

The statements following statement number 1 are processed when the contents of the variable ALPHA are 1 and the two variables ALPHA and BETA have the same contents. Statement number 2 is nested within the first)SEL statement.

Tip

Complex)SEL statements should, where possible, be avoided. They are difficult to understand and errors can arise inadvertently.

11.3.9)SET - Assignment Statement

The)SET statement assigns a value to a variable. The value may be an arithmetic expression. The variable is available for use in the ISPF environment, e.g. may be used for display in a panel. The variable is created if it does not currently exist.

Syntax:
```
)SET target-variable = variable | value [op variable | value]...
```

target-variable
>   The name of the result variable.

>   Note: This variable can have one of two forms:
·   Variable not prefixed by & (ampersand), this is the direct result, e.g.
>   `)SET ALPHA = 2`
>   sets 2 into ALPHA.
·   Variable prefixed by & means indirect result. This variable contains the name of the result variable, e.g.
>   `)SET ALPHA = BETA`
>   `)SET &ALPHA = 2`
>   sets 2 into BETA.

>   Note: The form of the)SET target variable conflicts with that used for CLISTs.

variable
>   The name of a variable prefixed by & (ampersand).

op

One of the following operators:
+   addition
-   subtraction

value

Either a numeric constant (e.g. 100), an alphanumeric literal (e.g. ALPHA), or variable (variable-name prefixed with &, e.g. &ALPHA). Only numeric constants or variables containing a numeric value may be used in arithmetic expressions.

Tip

The z system variable can be used to set a variable to blank, e.g.)SET ALPHA= &Z

Example 1:

statement	result	value
)SET ALPHA = 1	ALPHA	1
)SET BETA = &ALPHA	BETA	1
)SET GAMMA = &ALPHA + 2	GAMMA	3
)SET DELTA = IOTA	DELTA	IOTA
)SET &DELTA = 0	IOTA	0
)SET EPSILON = 'ALPHA'	EPSILON	'ALPHA'
)SET ZETA = &DELTA&BETA	ZETA	IOTA1

Example 2:
```
)SET DDNAME = SYSLIB
)DOT TEMP
//&DDNAME DD DSNAME=&DSN,DISP=SHR
)SET DDNAME = &Z
)ENDDOT
```
This example sets SYSLIB as the ddname of the first generated record.

11.3.10)TB - Set Tab Stops

The)TB statement sets tab stop positions within the output record. A maximum of 16 positions can be assigned. A tab is invoked by using the "tab" character and the default is "!".

Syntax:
```
)TB tab-position [tab-position]...
```

tab-position

The position in the output record where the tab is to be set. The tab-positions must be defined in increasing order, the first position in the output record is 1.
Default: 255.

Example:
```
1      )TB 10 20
2      ABC!DEF
```

Statement number 1 sets the TAB at positions 10 and 20.
Statement number 2 maps ABC into positions 1-3, "!" invokes the next TAB (=10),
DEF is mapped into positions 10-12.

Note: The tabbing to a non-existent tab stop causes a run-time error.

11.4 FILE TAILORING CONTROL DELIMITERS

The file tailoring control statements make use of certain delimiters for control
purposes. The standard values may be changed with the)DEFAULT statement.

·   An ampersand ("&") is used to prefix a variable name. The current value of the
    variable in the variable pool is substituted, e.g. &ALPHA is replaced by the value
    of the variable ALPHA;

·   A period (".") delimits a variable name; this delimiter is only required when
    the variable name is immediately followed by a literal (either alphanumeric or
    numeric), e.g.
    &ALPHA.2 requires the period
    &ALPHA&BETA requires no period;

·   A question mark ("?") in the last data column indicates that the following
    statement is a **continuation**. Figure 11.5 illustrates the processing of data
    record continuation. Example:
    ALPHABETA ?
    GAMMA
    generates the following output record:
    ALPHABETA GAMMA

·   An exclamation mark ("!") causes a **tab** to the next tab stop position.
    If a tab stop is at the current address pointer in the output record, a tab will
    position at the following tab stop, e.g.

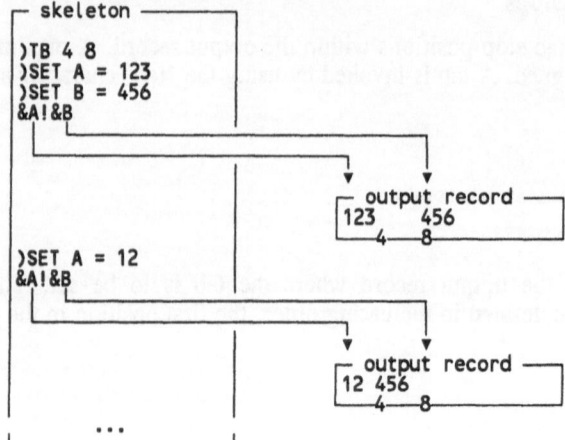

·   A less-than ("<"), break ("|"), and greater-than (">") define a **conditional substitution string**. A conditional substitution string has the following syntax:

    <variable | [string]>

variable
> The name (prefixed by "&") of the variable to be processed.

string
> The value to be substituted if the variable is null, otherwise the content of the variable is used.

Example:

    <&ALPHA|ZERO>

If the content of the variable ALPHA is null, the alphanumeric literal ZERO is to be substituted.

Two consecutive control delimiters in the data record are not interpreted as being control delimiters and are replaced in the output record by one of paired characters. Example:

&& generates &
!! generates !
<< generates <
|| generates |
>> generates >
.. generates .

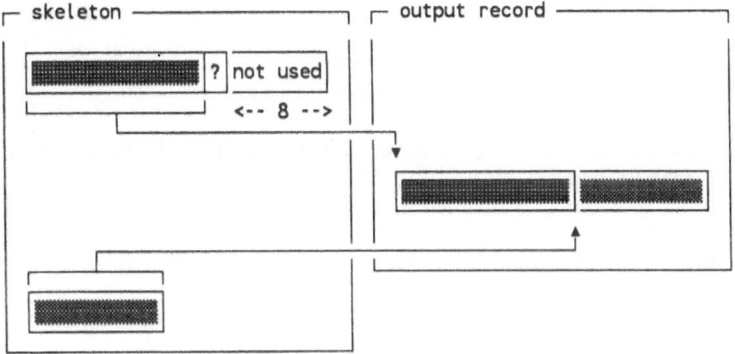

Figure 11.5 - Processing of data record continuation

11.5 FILE TAILORING DATA RECORD

The data record may also contain file tailoring information. The data record consists of the following items:

- Fixed data, e.g. ALPHA, 100.
- Variable data (variable names prefixed by "&"), e.g. &ALPHA.
- TAB character, "!" unless it has been redefined by the)DEFAULT control statement.
- A conditional substitution string, <variable | string>.
- Continuation character "?" unless it has been redefined by the)DEFAULT control statement.

These items may also be used in combination, e.g.
```
&ALPHA.&BETA   123!&GAMMA <&ALPHA|0>
```
Data records are mapped into the output record. Variable data are replaced by the current content. Blanks between items are retained unless tab is specified.

Example:
```
)TB 10 20
)SET ALPHA = A
)SET BETA = B
)SET GAMMA = C
&ALPHA.&BETA        12345!&GAMMA <&ALPHA|0>
```

These statements produce the following output record:

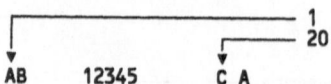

```
AB    12345    C A
```

Variable ALPHA (content A) is mapped into position 1;
variable BETA (content B) is concatenated into position 2;
five blanks follow;
12345 mapped into position 8 (the current position is now at 13), the tab character (!) causes a tab to the next tab position (20);
variable GAMMA (content C) is mapped into position 20;
one blank follows;
the conditional substitution string "<&ALPHA|0>" is replaced by the value of variable ALPHA (content A).

11.6 SYMBOLIC PARAMETERS

The following tables shows the use of symbolic parameters in skeleton control statements.

)BLANK *number*
)DOT   *table-name*
)IM   *skeleton-name* NT OPT
)SEL   *variable* op *value lop*
)SET   *target-variable variable*
)TB   *tab-position*

Note on the table: Variables may be used for italicised parameters, the variable must contain a correct value.

Example:
```
        )SET OPTN = OPT
        )IM TSSKL NT &OPTN
```
is equivalent to
```
        )IM TSSKL NT OPT
```

12

File Tailoring Applications

12.1 INTRODUCTION

This chapter describes application oriented processing using file tailoring services.

This worked example can be used in two ways:
- an annotated explanation of the various file tailoring statements;
- the solution with which the reader can compare his own answer.

12.2 EXAMPLE

The file tailoring example shown here uses the personnel data from the table services application and performs the following processing steps:
- The skeleton TSSKL000 contains the control statements.
- A temporary output file is to be created.
- The standard default delimiters "!" and "|" are to be replaced by "$" and "ə", respectively.
- The two PERSTAB columns NAME and PNO are to be copied to the output file, one output line per table row, two blanks separate each field.

· The two columns NAME and PNO from PERSTAB and the new variable PNUM are to be copied to positions 1, 20 and 30, respectively, in the output file when the following conditions are met:

```
2000 < PNO;

If PNO < 3000
  then PNUM = PNO+10000;

If PNUM = null
  then PNUM = "NULL";
```

Each table row copied to the output file has variable NAME as heading and is separated from the data for the next table row by a blank line.

12.3 WORKED EXAMPLE

Procedure statements for the invocation of file tailoring:

```
1       ISPEXEC FTOPEN TEMP
2       ISPEXEC FTINCL TSSKL000
3       ISPEXEC FTCLOSE
4       ISPEXEC VGET (ZTEMPF) SHARED
5       ISPEXEC BROWSE DATASET('&ZTEMPF')
```

Explanation:

1   The FTOPEN statement specifies that a non-permanent (TEMP) skeleton is to be created.

2   The FTINCL statement includes the skeleton TSSKL000 from the input library, the FTINCL invokes the file tailoring.

3   The FTCLOSE statement transfers the processed skeleton to the output file (temporary). The data set name of this temporary file is contained in the ZTEMPF system variable.

4   The VGET statement is required to make available the data set name.

5   The ISPF/PDF BROWSE function is used to display the processed skeleton.

TSSKL000 skeleton:

```
1       )DEFAULT )&?$<@>
2       )CM TABLE PROCESSING WITH TABBING
3       )DOT PERSTAB
4       &NAME    &PNO
5       )ENDDOT
6       )CM TABLE PROCESSING WITH SELECTION
7       )TB 20 30
```

```
 8        )DOT PERSTAB
 9        )SET PNUM = &Z
10        )SEL &PNO GT 2000
11        )SEL &PNO LT 3000
12        )SET PNUM = &PNO + 10000
13        )ENDSEL
14        NAME$PNO$PNUM
15        &NAME$&PNO$<&PNUM@NULL>
16        )BLANK 1
17        )ENDSEL
18        )ENDDOT
```

The skeleton will now be analysed in detail.

        1   )DEFAULT)&?$<@>
Redefine the default delimiters, "$" replaces "!" and "@" replaces "|".

        2   )CM TABLE PROCESSING WITH TABBING
Define a commentary line.

        3   )DOT PERSTAB
PERSTAB is to be processed row-wise. Each table row is to be processed according to the statements up to the following)ENDSEL (statement 5).

        4   &NAME   &PNO
Define a data record. The variable NAME is to be separated by 3 blanks from the variable PNO.

        5   )ENDDOT
Terminate the DOT-group introduced by statement 3. Every statement (control statement and data) within the DOT-group is processed for each table row, i.e. statement number 4 writes PNO and NAME from each row into the output file.

        7   )TB 20 30
Set the tab stops at 20 and 30.

        8   )DOT PERSTAB
PERSTAB is to be processed row-wise. Each table row is to be processed according to the statements up to the following)ENDSEL (statement 13).

        9   )SET PNUM = &Z
Set variable PNUM to null.

        10   )SEL &PNO GT 2000
Select the following statements for processing when variable PNO is greater than 2000.

        11   )SEL &PNO LT 3000
Select the following statements for processing when variable PNO is less than 3000. The select statement is within the previous select statement, the two selects are connected by logical AND.

        12   )SET PNUM = &PNO + 10000
Add 10000 to the variable PNO and set the result into the variable PNUM.

13   )ENDSEL

Terminate the innermost SEL-group introduced by statement 11. This SEL-group is equivalent to the following pseudo-code:

```
IF PNO < 3000 THEN
PNUM = PNO + 10000;
```

14   NAMEPNOPNUM

Define a data record. The text NAME is to be mapped into position 1 in the output record, the text PNO is to be mapped to the next tab stop (position 20) in the output record, the text PNAME is to be mapped to the next tab stop (position 30) in the output record. Note: The tab character has been changed from ! to $ by the)DEFAULT statement.

15   &NAME$&PNO$<&PNUM@NULL>

Define a data record. The variable NAME is to be mapped into position 1 in the output record, the variable PNO is to be mapped to the next tab stop (position 20) in the output record, the variable PNAME, if not null, otherwise the text NULL is to be mapped to the next tab stop (position 30) in the output record.

16   )BLANK 1

Generate a blank line in the output record.

17   )ENDSEL

Terminate the outermost SEL-group introduced by statement 10.

18   )ENDDOT

Terminate the DOT-group introduced by statement 8.

Figure 12.1 shows the output file, the formatted content of PERSTAB is shown in Figure 12.2.

```
ALPHA    1111
ALPHA    1112
BETA    2222
BETAETA    2223
GAMMAGAMMA    3333
NAME                PNO             PNUM
BETA                2222            12222

NAME                PNO             PNUM
BETAETA             2223            12223

NAME                PNO             PNUM
GAMMAGAMMA          3333            NULL
```

Figure 12.1 File tailoring output file

```
------------------- Selection Results ---------------
COMMAND ===>

Persno   Name
-----------------------------------------------------
  1111   ALPHA
  1112   ALPHA
  2222   BETA
  2223   BETAETA
  3333   GAMMAGAMMA
```

Figure 12.2 - **PERSTAB** content

13

Command Table

13.1 INTRODUCTION

A **command table**, as the name implies, is an ISPF table containing command definitions for the application. The default ISPF/PDF command table is used when no explicit command table is defined. The command table is a member of the **input table library** (ISPTLIB) and may be defined using the Command Table Utility. The member name is "*aaaa*CMDS" ("*aaaa*" is the application-id), e.g. the command table for the ISPF application (ISPF/PDF) is ISPCMDS.

Commands are entered in the panel command field and are executed before any)PROC section processing is performed.

There are two classes of commands:

·   Standard ISPF commands (e.g. print screen content, invoke help).
·   User defined commands, these can invoke a command procedure, program, etc.

Application command definitions can be used to disable or redefine standard commands, for example, the TSO command (which permits TSO commands to be executed within the ISPF environment) disabled.

13.2 COMMAND HIERARCHY

The command processing sequence is depicted in Figure 13.1; aaaa is the application-id

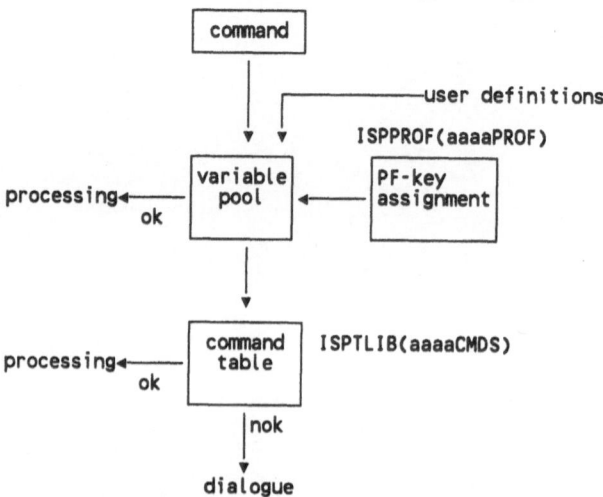

Figure 13.1 - Command processing sequence

13.3 COMMAND TABLE FORMAT

A command table entry has the following format:

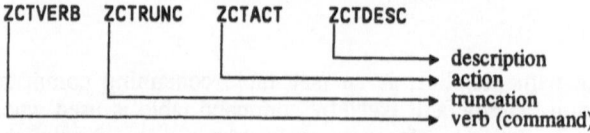

ZCTVERB, ZCTRUNC, ZCTACT and ZCTDESC are the column names in the command table.

13.3.1 ZCTVERB - Verb (Command)

The ZCTVERB column defines the **command name**. The command name is 2 to 8 characters long, the first of which must be alphabetic.

The command name may be either an ISPF system command name (e.g. HELP, KEYS, PRINT) or a user-defined command name.

Tip
User-defined commands which are to be processed by the panel do not need to be defined in the command table, as any command which is not defined in the command table is passed to the dialogue.

13.3.2 ZCTTRUNC - Truncation Length

The ZCTTRUNC column defines minimum length of the command which may be defined. Length 0 means that the command cannot be truncated.

For example

ZCTVERB	ZCTRUNC	
ALPHA	3	
BETA	0	

At least three characters (ALP, ALPH or ALPHA) must be specified for the ALPHA command and the BETA command cannot be truncated.

13.3.3 ZCTACT - Action

The ZCTACT column defines the action to be performed for the command.

The valid actions are:

· SELECT   Pass control to specified function.
· ALIAS   Specify command as being alias for another command.
· PASSTHRU Command is passed to dialogue without being processed.
· SETVERB   Command is passed to dialogue, operation (command) and operand are stored in variables.
           Operation - ZVERB
           Operand - panel command field, normally ZCMD.
· NOP   The command is disabled.
· blank   The entry is ignored.

A list of some of the system commands that can also be used in the action field follows:

· SPLIT   Perform horizontal screen split.
· SPLITV   Perform vertical screen split (only 3290).
· SWAP   Swap active screen.
· CURSOR   Position cursor at home position.
· PRINT   Print physical screen content.
· PRINT-HI Print physical screen content (highlighted).
· PRINTL   Print logical screen content.
· PRINTLHI Print logical screen content (highlighted).

Tip
A variable (variable name prefixed with & (ampersand)) may be used in the ZCTACT column. This variable must contain a valid action prior to the command being invoked. The use of a variable as an action can be used to impart flexibility into the application. The variable can be set to an action appropriate at that point.

For example, the following statement enables the PRINT command:

    ALPHA = 'PRINT'

and the following statement disables the PRINT command:

    ALPHA = 'NOP'

ZCTVERB	ZCTRUNC	ZCTACT
PRINT	0	&ALPHA

Note: The current setting also applies to any other commands having this command as alias.

13.3.3.1 SELECT - Pass Control to Specified Function. The SELECT action passes control to the specified function (program, command procedure or selection panel) before the dialogue is processed. Only the most important parameters are described briefly here; Section 3.2.2 has a complete description of all the parameters.

Syntax:

```
ISPEXEC SELECT
        { PANEL(panelname) [OPT(option)] [ADDPOP] }
        { CMD(command [parameter] ...])
                        [LANG(APL|CREX))]
                        [MODE(LINE|FSCR)]
                        [BARRIER]
                        [NEST]                              }
        { PGM(programname) [PARM(parameter)]
                        [MODE(LINE|FSCR)]                   }
        {{[NEWAPPL[applicationid|ISP)]] [PASSLIB]} | [NEWPOOL]} [SUSPEND]
```

PGM(programname)
    Programname is the name of the dialogue program which is to be invoked.

PARM(parameter)
    Parameter is passed to the program.

CMD([%]procname)
    Procname is the name of the command procedure which is to be invoked.

PANEL(selection-panel-name)
    Selection-panel-name is the name of the selection panel which is to be displayed.

OPT(option)
    Invoke the selection panel with **option**.

Example:

ZCTVERB	ZCTRUNC	ZCTACT
ALPHA	5	SELECT PGM(TSPGM01) PARM(99)

This example specifies that the ALPHA command invokes the TSPGM01 with parameter "99".

13.3.3.2 ALIAS - Define Alias. The ALIAS action defines the command as being an alias for another command.

Syntax:
```
ALIAS aliasname
```

aliasname
> The name of the command for which this entry is an alias.

Example:

ZCTVERB	ZCTRUNC	ZCTACT
HILFE	5	ALIAS HELP

This example defines HILFE as being an alias for the HELP command, i.e. HILFE and HELP are equivalent.

13.3.3.3 PASSTHRU - Pass Command to Dialogue. The PASSTHRU action passes the command to the dialogue. No processing is performed on the command.

Syntax:
```
PASSTHRU
```

Example:

ZCTVERB	ZCTRUNC	ZCTACT
PRINT	0	PASSTHRU

This example redefines the PRINT as being a command which will be processed by the dialogue, i.e. the processing of the ISPF PRINT command is now handled by the dialogue.

13.3.3.4 SETVERB - Pass Verb to Dialogue. The SETVERB action is similar to PASSTHRU. The verb is stored in the ZVERB variable and the operand is stored in the panel command field, no other processing is performed on the command.

Syntax:
```
SETVERB
```

Example:

ZCTVERB	ZCTRUNC	ZCTACT
TSO	3	SETVERB

This example passes the TSO command to the dialogue.

13.3.3.5 NOP - No-operation. The NOP action disables the command.

Syntax:
```
NOP
```

Example:

ZCTVERB	ZCTRUNC	ZCTACT
TSO	0	NOP

This example disables the TSO command, i.e. no TSO commands can be issued from this application.

Tip
The NOP command can be used to stop the user from invoking commands which could compromise the integrity of the system, for example by disabling the TSO command.

13.3.3.6 Blank. An entry with a blank action is ignored.

13.3.4 ZCTDESC - Description

The ZCTDESC column is used only as comment.

Example:

ZCTVERB	ZCTRUNC	ZCTACT	ZCTDESC
HILFE	3	ALIAS HELP	Help for German users

13.3.5 Example

ZCTVERB	ZCTRUNC	ZCTACT
HILFE	2	ALIAS HELP
SPLIT	0	NOP
COMPRESS	2	SELECT PANEL(TSCMP000)

This command table defines three entries (commands):

· HILFE   May be abbreviated to HI and is an alias for HELP.
· SPLIT   Disabled. The command cannot be abbreviated.
· COMPRESS   May be abbreviated to CO and invokes the TSCMP000 selection panel.

13.4 ISPCMDS - DEFAULT COMMAND TABLE

A selection of the contents of the default command table (ISPCMDS) is listed in Figure 13.2.

```
ZCTVERB   ZCTTRUNC  ZCTACT
UP        0         SETVERB
DOWN      0         SETVERB
LEFT      0         SETVERB
RIGHT     0         SETVERB
RFIND     0         SETVERB
RCHANGE   0         SETVERB
END       0         SETVERB
RETURN    0         SETVERB
HELP      0         SELECT PGM(ISPTUTOR) PARM(&ZPARM) NOFUNC
TSO       0         SELECT CMD(&ZPARM)
KEYS      0         SELECT PGM(ISPOPT) PARM(ISPOPT3)
NOP       0         NOP
SPLIT     0         SPLIT
SWAP      0         SWAP
CURSOR    0         CURSOR
PRINT     0         PRINT
PANELID   0         SELECT PGM(ISPOPI) PARM(&ZPARM) NOFUNC
PFSHOW    0         SELECT PGM(ISPOPF) PARM(&ZPARM) NOFUNC
ISPPREP   0         SELECT PGM(ISPPREP) NEWAPPL
```

Figure 13.2 - Partial contents of default command table (ISPCMDS)

13.5 PROGRAM FUNCTION KEYS (PF-KEYS)

Standard IBM terminals are equipped with 12 or 24 function keys, known as **program function** (PF) keys. These PF keys can be assigned a string of characters which is set into the panel command field when the PF key is pressed, i.e. PF keys can be assigned commands. A command assigned to a PF key is processed in the same way as a command entered in the command field.

The standard (default) definitions for the PF keys are stored in the application profile table (ISPPROF file). The PF keys are assigned the system variables:

```
ZPF01      PF key 1
ZPF02      PF key 2
  ...
ZPF24      PF key 24.
```

The PF keys may be assigned commands by the user. However, the key definition must be stored in the profile pool to be effective.

Example:
The procedure statements:

```
ZPF01 = 'ALPHA'
ADDRESS ISPEXEC "VPUT (ZPF01) PROFILE"
```

assign the command ALPHA to PF key 1.

The equivalent processing can be made in a panel:

```
)INIT
&ZPF01 = 'ALPHA'
VPUT (ZPF01) PROFILE
```

The .PFKEY system variable is set to contain the value of the pressed PF key (PF01 for PF key 1, PF02 for PF key 2, etc.). .PFKEY contains blanks if no PF key has been pressed. The control flow for PF key processing is depicted in Figure 13.3.

Tip
If the application redefines PF keys this should only be done in its own application, i.e. the function has been invoked with an application-id. This avoids conflicts in PF key usage with standard applications.

Similarly, to avoid the user himself redefining the application's PF keys, the KEYS command can be disabled (ZCTACT set to NOP) in the command table.

It should be remembered that certain PF keys are used for ISPF's own processing:

· PF1 HELP
· PF3 END
· PF12 CURSOR (Home), etc.

The application developer should, as far as possible, adhere to the standard PF key usage. However, application-oriented PF keys can greatly simplify user processing.

In any case, it is desirable for a user-friendly application that the current PF key assignments are displayed on a status line (or lines).

Figure 13.3 shows the control flow for PF key processing:

· The code for the PF key is set in the .PFKEY control variable.
· The value associated with the PF key (ZPFn system variable) is set into the panel command field (usually ZCMD).

* The standard name of the command field.

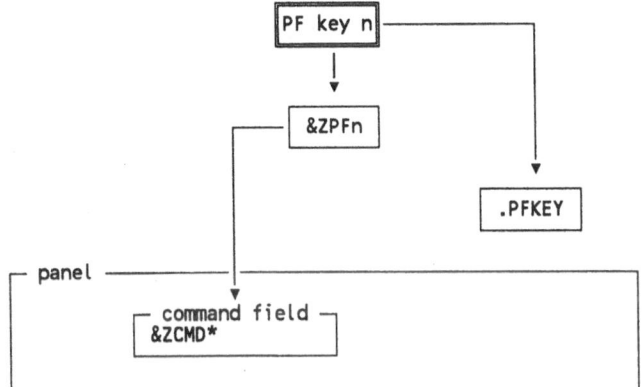

Figure 13.3 - Control flow for PF key processing

13.5.1 Keylists

A keylist associates PF keys with a panel. The keylists are stored as an ISPF table.

The keylist table has the following definition:
```
TBCREATE idKEYS
        KEYS(keylistname)
        NAMES( (KEYnDEF KEYnLAB KEYnATR)... )
```
$n = 1,...,24$ is the number of the corresponding PF-key.

idKEYS
> The keylist table name. **id** is specified in the)PANEL header in the panel definition.

keylistname
> The keylist-name as specified in the)PANEL header.

KEYnDEF
> The name of the associated command. NOP disables a key.

KEYnLAB
> The label that is shown if the PFSHOW command is used to display the key settings.

KEYnATR

One of the following attributes can be set:

NO   The key is not shown, although the function is active.

LONG   The key is shown in the function key area only for the initial display.

SHORT The key is shown in the function key area.

ISPF option 0 or a user-written procedure can be used to create keylists. Section 19.5.6 shows an example of a user-written procedure that creates a keylist.

Example:

```
Variable     T   A    Value
KEYLISTN     K        TEST
KEY1DEF      N        HELP
KEY1LAB      N        HELP
KEY1ATR      N        NO
KEY2DEF      N        NOP
KEY2LAB      N        NOP
KEY2ATR      N        NO
KEY3DEF      N        EXIT
KEY3LAB      N        EXIT
KEY3ATR      N        SHORT
   ...
KEY10DEF     N        ACTIONS
KEY10LAB     N        ACTIONS
KEY10ATR     N        SHORT
   ...
KEY13DEF     N        HELP
KEY13LAB     N        HELP
KEY13ATR     N        NO
   ...
KEY15DEF     N        EXIT
KEY15LAB     N        EXIT
KEY15ATR     N        SHORT
   ...
KEY22DEF     N        ACTIONS
KEY22LAB     N        ACTIONS
KEY22ATR     N        SHORT
   ...
```

This example shows the form of the key definitions. With exception of the PF2 entry, the inactivated key settings are not shown.

Associated panel header:
```
)PANEL KEYLIST(TEST)
```

14

Program Environment

14.1 INTRODUCTION

Up to now, the services have only been described as being invoked from a command procedure (REXX exec or CLIST). This is doubtless the easiest and most common way of using ISPF services. However, for some applications it is advantageous to call ISPF services from within an application program, e.g. where performance is important.

In the command environment, the variables are in a common (function) pool, and so may be directly accessed from both ISPF and command procedure applications. In the program environment, program variables are not directly accessible from ISPF and vice versa, and so special ISPF services are required to make the variables available.

14.2 ISPF PROGRAM INTERFACES

There are two interfaces available for programs to use ISPF services: ISPEXEC and ISPLINK. ISPEXEC is the same interface as described in the preceding chapters. The parameters for ISPEXEC are defined as a character string in a buffer; the address and length of this buffer are passed in the call. ISPLINK passes individual parameters. In most cases these two interfaces can be used interchangeably. Only in the case where values for variables are to be passed between the program and ISPF is it necessary to use ISPLINK.

14.2.1 ISPEXEC Call Interface

The content of the ISPEXEC buffer has the same form as for command procedure invocations; the call passes the address and size of the buffer. The maximum buffer size is 256 bytes.

The buffer entry can contain symbolic variables (ISPF variable name prefixed with an &). Such variables are resolved.

Example:
```
DCL BUFFER CHAR(80);
DCL BUFFER_LEN FIXED BIN(31,0) INIT(80);
   ...
BUFFER = 'DISPLAY PANEL(DMPAN000) MSG(DMMSG001)';
CALL ISPEXEC(BUFFER_LEN,BUFFER);
```

14.2.2 ISPLINK Call Interface

The ISPLINK interface requires that the necessary parameters are passed in the call. These parameters are positional and the sequence determines the meaning of the parameter. Optional parameters at the right-hand end of the call sequence may be omitted. Optional parameters within the call sequence are coded with blank content.

Tip

Specify even optional parameters with their value, because it helps in the understanding of your program by someone who may not be so familiar with ISPF.

Example:
```
DCL PAN_ID CHAR(8);
DCL MSG_ID CHAR(8);
   ...
PAN_ID = 'DMPAN000';
MSG_ID = 'DMMSG001';
CALL ISPLINK('DISPLAY',PAN_ID,MSG_ID);
```

14.2.3 Calls That Return Values Indirectly

Certain services do not return the required value directly, rather the name of a variable containing the value is returned. In the program environment a further service must be invoked to access this variable.

Example:
```
DCL TABNAME CHAR(8);
DCL VL FIXED BIN(31,0) INIT(4);
DCL NROWS FIXED BIN(31,0);
   ...
CALL ISPLINK,('TBQUERY',TABNAME,' ',' ','ALPHA')
CALL ISPLINK,('VCOPY','ALPHA',VL,NROWS,'MOVE')
```

This example returns the number of rows in the table TABNAME into the program variable NROWS, ALPHA is used as an intermediate variable (any name could have been used). Compare this with the equivalent CLIST processing:

```
ISPEXEC TBQUERY &TABNAME ROWNUM(NROWS)
```

14.3 PROGRAM INVOCATION

Programs which are to run in the ISPF environment (i.e. use ISPF services) can be invoked in one of two ways:

```
·   ISPEXEC SELECT PGM(program-name) ...
·   CALL 'library-name(program-name)' ...
```

The SELECT is required to create the ISPF environment for the program. A function pool is created for the first invocation of the application-id or reinstated for a subsequent invocation within the ISPF session.
Either CALL or SELECT may be used once the ISPF environment has been created.

Tip
The overhead is less using the CALL invocation.

14.4 PROGRAM CALLS

ISPF services conform to the standard IBM linkage conventions and may be called from programs written in the following programming languages:
· Assembler
· C/370
· COBOL
· PL/I
· APL2
· FORTRAN
· Pascal.

This book discusses only the first four languages. The call syntax examples will be shown in PL/I syntax.

14.5 LINKAGE TO SERVICES

Programs directly invoked by SELECT PGM or CALL may be passed a parameter. The manner of processing this parameter is dependent on the programming language.

In all cases, the name of the panel to be displayed is passed as parameter.

```
ISPEXEC SELECT PGM(DMPGM02) PARM(DMPAN000)
```

14.5.1 Invoked PL/I Program

The calling parameter must be specified with the VARYING attribute and be assigned to a fixed length field before being used in ISPF calls.

The execution parameter (here DMPAN000) must be prefixed by a slash ("/") for PL/I programs; parameters preceding the slash are interpreted as being run-time options. Example

```
ISPEXEC SELECT PGM(DMPGM01) PARM(/DMPAN000)
```

Example:

```
DMPGM01: PROC(PARM) OPTIONS(MAIN);
DCL 1 PARM CHAR(8) VARYING;
DCL 1 PANEL CHAR(8);
DCL ISPLINK ENTRY EXTERNAL OPTIONS(ASM,INTER,RETCODE);
  PANEL = PARM;
  CALL ISPLINK('DISPLAY',PANEL);
END DMPGM01;
```

14.5.2 Invoked COBOL Program

Because COBOL programs cannot easily process variable length parameters, only fixed length parameters should be passed. However, this parameter will be preceded by a halfword that contains the length of the following parameter.

Example:

```
IDENTIFICATION DIVISION.
PROGRAM-ID. DMPGM02.
  ...
WORKING-STORAGE SECTION.
  ...
77  P-DISPLAY                PIC  X(8) VALUE 'DISPLAY'.
  ...
LINKAGE SECTION.
  ...
01  PARM.
02  PARM-LEN                 PIC  S9(4) COMP.
02  PARM-DATA                PIC  X(8).
  ...
PROCEDURE DIVISION USING PARM.
  ...
    CALL 'ISPLINK' USING P-DISPLAY PARM-DATA.
  ...
    STOP RUN.
```

14.5.3 Invoked Assembler Program

The address of the calling parameter is contained in register 1. The first halfword of the parameter contains the (binary) length of the actual parameter.

Example:
```
DMPGM03  CSECT
*  ... set up base register and chain save-areas
*  (this coding is not shown)
          L     2,0(1)          address of parameter
          LH    1,0(2)          length of parameter
          LTR   1,1
          BZ    A100            no parameter
          SH    1,=H'1'         length code of parameter
          MVC   PANEL(0),2(1)   move panel name
          EX    1,*-6           use actual length
          CALL  ISPLINK,(DISPLAY,PANEL),VL
*  ... terminate program (this coding is not shown)
          ...
DISPLAY   DC    CL8'DISPLAY'
PANEL     DC    CL8' '
          END
```

14.5.4 Invoked C/370 Program

The calling parameter must be converted from C-format (null-terminated) to standard call format.

Example:
```
#pragma linkage(ISPLINK,OS)
#include <stdio.h>

void main(int argc, char *argv[])
{
  char panel[9];
  int rc;
  sprintf(panel,"%-8.8s",argv[1]); /* left-align to 8 characters */
  rc = ISPLINK("DISPLAY",panel);
  printf("RC:%d\n",rc); /* display ISPLINK ReturnCode */
}
```

14.6 PROGRAM LINKAGE TO SERVICES

The following section describes particular considerations for the most commonly used programming languages.

14.6.1 PL/I Program Invocation

PL/I programs must include the following statement:
```
DCL ISPLINK ENTRY EXTERNAL OPTIONS(ASM,INTER,RETCODE);
```

PL/I programs may use the return code from services by coding the following statement:
```
DCL PLIRETV BUILTIN;
```

Example:
```
CALL ISPLINK('DISPLAY',PANEL);
IF PLIRETV() = 0 THEN
   ...
```

14.6.2 COBOL Program Invocation

COBOL programs reference the return code from services in the reserved word
RETURN-CODE, e.g.

```
CALL 'ISPLINK' USING P-DISPLAY PANEL.
IF RETURN-CODE = ZERO THEN ...
```

14.6.3 Assembler Program Invocation

Assembler programs should always use the VL identifier at the end of the call to
denote a variable number of parameters. This isolates the program from any
changes in the number of parameters that the function can accept.

Assembler programs reference the return code from services in the general purpose
register 15, e.g.

```
CALL   ISPLINK,(DISPLAY,PANEL),VL
LTR    15,15
BZ     ...
```

14.6.4 C/370 Program Invocation

C/370 programs must define standard (MVS) linkage conventions for invoking
ISPLINK:

```
#pragma linkage (ISPLINK,OS)
```

The service return code is the function result. The length of character function
parameters does not include the terminating \x00.

Example:
```
#pragma linkage (ISPLINK,OS)
typedef int ISPLINK();

int rc;

rc = ISPLINK("DISPLAY ","PAN1   ");
if (rc != 0) ...
```

14.7 PROGRAM ISPF PARAMETERS

The parameters passed in calls to ISPF have the following forms:

· name
· service-name
· keyword
· name-list-string

· name-list-structure
· numeric value
· dataset-list.

Omitted parameters are defined by setting their content to blank. Certain languages (e.g. Assembler) support null parameters (zero address) in the call statement.

14.7.1 Name

A name is a left-justified character string that is delimited by a blank if it is shorter than the maximum length allowed for that particular parameter. The maximum length for parameters is 8 characters, except for:

· data set name (44 characters)
· volume serial (6 characters).

Example:
```
"ALPHA "    requires a blank because its length is less than 8 characters
"ALPHABET"  does not require a blank because its length is 8 characters.
```

In PL/I syntax:
```
DCL VN CHAR INIT('ALPHA ');
CALL ISPLINK,('VCOPY',VN,VL,VA,'MOVE');
```

Note: The delimiting blank may be used in all circumstances.

14.7.2 Service Name

A service name is a left-justified character string, e.g. "VCOPY"

In PL/I syntax:
```
CALL ISPLINK,('VCOPY',VN,VL,VA,'MOVE');
```

Tip
As far as possible, the variables used for service-names should be the same as the service-name. PL/I has the advantage of allowing the use of literals in the call. COBOL, however, has certain service-names (e.g. DISPLAY) as reserved words; VS COBOL II allows literals to be directly specified in the call statement using CALL BY CONTENT.

14.7.3 Keyword

A keyword is a left-justified character string, e.g. "MOVE"

In PL/I syntax:
```
CALL ISPLINK,('VCOPY',VN,VL,VA,'MOVE');
```

Tip

As far as possible, variables used for keywords should be the same as the keyword. PL/I has the advantage of allowing the use of literals in the call. COBOL, moreover, has certain keywords (e.g. MOVE) as reserved words.

14.7.4 Name List String

A name list string is a string of names, each separated by a blank or comma, and enclosed within apostrophes.

Example:
```
"(ALPHA BETA GAMMA)"
```

In PL/I syntax:
```
DCL 1 DSL CHAR INIT('(ALPHA BETA GAMMA)');
```

14.7.5 Name List Structure

A name list structure is a list of names, each eight characters, preceded by two binary fullwords containing the number of names in the structure and the value 8, respectively.

Example:

3	8
ALPHA	
BETA	
GAMMA	

In PL/I syntax:
```
DCL 1 VNA,
      2 VNA_N FIXED BIN(31,0) INIT(3),
      2 VNA_8 FIXED BIN(31,0) INIT(8),
      2 VNA_NAME(3) CHAR(8) INIT('ALPHA','BETA','GAMMA');
```

14.7.6 Numeric Value

A numeric value is a fullword binary value.

In PL/I syntax:
```
DCL 1 VL FIXED BIN(31,0) INIT(3);
```

14.7.7 Dataset List

A dataset list is a list of data set names, each separated by a comma or blank, contained within parentheses.

Example:
```
"('ISPF.SYST.ISPPLIB','TEST.ISPPLIB',USER.ISPPLIB)"
```

In PL/I syntax:
```
DCL 1 DSL CHAR
    INIT('('''ISPF.SYST.ISPPLIB'','''TEST.ISPPLIB'',USER.ISPPLIB)');
```
This example defines a list of three data set names; the first two are fully qualified (defined within apostrophes) and the third will be prefixed with the user's current prefix.

14.8 LINKAGE EDITOR PARAMETERS

The Linkage Editor (Binder) parameter REUS should not be used if split mode is enabled; if the program is invoked in both screens an endless loop results.

14.9 PROGRAM VARIABLE SERVICES

The use of ISPF services from programs involves two aspects:

· invoke services
· pass data values between ISPF and program.

The invocation of ISPF services is similar to that from a command procedure. The transfer of data values between ISPF and the program requires that the program informs ISPF of the address and attributes of its data field associated with a particular variable (name). Special program **variable services** are available and are listed below in alphabetic order:

· VCOPY   Copy pool variable into program variable.
· VDEFINE Make program variable available as pool variable.
· VDELETE Remove availability of program variable as pool variable.
· VMASK   Specify mask processing.
· VREPLACE Replace pool variable with program variable.
· VRESET   Remove availability of all defined program variables.

In addition, the VGET and VPUT services are available to transfer variables from shared (or profile) pool into function pool, and vice versa. The VERASE service removes variables from a pool (shared, profile, or both). The VERASE, VGET and VPUT services can be invoked both from programs and procedures. However, these two services are not directly related to the program processing of ISPF variables. These three services are described in Chapter 6.

The VDEFINE service makes the value for the specified variable **implicitly** available. The values in the function pool and in the program are **automatically** updated. The VCOPY and VREPLACE services must be **explicitly** called to make the value for the specified variable available. Whether VDEFINE or VCOPY and VREPLACE is used depends, largely, on the application developer's own preferences. To some extent, VDEFINE is simpler and performs certain data conversions automatically. However, VDEFINE creates a new version of the current variable each time it is called and there is the danger, especially in complicated processing, of accessing the wrong value, i.e. the variables are **stacked**. The use of VCOPY and VREPLACE has the advantage that the application developer has full control over the processing.

Tip

VCOPY and VREPLACE rather than VDEFINE (and VDELETE) should be used when the calling program is loaded more than once or when a subprogram is called more than once from the main program.

14.9.1 VCOPY - Copy ISPF Variable into Program Variable

The VCOPY service copies the current value of the specified ISPF variable into the specified program variable. The ISPF variable is not changed.

The dialogue pools are searched in the following order:

- defined function pool (variables defined with VDEFINE)
- function pool
- shared pool
- profile pool.

Syntax:
```
CALL ISPLINK,('VCOPY',name-list
       ,length-array
       ,value-array
       [,'LOCATE'|'MOVE']);
```

name-list

>The list of the names of variables to be copied from dialogue pool and made available as program variables.

length-array

>The array of program variables which is to contain the lengths of the values.

>In MOVE mode, each length-array element must be initialised with the length of the corresponding value-array element.

>On return each length-array element contains the length of the corresponding value-array element. This means that the array must be re-initialised before each call.

value-array

>The array of program variables which is to contain the values (MOVE parameter) or addresses of the values (LOCATE mode).

LOCATE

>The addresses of the variables are to be returned. Each **value-array** element is a fullword containing the address of the corresponding variable. The length of the value is contained in the corresponding **length-array** element. Default: LOCATE.

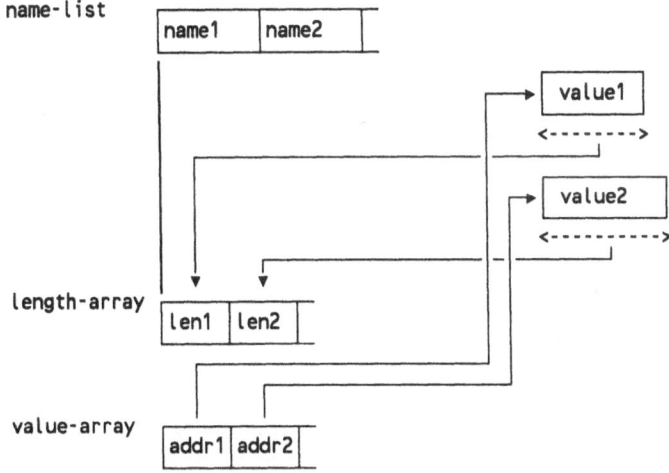

MOVE

The values of the variables are to be returned. Each **value-array** element is a fullword containing the value of the corresponding variable. The length of the value is contained in the corresponding **length-array** element.

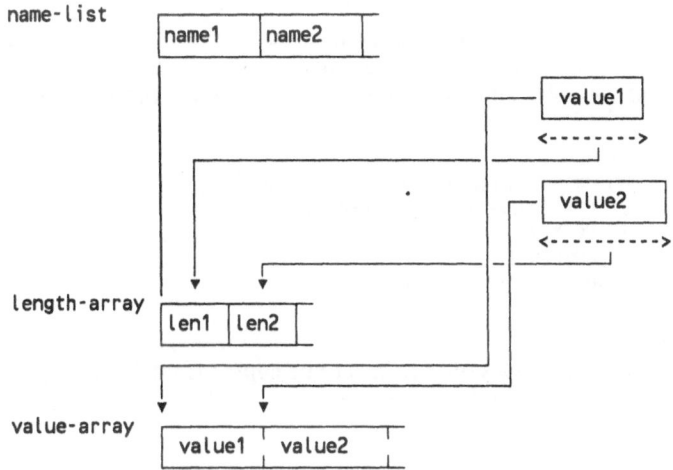

The service sets one of the following return codes:

  0 Normal completion.
  8 One or more variables do not exist.
  16 Truncation has occurred, the length specified was not sufficient to contain a variable.
  20 Severe error.

Example:
```
DCL 1 VNA,
      2 VNA_N FIXED BIN(31,0),
      2 VNA_8 FIXED BIN(31,0) INIT(8),
      2 VNA_NAME(10) CHAR(8);
DCL 1 VLA(10) FIXED BIN(31,0);
DCL 1 VAA CHAR(256);

VNA_N=2;
VNA_NAME(1)='PNO';
SUBSTR(VAA,1,4)='9999';
VLA(1) = 4;
VNA_NAME(2)='NAME';
SUBSTR(VAA,5,6)='NONAME';
VLA(2) = 6;
CALL ISPLINK('VCOPY',VNA,VLA,VAA,'MOVE');
```

This program copies the pool values for the two ISPF variables PNO and NAME into the program variable VAA. The value for PNO occupies the first 4 bytes and the value for NAME the next 6 bytes.

14.9.2 VDEFINE - Make ISPF Variable Available as Program Variable

The VDEFINE service defines the specified variable in the **defined function pool** and makes an implicit direct connection between that variable and the associated program field. An alteration in one of the values is automatically reflected in the other value. A new pool variable is created each time VDEFINE is called. This can lead to multiple variables having the same name but differing values. **Defined function pool** variables are removed with the VDELETE (or VRESET) service.

Syntax:
```
CALL ISPLINK,('VDEFINE',name-list,value-array
             ,( CHAR|FIXED|BIT|HEX|USER),length
             [ ,COPY ]
             [ ,NOSCAN ]
             [ ,user-subroutine-address ])
```

name-list

> The list of the names of variables to be copied from dialogue pool and made available as program variables.

value-array

> The array of program variables which is to contain the values, the number of entries in **name-list** determines the dimension of this array.

CHAR

> The data is to be stored in **character** format (left-justified, padded with blanks). No data conversion is performed.
> Default: CHAR.

Example:
```
DCL VL FIXED BIN(31,0) INIT(8);
DCL VA CHAR(8);
...
CALL ISPLINK('VDEFINE','FLD',VA,'CHAR',VL);
```

```
          < 8 bytes >
           ┌─ FLD ─┐
          │0010 0111│
           └───┬───┘
               │
               │       ┌─── VA ──────────┐
               └─► C'│0 0 1 0 0 1 1 1│'
                       └─────────────────┘
                       <--- 8 bytes --->
```

FLD is the panel field
VA is the program field.

FIXED

The data is to be stored in **binary integer** format. Fields with length 4 bytes are signed (x'80000000' represents a null (missing) value).

Example:
```
DCL VL FIXED BIN(31,0) INIT(4);
DCL VA FIXED BIN(31,0);
...
CALL ISPLINK('VDEFINE','FLD',VA,'FIXED',VL);
```

```
          < 8 bytes >
           ┌─ FLD ─┐
          │0010 0111│
           └───┬───┘
               │
               │     ┌─── VA ─────┐
               └─► F'│00 10 01 11│'
                     └───────────┘
                     <- 4 bytes ->
```

FLD is the panel field
VA is the program field.

BIT

The data are to be stored in **bit** format (left-justified, padded with 0). A bit string may only contain the two characters 0 and 1.

Example:
```
DCL VL FIXED BIN(31,0) INIT(1);
DCL VA CHAR(1);
...
CALL ISPLINK('VDEFINE','FLD',VA,'BIT',VL);
```

```
              < 8 bytes >
              ┌─ FLD ──┐
              │0010 0111│
              └─────────┘
                    │
                    │        ┌── VA ──┐        ┌VA┐
                    └──→  B' │0010 0111│ ' = X' │27│ '
                             └─────────┘        └──┘
                         <- 1 byte->
```

FLD is the panel field
VA is the program field.

HEX

The data are to be stored in **hexadecimal** format (left-justified, padded with
0). A hexadecimal string may only contain the characters 0 - 9 and A - F.

Example:
```
DCL VL FIXED BIN(31,0) INIT(4);
DCL VA CHAR(4);
 ...
CALL ISPLINK('VDEFINE','FLD',VA,'HEX',VL);
```

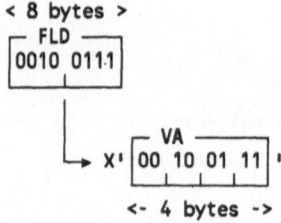

```
              < 8 bytes >
              ┌─ FLD ──┐
              │0010 0111│
              └─────────┘
                    │
                    │        ┌──── VA ────┐
                    └──→  X' │00 10 01 11 │ '
                             └────────────┘
                         <- 4 bytes ->
```

FLD is the panel field
VA is the program field.

USER

A user-supplied subroutine is to be used for data conversion.

length

The length of each **value-array** element. **Length** is a binary fullword.

COPY

A dialogue variable, if present, is to be used to initialise the program field.

The dialogue pools are searched in the following order:
- function pool
- shared pool
- profile pool.

NOSCAN

Any trailing blanks are not to be stripped from the variable.

user-subroutine-address

User-subroutine-address is the address of the user's conversion routine.
This parameter is mandatory when the USER parameter has been specified.
The requirements for such subroutines are described in the following
section.

The service sets one of the following return codes:

0   Normal completion.

8   One or more variables do not exist.

16   Truncation has occurred, the length specified was not sufficient to
contain a variable.

20   Severe error.

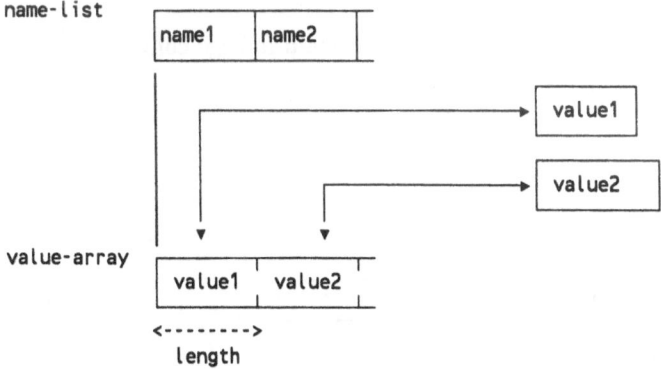

Note: A translation error (return code) occurs on a subsequent display if the panel
field contains invalid data for the particular format. Consider the following
example where we have a panel field containing "1234" in conjunction with VDEFINE
format BIT.

```
DCL 1 VNA,
      2 VNA_N FIXED BIN(31,0),
      2 VNA_8 FIXED BIN(31,0) INIT(8),
      2 VNA_NAME(10) CHAR(8);
DCL 1 VL FIXED BIN(31,0);
DCL 1 VAA CHAR(256);

  VNA_N=2;
  VNA_NAME(1)='PNO';
  SUBSTR(VAA,1,4)='9999';
  VL = 4;
  VNA_NAME(2)='NAME';
  SUBSTR(VAA,5,6)='NONAME';
  CALL ISPLINK('VDEFINE',VNA,VAA,'CHAR',VL);
```

This sample program shows how the two ISPF variables PNO and NAME are made available as program variables.

Note: Only 4 characters "NONA" are actually assigned to the variable NAME.

14.9.2.1 User Conversion Routine. The VDEFINE service permits the application developer to define his own subroutines for data conversion. The address of a structure containing the entry point address of the subroutine, and any parameters to be passed to it, is specified as the user-subroutine-address of the VDEFINE call.

The structure has the following form:
```
DCL conversion-routine-name ENTRY EXTERNAL;
DCL 1 USERDATA,
      2 CVT_ADDR ENTRY VARIABLE,
      2 CVT_DATA CHAR(length) INIT('parameter');

CVT_ADDR = conversion-routine-name;
```

The conversion routine conforms to the standard linkage conventions and receives the following seven parameters:

```
1   ┌─────────┬─────────┬─────────┬─────────┐
    │    0    │    0    │    0    │    0    │
    ├─────────┴─────────┤─────────┴─────────┘
    │ length of parameter │
    ├───────────────────┬───────────────────────────────┐
    │ parameter         │                               │
    └───────────────────┴───────────────────────────────┘

2   ┌─────────────────────┬───────────────────┐
    │ service request code │                   │
    └─────────────────────┴───────────────────┘

3   ┌─────────────────────┐
    │ length              │
    ├───────────────────┬─────────────────────────────┐
    │ name of variable  │                             │
    └───────────────────┴─────────────────────────────┘

4   ┌─────────────────────┬───────────────────┐
    │ length VDEFINE data  │                   │
5   ├─────────────────────┴──────────────────────────┐
    │ VDEFINE data                                   │
    └────────────────────────────────────────────────┘

6   ┌─────────────────────────┬───────────────────┐
    │ length ISPF (panel) data │                   │
7   ├─────────────────────────┴──────────────────────┐
    │ ISPF (panel) data                              │
    └────────────────────────────────────────────────┘
```

As such conversion routines will normally be written in Assembler language, the parameters will be described in Assembler syntax:

Parameter 1: User parameter
```
DS    A   always 0
DS    H   length of user data (refer to note)
DS    CLn user parameter
```

Note: The length field is only present if the user parameter has been defined as being VARYING.

Parameter 2: Request code
```
DS    F   0 = read request, 1 = write request
```

"Read" means data being read from the calling program. "Write" means data being written to the calling program.

Parameter 3: Name of variable
```
DS    AL1 length of name
DS    CLn name of variable, left justified.
```

Parameter 4 and 5: VDEFINE data
```
DS    F   length of VDEFINE data
DS    CLn VDEFINE data
```

The VDEFINE data is the data defined in the calling program.

Parameter 6 and 7: ISPF data
```
DS    F   length of ISPF data
DS    CLn ISPF data
```

The ISPF data is the data being passed to ISPF for a write request and the data being obtained from ISPF for a read request.

Example:
The following PL/I program (DMPGM03) uses the Assembler conversion routine (DMCVT00) to perform the simple conversion of returning the string "MYDATA" for a write request.

```
DMPGM03: PROC OPTIONS(MAIN);
DCL PLIRETV BUILTIN;
DCL 1 PANEL CHAR(8) INIT('DMPAN000');
DCL 1 VN CHAR(8) INIT('NAME');
DCL 1 VL FIXED BIN(31,0);
DCL 1 VA CHAR(16) INIT('PGM DATA');
DCL ISPLINK ENTRY EXTERNAL OPTIONS(ASM,INTER,RETCODE);
DCL QTCVT00 ENTRY EXTERNAL;
DCL 1 USERDATA,
    2 CVT_ADDR ENTRY VARIABLE,
    2 CVT_DATA CHAR(9) INIT('PARM DATA');
A120:
 VL = LENGTH(VA);
 CVT_ADDR = DMCVT00;
 CALL ISPLINK('VDEFINE',VN,VA,'USER',VL,' ',USERDATA);
 CALL ISPLINK('DISPLAY',PANEL);
 IF PLIRETV() < 8 THEN GOTO A120;
END DMPGM03;
```

```
               TITLE 'VDEFINE conversion routine'
DMCVT00  CSECT
* initialise addressing
               STM   14,12,12(13)              save registers
               BALR  12,0                      base register
               USING *,12
               LA    15,SA                     A(save-area)
               ST    13,4(15)                  backward ptr
               ST    15,8(13)                  forward ptr
               LR    13,15                     A(new save-area)
               B     SA_END                    jump over save-area
SA       DS    18A                             save-area
SA_END   DS    OH
               LM    2,8,0(1)
* P1: user data
* P2: request code, 0 = read, 1 = write
* P3: name string
* P4: defined area length
* P5: defined area
* P6: ISPF data length
* P7: ISPF data
               L     0,0(3)                    service code
               LTR   0,0
               BNZ   WRITE
* else read (from routine)
               LA    1,L'DATAAREA
               ST    1,0(7)                    data length
               LA    1,DATAAREA
               ST    1,0(8)                    data address
WRITE    DS    OH
               L     13,4(13)                  restore A(old save-area)
               RETURN (14,12),RC=(15)
DATAAREA DC    CL8'MYDATA'
               END
```

14.9.3 VDELETE - Remove Availability of ISPF Variable

The VDELETE service removes the availability of the specified variables from the
defined function pool.

Syntax:
```
     CALL ISPLINK,('VDELETE',( name-list | '*' ))
```

name-list
> The list of the names of variables to be deleted from the defined function
> pool.

'*'

> Delete all variables previously defined by the program module from the
> defined function pool.

The service sets one of the following return codes:

 0 Normal completion.
 8 One or more variables do not exist.
20 Severe error.

Example:
```
CALL ISPLINK('VDELETE','(PNO,NAME)');
```
Delete the two variables PNO and NAME from the defined function pool.

14.9.4 VMASK - Specify Mask Processing

The VMASK associates an edit mask with the dialogue variable defined from a program variable. The edit mask is a pattern that is used to validate the data input in the variable. The mask characters are removed from the data entry before it is stored in the function pool. The mask characters are inserted when the data entry is displayed.

The VEDIT processing section statement is used to identify such variables in the corresponding panel (or panels).

Syntax:
```
CALL ISPLINK,('VMASK',namelist,
      'FORMAT '[,format] | 'USER ','mask',masklen)
```

namelist
> The list of the names of dialogue variables whose values are to be associated with the specified mask pattern.

FORMAT
> A predefined mask format is to be used.

format
> The name of the predefined format mask:
>
> IDATE   Internal date: yymmdd.
>
>   Representative display format: yy/mm/dd. The delimiter (shown as /) and the sequence depends on the national language.
>
> STDDATE   Internal date: yyyymmdd.
>
>   Representative display format: yyyy/mm/dd. The delimiter (shown as /) and the sequence depends on the national language.
>
> ITIME   Internal time: hhmm.
>
>   Representative display format: hh:mm. The delimiter (shown as :) depends on the national language. Hours are specified using the 24-hour clock.

STDTIME   Internal time: hhmmss.
             Representative display format: hh:mm:ss. The delimiter
             (shown as :) depends on the national language. Hours are
             specified using the 24-hour clock.
JDATE   Internal date: yyddd. ddd is the day of the year.
             Representative display format: yy.ddd.
JSTD   Internal date: yyyyddd. ddd is the day of the year.
             Representative display format: yyyy.ddd.

USER

A user-defined mask format is to be used.

mask

A user-defined mask.
The mask can contain the following pattern characters:

A   An alphabetic character (A-Z, a-z)
B   A blank
H   A hexadecimal digit (0-9, A-F, a-f)
N   A numeric digit or alphabetic character (0-9, A-Z, a-z)
V   Implied decimal point
S   Signed numeric data (if specified, this must be in the first position)
X   Any character
9   A numeric digit (0-9).
x   One of the special characters: ( ) - / , .

The mask must contain at least one of the following symbols: A, H, N, X or
9. The data represented by B, V or special characters are removed when the
data are stored.

masklen

The length of the mask. The mask has a maximum length of 20 characters.

The service sets one of the following return codes:

0   Normal completion.
8   Variable not found.
20   Severe error.

Example:
The following example program shows the use of both predefined format and user-
defined masks.

```
IDENTIFICATION DIVISION.
PROGRAM-ID. TVMASK.
ENVIRONMENT DIVISION.
DATA DIVISION.
WORKING-STORAGE SECTION.
01 C-DISPLAY PIC X(8) VALUE 'DISPLAY'.
01 C-VGET PIC X(8) VALUE 'VGET'.
01 C-VDEFINE PIC X(8) VALUE 'VDEFINE'.
```

```
01 C-VMASK PIC X(8) VALUE 'VMASK'.
01 C-FORMAT PIC X(8) VALUE 'FORMAT'.
01 C-MASK PIC X(8) VALUE 'MASK'.
01 C-USER PIC X(8) VALUE 'USER'.
01 C-CHAR PIC X(8) VALUE 'CHAR'.
01 C-FIXED PIC X(8) VALUE 'FIXED'.
01 C-IDATE PIC X(8) VALUE 'IDATE'.
01 P-UDATE PIC X(8) VALUE 'UDATE'.
01 P-UVAL PIC X(8) VALUE 'UVAL'.
01 V-UDATE PIC X(6).
01 V-UVAL PIC S9(9) BINARY.
01 V-MASK PIC X(11) VALUE 'S999,999.99'.
01 PN PIC X(8).
01 VD PIC X(80).
01 VL PIC 9(9) BINARY.
01 RC PIC 9(4) COMP.
PROCEDURE DIVISION.
* define program variables
    MOVE 6 TO VL
    CALL 'ISPLINK' USING C-VDEFINE P-UDATE V-UDATE
     C-CHAR VL
    MOVE 4 TO VL
    CALL 'ISPLINK' USING C-VDEFINE P-UVAL V-UVAL
     C-FIXED VL
* standard-FORMAT VMASK
    CALL 'ISPLINK' USING C-VMASK P-UDATE C-FORMAT C-IDATE
    DISPLAY 'VMASK RC:' RETURN-CODE
* user-format VMASK
    DISPLAY 'VMASK'
    MOVE 11 TO VL
    CALL 'ISPLINK' USING C-VMASK P-UVAL C-USER V-MASK VL
    DISPLAY 'VMASK RC:' RETURN-CODE
* display panel with VEDIT
    MOVE 'XVEDIT' TO PN
    CALL 'ISPLINK' USING C-DISPLAY PN
* 98/12/31 -> 981231
    DISPLAY 'VUDATE:' V-UDATE
    DISPLAY 'VUVAL:' V-UVAL
    STOP RUN.
```

Associated (VEDIT) panel:

```
)BODY
+       date:_UDATE   +
+user value:_UVAL        +
)INIT
&UDATE= '98/12/31'
&UVAL= '-123,456.78'
)PROC
 VEDIT (UDATE)
 VEDIT (UVAL)
)END
```

14.9.5 VREPLACE - Replace Function Pool Variable with Program Variable

The VREPLACE service replaces the specified function pool variables with the program variable values. Any variables which do not exist will be created.

If the variables are to be placed in a specific pool (shared or profile), the VREPLACE request must be followed by the appropriate VPUT service request.

Syntax:
```
CALL ISPLINK,('VREPLACE',namelist
       ,length-array
       ,value-array)
```

namelist

The list of the names of dialogue variables to be replaced in the function pool.

length-array

The array of program variables that contain the lengths of the corresponding values in the **value-array.** Each element is a binary fullword.

value-array

The array of program variables that contain the values to be transferred to the function pool. The length of array element is specified in the corresponding **length-array** element.

The service sets one of the following return codes:

    0   Normal completion.
  20   Severe error.

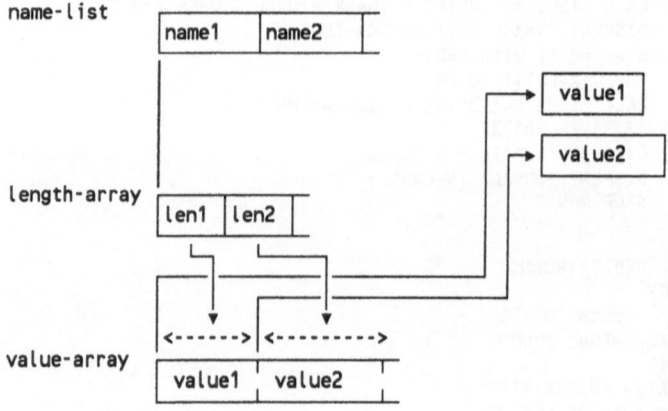

Example:
```
DCL 1 EMPLOYEE_NUMBER  CHAR(4) INIT('1234');
DCL 1 VL   FIXED BIN(31,0) INIT(4);

    CALL ISPLINK('VREPLACE','PNO',VL,EMPLOYEE_NUMBER);
```
Replace the variable PNO in the function pool with the value "1234".

14.9.6 VRESET - Remove Variables from the Defined Function Pool

The VRESET service removes all references for defined **variables**.

Syntax:
```
CALL ISPLINK,('VRESET')
```

The service sets one of the following return codes:

   0   Normal completion.
   20   Severe error.

Example:
```
DCL ISPLINK ENTRY EXTERNAL OPTIONS(ASM,INTER,RETCODE);
  CALL ISPLINK('VRESET');
```
Make all program variables inaccessible from ISPF.

14.10 PANEL EXIT

The PANEXIT statement can be used to temporarily pass control from a panel to a program exit routine. A panel exit routine may be called from those sections concerned with field processing, i.e.)INIT,)REINIT and)PROC sections. The exit routine receives names of variables and their current value from the panel and may return updated values. The exit routine can be used to perform processing which cannot be performed in the panel, etc. Panel exit routines are subject to certain conditions:

· The exit routine must be preloaded. The address of the loaded routine must be set into an ISPF variable (fullword) using the VDEFINE service;
· The exit routine may not invoke any ISPF services;
· The exit routine may change the value of variables but not their length.

The exit routine is called in 31-bit addressing mode (AMODE 31) using the standard linkage conventions. The exit routine is passed the following parameter list:

```
1  | value of exit-data variable                        |

2  | panel name              |

3  | section  |

4  | message-id              |

5  | number of variables (=n)         |
```

6 | variable name$_1$ | |
    | variable name$_2$ | |

    | variable name$_n$ | |

7 | length data$_1$ |
    | length data$_2$ |

    | length data$_n$ |

8 | data$_1$ | |
    | data$_2$ | |

    | data$_n$ | |

Because such exit routines are normally written in Assembler language, the parameters will be described in Assembler syntax:

Parameter 1: Value of exit-data variable. This is the value of the optional exit-data dialogue variable passed in the PANEXIT statement. This parameter contains 0 if no exit-data is specified.
```
DS    F
```

Parameter 2: Panel name. This is the name of the panel which issues the PANEXIT statement.
```
DS    CL8
```

Parameter 3: Section. This parameter contains the identification of the panel section which invoked the exit.
```
DS    CL1 I = )INIT, P = )PROC, R = )REINIT
```

Parameter 4: Message identifier. The exit routine can return the message-id of the message to be displayed if the exit-routine return code is set to 8. If no message identifier is specified, either the message specified in the panel exit or a default message will be displayed in an error situation.
```
DS    CL8
```

Parameter 5: Number of variables. This parameter contains the number of variables returned. The variable name, its value and the length of the value are returned in the respective parameters.
```
DS    F    number of variables (=n)
```

Parameter 6: Array of variable names. The name of each variable specified in the PANEXIT statement is stored in this parameter. Parameter 5 contains the number of elements in this array.
```
DS    nCL8   variable names
```

Parameter 7: Array of variable value lengths. The length of the corresponding value for each variable name is contained as an element of this array. Parameter 5 contains the number of elements in this array.
```
DS    nF    length of corresponding value
```

Parameter 8: Array of values. The value for each variable specified in the PANEXIT statement is stored in this parameter. The values are stored as a string of characters. Parameter 5 contains the number of elements in this array. Parameter 7 contains the length of each element in this array.
```
DS    CLm   values
```

Example:
If the variables PNO and NAME contain 4096 and ALPHA, respectively, the statement
```
PANEXIT ((PNO,NAME),PGM,&EXAD,MSG=DMMMM999)
```
invoked from the)PROC section passes the following parameters to the exit routine:
```
DC    F'0'
DC    CL8'panelname'
DC    C'P'
DC    CL8'DMMMM999'
DC    F'2'
DC    CL8'PNO',CL8'NAME'
DC    F'4',F'5'
DC    C'4096ALPHA'
```

Note: The variable EXAD must have been previously defined with the address of the exit routine. Section 14.12 contains a fully worked example of a panel exit program.

The panel exit routine must set one of the following return codes:

    0   Normal completion; no message will be displayed.

    8   Exit routine has detected an error; the associated message will be displayed.

  20 Severe error. This code is also set if the exit routine sets a code other than 0 or 8.

14.11 PROGRAM EXAMPLES

A simple example program written in PL/I, COBOL, Assembler and C/370 follows. This program uses the ISPLINK and ISPEXEC services to display and redisplay a panel. The redisplay is made by setting the panel name to blank and reinvoking the service. For simplicity, the programs incorporate limited error handling — the service return code is only displayed (except for Assembler which does not have any standard service to display a numeric value).

For flexibility, all the programs dynamically load the ISPF service routines. COBOL supports dynamic loading automatically (by setting the DYNAM (standard) compiler option).

The equivalent CLIST:

```
SET &PN = XPAN
ISPEXEC DISPLAY PANEL(&PN)
WRITE &LASTCC /* display service return code */
SET &PN = &STR() /* clear &PN */
ISPEXEC DISPLAY PANEL(&PN)
WRITE &LASTCC /* display service return code */
```

This sample program illustrates the compactness of a CLIST application compared with program implementations.

14.11.1 Sample PL/I Program

```
PXSPF: PROC OPTIONS(MAIN);
DCL PLIRETV BUILTIN;
DCL SYSPRINT FILE STREAM OUTPUT PRINT EXTERNAL;

DCL ISPLINK ENTRY EXTERNAL OPTIONS(ASM,INTER,RETCODE);
DCL ISPEXEC ENTRY EXTERNAL OPTIONS(ASM,INTER,RETCODE);

DCL 1 PANEL CHAR(8) INIT('XPAN1');
DCL 1 BUF CHAR(20) INIT('DISPLAY PANEL(XPAN1)');
DCL 1 BUFL FIXED BIN(31,0) INIT(0);
/* ISPLINK invocation */
FETCH ISPLINK;              /* load address of entry point */
CALL ISPLINK('DISPLAY',PANEL);
PUT SKIP LIST('RC:',PLIRETV);

PANEL = ' ';
CALL ISPLINK('DISPLAY',PANEL);
PUT SKIP LIST('RC:',PLIRETV);

/* ISPEXEC invocation */
FETCH ISPEXEC;              /* load address of entry point */
BUFL = 20; /* BUFFER LENGTH */
CALL ISPEXEC(BUFL,BUF);
PUT SKIP LIST('RC:',PLIRETV);

BUFL = 7;
CALL ISPEXEC(BUFL,BUF);
PUT SKIP LIST('RC:',PLIRETV);

END;
```

14.11.2 Sample COBOL Program

```
IDENTIFICATION DIVISION.
PROGRAM-ID. BXSPF.
ENVIRONMENT DIVISION.
DATA DIVISION.
WORKING-STORAGE SECTION.
01 V-DISPLAY PIC X(8) VALUE 'DISPLAY'.
01 V-PANEL PIC X(8).
```

```
       *
       01 BUF-LEN PIC S9(9) BINARY.
       01 BUF PIC X(80).
       PROCEDURE DIVISION.
       * ISPLINK invocation
           MOVE 'PAN1' TO V-PANEL
           CALL 'ISPLINK' USING V-DISPLAY V-PANEL
           DISPLAY 'RETURN-CODE:' RETURN-CODE
       * redisplay
           MOVE ' ' TO V-PANEL
           CALL 'ISPLINK' USING V-DISPLAY V-PANEL
           DISPLAY 'RETURN-CODE:' RETURN-CODE
           MOVE 'DISPLAY PANEL(PAN1)' TO BUF
       * ISPEXEC invocation
           MOVE 19 TO BUF-LEN
           CALL 'ISPEXEC' USING BUF-LEN BUF
           DISPLAY 'RETURN-CODE:' RETURN-CODE
       * redisplay
           MOVE 8 TO BUF-LEN
           CALL 'ISPEXEC' USING BUF-LEN BUF
           DISPLAY 'RETURN-CODE:' RETURN-CODE
           STOP RUN.
```

14.11.3 Sample Assembler Program

```
AXSPF    CSECT
* initialise addressing
         STM    14,12,12(13)  save registers
         BALR   12,0  set base register
         USING  *,12
         LA     15,SA  A(save-area)
         ST     13,4(15)  backward ptr
         ST     15,8(13)  forward ptr
         LR     13,15  A(new save-area)
** load ISPLINK
         LOAD EP=ISPLINK
         LR     2,0  save ISPLINK load-point address
**
         LR     15,2
         CALL   (15),(DISPLAY,PAN),VL
         LTR    15,15  test return code
* redisplay
         LR     15,2
         MVC    PAN,=CL8' '
         CALL   (15),(DISPLAY,PAN),VL
         LTR    15,15  test return code
** load ISPEXEC
         LOAD EP=ISPEXEC
         LR     2,0    save ISPEXEC load-point address
**
         LR     15,2
         MVC    BUFL,=F'20'
         CALL   (15),(BUFL,BUF)
         LTR    15,15  test return code
* redisplay
         LR     15,2
         MVC    BUFL,=F'7'
         CALL   (15),(BUFL,BUF)
```

```
          LTR   15,15   test return code
**
          L     13,4(13)   restore A(old save-area)
          RETURN (14,12)
SA        DS    18F
DISPLAY   DC    CL8'DISPLAY'
PAN       DC    CL8'XPAN1'
BUFL      DS    F
BUF       DC    C'DISPLAY PANEL(XPAN1)'
          END
```

14.11.4 Sample C/370 Program

```c
/* CXSPF */
#pragma linkage (OSFUNC,OS)
typedef int OSFUNC();

#include <stdlib.h>
#include <string.h>
#include <stdio.h>

void main()
{
  int rc;
  OSFUNC *fptr;
  char pan[9];
  char buf[256];
  int buflen;

  /* ISPLINK invocation */
  fptr = (OSFUNC *)fetch("ISPLINK");
  if (fptr == NULL)
  {
    puts("fetch error");
    exit(4);
  }
  strcpy(pan,"PAN1    ");
  rc = (*fptr)("DISPLAY ",pan);
  printf("RC:%d\n",rc);

  /* redisplay */
  strcpy(pan," ");
  rc =  (*fptr)("DISPLAY ",pan);
  printf("RC:%d\n",rc);

  /* ISPEXEC invocation */
  fptr = (OSFUNC *)fetch("ISPEXEC");
  if (fptr == NULL)
  {
    puts("fetch error");
    exit(4);
  }

  strcpy(buf,"DISPLAY PANEL(PAN1)");
  buflen = strlen(buf);
  rc = (*fptr)(buflen,buf);
  printf("RC:%d\n",rc);
```

```
/* redisplay */
strcpy(buf,"DISPLAY");
buflen = strlen(buf);
rc = (*fptr)(buflen,buf);
printf("RC:%d\n",rc);

return;
}
```

14.12 SAMPLE PANEL EXIT

Panel:

```
)ATTR
)BODY
%EX01 ------ Display Panel -----------+
%COMMAND ===>_ZCMD
+
+Persno. ===>_PNO +
+Name     ===>_NAME                    +
+
)INIT
)PROC
IF (.RESP EQ ENTER)
  PANEXIT ((PNO,NAME),PGM,&EXAD)
)END
```

The panel exit program consists of two parts:
· initialisation
· panel exit processing.

The initialisation sets the address of the panel exit processing routine in the ISPF variable EXAD and then displays the panel as defined above.

The panel exit processing routine is invoked by the following statement.

```
PANEXIT ((PNO,NAME),PGM,&EXAD)
```

This invocation passes two variables (PNO and NAME) to the exit processing routine. The sample exit processing routine determines whether the personnel number (PNO) is divisible by 3. An error message (DMMMM001) is issued and the return code is set to 8 if the validation fails.

Sample panel exit program:

```
DMPGM03  CSECT
* Initialisation section
* Initialise addressing
         STM   14,12,12(13)        save registers
         BALR  12,0                set base register
         USING *,12
         LA    15,SA1              A(save-area)
```

```
              ST     13,4(15)              backward ptr
              ST     15,8(13)              forward ptr
              LR     13,15                 A(new save-area)
              SPACE
* pass address of exit routine to ISPF
              CALL   ISPLINK,(VDEFINE,VN_EXAD,EXADDR,FIXED,VL_4),VL
REDISPL  CALL   ISPLINK,(DISPLAY,PN),VL display panel
              CH     15,=H'4'              check for END
              BNH    REDISPL               redisplay
              L      13,4(13)              restore A(old save-area)
              LA     15,0                  set ReturnCode
              RETURN (14,12),RC=(15)
SA1           DS     18A                   save-area
* ISPF constants
VDEFINE  DC     CL8'VDEFINE'
FIXED    DC     CL8'FIXED'
DISPLAY  DC     CL8'DISPLAY'
PN       DC     CL8'EX01'             panel name
VN_EXAD  DC     CL8'EXAD'             name of variable containing
VL_4     DC     F'4'                  constant
EXADDR   DC     A(PANEXIT)            address of exit routine
              DROP   12

PANEXIT  DS     0H
* Actual exit routine,
* personnel number (first data field) must be a multiple of 3.
* Initialise addressing
              STM    14,12,12(13)          save registers
              BALR   12,0                  set base register
              USING  *,12
              LA     15,SA2                A(save-area)
              ST     13,4(15)              backward ptr
              ST     15,8(13)              forward ptr
              LR     13,15                 A(new save-area)
              LM     2,9,0(1)
* P1: A(EXDATA)
* P2: A(PANNAME); panel name (CL8)
* P3: A(PANSECT); panel section (CL1)
* P4: A(MSGID); message-id (CL8)
* P5: A(ARAYDIM); dimension of VARNAME and VARLEN (=n)
* P6: A(VARNAME); array of dialogue variable names (nCL8)
* P7: A(VARLEN); array of variable lengths (nFL4)
* P8: A(VARVAL); array of dialogue variable values
              L      1,0(8)                L(PNO variable)
              BCTR   1,0                   LC(PNO variable)
              EX     1,PACK                pack into dwd
              LA     15,0                  preset ReturnCode (ok)
              DP     D,=P'3'               divide by 3
              CP     D+7(1),=P'0'          check remainder
              BE     RETURN                :ok
              LA     15,8                  set ReturnCode (nok)
              MVC    0(8,5),MSGID          set message
RETURN   L      13,4(13)              restore A(old save-area)
              RETURN (14,12),RC=(15)
SA2      DS     18A                   save-area
PACK     PACK   D,0(0,9)              EX instruction
D        DS     PL8                   doubleword (work-area)
MSGID    DC     CL8'DMMMM001'
              END
```

14.12.1 Generalised Panel Exit

Because Dialog Manager applications are usually written in REXX, it would be natural also to write panel exits in REXX. Unfortunately, the panel exit routine must be a program. The following generalised panel exit program passes control to the specified REXX procedure, which then performs the required processing. This REXX procedure is subject to the same restrictions as for panel exit programs (i.e. it cannot invoke ISPF services, and the lengths of the passed parameters cannot be changed).

14.12.2.1 Invocation Sequence. As for panel exits, this PANEXIT statement appears in the processing section.

```
PANEXIT ((procname,ddname[,var]...),LOAD,PANEXPGM)
```

procname
> The name of the REXX procedure that is to be invoked.

ddname
> The name of the file that contains the REXX procedure.

var
> The name of a dialogue variable whose content is to be passed to the REXX procedure.

Example ()PROC panel statements):
```
&PROCNAME = RX2 /* name of REXX exec */
&DDNAME = SYSPROC /* DDname of the library that contains the REXX exec
*/
&VAR2 = '               ' /* clear target field in the maximum length */
PANEXIT ((PROCNAME,DDNAME,VAR1,VAR2),LOAD,PANEXPGM)
```

RX2 REXX procedure:
```
/* REXX - RX2 */
/* convert ISPF variable from hex to character */
PARSE ARG P1, L1, P2, L2;
inparm = STORAGE(P1,L1); /* source variable */
outparm = X2C(inparm);
outparm =LEFT(outparm,L2,' ');
x = STORAGE(P2,L2,outparm); /* target variable */
EXIT 0; /* normal return */
```

This procedure receives a character string as input (first) parameter and returns the hexadecimal equivalent as output (second) parameter. For example, "123A" is returned as "F1F2F3C1".

Because parameter addresses and lengths are passed to the panel exit routine, the REXX STORAGE function must be used to associate REXX variables with these data areas.

14.12.2.2 PANEXPGM Program Code.

```
PANEXPGM CSECT
PANEXPGM AMODE 31
PANEXPGM RMODE ANY
         BAKR  14,0                  save regs and return address
         BALR  12,0                  set base register
         USING *,12
         LM    5,8,16(1)             get arguments
* R5: A(array dimension)
* R6: A(varname-array, each element CHAR(8))
* R7: A(varlen-array, each element F)
* R8: A(varvalue-array)
*     The first element is the name of the processing REXX exec,
*     the second element is the name of the DD for the exec,
*     the subsequent elements are application-specific
         LA    13,SA
         MVC   4(4,13),=C'F1ST'      indicate stack used
         L     3,0(5)                dimension (no. of entries)
         CH    3,=H'2'               minimum(2 parameters)
         BL    ERROR                 error (invalid no. of parms)
         CH    3,=AL2(MAXPARM)
         BH    ERROR                 error (too many parms)
* first value (exec-name)
         L     2,0(7)                L(first value)
         CH    2,=H'8'
         BH    ERROR                 too long
         SH    2,=H'1'               LC
         BM    ERROR                 omitted
         MVC   EXEC_MEMBER(0),0(8)
         EX    2,*-6                 move member name
         LA    8,1(2,8)              A(next value)
         LA    7,4(7)                update ptr
* second value (DD-name)
         L     2,0(7)                L(second value)
         CH    2,=H'8'
         BH    ERROR                 too long
         SH    2,=H'1'               LC
         BM    ERROR                 omitted
         MVC   EXEC_DDNAME(0),0(8)
         EX    2,*-6                 move DDNAME
         LA    8,1(2,8)              A(next value)
         LA    9,ARGENTRY
         LA    10,PARMEXEC
         USING WKDSECT,10
         B     USERPARM
* user-parameters
LOOP     LA    7,4(7)                length-ptr
         ST    8,WORD                A(data)
         BAL   14,CTOX               convert to hex-format
         LA    1,HEX
         ST    1,0(9)                A(data)
         LA    1,8
         ST    1,4(9)                length
         L     2,0(7)
         CVD   2,PL8
         UNPK  WK,PL8
         OC    WK,=8C'0'
         LA    1,WK
```

```
            ST     1,8(9)            A(data)
            LA     1,8
            ST     1,12(9)           length
            LA     8,0(2,8)          A(next value)
            LA     9,16(9)
            LA     10,16(10)         A(next exec parameter)
USERPARM BCT     3,LOOP
            MVC    0(8,9),=2F'-1'    set end of ArgList
            CALL   IRXEXEC,                                              X
                   (AEXECBLK,AARGLIST,FLAGS,A0,A0,AEVALBLK,A0,A0),VL
            SR     15,15             zeroise
            IC     15,EVAL_EVDATA    ReturnCode from exec
            N      15,=X'0000000F'   clear high-order
EOJ         PR     ,                 terminate program
ERROR       LA     15,4              processing error
            B      EOJ
CTOX        DS     0H  convert characters (WORD) to hex (HEX)
            LA     1,WORD            A(source)
            LA     0,4               length
            LA     15,HEX            A(target)
CTOXLOOP MVC    0(1,15),0(1)      1st half-byte
            TR     0(1,15),TRTAB1
            MVC    1(1,15),0(1)      2nd half-byte
            TR     1(1,15),TRTAB2
            LA     1,1(1)
            LA     15,2(15)
            BCT    0,CTOXLOOP
            BR     14                return
            LTORG
** data areas
MAXPARM  EQU    10                maximum number of arguments
SA          DS     18F
WORD        DS     F
PL8         DS     0D,PL8
A0          DC     A(0)              zero constant
AARGLIST DC     A(ARGENTRY)
** ARGLIST definition
ARGENTRY DS     (MAXPARM*4)A      pointer, length
            DC     2F'-1'            end
PARMEXEC DS     (MAXPARM*2)CL8
FLAGS       DC     X'80000000'       exec invoked as command
AEXECBLK DC     A(EXECBLK)
** EXECBLOCK definition
EXECBLK  DC     CL8'IRXEXECB'
            DC     A(EXECBLKE-EXECBLK) L(EXECBLK)
            DS     F                 reserved
EXEC_MEMBER DC CL8' '               member name
EXEC_DDNAME DC CL8' '               DDname name
            DC     CL8' ',A(0),A(0)
EXECBLKE EQU    *                 end of EXECBLOCK
AEVALBLK DC     A(EVALBLOCK)
** EVALBLOCK definition
EVALBLOCK   DS 0F
EVAL_EVPAD1 DC F'0'
EVAL_EVSIZE DC A((EVALBLOCKE-EVALBLOCK)/8)
EVAL_EVLEN  DS F
EVAL_EVPAD2 DC F'0'
EVAL_EVDATA DS CL8
EVALBLOCKE EQU *                     end of EVALBLOCK
```

```
* translation tables
TRTAB1  DC      16C'0',16C'1',16C'2',16C'3',16C'4',16C'5',16C'6',16C'7'
        DC      16C'8',16C'9',16C'A',16C'B',16C'C',16C'D',16C'E',16C'F'
TRTAB2  DC      16C'0123456789ABCDEF'
** DSECTs
WKDSECT DSECT
HEX     DS      CL8
WK      DS      CL8
        END
```

15

Help Mode

15.1 INTRODUCTION

Help mode can be considered as being a **sub-application** running parallel to the main application. This sub-application consists of **help panels**. These help panels can be linked together to form a dialogue. The help dialogue is controlled by the **help tutorial program** (ISPTUTOR).

Help mode may be entered in the following ways:

· Invoke HELP. If a message has been displayed, help information associated with the message (e.g. long message) is displayed. If no message has been displayed, depending on the cursor position, help information associated with the panel, or field (field-help) or reference phrase is displayed. The .HELP control variable contains the name of the associated help panel.
· Invoke the HELP program. The HELP program is called with the name of the help panel to be displayed as parameter.

In help mode a number of specific commands are available to navigate through the help dialogue:

· TOC (or T) — display table of contents;
· INDEX (or I) — display index;
· SKIP (or S) — display next topic;
· UP (or U) — display higher level topic;
· BACK (or B) — display previous help panel.

Help panels can be directly associated with:

· messages
· display or select panels
· named fields (field-help)
· text (reference phrases).

The relationship between application dialogue and help is shown in Figure 15.1.

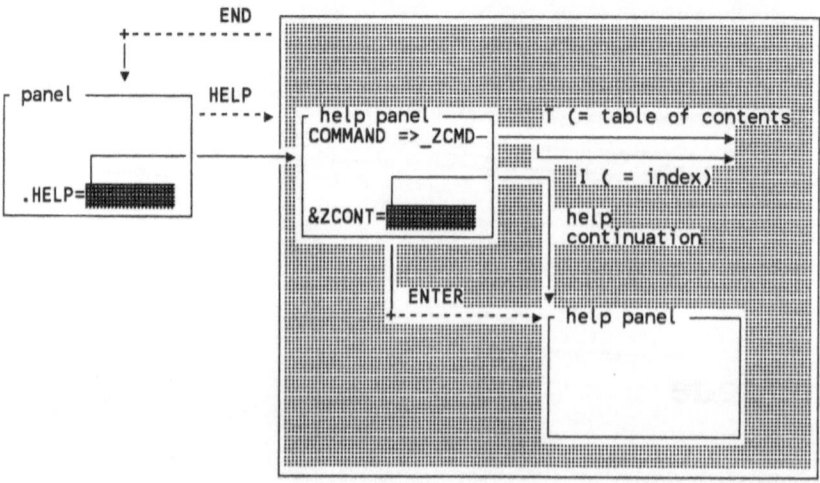

:::::: help environment

Figure 15.1 - Relationship between application dialogue and help

15.2 HELP PANEL

A help panel has the form of a display panel with the following restrictions:

· The panel must have a command field named zcmd.
· The name of the next (help) panel to be displayed is contained in the field zsel.

Table 15.1 lists those following system control variables which may be used in the help dialogue. These variables may be set in panels, CLISTs, etc.

Table 15.1 - System control variables which may be used in the help dialogue.

ZUP	Name of parent panel
ZCONT	Name of the continuation help panel
ZHTOP	Name of the "top" help panel
ZHINDEX	Name of the index panel
ZIND	ZIND=YES, identifies the index panel

15.3 STANDARD HELP PANEL

A **standard** help panel is displayed in response to the help command. The help panel is associated with either a message or a panel. A **logical** help panel can consist of continuation help panels. The ZCONT system variable contains the name of the continuation help panel. This panel is displayed by pressing the ENTER key. If no continuation help panel is defined, the table of contents help panel is displayed. Control is returned to the original panel by pressing the END key.

The relationship between message, panel and help panel is illustrated in Figure 15.2; ▮▮▮▮▮▮▮ represents the name of a help panel.

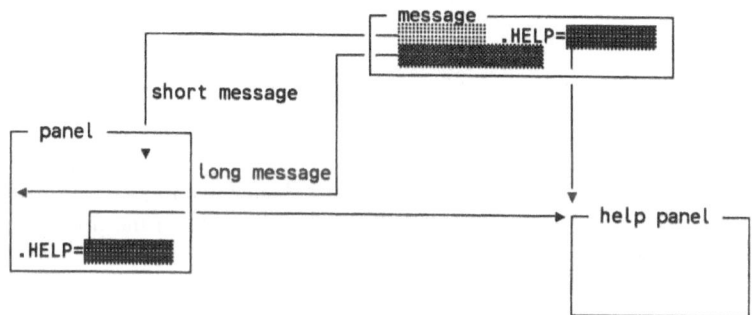

Figure 15.2 - Relationship between message, panel and help panel

15.4 TABLE OF CONTENTS

The **table of contents** help panel is that panel named in the ZHTOP system variable or the panel name passed as parameter to the tutorial program:

· ZHTOP = panelname
· ISPEXEC SELECT PGM(ISPTUTOR) PARM(panelname)

The table of contents help panel is displayed by entering the TOC command while in help mode. Figure 15.3 shows the relationship of the table of contents.

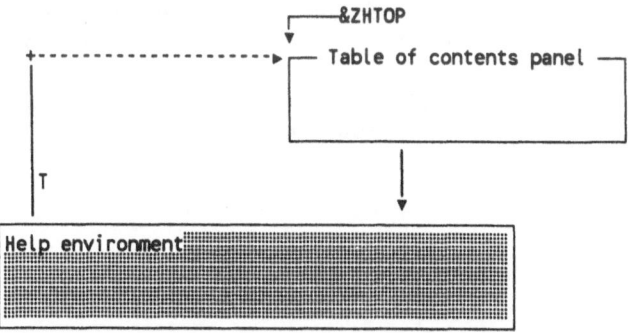

Figure 15.3 — Table of contents

The table of contents can be used in one of two ways:

- A specific (help) **topic** is selected.
- Help topics are displayed sequentially.

Note: A topic is a logical help panel, i.e. a series of one or more physical help panels linked by ZCONT.

The name of the help panel to be displayed is set in the ZSEL variable. The order in which topics are sequentially displayed is defined in the TRANS list. A table of contents may be continued by setting the name of the continuation panel in the ZCONT variable.

Example:
```
&ZSEL = TRANS(&ZCMD
      1,TSEXMH01
      2,TSEXMH02
      3,TSEXMH10)
```
Option 1 displays help panel TSEXMH01, option 2 displays help panel TSEXMH02, etc.; sequential processing (no option input) displays the topics in the order: TSEXMH01, TSEXMH02, TSEXMH10.

If the panel name in the selection list is prefixed with "*" (asterisk), that panel is not displayed during sequential (tutorial) processing, e.g.
```
&ZSEL = TRANS(&ZCMD
      1,TSEXMH01
      2,*TSEXMH02
      3,TSEXMH10)
```
displays the topics in the order: TSEXMH01, TSEXMH10 during sequential processing.

Note: There is no restriction in the number of table of contents defined in the help application. However, only one table of contents may be active at any one time, namely that defined in ZHTOP.

15.5 INDEX

The **index** help panel is that panel named in the ZHINDEX system variable. This panel must identify itself as being the index panel by setting &ZIND=YES in its initialisation section.

The index help panel is displayed by entering the INDEX command while in help mode. Figure 15.4 shows an index structure.

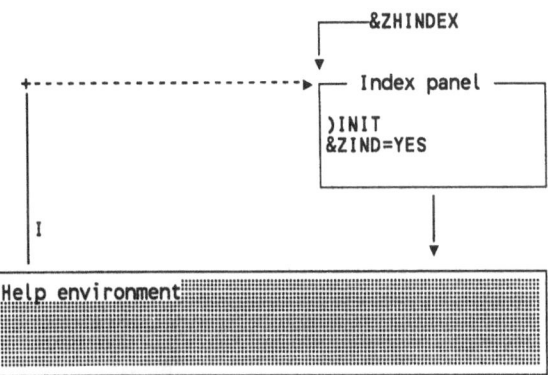

Figure 15.4 — Index structure

An **index** is essentially the same as a table of contents, it offers another means of navigating through the help panels. The only difference is that with an index the table of contents is displayed at the end of sequential processing. The name of the next help panel to be displayed is set in the ZSEL variable. The order in which topics are sequentially displayed is defined in the TRANS list. Control is passed to the table of contents at the end of the list.

An index may be continued by setting the name of the continuation index panel in the ZCONT variable.

Example:
```
&ZSEL = TRANS(&ZCMD
        1,TSEXMH11
        2,TSEXMH12
        3,TSEXMH20)
```
Option 1 displays help panel TSEXMH11, option 2 displays help panel TSEXMH12, etc.; sequential processing (no option input) displays the topics in the order: TSEXMH11, TSEXMH12, TSEXMH20.

If the panel name in the selection list is prefixed with "*" (asterisk), that panel is not displayed during sequential processing, e.g.
```
&ZSEL = TRANS(&ZCMD
        1,TSEXMH11
        2,*TSEXMH12
        3,TSEXMH20)
```
displays the topics in the order: TSEXMH11, TSEXMH20 and the table of contents, if one exists, during sequential processing.

15.6 HELP PANEL HIERARCHY

The hierarchy of help panels is illustrated in Figure 15.5.

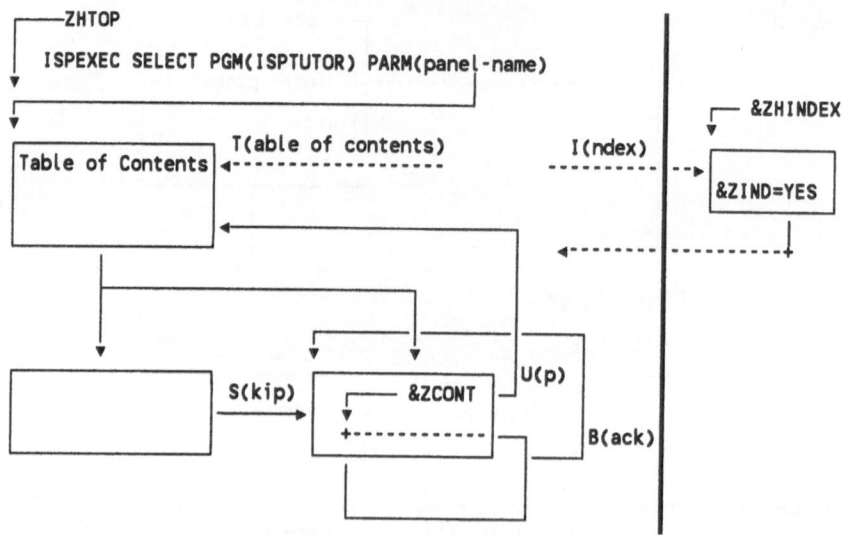

Figure 15.5 - Help panel hierarchy

Tip

There is no major difference between an index panel and a table of contents. They should be used to represent two distinct access paths to the help panels:

·   by a (sorted) index
·   by topic.

15.7 FIELD-HELP

Field-help refers to a help panel that is associated with a named field. Field helps are defined in the)HELP section, in which fields are linked to a help panel. Field-help takes priority over panel help; if the cursor is positioned in a field for which field-help has been defined and the HELP PF-key is pressed, the associated help panel is shown (otherwise the panel help panel is shown).

Example:

```
)ATTR
# TYPE(INPUT)
a TYPE(OUTPUT)
+ TYPE(TEXT)
)BODY
+  Surname :#SNAME          +
+First Name:#FNAME          +
)INIT
.HELP = PAN1H /* panel help
)HELP
 FIELD(SNAME) PANEL(PANF1H)
 FIELD(FNAME) PANEL(PANF2H)
)END
```

15.8 REFERENCE PHRASE

Reference phrases are similar to field help, but are used to associate a help panel with a text field. Because a text field does not have a name, a pseudo-name (zRPmmnnn; mm = scrollable area number (00 = normal field); nnn = reference phrase number within the scrollable area or body section (for normal field) is assigned to the reference phrases. Reference phrases have the RP attribute. Reference phrase helps are defined in the)HELP section, in which the reference phrases are linked to a help panel. Reference phrases take priority over panel help; if the cursor is positioned in a reference phrase and the HELP PF-key is pressed, the associated help panel is shown (otherwise the panel help panel is shown).

Example:
```
)ATTR
# TYPE(INPUT)
a TYPE(RP)
+ TYPE(TEXT)
)BODY
a  Surname :#SNAME          +
aFirst Name:#FNAME          +
)INIT
 .HELP = PAN1H /* panel help
)HELP
 FIELD(ZRP00001) PANEL(PANF1H) /* surname
 FIELD(ZRP00002) PANEL(PANF2H) /* first name
)END
```

15.9 DEFINITION OF HELP PANELS

Although a help panel has the general form of a display panel, there are some aspects that affect the definition of help panels.

Most well-implemented applications offer extensive online help. For example, one or more help panels for the display panel, field helps for each input field, reference phrase (helps) for each explanatory text, etc. (together with an associated tutorial). This means that a small application with ten panels, each of which has ten input fields, could easily have more than two hundred help panels (10 panel helps, 100 field helps, 100 reference phrase helps). This large number of panels has maintenance repercussions; the change to a single display panel may affect up to 21 associated help panels. Dynamic formatting of help panels can be used to greatly reduce the number of help panels.

15.9.1 Dynamically Formatted Help Panels

Dynamically formatted help panels are help panel skeletons that contain one or more text fields (or variables) that the associated panel sets at invocation time. For example, each display panel in the previous example could use the same set of field-level help panels, which are assigned the appropriate text on invocation. If dynamic areas are used in the help panels, the assigned data can incorporate attribute characters (for highlighting, etc.). This method is appropriate only when the help panels have the same form.

Example:

The following example has two display panels, each of which has two input fields.
Each panel assigns the appropriate help text to the two text fields in the field help
panels. For simplicity, only a single line of the help text is shown, although
multiple lines could be used. Similarly, because the panel-level helps (PAN1H and
PAN2H) are not directly concerned with dynamically formatted help panels, they are
omitted from the example (although the same method can be used in such panels).

Panel 1:

```
)ATTR
# TYPE(INPUT)
@ TYPE(OUTPUT)
+ TYPE(TEXT)
)BODY
+  Surname :#SNAME          +
+First Name:#FNAME          +
)INIT
 .HELP = PAN1H /* panel help
 &HTEXT1 = 'Surname help.'
 &HTEXT2 = 'First name help.'
)HELP
 FIELD(SNAME) PANEL(PANF1H)
 FIELD(FNAME) PANEL(PANF2H)
)END
```

Panel 2:

```
)ATTR
# TYPE(INPUT)
@ TYPE(OUTPUT)
+ TYPE(TEXT)
)BODY
+    Dialing Code:#DCODE        +
+Telephone Number:#TELNUM    +
)INIT
 .HELP = PAN2H /* panel help
 &HTEXT1 = 'Dialing code help.'
 &HTEXT2 = 'Telephone number help.'
)HELP
 FIELD(DCODE) PANEL(PANF1H)
 FIELD(TELNUME) PANEL(PANF2H)
)END
```

Help Panel 1:

```
)ATTR
+ TYPE(TEXT)
)BODY
+     Field Help
+&HTEXT1
)END
```

Help Panel 2:

```
)ATTR
+ TYPE(TEXT)
)BODY
+     Field Help
+&HTEXT2
)END
```

15.10 EXAMPLE

```
┌─ TSPAN001 panel ──────────────────────────────
│)BODY
│+----------------------------------------------------
│%COMMAND ===>_ZCMD
│+
│%Employee number ===>_PNO +
│%Surname          ===>_NAME            +
│)INIT
│.HELP=TSPANH01
│&ZHTOP=TSPANT00
│&ZHINDEX=TSPANX00
│)PROC
│ VER(&PNO,NB,NUM,MSG=TSMSG005)
│)END
```

Panel TSPAN001 makes the following definitions:

- Panel help TSPANH01
- Table of contents panel TSPANT01
- Index panel TSPANX01.

The following message definition TSMSG005 has TSMSGH04 as the associated help panel:

```
┌─ TSMSG005 message ───────────────
│TSMSG005 'NOT NUMERIC' .HELP=TSMSGH04
│'PERSONNEL NUMBER &PNO NOT NUMERIC'
```

TSPANH01 help panel:

```
┌─ TSPANH01 help panel ──────────────────────────────────────┐
│ )BODY                                                        │
│ +------------------------------------------------------     │
│ %COMMAND ===>_ZCMD                                           │
│ +                                                            │
│ %This is a help panel for panel TSPAN001;                    │
│ %there is continuation for this help panel.                  │
│ +                                                            │
│ %ENTER - display help table of contents                      │
│ %END   - return to original display panel                    │
│ )INIT                                                        │
│ )END                                                         │
└────────────────────────────────────────────────────────────┘
```

The two help panels (TSMSGH05 is a continuation of TSMSGH04) for message TSMSG005 follow:

```
┌─ TSMSGH04 help panel ──────────────────────────────────────┐
│ )BODY                                                        │
│ +------------------------------------------------------     │
│ %COMMAND ===>_ZCMD                                           │
│ +                                                            │
│ %This is a help panel for message TSMSG004;                  │
│ +                                                            │
│ %ENTER - continue                                            │
│ %END   - return to original display panel                    │
│ )INIT                                                        │
│ &ZCONT=TSMSGH05                                              │
│ )END                                                         │
└────────────────────────────────────────────────────────────┘
```

```
┌─ TSMSGH05 help panel ──────────────────────────────────────┐
│ )BODY                                                        │
│ +------------------------------------------------------     │
│ %COMMAND ===>_ZCMD                                           │
│ +                                                            │
│ %This is the continuation of panel TSMSGH04;                 │
│ %this panel has no continuation.                             │
│ +                                                            │
│ %ENTER - display help table of contents                      │
│ %END   - return to original display panel                    │
│ )END                                                         │
└────────────────────────────────────────────────────────────┘
```

```
┌─ TSPANT01 table of contents ──────────────────────────┐
│)BODY                                                   │
│+------------------------------------------------------ │
│%COMMAND ===>_ZCMD                                      │
│+                                                       │
│%This is the TABLE OF CONTENTS,                         │
│%either select topic or press ENTER for tutorial.       │
│+                                                       │
│%1+topic 1                                              │
│%2+topic 2                                              │
│%3+topic 3                                              │
│+                                                       │
│)INIT                                                   │
│)PROC                                                   │
│ &ZSEL=TRANS(&ZCMD                                      │
│         1,TSPANH01                                     │
│         2,*TSPANH22                                    │
│         3,TSPANH13)                                    │
│)END                                                    │
└────────────────────────────────────────────────────────┘
```

Panel TSPANT01 is the table of contents. Three topics may be explicitly selected:
· Topic 1 TSPANH01
· Topic 2 TSPANH22
· Topic 3 TSPANH13.

TSPANH22 is not displayed in tutorial mode (panel name prefixed by *).

```
┌─ TSPANX01 index ──────────────────────────────────────┐
│)BODY                                                   │
│+------------------------------------------------------ │
│%COMMAND ===>_ZCMD                                      │
│+                                                       │
│%This is the INDEX                                      │
│%please select topic.                                   │
│+                                                       │
│%1+topic 1                                              │
│%2+topic 2                                              │
│%3+topic 3                                              │
│+                                                       │
│+                                                       │
│)INIT                                                   │
│ &ZIND=YES                                              │
│)PROC                                                   │
│ &ZSEL=TRANS(&ZCMD                                      │
│         1,TSPANH01                                     │
│         2,*TSPANH02                                    │
│         3,TSPANH03)                                    │
│)END                                                    │
└────────────────────────────────────────────────────────┘
```

Panel TSPANX01 is the index. Three topics may be explicitly selected:
· Topic 1 TSPANH01
· Topic 2 TSPANH02
· Topic 3 TSPANH03.

TSPANH02 is not displayed in tutorial mode (panel name prefixed by *). &ZIND=YES must be set in the index panel.

16

Miscellaneous Display Services

16.1 INTRODUCTION

Besides the object (panel, table, etc.) oriented services, ISPF provides several
miscellaneous **display** services. Although the display services are PDF components,
there are often requirements to make use of them in ISPF applications, for example,
to display a file. Furthermore, **edit macros** may be used by the edit services to
automate file processing. The features offered by edit macros are only indirectly
related to topics covered in this book and so are not discussed here.

The miscellaneous display services are listed in alphabetic order:

- BRIF   Browse interface.
- BROWSE Browse a dataset or library member.
- EDIF   Edit interface.
- EDIREC Initialise edit recovery.
- EDIT   Edit a dataset or library member.
- VIEW   View a dataset or library member.

BROWSE, EDIREC, EDIT, and VIEW are ISPEXEC services, i.e. can be invoked from a
command procedure. BRIF and EDIF are ISPLINK services, i.e. they are program
services that must be invoked from a program (e.g. Assembler).

For simplicity, the sample programs for the BRIF and EDIF services use
internally generated records rather than external files.

The processing routines (read routine, write routine, etc.) are invoked with the
standard linking conventions. All the routines operate in 31-bit addressing mode.

16.2 BRIF — BROWSE INTERFACE

The browse interface service provides browsing functions for an application program. For example, this gives an application program a simple means of displaying data that is stored in a non-supported format (e.g. DB2 table data, or installation-specific data storage methods). The application program is responsible for reading the data and any associated tasks (e.g. serialisation).

Syntax:
```
CALL ISPLINK ('BRIF',dataname,recordformat,recordlength,readroutine,
   [commandroutine],[dialoguedata],[panelname],[formatname],[dbcs]);
```

dataname
> The (optional) data name that appears in the title line of the browse panel. The first blank character terminates the name; maximum length: 54 characters.

recordformat
> The record format of the data to be browsed. The format is terminated with a blank.
>
> F   fixed
>
> FA   fixed (with ASA printer control character)
>
> FM   fixed (with machine printer control character)
>
> V   variable
>
> VA   variable (with ASA printer control character)
>
> VM   variable (with machine printer control character)
>
> U   undefined.

recordlength
> The record length (in bytes) of the data to be browsed (maximum record length for U and V format records). Format: Fullword (maximum value: 32,760).

readroutine
> The address of the entry-point of the routine that supplies the read records.

commandroutine
> The (optional) address of the entry-point of the routine that processes browse primary commands.

dialoguedata
> The (optional) address of the data area that is passed to the processing routines.

panelname
> The (optional) name of the panel that is used for the data display. Format: CL8. Default: The standard browse panel.

formatname

The (optional) name of the format that is used to reformat the data. This parameter is used only with DBCS on an IBM 5550 display terminal. Format: CL8.

dbcs

This keyword specifies whether mixed-mode DBCS data is present (YES). Default: NO.

The service sets one of the return codes:

- 0 Normal completion.
- 12 No data.
- 16 Unexpected return code received from a processing routine.
- 20 Severe error.

16.2.1 Read Routine

The read routine is called repeatedly to supply a record until the read routine signals end-of-data.

The read routine has the following interface conditions.

16.2.1.1 Entry Parameters

Parameter 1 (address) — Pointer to the read record (set by the read routine).

Parameter 2 (fullword) — The length of the read record (set by the read routine for U and V format record).

Parameter 3 (fullword) — The relative record number.

Parameter 4 (address) — Pointer to the dialogue data area.

16.2.1.2 Exit Parameters

Return code (register 15):

- 0 Normal return.
- 4 Temporary end-of-file.
- 8 Permanent end-of-file.
- 16 Read error.
- 20 Severe error.

If end-of-file is set, the read routine must set the corresponding relative record number in parameter 3.

16.2.2 Command Routine

If present, the command routine processes the BROWSE primary commands and any dialogue-specific primary commands.

16.2.2.1 Entry Parameters

Parameter 1 (fullword) — Command type:

    10   Recursive browse

    20   Non-BROWSE command; the ZCMD variable contains the command.

Parameter 2 (address) — Pointer to the dialogue data area.

16.2.2.2 Exit Parameters

Return code (register 15):

    0   Normal return.

    4   ISPF/PDF should process the command.

    12   Command deferred (redisplay with input command).

    20   Severe error.

16.2.3 Example

The sample program generates 80 records. Each record is one byte longer than the previous record (the first record is 40 bytes long).

Sample program:

```
      * driver routine
      TBRIF   CSECT
      TBRIF   AMODE 31
              BAKR  14,0                save return address and registers
              BALR  10,0                set base register
              USING *,10
              LA    13,SA               set internal save-area
              MVC   4(4,13),=C'F1SA'    indicate stack used
      * invoke Browse Interface
              CALL  ISPLINK,(VBRIF,DATANAME,RECFM,LRECL,AREADRTN),VL
      EOJ     PR    ,                   terminate driver program
      ** read routine
      READRTN BALR  15,0
              USING *,15
              STM   0,14,RSA
              BALR  11,0
              USING *,11
              LM    2,5,0(1)
      * GPR2: A(record)
      * GPR3: F'record length'
      * GPR4: F'record number'
      * GPR5: A(dialog data area)
              LA    0,MYREC
              ST    0,0(2)
              L     0,0(4)              record no.
              CVD   0,RECNO
              C     0,=F'80'
              BH    READEOF
      * R0: record number
      * generate record size (40 + <RECNO>)
              LA    1,40
              AR    1,0                 40 + <RECNO>
```

```
          ST     1,0(3)            record size
          LA     15,0
READRTNX  LM     0,14,RSA
          BR     14     return
READEOF   LA     15,4              EOF
          B      READRTNX          exit
**
MYREC     DC     100C'12345'
VBRIF     DC     CL8'BRIF'
DATANAME  DC     C'MY-FILE '
RECFM     DC     C'V '
LRECL     DC     F'60'
AREADRTN  DC     A(READRTN)
SA        DS     18F
RSA       DS     18F
          END
```

16.3 BROWSE - BROWSE A DATASET OR LIBRARY MEMBER

The BROWSE service invokes the PDF browse service to display a dataset or library member.

Syntax:
```
ISPEXEC BROWSE DATASET(datasetname)
        [VOLUME(volumeserial)]
        [PASSWORD(password)]
        [PANEL(panelname)]
```

DATASET(datasetname)
> **Datasetname** is the name of the dataset or library (partitioned dataset) to be browsed. **Datasetname** is specified in TSO syntax. A fully qualified dataset name is specified within apostrophes. The current TSO userid prefix is appended in front of a dataset name specified without apostrophes.

> Example of fully qualified dataset name:
> ```
> DATASET('ALPHA.DATA')
> ```

> Example of implicit dataset name:
> ```
> DATASET(ALPHA.DATA)
> ```
> If the TSO userid prefix is TSAB123, this dataset name specification is equivalent to the fully qualified dataset name:
> ```
> DATASET('TSAB123.ALPHA.DATA')
> ```

> If a partitioned dataset is being processed, the member name may be specified within parentheses, otherwise a member list will be displayed.

> Example:
> ```
> DATASET('ALPHA.DATA(BETA)')
> ```
> This example specifies member BETA from the dataset 'ALPHA.DATA'.

VOLUME(volumeserial)

Volumeserial is the serial number of the volume containing the dataset. This parameter is only required for datasets which are not catalogued.

Example:
```
DATASET('ALPHA.DATA') VOLUME(123456)
```
This example specifies that the dataset 'ALPHA.DATA' is contained on the volume with serial number 123456.

PASSWORD(password)

Password is the password required to access the dataset. This parameter is only required for datasets which are password protected.

PANEL(panelname)

Panelname is the name of the panel which is to be used for the dataset display. This panel must conform to the specifications for a customised browse panel (described in the IBM manual: ISPF and ISPF/PDF Installation and Customization).

The service sets one of the following return codes:

    0   Normal completion.
   12   Empty member or dataset.
   14   Member not found.
   16   Partitioned dataset specified contains no members.
   20   Severe error.

Example:
```
ISPEXEC BROWSE DATASET(ALPHA.TEXT)
```
Browse (display) the dataset ALPHA.TEXT.

Tip

The browse service is useful to list the content of temporary files created by file tailoring, e.g.
```
ISPEXEC VGET (ZTEMPF) SHARED
ISPEXEC BROWSE DATASET('&ZTEMPF')
```

16.4 EDIF — EDIT INTERFACE

The edit interface service provides editing functions for an application program. For example, this gives an application program a simple means of changing data that is stored in a non-supported format (e.g. DB2 table data, or installation-specific data storage methods). The application program is responsible for reading and writing the data and any associated tasks (e.g. serialisation).

Syntax:
```
    CALL ISPLINK ('EDIF',dataname,profilename,recordformat,recordlength,

    readroutine,writeroutine,[commandroutine],[dialoguedata],[editlength],
        [panelname],[macroname],[formatname],[dbcs],[recovery]);
```

dataname
>   The (optional) data name that appears in the title line of the edit panel. The
>   first blank character terminates the name; maximum length: 54 characters.

profilename
>   The name of the associated edit profile. This parameter is mandatory if the
>   recovery request is NO. Format: CL8.

recordformat
>   The record format of the data to be edited. 'F ' = fixed; 'V ' = variable.

recordlength
>   The record length (in bytes) of the data to be edited (maximum record
>   length for U and V format records). Maximum value: 32,760 (255 prior to
>   ISPF 4.1). Format: Fullword.

readroutine
>   The address of the entry-point of the routine that supplies the read records.

writeroutine
>   The address of the entry-point of the routine that processes the records to be
>   written.

commandroutine
>   The (optional) address of the entry-point of the routine that processes edit
>   primary commands.

editlength
>   The (optional) length of the data to be edited. The edit-length must be less
>   than or equal to the record-length. Format: Fullword.

dialoguedata
>   The (optional) address of the data area that is passed to the processing
>   routines.

panelname
>   The (optional) name of the panel that is used for the data display. Default:
>   The standard edit panel. Format: CL8.

macroname
>   The (optional) name of the initial macro that is to be executed. Default: No
>   initial macro. Format: CL8.

formatname
> The (optional) name of the format that is used to reformat the data. This parameter is used only with DBCS on an IBM 5550 display terminal. Format: CL8.

dbcs
> This keyword specifies whether mixed-mode DBCS data is present (YES). Default: NO.

recovery
> This keyword specifies whether a pending error recovery is to proceed (YES). Default: NO.

The profile-name, edit-length, panel-name, format-name and dbcs cannot be specified in conjunction with YES recovery.

The service sets one of the following return codes:

> 0   Normal completion.
> 4   Normal completion, but no data was saved.
> 16   Unexpected return code received from a processing routine.
> 20   Severe error.

16.4.1 Read Routine

The read routine is called repeatedly to supply a record until the read routine signals end-of-data.

The read routine has the following interface conditions.

16.4.1.1 Entry Parameters

Parameter 1 (address) — Pointer to the read record (set by the read routine).

Parameter 2 (fullword) — The length of the read record (set by the read routine for V format record).

Parameter 3 (fullword) — The request code:
> 0   Read next record
> 1   Read first record.

Parameter 4 (address) — Pointer to the dialogue data area.

16.4.1.2 Exit Parameters

Return code (register 15):
> 0   Normal return.
> 8   End-of-file.
> 16   Read error.
> 20   Severe error.

16.4.2 Write Routine

The write routine is called repeatedly for each edited record when a save is made (explicitly or implicitly). The write routine is not called for records that have been deleted.

The write routine has the following interface conditions.

16.4.2.1 Entry Parameters

Parameter 1 (address) — Pointer to the record to be written.

Parameter 2 (fullword) — The length of the record, if V format record.

Parameter 3 (fullword) — The source and change bits for the record.

Source bits:
1	original record
2	Move line command
3	Copy/Repeat line command
4	Move primary command
5	Copy/Repeat primary command
6	TE line command
7	Insert line command.

Change bits:
8	record changed
9	data overtyped
10	Change primary command or Overlay line command
11	(, ((,), or)) line command
12	<, <<, >, or >> line command
13	text changed
14	record renumbered.

Parameter 4 (fullword) — The request code:
0	Write next record.
1	First write request
2	Last write request
3	First and last write request
4	No data records to write.

Parameter 5 (address) — Pointer to the dialogue data area.

16.4.2.2 Exit Parameters

Return code (register 15):
0	Normal return.
16	Read error.
20	Severe error.

16.4.3 Command Routine

If present, the command routine processes the EDIT primary commands and any dialogue-specific primary commands. The ZCMD dialogue variable contains the specified command.

16.4.3.1 Entry Parameters

Parameter 1 (fullword) — Command type:

1n	Move
2n	Copy
3n	Create
4n	Replace
5n	Recursive edit.

n has one of the values:

0	start of function
1	successful completion
2	unsuccessful completion.

Parameter 2 (address) — Pointer to the dialogue data area.

16.4.3.2 Exit Parameters

Return code (register 15):

0	Normal return.
8	End of data (no data record returned).
16	Read error.
20	Severe error.

16.4.4 Example

The sample program generates variable length records. Each stored record is prefixed with the length of the record. The entry with length 0 indicates the end of the internal table.

Sample program:

```
* driver program
TEDIF     CSECT
TEDIF     AMODE 31
          BAKR  14,0               save return address and registers
          BALR  10,0               set base register
          USING *,10
          LA    13,SA              set internal save-area
          MVC   4(4,13),=C'F1SA'   indicate stack used
* invoke Edit Interface
          CALL  ISPLINK,(VEDIF,DATANAME,EDPROF,RECFM,LRECL,AREADRTN,   X
                AWRITRTN),VL
EOJ       PR    ,                  terminate program
** read routine
READRTN   BALR  15,0
          USING *,15
```

```
              STM    0,14,RSA
              BALR   11,0
              USING  *,11
              LM     2,5,0(1)
* GPR2: A(record read)
* GPR3: F'record length'
* GPR4: F'request code'
** 0 = read next record
** 1 = read first record
* GPR5: A(dialog data area)
              L      4,0(4)
              CH     4,=H'1'
              BNE    *+10
              MVC    AREC,=A(RECTABLE)   1st call
              L      9,AREC
              LA     15,8                preset ReturnCode
              LH     1,0(9)              record length
              LTR    1,1
              BZ     EOF                 end-of-file
              ST     1,0(3)              next record length
              LA     0,2(9)              record address
              ST     0,0(2)
              LA     9,2(1,9)            next record entry
              ST     9,AREC
              LA     15,0                normal return
EOF           LM     0,14,RSA            restore registers
              BR     14     return
              DROP   11
** write routine
WRITRTN       BALR   15,0
              USING  *,15
              STM    0,14,RSA
              BALR   11,0
              USING  *,11
              LM     2,6,0(1)
* GPR2: A(record)
* GPR3: F'record length'
* GPR4: XL4'status bits'
* GPR5: F'request code'
* GPR6: A(dialog data area)
              L      2,0(2)
              L      1,0(4)
              LM     0,14,RSA
              LA     15,0
              BR     14     return
              DROP   11
**
RSA        DS     15A
MSG        DS     CL8
AREC       DS     A
VEDIF      DC     CL8'EDIF'
EDPROF     DC     CL8'MYPROFIL'
DATANAME   DC     C'MY-FILE '
RECFM      DC     C'V '
LRECL      DC     F'200'
AREADRTN   DC     A(READRTN)
AWRITRTN   DC     A(WRITRTN)
SA         DS     18F
RECTABLE   DC     HL2'41',CL41'line1'
```

```
DC      HL2'42',CL42'line2'
DC      HL2'43',CL43'line3'
DC      HL2'44',CL44'line4'
DC      HL2'45',CL45'line5'
DC      HL2'46',CL46'line6'
DC      HL2'47',CL47'line7'
DC      HL2'48',CL48'line8'
DC      HL2'49',CL49'line9'
DC      HL2'0'  end of table
END
```

16.5 EDIREC — INITIALISE EDIT RECOVERY

The EDIREC service initialises an edit recovery table to be used the EDIF service. The EDIREC service also prompts should an EDIF recovery be pending.

Syntax:
```
CALL ISPLINK ('EDIREC','INIT     ',[commandname]);
```
or
```
CALL ISPLINK ('EDIREC',option);
```

option (CL8)

> INIT   Initialise an edit recovery table in the user's profile.
>
> QUERY Search the edit recovery table for a pending recovery. The ZEDMODE system variable contains either E (for EDIT) V (for VIEW).
>
> CANCEL Cancel edit recovery.
>
> DEFER Defer edit recovery.

commandname (CL8)

> The (optional) command procedure used to initialise the EDIF table. Default: ISREIRTI.

16.6 EDIT - EDIT A DATASET OR LIBRARY MEMBER

The EDIT service invokes the PDF edit service to edit a dataset or library member.

Syntax:
```
ISPEXEC EDIT DATASET(datasetname)
        [VOLUME(volumeserial)]
        [PASSWORD(password)]
        [PANEL(panelname)]
        [MACRO(macroname)]
        [PROFILE(profilename)]
```

DATASET(datasetname)

> **Datasetname** is the name of the dataset or library (partitioned dataset) to be edited. **Datasetname** is specified in TSO syntax. A fully qualified dataset

name is specified within apostrophes. The current TSO userid prefix is appended in front of a dataset name specified without apostrophes.

Example of fully qualified dataset name:
```
DATASET('ALPHA.DATA')
```

Example of implicit dataset name:
```
DATASET(ALPHA.DATA)
```
If the TSO userid prefix is TSAB123, this dataset name specification is equivalent to the fully qualified dataset name:
```
DATASET('TSAB123.ALPHA.DATA')
```

If a partitioned dataset is being processed, the member name may be specified within parentheses; the member will be created, if it does not exist. A member list will be displayed, if a partitioned dataset without member name is specified.

Example:
```
DATASET('ALPHA.DATA(BETA)')
```
This example specifies member BETA from the dataset 'ALPHA.DATA'.

VOLUME(volumeserial)
Volumeserial is the serial number of the volume containing the dataset. This parameter is only required for datasets which are not catalogued.

Example:
```
DATASET('ALPHA.DATA') VOLUME(123456)
```
This example specifies that the dataset 'ALPHA.DATA' is contained on the volume with serial number 123456.

PASSWORD(password)
Password is the password required to access the dataset. This parameter is only required for datasets which are password protected.

PANEL(panelname)
Panelname is the name of the panel which is to be used for the dataset display, this panel must conform to the specifications for a customised edit panel (described in the IBM manual: ISPF and ISPF/PDF Installation and Customization).

MACRO(macroname)
Macroname is the name of the edit macro to be invoked after the dataset (library member) is read but before it is displayed. An edit macro is a special command procedure used to perform edit operations.

PROFILE(profilename)
Profilename is the name of the edit profile to be used. The edit profile is contained in the *apid*EDIT profile member (*apid* is the current application-id). If not edit profile is specified, the profile associated with the last

qualifier of the dataset (library) name is used. **profilename** has a maximum length of 8 characters.

The service sets one of the following return codes:

- 0   Normal completion, data was saved.
- 4   Normal completion, data was not saved.
- 14   Dataset in use.
- 16   Partitioned dataset specified contains no members.
- 20   Severe error.

Example:
```
ISPEXEC EDIT DATASET(ALPHA.TEXT) MACRO(GAMMA) PROFILE(ASM)
```
Edit the dataset ALPHA.TEXT using ASM profile; the GAMMA edit macro will be invoked.

16.7 VIEW - VIEW A DATASET OR LIBRARY MEMBER

The VIEW service invokes the PDF view service to view a dataset or library member. The VIEW service is similar to the EDIT service (e.g. EDIT commands and macros can be used), but does not permit changes to be made to the data. Unlike BROWSE, the VIEW service sets an ENQ (lock) on the dataset.

Note: Because the VIEW service does not perform a view recovery, the EDIREC service must be explicitly invoked if the changed dataset is to be viewed following an abnormal view termination.

Syntax:
```
ISPEXEC VIEW DATASET(datasetname)
        [VOLUME(volumeserial)]
        [PASSWORD(password)]
        [PANEL(panelname)]
        [MACRO(macroname)]
        [PROFILE(profilename)]
        [CONFIRM(YES|NO)]
```

DATASET(datasetname)

Datasetname is the name of the dataset or library (partitioned dataset) to be viewed. **Datasetname** is specified in TSO syntax. A fully qualified dataset name is specified within apostrophes. The current TSO userid prefix is appended in front of a dataset name specified without apostrophes.

Example of fully qualified dataset name:
```
DATASET('ALPHA.DATA')
```

Example of implicit dataset name:
```
DATASET(ALPHA.DATA)
```
If the TSO userid prefix is TSAB123, this dataset name specification is equivalent to the fully qualified dataset name:

```
DATASET('TSAB123.ALPHA.DATA')
```

If a partitioned dataset is being processed, the member name may be specified within parentheses; the member will be created, if it does not exist. A member list will be displayed, if a partitioned dataset without member name is specified.

Example:
```
DATASET('ALPHA.DATA(BETA)')
```
This example specifies member BETA from the dataset 'ALPHA.DATA'.

VOLUME(volumeserial)

Volumeserial is the serial number of the volume containing the dataset. This parameter is only required for datasets which are not catalogued.

Example:
```
DATASET('ALPHA.DATA') VOLUME(123456)
```
This example specifies that the dataset 'ALPHA.DATA' is contained on the volume with serial number 123456.

PASSWORD(password)

Password is the password required to access the dataset. This parameter is only required for datasets which are password protected.

PANEL(panelname)

Panelname is the name of the panel which is to be used for the dataset display, this panel must conform to the specifications for a customised view panel (described in the IBM manual: ISPF and ISPF/PDF Installation and Customization).

MACRO(macroname)

Macroname is the name of the view macro to be invoked after the dataset (library member) is read but before it is displayed. An edit macro is a special command procedure used to perform edit operations.

PROFILE(profilename)

Profilename is the name of the view profile to be used. The view profile is contained in the *apid*EDIT profile member (*apid* is the current application-id). If not view profile is specified, the profile associated with the last qualifier of the dataset (library) name is used. **profilename** has a maximum length of 8 characters.

CONFIRM(YES|NO)

Keyword to indicate whether a prompt panel is displayed if the VIEW service is terminated when data has been changed in the viewed dataset. Although the VIEW service does not permit the changed data to be saved directly, the changed data can be stored in some other dataset.

The service sets one of the following return codes:

    0   Normal completion.
  14   Dataset in use.
  16   Partitioned dataset specified contains no members.
  20   Severe error.

Example:
```
ISPEXEC VIEW DATASET(ALPHA.TEXT) MACRO(GAMMA) PROFILE(ASM) CONFIRM(NO)
```
View the dataset ALPHA.TEXT using ASM profile. The GAMMA edit macro will be invoked. No confirmation panel is displayed if the VIEW service is terminated when data has been changed.

Chapter 17

Library Management

17.1 INTRODUCTION

Although the library management services are only indirectly associated with dialog management, they can be useful for creating practical Dialog Manager applications.

The library management services are principally concerned with file management, both at the file level and member level.

17.1.1 Service Identifier

The two initialisation services (LMDINIT and LMINIT) return an identifier to the associated dataset or dataset list. This identifier is used to associate the subsequent services with this dataset or dataset list.

REXX Example:
```
ADDRESS ISPEXEC
"LMINIT DATAID(did) DATASET(my.file) ENQ(SHR)"
IF rc = 0 THEN "LMOPEN DATAID("did")"
```

CLIST Example:
```
ISPEXEC LMINIT DATAID(did) DATASET(my.file) ENQ(SHR)
IF &LASTCC = 0 THEN ISPEXEC LMOPEN DATAID(&did)
```

LMINIT specifies the name of a variable (here DID) in which the associated identifier is to be stored. Note DID is the name of a variable, whereas MY.FILE is a literal (the

dataset name). The subsequent library management services (e.g. LMOPEN) use the
value contained in this variable to access the associated dataset (or dataset list).

17.1.2 Error Handling

To avoid over-complication, the examples shown in the individual sections
perform only limited error processing. The worked example in Section 17.4 has
comprehensive error handling.

17.2 LIBRARY MANAGEMENT SERVICES

ISPF provides the following Library Management Services:

- LMCLOSE   Close dataset
- LMCOMP   Compress a library
- LMCOPY   Copy library members
- LMDDISP   Dataset display
- LMDFREE   Free a dataset-list
- LMDINIT   Initialise a dataset-list
- LMDLIST   List a dataset
- LMERASE   Erase (delete) a dataset
- LMFREE   Free a dataset association
- LMGET   Read a logical record
- LMINIT   Initialise a data-id for a dataset
- LMMADD   Add member
- LMMDEL   Delete a member
- LMMDISP   Member list service
- LMMFIND   Find member
- LMMLIST   List library members
- LMMOVE   Move library members
- LMMREN   Rename member
- LMMREP   Replace member
- LMMSTATS   Set member statistics
- LMOPEN   Open a dataset
- LMPRINT   Print a dataset or member
- LMPUT   Write a logical record
- LMQUERY   Retrieve dataset information
- LMRENAME   Rename a dataset

The following services are used for configuration management and are not handled in this book:

- `LMACT`   Activate a promotion hierarchy
- `LMDEACT`   Deactivate a promotion hierarchy
- `LMHIER`   Create a table with the hierarchy structure
- `LMPROM`   Promote a dataset or member
- `LMREVIEW` Create a dataset that contains control information.

17.2.1 LMCLOSE — Close Dataset

Close the associated dataset.

Syntax:
```
    ISPEXEC LMCLOSE DATAID(dataid)
```
or
```
    CALL ISPLINK ('LMCLOSE',dataid);
```

dataid
The dataid of the associated dataset returned by the `LMINIT` service.

Return code:

0	Normal completion.
8	Error; dataset is not open.
10	Invalid dataid.
20	Severe error.

Example:
```
    /* rexx */
    ADDRESS ISPEXEC
    "LMINIT DATAID(did) DATASET(my.file) ENQ(SHR)"
    IF rc = 0 THEN DO
      "LMOPEN DATAID("did")"
      "LMGET DATAID("did") MODE(INVAR) DATALOC(vdata)",
      "DATALEN(vlen) MAXLEN(80)"
      IF rc > 0 THEN LEAVE /* EOF or error */
      SAY rc vdata vlen
    END
    "LMCLOSE DATAID("did")"
```

17.2.2 LMCOMP - Compress a Library

Compress a library.

Syntax:
```
    ISPEXEC LMCOMP DATAID(dataid)
```
or
```
    CALL ISPLINK ('LMCOMP',dataid);
```

dataid
>   The dataid of the associated dataset returned by the LMINIT service.

Return code:
>   0   Normal completion.
>   10   Invalid dataid.
>   12   Dataset error.
>   20   Severe error.

Example:
```
/* rexx */
ADDRESS ISPEXEC
"LMINIT DATAID(did) DATASET(po.file) ENQ(EXCLU)"
IF rc = 0 THEN DO
  "LMCOMP DATAID("did")"
END
```

17.2.3 LMCOPY - Copy Library Members

Copy a selected member of a library or a sequential dataset to a library or sequential dataset.

Syntax:
```
ISPEXEC LMCOPY FROMID(from-dataid) [FROMMEM(from-member)]
        TODATAID(to-dataid) [TOMEM(to-member)]
        [REPLACE]
        [PACK]
        [TRUNC]
        [LOCK]
```
or
```
CALL ISPLINK ('LMCOPY',from-dataid,[from-member]
        ,to-dataid,[to-member]
        ,['REPLACE']
        ,['PACK']
        ,['TRUNC']
        ,['LOCK']);
```

from-dataid
>   The dataid of the associated input (source) dataset returned by the LMINIT service.

from-member
>   The name of the member to be copied if the input dataset is partitioned.

to-dataid
>   The dataid of the associated output (target) dataset returned by the LMINIT service.

to-member
>   The name to be assigned to the member copied into the output dataset. If omitted, the member name from the input library is used.

REPLACE

Replace a member in the output library having the same name. Default: Do not replace an existing member.

PACK

Store data in packed format. Default: Store data in unpacked (normal) format.

TRUNC

Right-truncate any records that are too long to be stored in the output dataset. Default: Terminate the copy if the record length of the output dataset is less than the input dataset.

LOCK

Lock members (the dataset must be a LMF-controlled library). No other user can change a locked member until it has been promoted. Default: No locking.

Return code:

0	Normal completion.
4	Member not available.
8	Input member not found.
10	Invalid dataid.
12	Dataset error.
16	Truncation error.
20	Severe error.

Example:

```
/* rexx - copy contents of PO-file to PS-file */
ADDRESS ISPEXEC
"LMINIT DATAID(didi) DATASET('tsouser.po.file') ENQ(SHR)"
"LMINIT DATAID(dido) DATASET(ps.file) ENQ(MOD)"
"LMOPEN DATAID("didi")"
IF rc = 0 THEN DO
  memname = ' '
  DO i = 0 TO 999 WHILE rc = 0
    memname.i = memname
    "LMMLIST DATAID("didi") OPTION(LIST) MEMBER(memname)"
  END
  memname.0 = (i-1)
  DO i = 1 TO memname.0
    "LMCOPY FROMID("didi") FROMMEM("memname.i") TODATAID("dido")"
    IF rc = 0
      THEN SAY memname.i 'copied'
      ELSE SAY memname.i 'copy error:' rc
  END
  "LMMLIST DATAID("didi") OPTION(FREE)"
  "LMCLOSE DATAID("didi")"
END
```

17.2.4 LMDDISP - Dataset Display

Display a list of the associated dataset names.

Syntax:
```
ISPEXEC LMDDISP LISTID(dslist-id)
        [VIEW(VOLUME|ATTRIB|SPACE|TOTAL)]
        [CONFIRM(YES|NO)]
        [PANEL(ISRUDSLO|panelname)]
```
or
```
CALL ISPLINK ('LMDDISP',dslist-id
        ,['VOLUME'|'ATTRIB'|'SPACE'|'TOTAL')]
        ,['YES'|'NO']
        ,['ISRUDSLO'|panelname] );
```

dslist-id

The dslist-id returned by the LMDINIT service.

VIEW(keyword)

The associated information that is shown on the display:

VOLUME   The volume on which the dataset resides. Default.

ATTRIB   The dataset attributes (organisation, record format, record length, block size).

SPACE   The amount of space that the dataset occupies.

TOTAL   The complete information (each dataset entry occupies two lines).

CONFIRM(keyword)

Whether a confirmation message is displayed before a marked dataset is deleted. Default: YES.

PANEL(keyword)

The name of the panel that is used to display the dataset information. Default: to Whether a confirmation message is displayed before a marked dataset is deleted. Default: The standard panel ISRUDSLO.

Return code:

0   Normal completion.

10   Invalid dataid.

12   Dataset error.

20   Severe error.

Example:
```
ADDRESS ISPEXEC
"LMDINIT LISTID(lid) LEVEL(tsouser)"
IF rc = 0 THEN DO
  "LMDDISP LISTID("lid") VIEW(ATTRIB)
  "LMDFREE LISTID("lid")"
END
```

17.2.5 LMDFREE - Free a Dataset-List

Free a dataset-list that was created by the LMDINIT service. Every LMDINIT call should have a corresponding LMFDREE.

Syntax:
```
     ISPEXEC LMDFREE LISTID(dslist-id)
```
or
```
     CALL ISPLINK ('LMDFREE',dslist-id);
```

dslist-id
> The dslist-id returned by the LMDINIT service.

Return code:
> 0   Normal completion.
>
> 8   Processing error.
>
> 10   Invalid dslist-id.
>
> 20   Severe error.

Example:
```
     /* rexx */
     ADDRESS ISPEXEC
     "LMDINIT LISTID(lid) LEVEL(tsu0001)"
     /* ... */
     "LMDFREE LISTID("lid")"
```

17.2.6 LMDINIT - Initialise a Dataset List

Initialize a dataset-list. The initialized list is identified by the dslist-id that the LMDINIT service returns. The dslist-id is returned as a dialog variable, which is used in subsequent services (or until freed by the LMDFREE service).

Syntax:
```
     ISPEXEC LMDINIT LISTID(dslist-id-var)
             [LEVEL(dsname-level)]
             [VOLUME(volume)]
```
or
```
     CALL ISPLINK ('LMDINIT',dslist-id-var
            ,[dsname-level]
            ,[volume]);
```

dslist-id-var
> The name of the variable into which the assigned dslist-id is to be placed.

dsname-level
> The first level qualifier for which the dataset-list is to be created.

volume
> The serial-id of the volume for which the dataset-list is to be created.

Note: Either dsname-level or volume must be specified.

Return code:
    0   Normal completion.
    8   Error; dslist-id not created.
    12 A keyword value was incorrect.
    16 A dialogue variable error occurred.
    20 Severe error.

Example:
```
ADDRESS ISPEXEC "LMDINIT LISTID(lid) LEVEL(tsu0001)"

DO WHILE rc = 0
  "LMDLIST LISTID("lid") OPTION(LIST) DATASET(dsn)"
  IF rc = 0 THEN SAY dsn
END

"LMDLIST LISTID("lid") OPTION(FREE)"
"LMDFREE LISTID("lid")"
```

17.2.7 LMDLIST - List a Dataset

List a dataset. The data list applies the associated datasets that satisfy the criteria
specified for the LMDINIT service. There are two major call types: the LIST option
returns the dataset name (and additional optional information) of the next entry;
the SAVE option writes the list to an external file.

Syntax:
```
ISPEXEC LMDLIST LISTID(dslist-id)
        [OPTION(LIST|FREE|SAVE)]
        DATASET[(dataset-var)]
        [STATS(YES|NO)]
        [GROUP(group)]
```
or
```
CALL ISPLINK ('LMDLIST',dslist-id
        ,['LIST'|'FREE'|'SAVE']
        ,dataset
        ,['YES'|'NO']
        ,[group]);
```

dslist-id
    The dslist-id returned by the LMDINIT service.

OPTION
    LIST   First call: Create an internal list of the dataset-names that satisfy the
           selection criterion specified in the LMDINIT service. If dataset-var is
           initialised to blank, the first entry in the list is returned.
           Subsequent calls: Return the next entry in the list.

FREE   Free the internal list that was created by the corresponding LMDLIST
        OPTION(LIST).

SAVE   Write the internal list to a physical file. The form of the generated
        dataset name is governed by the presence of the group parameter.

dataset-var
> Input: The starting position in the list.
> Output: The next name in the list.

STATS(YES|NO)
> Indicator whether file statistics are to be returned:
> YES   return statistics
> NO   do not return statistics.
> The file statistics are returned as the following dialog variables:

ZDLVOL	Volume serial-id.
ZDLDEV	Device type.
ZDLDSORG	Dataset organisation.
ZDLRECFM	Record format.
ZDLLRECL	Logical record length.
ZDLBLKSZ	Blocksize.
ZDLSIZE	Dataset size (in tracks).
ZDLUSED	Percentage of used tracks.
ZDLEXT	Number of extents used.
ZDLCDATE	Creation date.
ZDLEDATE	Expiry date.
ZDLRDATE	Last-referenced date.
ZDLMIGR	Dataset migration state (YES, NO).
ZDLDSNTP	Dataset type.

group
> If specified, the second level qualifier to be used for the dataset name
> assigned to the SAVE dataset, which has the form: <userid>.<group>.
> DATASETS. If omitted, the SAVE dataset is written to the ISPF list dataset.

Return code:
> 0   Normal completion.
> 4   The LMDINIT service returned no datasets.
> 8   End of the list.
> 10   Invalid dslist-id.
> 12   A keyword value was incorrect.
> 16   A dialogue variable error occurred.
> 20   Severe error.

Example 1:
```
/* REXX */
ADDRESS ISPEXEC
"LMDINIT LISTID(lid) LEVEL(tsouser)"
IF rc = 0 THEN DO
  dsn = 'TSOUSER.Q' /* start criterion */
  DO WHILE rc = 0
    "LMDLIST LISTID("lid") OPTION(LIST) DATASET(dsn)"
    IF rc = 0 THEN SAY dsn
  END
  "LMDLIST LISTID("lid") OPTION(FREE)"
END
"LMDFREE LISTID("lid")"
```
List the TSOUSER datasets starting with TSOUSER.Q... .

Example 2:
```
/* REXX */
ADDRESS ISPEXEC
"LMDINIT LISTID(lid) LEVEL(tsu0001)"

IF rc = 0 THEN DO
  "LMDLIST LISTID("lid") OPTION(SAVE) DATASET(dsn) STATS(YES)
GROUP(LIST)"
  /* userid.LIST.DATASETS or userid.SPFn.LIST (printed at session end */
  "LMDFREE LISTID("lid")"
END
```

17.2.8 LMERASE - Erase (Delete) a Dataset

Delete a library (dataset). The name of the dataset is specifed either as a three-level quaified name (project.group.type) or as an explicit dataset name.

Syntax:
```
ISPEXEC LMERASE
        {PROJECT(project) GROUP(group) TYPE(type)} | {[DATASET(dsname)]}
        [VOLUME(volume)]
        [PASSWORD(password)]
        [PURGE(YES|NO)]
```
or
```
CALL ISPLINK('LMERASE '
        ,[project],[group],[type]
        ,['YES'|'NO']
        ,[dsname]
        ,[volume]
        ,[password]);
```

project
> The project (highest level qualifier).

group
> The second level qualifier.

type
> The type (third level qualifier).

dsname
>   The dataset name in TSO conventions. If **dsname** is specified without quotes, the user's TSO prefix is appended. If both a dataset name and a three-level qualified name are specified, **dsname** takes precedence.

volume
>   The volume if the dataset is not catalogued.

password
>   The password if the dataset is password protected.

PURGE
>   YES   Delete the dataset irrespective of whether the expiry date has been reached.
>
>   NO   Delete the dataset only if the expiry date has been reached. Default.

Return code:
>   0   Normal completion.
>   8   Error; dataset error.
>   12   Error; expiration date not reached and PURGE(YES) not specified.
>   20   Severe error.

Example:
```
/* rexx */
ADDRESS ISPEXEC
"LMERASE PROJECT(tsouser) GROUP(jcl) TYPE(cntl) NEWGROUP(ex)
```
Delete the 'TSOUSER.JCL.CNTL' dataset.

17.2.9 LMFREE - Free a Dataset Association

Free the association with the dataset specified with the LMINIT service. Each LMINIT should have a matching LMFREE.

Syntax:
```
ISPEXEC LMFREE DATAID(dataid)
```
or
```
CALL ISPLINK ('LMFREE',dataid);
```

dataid
>   The dataid of the associated dataset returned by the LMINIT service.

Return code:
>   0   Normal completion.
>   8   Error.
>   10   Invalid dslist-id.
>   20   Severe error.

Example:
```
/* rexx */
ADDRESS ISPEXEC
"LMINIT DATAID(did) DATASET(my.file) ENQ(SHR)"
  /* processing... */
"LMFREE DATAID("did")"
```

17.2.10 LMGET - Read a Logical Record

Read a logical record from the associated dataset. The first LMGET invocation
returns the first record; each subsequent invocation returns the next logical record.
If the dataset is partitioned, the LMMFIND service must be used to position to the
required member.

Syntax:
```
ISPEXEC LMGET DATAID(dataid)
        MODE(INVAR|LOCATE|MOVE)
        DATALOC(dataloc-var)
        DATALEN(datalen-var)
        MAXLEN(maxlen)
```
or
```
CALL ISPLINK ('LMGET',dataid
        ,'INVAR'|'LOCATE'|'MOVE'
        ,dataloc-var
        ,datalen-var
        ,maxlen);
```

dataid
> The dataid of the associated dataset returned by the LMINIT service.

MODE(keyword)
> The access mode for the read record.
>
> INVAR   The data record is stored in the specified variable.
>
> LOCATE   The address of the data record is placed in the specified
>   variable.
>
> MOVE   The data record is moved to the location whose address is
>   contained in the specified variable.

dataloc-var
> The name of the data location variable. The MODE keyword specifies the
> form of this variable.

datalen-var
> The name of the variable in which the length of the read record is placed.

maxlen
> The maximum length of the record to be read. This parameter is ignored in
> LOCATE mode.

Return code:

    0   Normal completion.

    8   End of dataset.

   10 Invalid dslist-id.

   12 Error: dataset not open for input; no member located for library; invalid parameter.

   16 Truncation error.

   20 Severe error.

Example 1:

```
/* rexx */
ADDRESS ISPEXEC
"LMINIT DATAID(did) DATASET(my.file) ENQ(SHR)"
IF rc = 0 THEN DO
  "LMOPEN DATAID("did")"
  "LMGET DATAID("did") MODE(INVAR) DATALOC(vdata)",
  "DATALEN(vlen) MAXLEN(80)"
  IF rc > 0 THEN LEAVE /* EOF or error */
  SAY vlen vdata /* display length and contents */
END
"LMCLOSE DATAID("did")"
```

Example 2:

```
/* rexx - LMGET LOCATE */
ADDRESS ISPEXEC
"LMINIT DATAID(did) DATASET(my.file) ENQ(SHR)"
IF rc = 0 THEN DO
  "LMOPEN DATAID("did")"
  IF rc > 0 THEN LEAVE /* open error */
  "LMGET DATAID("did") MODE(LOCATE) DATALOC(vaddr)",
  "DATALEN(vlen) MAXLEN(80)"
  SAY STORAGE(D2X(vaddr),vlen) /* display record contents */
END
"LMCLOSE DATAID("did")"
```

17.2.11 LMINIT - Initialise a Dataid for a Dataset

Initialise a dataid for the specified dataset. The dataid is returned as a dialog variable that is used in subsequent Library Management services. The LMFREE service should be used to free the association when it is no longer required.

Syntax:

```
ISPEXEC LMINIT LISTID(dataid-var)
        dataset
        [VOLUME(volume)]
        [PASSWORD(password)]
        [ENQ(SHR|EXCLU|SHRW|MOD)]
        [ORG(org-var)]
```

or

```
CALL ISPLINK ('LMINIT',dataidvar
        ,project,group1,[group2],[group3],[group4],type
        ,dsname
        ,ddname
        ,[volume]
        ,[password]
        ,['SHR'|'EXCLU'|'SHRW'|'MOD']
        ,[org-var]);
```

The *dataset* may be specified in three ways (in the following search sequence):

```
DDNAME(ddname)
```

or

```
DATASET(dsname) [VOLUME(volume)]
```

or

```
PROJECT(project) GROUP1(group1) TYPE(type) [GROUP2(group2)]
[GROUP3(group3)] [GROUP4(group4)]
```

In the program invocation, only one of these entries needs to be made (non-applicable entries should be set to blank).

dataid-var

The name of the variable into which the assigned dataid is to be placed.

password

The password, if the dataset is MVS password-protected.

ENQ(keyword)

The synchronisation (shareability) of the dataset:

SHR	Input data can be shared; default.
EXCLU	Exclusive use of data.
SHRW	Shared write for (partitioned) data. More than one user can read dataset members, but writing of members is enqueued.
MOD	Records are written at the end of a sequential dataset. The EXCLU option causes a sequential dataset to be overwritten.

ddname

The DD-name associated with the previously allocated dataset.

dsname

The dataset-name of an existing dataset. The name may be either fully qualified (written within single quotation marks) or non-qualified, in which case the TSO user prefix is implicitly placed before the specified dataset-name.

org-var

The name of the variable into which the dataset-set organisation (PO, PS) is to be placed.

volume
>The serial-id of the volume on which the dataset resides.

Note: Either dsname-level or volume must be specified.

project
>The project (highest level qualifier).

group1
>The first in the list of the second level qualifiers.

group2
>The second in the list of the second level qualifiers.

group3
>The third in the list of the second level qualifiers.

group4
>The fourth in the list of the second level qualifiers.

type
>The type (third level qualifier).

Return code:

0	Normal completion.
8	Error; dslist-id not created.
12	A keyword value was incorrect.
16	A dialogue variable error occurred.
20	Severe error.

Example 1:
```
/* rexx */
ADDRESS ISPEXEC
"LMINIT DATAID(did) DATASET(my.file) ENQ(SHR)"
IF rc = 0 THEN DO
  "LMOPEN DATAID("did")"
END
```

Example 2:
```
/* rexx */
ADDRESS ISPEXEC
"LMINIT DATAID(did) PROJECT(tsouser) GROUP1(jcl) GROUP2(ex) TYPE(cntl)
ENQ(SHR)"
IF rc = 0 THEN DO
  "LMOPEN DATAID("did")"
  "LMMFIND DATAID("did") MEMBER(a2) GROUP(group)"
END
```

17.2.12 LMMADD - Add Member

Add the specified member in the associated dataset.

Syntax:
```
ISPEXEC LMMADD DATAID(dataid)
        MEMBER(member)
        [STATS(YES|NO)]
```
or
```
CALL ISPLINK ('LMMADD',dataid
        ,member
        [,'YES'|'NO')]);
```

dataid
> The dataid of the associated dataset returned by the LMINIT service.

member
> The name of the member to be added.

STATS(YES|NO)
> Indicates whether member statistics are to be set:
>
> YES   set member statistics
>
> NO   do not set member statistics (default).
>
> The following dialog variables specify the statistics to be set:
>
> | | |
> |---|---|
> | ZLVERS | The version number. |
> | ZLMOD | The modification level. |
> | ZLCDATE | The creation date. |
> | ZLMDATE | The last-modified date. |
> | ZLMTIME | The last-modified time (hh:mm). |
> | ZLMSEC | The last-modified seconds value. |
> | ZLINORC | The current number of records. |
> | ZLMNORC | The original number of records. |
> | ZLUSER | The userid of the person who last modified the member. |

Return code:
> | | |
> |---|---|
> | 0 | Normal completion. |
> | 4 | Member already present. |
> | 10 | Invalid dataid. |
> | 12 | Dataset error. |
> | 14 | No records have been written. |
> | 16 | A dialogue variable error occurred. |
> | 20 | Severe error. |

Example:
```
/* rexx - LMMADD */
ADDRESS ISPEXEC
"LMINIT DATAID(did) DATASET(pov.file) ENQ(SHRW)"
"LMOPEN DATAID("did") OPTION(OUTPUT)"
```

```
vdata = "alpha        "
vlen = LENGTH(vdata)
"LMPUT DATAID("did") MODE(INVAR) DATALOC(vdata) DATALEN("vlen")"
"LMMADD DATAID("did") MEMBER(a2)"
"LMCLOSE DATAID("did")"
```

17.2.13 LMMDEL - Delete a Member

Delete the specified member from the associated dataset.

Syntax:
```
ISPEXEC LMMDEL DATAID(dataid) MEMBER(member)
```
or
```
CALL ISPLINK ('LMMDEL',dataid,member);
```

dataid
>The dataid of the associated dataset returned by the LMINIT service.

member
>The name of the member to be deleted.

Return code:

0	Normal completion.
8	Member not present.
10	Invalid dataid.
12	Dataset error.
20	Severe error.

Example:
```
/* rexx */
ADDRESS ISPEXEC
"LMINIT DATAID(did) DATASET(pov.file) ENQ(SHRW)"
"LMOPEN DATAID("did") OPTION(OUTPUT)"
"LMMDEL DATAID("did") MEMBER(a2)"
"LMCLOSE DATAID("did")"
```

17.2.14 LMMDISP - Member List Service

The LMMDISP service has five options that perform various member list processing:

- DISPLAY Create and display member list.
- GET   Get next member.
- PUT   Save information for a member.
- ADD   Add a new member.
- FREE   Free member list.

The default panel displays the member list in the standard ISPF format. LMMDISP cannot be used with the save dataid as LMLIST, and vice versa.

Member information is returned in ISPF variables:

ZLMEMBER	Member name of selected member
ZLLCMD	Line command that selected the member
ZLUDATA	User data area on member list.

The following variables apply only if STATS(YES) is specified:

ZLLIB	The library concatenation number.
ZLVERS	Member version number
ZLMOD	Member modification number
ZLCDATE	Member creation date
ZLMDATE	Date member was last modified
ZLMTIME	Time member was last modified
ZLMSEC	Seconds value of the last modified time
ZLCNORC	Current number of records in member
ZLINORC	Initial number of records in member
ZLMNORC	Number of modified records in member
ZLUSER	Userid that last modified member
ZLPDSUDA	Value of member directory user data area

17.2.14.1 DISPLAY. Create and display a member list.

Syntax:
```
ISPEXEC LMMDISP DATAID(dataid)
        OPTION(DISPLAY)
        [MEMBER(pattern)]
        [STATS(YES|NO)]
        [PANEL(panelname)]
        [CURSOR(ZCMD|ZLLCMD|ZLUDATA)]
        [TOP(toprow)]
        [COMMANDS(S|ANY)]
        [FIELD(1|9)]
```
or
```
CALL ISPLINK('LMMDISP', dataid
        ,'DISPLAY '
        ,[pattern]
        ,['YES'|'NO']
        ,[panelname]
        ,['ZCMD'|'ZLLCMD'|'ZLUDATA ']
        ,[toprow]
        ,' ',' '
        ,['S '|'ANY ']
        ,[1|9];
```

dataid
    The dataid of the associated dataset returned by the LMINIT service.

MEMBER(pattern)
    The character string that specifies the members to be displayed. Example:
    ISP*

STATS(YES|NO)

Indicates whether member statistics are to be returned:

YES   return statistics

NO   no statistics.

Statistics are returned as ISPF variables:

PANEL(panelname)

The name of the panel to be used for the member list display.

Default: ISRML000.

CURSOR(ZCMD|ZLLCMD|ZLUDATA)

The name of the panel field where the cursor is to be placed.

TOP(toprow)

The name that designates the member that is to appear in the top row of the display.

COMMANDS(S|ANY)

The valid member selection commands:

S   only s selection

ANY   any line selection command is valid.

FIELD(1|9)

The length of the line selection field.

Service return code:

0	Normal processing.
4	No members selected.
8	END or RETURN entered.
10	No dataid.
12	Dataset error.
16	Truncation.
20	Severe error.

17.2.14.2 GET. Get information for subsequent members. Each GET invocation returns information for the next member. The DISPLAY option returns information for the first selected member.

Syntax:

```
ISPEXEC LMMDISP DATAID(dataid)
        OPTION(GET)
        [STATS(YES|NO)]
```

or

```
CALL ISPLINK('LMMDISP ', dataid
        ,'GET'
        ,' '
        ,['YES'|'NO']);
```

dataid

> The dataid of the associated dataset returned by the LMINIT service.

STATS(YES | NO)

> Indicates whether member statistics are to be returned:
>
> YES   return statistics
>
> NO   no statistics.
>
> Statistics are returned as ISPF variables.

Service return code:

0	Normal processing.
8	No more members selected.
10	No dataid.
12	Dataset error.
16	Truncation.
20	Severe error.

17.2.14.3 PUT. Save information in the line command field and user data field.

Syntax:

```
ISPEXEC LMMDISP DATAID(dataid)
        OPTION(PUT)
        MEMBER(membername)
        [ZLLCMD(lcmdvalue)]
        [ZLUDATA(udatavalue)]
```

or

```
CALL ISPLINK('LMMDISP', dataid
        ,'PUT'
        ,membername
        ,' ',' ',' ',' '
        ,[lcmdvalue]
        ,[udatavalue]);
```

dataid

> The dataid of the associated dataset returned by the LMINIT service.

MEMBER(membername)

> The name of the member for which the information is to be saved.

ZLLCMD(lcmdvalue)

> The value to be stored in the line command field.

ZLUDATA(udatavalue)

> The value to be stored in the user data field. Maximum length 8 bytes
> (blank delimited).

Service return code:

    0   Normal processing.

    8   Specified member does not exist.

   10 No dataid.

   12 Dataset error.

   16 Truncation.

   20 Severe error.

17.2.14.4 ADD. Add a member to a member list.

Syntax:
```
ISPEXEC LMMDISP DATAID(dataid)
        OPTION(ADD)
        MEMBER(membername)
        [ZLLCMD(lcmd-value)]
        [ZLUDATA(udata-value)]
```
or
```
CALL ISPLINK('LMMDISP ', dataid
        ,'ADD '
        ,member-name
        ,' ',' ',' ',' '
        ,[lcmd-value]
        ,[udata-value] );
```

dataid

    The dataid of the associated dataset returned by the LMINIT service.

MEMBER(membername)

    The name of the member to be added.

ZLLCMD(lcmdvalue)

    The value to be stored in the line command field.

ZLUDATA(udatavalue)

    The value to be stored in the user data field. Maximum length 9 bytes.

Service return code:

    0   Normal processing.

    8   Specified member exists already.

   10 No dataid.

   12 Dataset error.

   16 Truncation.

   20 Severe error.

17.2.14.5 FREE. Free a member list.

Syntax:
```
ISPEXEC LMMDISP DATAID(data-id)
        OPTION(FREE)
```
or
```
CALL ISPLINK('LMMDISP ', dataid
        ,'FREE ');
```

dataid
> The dataid of the associated dataset returned by the LMINIT service.

Service return code:

> 0   Normal processing.
> 8   No member list exists.
> 10 No dataid.
> 12 Dataset error.
> 16 Truncation.
> 20 Severe error.

17.2.14.6 Example.
```
/* REXX */
ADDRESS ISPEXEC
"LMINIT DATAID(didi) DATASET(demo.ispplib) ENQ(SHR)"
"LMINIT DATAID(dido) DATASET(ps.file) ENQ(MOD)"
"LMOPEN DATAID("didi")"
DO FOREVER
  "LMMDISP DATAID("didi") OPTION(DISPLAY) COMMANDS(S)",
   "FIELD(1)"
  IF RC > 0 THEN LEAVE
  DO WHILE RC = 0
    "LMCOPY FROMID("didi") FROMMEM("zlmember")",
     "TODATAID("dido")"
    IF RC = 0
      THEN msg = '*copied'
      ELSE msg = 'RC:'RC
      "LMMDISP DATAID("didi") OPTION(PUT)",
       MEMBER("zlmember") ZLUDATA("msg")"
    "LMMDISP DATAID("didi") OPTION(GET)"
  END
END
"LMMDISP DATAID("didi") OPTION(FREE)"
"LMCLOSE DATAID("didi")"
```

This example copies selected members onto the PS.FILE dataset. A confirmation message (or error message) is set into the corresponding member display.

17.2.15 LMMFIND - Find Member

Find the specified member in the associated (partitioned) dataset.

Syntax:
```
ISPEXEC LMMFIND DATAID(dataid)
        MEMBER(member)
        [LOCK]
        [LRECL(lrecl-var)]
        [RECFM(recfm-var)]
        [GROUP(group-var)]
        [STATS(YES|NO)]
```
or
```
CALL ISPLINK ('LMMFIND',dataid
        ,member
        ,['LOCK']
        ,[lrecl-var]
        ,[recfm-var]
        ,[group-var]
        [,'YES'|'NO']);
```

dataid
> The dataid of the associated dataset returned by the LMINIT service.

member
> The name of the member to be found. If the associated dataset was defined (with the LMINIT service) with more than one group entry, the datasets are searched in group number sequence (i.e. GROUP1 before GROUP2).

LOCK
> Lock members (the dataset must be a LMF-controlled library). No other user can change a locked member until it has been promoted. Default: No locking.

lrecl-var
> The name of the variable into which the logical record length is to be placed.

recfm-var
> The name of the variable into which the record format is to be placed.

group-var
> The name of the variable into which the group name that contains the member is to be placed.

STATS(YES|NO)
> Indicates whether member statistics are to be returned:
>
> YES   return statistics
>
> NO   no statistics.

The following statistics are returned as dialog variables (in the function pool):

ZLLIB	The position in the concatenated dataset sequence.
ZLVERS	The version number.
ZLMOD	The modification level.
ZLCDATE	The creation date.
ZLMDATE	The last-modified date.
ZLMTIME	The last-modified time (hh:mm).
ZLMSEC	The last-modified seconds value.
ZLINORC	The current number of records.
ZLMNORC	The original number of records.
ZLUSER	The userid of the person who last modified the member.

Return code:

0	Normal completion.
4	Member not available.
8	Member not found.
10	Invalid dataid.
12	Dataset error.
16	A dialogue variable error occurred.
20	Severe error.

Example:

```
/* rexx */
ADDRESS ISPEXEC
"LMINIT DATAID(did) PROJECT(tsouser) GROUP1(jcl) TYPE(cntl) ENQ(SHR)"
"LMOPEN DATAID("did")"
"LMMFIND DATAID("did") MEMBER(a2) GROUP(group) STATS(YES)"
SAY 'Group:' group /* JCL */
SAY 'Sequence:' zllib /* 1 */
DO WHILE rc = 0
  "LMGET DATAID("did") MODE(INVAR) DATALOC(vdata) DATALEN(vlen)",
    "MAXLEN(80)"
  IF rc = 0 THEN SAY rc vlen vdata
END
"LMCLOSE DATAID("did")"
END
```

This example displays the records from member A2 of the partitioned dataset 'TSOUSER.JCL.CNTL'.

17.2.16 LMMLIST - List Library Members

List the members of a library. The list applies the associated members that satisfy the criteria specified for the LMINIT service. There are two major call types: the LIST option returns the member name (and additional optional information) of the next entry; the SAVE option writes the list to an external file.

Syntax:
```
ISPEXEC LMMLIST DATAID(dataid)
       [OPTION(LIST|FREE|SAVE)]
       MEMBER(member-var)
       [STATS(YES|NO)]
       [GROUP(group)]
```
or
```
CALL ISPLINK ('LMMLIST',dataid
       ,['LIST'|'FREE'|'SAVE']
       ,member-var
       ,['YES'|'NO']
       [group] );
```

dataid

> The dataid of the associated input (source) dataset returned by the LMINIT service.

OPTION

> LIST   First call: Create an internal list of the member-names for the library identified with the LMINIT service. If member-var is initialised to blank, the first entry in the list is returned.
> Subsequent calls: Return the next entry in the list.

> FREE   Free the internal list that was created by the corresponding LMMLIST OPTION(LIST).

> SAVE   Write the internal list to a physical file. The form of the generated dataset name is governed by the presence of the group parameter.

member-var

> Input: The starting position in the list.
> Output: The next name in the list.

STATS(YES|NO)

> Indicator whether member statistics are to be returned:
> YES   return statistics
> NO   no statistics.

> The following statistics are returned as dialog variables (in the function pool):

ZLLIB	The position in the concatenated dataset sequence.
ZLVERS	The version number.
ZLMOD	The modification level.
ZLCDATE	The creation date.
ZLMDATE	The last-modified date.
ZLMTIME	The last-modified time (hh:mm).
ZLMSEC	The last-modified seconds value.
ZLINORC	The current number of records.

ZLMNORC	The original number of records.
ZLUSER	The userid of the person who last modified the member.

group

If specified, the second level qualifier to be used for the dataset name assigned to the SAVE dataset, which has the form: <userid>.<group>. MEMBERS. If omitted, the SAVE dataset is written to the ISPF list dataset. Note: The ISPF list dataset is open during the ISPF session.

Return code:

0 Normal completion.

4 Empty member list.

8 Exception condition:

LIST: End of the member list

FREE: Member does not exist

SAVE: SAVE made after LIST without FREE being made.

10 Invalid dataid.

12 Dataset error.

16 Truncation error.

20 Severe error.

Example 1:

```
/* rexx - display member names */
ADDRESS ISPEXEC
"LMINIT DATAID(did) DATASET('tsouser.po.file') ENQ(SHR)"
"LMOPEN DATAID("did")"
DO WHILE rc = 0
  "LMMLIST DATAID("did") OPTION(LIST) MEMBER(memname) STATS(YES)"
  IF rc = 0 THEN DO
    SAY memname ZLINORC /* no. of records */
  END
END
"LMMLIST DATAID("did") OPTION(FREE)"
```

This example displays the member names together with the number of records in the member.

Example 2:

```
/* rexx - copy contents of PO-file to PS-file */
ADDRESS ISPEXEC
"LMINIT DATAID(didi) DATASET(ex.exec) ENQ(SHR)"
"LMINIT DATAID(dido) DATASET(ps.file) ENQ(MOD)"
"LMOPEN DATAID("didi")"
memname = 'GET'
"LMMLIST DATAID("didi") OPTION(LIST) MEMBER(memname)"
DO FOREVER WHILE rc = 0
  IF LEFT(memname,3) > 'GET' THEN LEAVE
  "LMCOPY FROMID("didi") FROMMEM("memname") TODATAID("dido")"
  SAY memname RC
  "LMMLIST DATAID("didi") OPTION(LIST) MEMBER(memname)"
END
```

```
"LMMLIST DATAID("didi") OPTION(FREE)"
"LMCLOSE DATAID("didi")"
```

This example copies those members whose name commences with GET to the
PS.FILE output dataset.

Example 3:
```
/* rexx */
ADDRESS ISPEXEC
"LMINIT DATAID(did) DATASET(ex.exec) ENQ(SHR)"
"LMOPEN DATAID("did")"
"LMMLIST DATAID("did") OPTION(SAVE) GROUP(MLIST)"
"LMCLOSE DATAID("did")"
```

This example writes the member list for the EX.EXEC input dataset to the
userid.MLIST.MEMBERS dataset.

17.2.17 LMMOVE - Move Library Members

Move a selected member of a library or a sequential dataset to a library or
sequential dataset.

Note: The source data (member or dataset) are deleted after being moved.

Syntax:
```
ISPEXEC LMMOVE FROMID(from-dataid) [FROMMEM(from-member)]
        TODATAID(to-dataid) [TOMEM(to-member)]
        [REPLACE]
        [PACK]
        [TRUNC]
        [LOCK]
```
or
```
CALL ISPLINK ('LMMOVE',from-dataid,[from-member]
        ,to-dataid,[to-member]
        ,['REPLACE']
        ,['PACK']
        ,['TRUNC']
        ,['LOCK']);
```

from-dataid
>   The dataid of the associated input (source) dataset returned by the LMINIT
>   service.

from-member
>   The name of the member to be copied if the input dataset is partitioned.

to-dataid
>   The dataid of the associated output (target) dataset returned by the LMINIT
>   service.

to-member
>   The name to be assigned to the member copied into the output dataset. If
>   omitted, the member name from the input library used.

REPLACE

Replace a member in the output library having the same name. Default: Do not replace an existing member.

PACK

Store data in packed format. Default: Store data in unpacked (normal) format.

TRUNC

Right-truncate any records that are too long to be stored in the output dataset. Default: Terminate the move if the record length of the output dataset is less than the input dataset.

LOCK

Lock members (the dataset must be a LMF-controlled library). No other user can change a locked member until it has been promoted. Default: No locking.

Return code:

0	Normal completion.
4	Member not available.
8	Input member not found.
10	Invalid dataid.
12	Dataset error.
16	Truncation error.
20	Severe error.

Example:

```
/* rexx - MOVE contents of PS-file */
ADDRESS ISPEXEC
"LMINIT DATAID(didi) DATASET(ps1.file) ENQ(SHR)"
"LMINIT DATAID(dido) DATASET(ps2.file) ENQ(EXCLU)"
"LMOPEN DATAID("didi")"
IF rc = 0 THEN DO
  "LMMOVE FROMID("didi") TODATAID("dido")"
  IF rc = 0
    THEN SAY 'dataset moved'
    ELSE SAY 'move error:' RC
END
"LMMLIST DATAID("didi") OPTION(FREE)"
"LMCLOSE DATAID("didi")"
```

17.2.18 LMMREN - Rename Member

Rename the specified member in the associated dataset.

Syntax:

```
ISPEXEC LMMREN DATAID(dataid)
        MEMBER(old-member-name)
        NEWNAME(new-member-name)
```

or
```
CALL ISPLINK ('LMMREP',dataid,
       ,old-member-name
       ,new-member-name);
```

dataid
> The dataid of the associated dataset returned by the LMINIT service.

old-member-name
> The name of the member to be renamed.

new-member-name
> The new name of the member.

Return code:

0	Normal completion. Member replaced.
4	New name exists already.
8	Member not found.
10	Invalid dataid.
12	Dataset error.
20	Severe error.

Example:
```
/* rexx */
ADDRESS ISPEXEC
"LMINIT DATAID(did) DATASET(pov.file) ENQ(SHRW)"
"LMOPEN DATAID("did") OPTION(OUTPUT)"
"LMMREN DATAID("did") MEMBER(a1) NEWNAME(a2)"
"LMCLOSE DATAID("did")"
```

17.2.19 LMMREP - Replace Member

Replace (or add) the specified member in the associated dataset.

Syntax:
```
ISPEXEC LMMREP DATAID(dataid)
        MEMBER(member)
        [STATS(YES|NO)]
```
or
```
CALL ISPLINK ('LMMREP',dataid,member[,'YES'|'NO']);
```

dataid
> The dataid of the associated dataset returned by the LMINIT service.

member
> The name of the member to be replaced.

STATS(YES | NO)

Indicates whether member statistics are to be set:

YES   set statistics

NO   do not set statistics.

The following dialog variables specify the statistics:

ZLVERS	The version number.
ZLMOD	The modification level.
ZLCDATE	The creation date.
ZLMDATE	The last-modified date.
ZLMTIME	The last-modified time (hh:mm).
ZLMSEC	The last-modified seconds value.
ZLINORC	The current number of records.
ZLMNORC	The original number of records.
ZLUSER	The userid of the person who last modified the member.

Return code:

0	Normal completion. Member replaced.
8	Normal completion. Member added.
10	Invalid dataid.
12	Dataset error.
14	No records have been written.
16	A dialogue variable error occurred.
20	Severe error.

Example:

```
/* rexx */
ADDRESS ISPEXEC
"LMINIT DATAID(did) DATASET(pov.file) ENQ(SHRW)"
"LMOPEN DATAID("did") OPTION(OUTPUT)"
vdata = "alpha        "
vlen = LENGTH(vdata)
"LMPUT DATAID("did") MODE(INVAR) DATALOC(vdata) DATALEN("vlen")"
"LMMREP DATAID("did") MEMBER(a2)"
"LMCLOSE DATAID("did")"
```

17.2.20 LMMSTATS - Set Member Statistics

Set the specified ISPF statistics for the specified member of the associated partitioned dataset.

Syntax:
```
ISPEXEC LMMSTATS DATAID(dataid)
        MEMBER(member)
        [VERSION(version-no)]
        [MODLEVEL(mod-level)]
        [CREATED(creation-date)]
        [MODDATE(modified-date)]
        [MODTIME(modified-time)]
        [CURSIZE(current-size)]
        [INITSIZE(initial-size)]
        [MODRECS(records-modified)]
        [USERID(user-id)]
        [DELETE]
```
or
```
CALL ISPLINK ('LMMSTATS',dataid
        ,member
        , [version-no]
        , [mod-level]
        , [creation-date]
        , [modified-date]
        , [modified-time]
        , [current-size]
        , [initial-size]
        , [records-modified]
        , [user-id]
        , ['DELETE']);
```

dataid
> The dataid of the associated dataset returned by the LMINIT service.

member
> The name of the member for which the statistics are to be set. The member name

version-no
> The version number, an integer in the range 1 through 99.

mod-level
> The modification level, an integer in the range 1 through 99.

creation-date
> The creation date of the member. The format is dependent on the default ISPF/PDF language. The English format is yy/mm/dd.

modified-date
> The date when the member was last modified. The format is dependent on the default ISPF/PDF language. The English format is yy/mm/dd. For example, 95/12/31.

modified-time
> The time when the member was last modified. The format is hh:mm. For example, 23:59.

current-size
> The current number of records in the member, an integer in the range 0 through 65535.

initial-size
> The initial number of records in the member, an integer in the range 0 through 65535.

records-modified
> The number of records modified in the member, an integer in the range 0 through 65535.

user-id
> The user-id that last modified the member data.

DELETE
> Remove the member statistics.

Return code:
0	Normal completion.
4	No matching members found or member empty.
8	Member not found.
10	Invalid dataid.
12	Dataset error.
20	Severe error.

Example 1:
```
/* rexx */
ADDRESS ISPEXEC
"LMINIT DATAID(did) DATASET(po.file) ENQ(SHRW)"
IF rc = 0 THEN
  "LMMSTATS DATAID("did") MEMBER(a2)",
   "VERSION(3) CREATED(95/12/31) MODTIME(23:59) USER(tsouser)"
```

Example 2:
```
/* rexx */
ADDRESS ISPEXEC
"LMINIT DATAID(did) DATASET(pov.file) ENQ(SHRW)"
IF rc = 0 THEN DO
  "LMMSTATS DATAID("did") MEMBER(ax*)",
    "VERSION(3) MODLEVEL(1)"
  "LMMSTATS DATAID("did") MEMBER(b*) DELETE"
END
```
Set 3.1 as version-level for all members whose names start with AX. Remove ISPF statistics for all members whose names start with B.

17.2.21 LMOPEN - Open a Dataset

Open a dataset.

Syntax:

```
ISPEXEC LMOPEN DATAID(dataid)
      [OPTION(INPUT|OUTPUT)]
      [LRECL(lrecl-var)]
      [RECFM(recfm-var)]
      [ORG(org-var)]
```

or

```
CALL ISPLINK ('LMOPEN',dataid,
      ,['INPUT'|'OUTPUT']
      ,[lrecl-var]
      ,[recfm-var]
      ,[org-var]):
```

dataid
>The dataid of the associated dataset returned by the LMINIT service.

OPTION

INPUT	Open the dataset in read-only mode. No changes can be made to the dataset.
OUTPUT	Open the dataset for output.

lrecl-var
>The name of the variable into which the logical record length is to be placed.

recfm-var
>The name of the variable into which the record format is to be placed.

org-var
>The name of the variable into which the dataset-set organisation (PO, PS) is to be placed.

Return code:

0	Normal completion.
8	Error; dataset error.
20	Severe error.

Example:

```
/* rexx */
ADDRESS ISPEXEC
"LMINIT DATAID(did) DATASET(pov.file) ENQ(SHR)"
"LMOPEN DATAID("did") OPTION(INPUT)"
"LMPRINT DATAID("did") INDEX"
"LMCLOSE DATAID("did")"
"LMFREE DATAID("did")"
```

17.2.22 LMPRINT - Print a Dataset or Member

Print the index of a partitioned dataset or the contents of a sequential dataset (or member of a partitioned dataset). Either INDEX or MEMBER must be specified for a partitioned dataset.

Syntax:
```
ISPEXEC LMPRINT DATAID(dataid)
        [MEMBER(member-name)]
        [INDEX]
        [FORMAT(YES|NO)]
```
or
```
CALL ISPLINK ('LMPRINT',dataid
        , [member-name]
        , ['INDEX']
        [, 'YES'|'NO']);
```

dataid
> The dataid of the associated dataset returned by the LMINIT service.

member
> The name of the member to be printed.

FORMAT
> YES   Format the print output for dataset list. Default. The formatted output contains heading lines, etc.
>
> NO   Do not format the print output for dataset list.

INDEX
> Print the index for a partitioned dataset.

Return code:
> 0   Normal completion.
>
> 8   Error; dataset error.
>
> 20 Severe error.

Example:
```
/* rexx - LMPRINT */
ADDRESS ISPEXEC
"LMINIT DATAID(did) DATASET(pov.file) ENQ(SHR)"
"LMOPEN DATAID("did") OPTION(INPUT)"
"LMPRINT DATAID("did") INDEX"
"LMPRINT DATAID("did") MEMBER(a2) FORMAT(NO)"
"LMCLOSE DATAID("did")"
"LMFREE DATAID("did")"
```

Sample index output:
```
DATASET:   TSOU002.POV.FILE

  GENERAL DATA:                        GENERAL DATA:
    MANAGEMENT CLASS:  STANDARD          RECORD FORMAT:        VB
    STORAGE CLASS:     WORK              RECORD LENGTH:        80
    DATA CLASS:                          BLOCK SIZE:        23,440
    VOLUME SERIAL:     WORK01            1ST EXTENT SIZE:       1
    DEVICE TYPE:       3380              SECONDARY QUAN:        1
    ORGANIZATION:         PO
    DATA SET NAME TYPE:  PDS
    CREATION DATE:     95/12/31
    EXPIRATION DATE:   **None**
    MEMBER    TTR   VERS.MOD  CREATION   DATE AND TIME    CURRENT
    NAME     (HEX)   LEVEL      DATE     LAST MODIFIED   NO. LINES
    A1      000007  03.01    95/07/25   95/07/25 07:44      1
    A2      000005  03.01    94/12/31   95/07/24 23:59      2
    B1      000009
    MAXIMUMS:        03.01    95/07/25   95/07/25 07:44      2
    TOTALS:                                                  3
    END OF MEMBER LIST
```

17.2.23 LMPUT - Write a Logical Record

Put (write) a logical record into the associated dataset. The first LMPUT invocation writes the first record; each subsequent invocation writes the next logical record. If the dataset is partitioned, the LMMFIND service must be used to position to the required member.

Syntax:
```
ISPEXEC LMPUT DATAID(dataid)
        MODE(INVAR|MOVE)
        DATALOC(dataloc-var)
        DATALEN(datalen-var)
        [NOBSCAN]
```
or
```
CALL ISPLINK ('LMPUT',dataid
        ,'INVAR'|'MOVE'
        ,dataloc
        ,datalen
        [,'NOBSCAN']);
```

dataid
   The dataid of the associated dataset returned by the LMINIT service.

MODE(keyword)
   The access mode for the record to be written:

   INVAR   The data record is written from the specified variable.

   MOVE   The data record is written from the location whose address is contained in the specified variable.

dataloc-var
> The name of the data location variable. The MODE keyword specifies the form of this variable.

datalen-var
> The length of the record to be written.

NOBSCAN
> No backscan; trailing blanks are not to be removed from variable length records.

Return code:

0	Normal completion.
4	Error; no dataset associated with the dataid.
12	Error; dataset error.
16	Error; truncation.
20	Severe error.

Example:
```
/* rexx */
ADDRESS ISPEXEC
"LMINIT DATAID(did) DATASET(pov.file) ENQ(SHRW)"
"LMOPEN DATAID("did") OPTION(OUTPUT)"
vdata = "alpha       "
vlen = LENGTH(vdata)
"LMPUT DATAID("did") MODE(INVAR) DATALOC(vdata) DATALEN("vlen")"
vdata = "beta        "
vlen = LENGTH(vdata)
"LMPUT DATAID("did") MODE(INVAR) DATALOC(vdata) DATALEN("vlen") NOBSCAN"
"LMMREP DATAID("did") MEMBER(a2)"
"LMCLOSE DATAID("did")"
```

17.2.24 LMQUERY - Retrieve Dataset Information

The LMQUERY service retrieves information that was provided to the LMINIT service.

Syntax:
```
ISPEXEC LMQUERY DATAID(dataid)
        [PROJECT(project-var)]
        [GROUP1(group1-var)]
        [GROUP2(group2-var)]
        [GROUP3(group3-var)]
        [GROUP4(group4-var)]
        [TYPE(type-var)]
        [DATASET(dsname-var)]
        [DDNAME(ddname-var)]
        [VOLUME(volume-var)]
        [ENQ(enq-var)]
```

or

```
CALL ISPLINK ('LMQUERY',dataid
         , [project-var]
         , [group1-var]
         , [group2-var]
         , [group3-var]
         , [group4-var]
         , [type-var]
         , [dsname-var]
         , [ddname-var]
         , [volume-var]
         , [enq-var] );
```

dataid
> The dataid of the associated dataset returned by the LMINIT service.

project-var
> The name of the variable into which the project (highest level qualifier) is to be placed.

group1-var
> The name of the variable into which the first of the second level qualifiers is to be placed.

group2-var
> The name of the variable into which the second of the second level qualifiers is to be placed.

group3-var
> The name of the variable into which the third of the second level qualifiers is to be placed.

group4-var
> The name of the variable into which the fourth of the second level qualifiers is to be placed.

type-var
> The name of the variable into which the type (third level qualifier) is to be placed.

dsname-var
> The name of the variable into which the dataset name is to be placed.

ddname-var
> The name of the variable into which the DD name is to be placed.

volume-var
> The name of the variable into which the volume is to be placed.

ENQ(enq-var)

The synchronisation (shareability) of the dataset:

SHR   Input data can be shared; default.

EXCLU   Exclusive use of data.

SHRW   Shared write for (partitioned) data. More than one user can read dataset members, but writing of members is enqueued.

MOD   Records are written at the end of a sequential dataset. The EXCLU option causes a sequential dataset to be overwritten.

ddname

The DD-name associated with the previously allocated dataset.

dsname

The dataset-name of an existing dataset. The name may be either fully qualified (written within single quotation marks) or non-qualified, in which case the TSO user prefix is implicitly placed before the specified dataset-name.

Return code:

0   Normal completion.

4   No information available for one or more keywords.

10   Error; no dataset associated with the dataid.

16   Error; truncation.

20   Severe error.

Example:
```
/* rexx */
ADDRESS ISPEXEC
"LMINIT DATAID(did) DATASET(po.file) ENQ(SHRW)"
"LMQUERY DATAID("did") DATASET(dsn) DDNAME(ddn)"
SAY dsn /* PO.FILE */
SAY ddn /* ISPnnnnn (nnnnn assigned) */
```

17.2.25 LMRENAME - Rename a Dataset

Rename a dataset.

Syntax:
```
ISPEXEC LMRENAME
        PROJECT(project)
        GROUP(group)
        TYPE(type)
        [NEWPROJECT(newproject)]
        [NEWGROUP(newgroup)]
        [NEWTYPE(newtype)]
```

or

```
CALL ISPLINK ('LMRENAME'
         ,project
         ,group
         ,type
         ,[newproject]
         ,[newgroup]
         ,[newtype]);
```

project
> The project (highest level qualifier).

group
> The second level qualifier.

type
> The type (third level qualifier).

newproject
> The new project (highest level qualifier). Default: the original project.

newgroup
> The new second level qualifier. Default: the original group.

newtype
> The new type (third level qualifier). Default: the original type.

Return code:
0	Normal completion.
4	Error; the new library exists already.
8	Error; dataset error.
12	A keyword value was incorrect.
20	Severe error.

Example:
```
/* rexx */
ADDRESS ISPEXEC
"LMRENAME PROJECT(tsouser) GROUP(jcl) TYPE(cntl) NEWGROUP(ex)
```
Rename the 'TSOUSER.JCL.CNTL' library (dataset) to 'TSOUSER.EX.CNTL'.

17.3 PROGRAM INVOCATION EXAMPLE

Although the previous section described the syntax for both command procedure invocation and for program invocation, for simplicity, all examples were shown as REXX execs. For completeness, this section shows an example of library management routines invoked from a program.

17.3.1 Invocation Forms

As for general ISPF services (e.g. ADDPOP), either the ISPEXEC or the ISPLINK service can be used to invoke Library Management routines.

If ISPLINK is used, two arguments are supplied. The first argument has the same form (with keywords) as for command procedure invocation. The second argument specifies the length of the first argument string.

If ISPEXEC is used, the arguments are positional. A dummy argument (blank content or address 0 (where supported, e.g. Assembler) must be specified if an argument is omitted; this does not apply for optional omitted arguments at the end of the argument list.

17.3.2 Data Type for Program Invocation

When ISPLINK is used to invoke a service the program arguments must be in the appropriate form.

In particular:
·   numeric fields are full-word binary (4 bytes)
·   character fields, unless otherwise specified, are 8 bytes, except for the dataset name field which is 44 bytes.

17.3.3 Sample Program

```
IDENTIFICATION DIVISION.
PROGRAM-ID. LM1.
ENVIRONMENT DIVISION.
DATA DIVISION.
WORKING-STORAGE SECTION.
01 C-VCOPY PIC X(8) VALUE 'VCOPY'.
01 C-VDEFINE PIC X(8) VALUE 'VDEFINE'.
01 C-LMINIT PIC X(8) VALUE 'LMINIT'.
01 C-LMFREE PIC X(8) VALUE 'LMFREE'.
01 C-MOVE PIC X(8) VALUE 'MOVE'.
01 C-CHAR PIC X(8) VALUE 'CHAR'.
01 P-DATAID PIC X(8) VALUE 'DID'.
01 P-PROJECT PIC X(8) VALUE 'TSOUSER'.
01 P-GROUP1 PIC X(8) VALUE 'PO'.
01 P-GROUP2 PIC X(8) VALUE ' '.
01 P-GROUP3 PIC X(8) VALUE ' '.
01 P-GROUP4 PIC X(8) VALUE ' '.
01 P-TYPE PIC X(8) VALUE 'FILE'.
01 V-DATAID PIC X(8).
01 DATAID PIC X(8).
01 VN PIC X(8).
01 VD PIC X(80).
01 VL PIC 9(9) BINARY.
01 RC PIC 9(4) COMP.
PROCEDURE DIVISION.
    MOVE 8 TO VL
    CALL 'ISPLINK' USING C-VDEFINE P-DATAID V-DATAID
    C-CHAR VL
    CALL 'ISPLINK' USING C-LMINIT P-DATAID P-PROJECT
    P-GROUP1 P-GROUP2 P-GROUP3 P-GROUP4 P-TYPE
```

```
        IF RETURN-CODE > 0 PERFORM
           DISPLAY 'RC:' RETURN-CODE
           MOVE 'ZERRSM' TO VN
           MOVE 80 TO VL
           CALL 'ISPLINK' USING C-VCOPY VN VL VD C-MOVE
           DISPLAY 'VN' VD
           MOVE 'ZERRLM' TO VN
           MOVE 80 TO VL
           CALL 'ISPLINK' USING C-VCOPY VN VL VD C-MOVE
           DISPLAY 'VN' VD
        END-PERFORM
     END-IF
 * processing
     CALL 'ISPLINK' USING C-LMFREE V-DATAID
     STOP RUN.
```

This example opens the file 'TSOUSER.PO.FILE'. The file is freed at the end of the
processing.

17.4 WORKED EXAMPLE

The sample procedure illustrates the use of a wide range of Library Management
services (and other ISPF services) in a practical application.

The procedure matches the statistics of the members of two libraries (the
primary library and the secondary library). The member list display of the primary
library is marked with a flag that indicates the status compared with the
corresponding member in the secondary library: *UPD indicates that the last
modified timestamp (date and time) is more recent in the primary library; *OLD
indicates that the last modified timestamp is older in the primary library; *NEW
indicates that the member is new (the member is not present in the secondary
library).

One or more line commands can be entered in the member display: s views the
member in the primary library (the ISPF BROWSE service is used to perform the
display); D deletes the member from the primary library. The processing status is
set into the user data field in the display. The member display remains until
terminated with the END key.

To make the code robust, the sample code performs comprehensive error
handling. The CONTROL ERRORS RETURN statement causes ISPF errors (return code >
8) to be handled by the procedure rather than being subject to default error
processing (error display and procedure termination). The SIGNAL ON ERROR REXX
statement avoids having to explicitly check the return code after each service
invocation (the named error handler is invoked if a service sets a non-zero return
code). The error signalling must be temporarily disabled in those cases where a
non-zero return code is expected (e.g. the END key pressed to end the display).

The sample code uses a REXX technique to simulate associative storage. The
MEM.n.i stem variable (n = 1 or 2 for the primary or secondary library,
respectively; i = member number in the corresponding library) contains the
corresponding member name. The MEM.n.*mname* stem variable (*mname* is the
member name) contains the index to the associated member data stem (0 indicates
that there is no associated member). This makes it easy to determine whether the

same member is in both libraries and to locate the associated entries. The following scheme illustrates this processing.

To illustrate associative storage processing, it is assumed that the primary library has three members (ALPHA, BETA and GAMMA) and the secondary library has two members (BETA and DELTA):

```
MEM.1.1 = ALPHA
MEM.1.2 = BETA
MEM.1.3 = GAMMA
MEM.1.ALPHA = 1
MEM.1.BETA = 2
MEM.1.GAMMA = 3

MEM.2.1 = BETA
MEM.2.2 = DELTA
MEM.2.BETA = 1
MEM.2.DELTA = 2
```

Because MEM.2.ALPHA and MEM.2.GAMMA do not exist (i.e. these stems do not contain an index value), the corresponding members names (ALPHA and GAMMA) do not exist in the secondary library, i.e. new entries.

The example illustrates the use of the following services: LMINIT, LMOPEN, LMFREE, LMMDISP OPTION(DISPLAY), LMMDISP OPTION(PUT), LMMDISP OPTION(GET), LMMLIST OPTION(LIST), LMMDEL, and BROWSE.

```
/* REXX */
ADDRESS ISPEXEC
"CONTROL ERRORS RETURN" /* accept ISPF errors */
SIGNAL ON ERROR NAME ErrorHandler /* enable errors */
/* primary library */
dsn1 = "'tsouser.new.jcl'"
"LMINIT DATAID(did1) DATASET("dsn1") ENQ(SHR)"
"LMOPEN DATAID("did1")"
/* secondary library */
dsn2 = "'tsouser.new.jcl'"
"LMINIT DATAID(did2) DATASET("dsn2") ENQ(SHR)"
"LMOPEN DATAID("did2")"

mem. = 0 /* initialise */
CALL GetMembers 1 did1
CALL GetMembers 2 did2
DO i = 1 TO mem.1.0
  mname = mem.1.i /* member name */
  name.i = mname
  x = mem.2.mname /* index in secondary library */
  /* test whether member exists in secondary library */
  IF x = 0
    THEN DO
      msg.i = '*new'
    END
```

```
        ELSE DO
          msg.i = '*old' /* default message - primary member older */
          /* compare last-update timestamps */
          IF date.1.i < date.2.x THEN ITERATE
          IF date.1.i = date.2.x ,
           & time.1.i <= time.2.x THEN ITERATE
          msg.i = '*upd' /* primary member newer */
        END
END
"LMFREE DATAID("did1")"
"LMINIT DATAID(did1) DATASET("dsn1") ENQ(SHRW)"
"LMOPEN DATAID("did1") OPTION(OUTPUT)"
SIGNAL OFF ERROR /* disable errors */
"CONTROL NONDISPL END" /* suppress initial display */
"LMMDISP DATAID("did1") OPTION(DISPLAY) STATS(NO) COMMANDS(ANY)"
IF RC > 8 THEN SIGNAL ErrorHandler
DO i = 1 TO mem.1.0
  "LMMDISP DATAID("did1") OPTION(PUT)",
   "MEMBER("name.i") ZLUDATA("msg.i")"
  IF RC > 8 THEN SIGNAL ErrorHandler
END
DO FOREVER /* outer (display) loop */
  "LMMDISP DATAID("did1") OPTION(DISPLAY) STATS(YES)"
  DO UNTIL RC > 0 /* inner processing loop */
    IF rc > 0 THEN LEAVE /* last selection */
    msg = '*select' /* default message */
    member = STRIP(zlmember)
    SELECT
      WHEN zllcmd = 'S' /* show */
        THEN "BROWSE DATAID("did1") MEMBER("member")"
      WHEN zllcmd = 'D' /* delete */
        THEN DO
          "LMMDEL DATAID("did1") MEMBER("member")"
          IF RC > 8 THEN SIGNAL ErrorHandler
          msg = '*delete'
        END
      OTHERWISE /* invalid selection */
        msg = '*selerr' /* default message */
    END
    "LMMDISP DATAID("did1") OPTION(PUT)",
     "MEMBER("zlmember") ZLUDATA("msg")"
    IF RC > 8 THEN SIGNAL ErrorHandler
    "LMMDISP DATAID("did1") OPTION(GET) STATS(YES)"
  END
END
"LMFREE DATAID("did1")"
"LMFREE DATAID("did2")"
EXIT

GetMembers:
  PARSE ARG n did
  memname = ' '
  rc = 0
```

```
      DO i = 0 TO 999 WHILE rc = 0
        mname = STRIP(memname) /* member name */
        mem.n.i = mname
        mem.n.mname = i /* index to statistics entry */
        date.n.i = zlmdate /* last-update date */
        time.n.i = zlmtime /* last-update time */
        "LMMLIST DATAID("did") OPTION(LIST) MEMBER(memname) STATS(YES)"
        SIGNAL OFF ERROR /* disable errors */
      END
      mem.n.0 = (i-1) /* no. of entries */
      RETURN

  ErrorHandler:
      SAY 'RC:'rc /* service return code */
      SAY "Stmt:"SIGL SOURCELINE(SIGL) /* error statement */
      SAY zerrlm /* error message text */
      EXIT 8 /* terminate */
```

18

DTL Example

18.1 INTRODUCTION

Because the DTL (Dialog Tag Language) is a language in its own right, this book does not provide a detailed coverage.

The example shown in this chapter provides a short introduction to basic DTL facilities and how they relate to the dialogue elements described previously in this book.

The simple application displays a panel in which a day-of-week (mon,...,sun) and a calendar week (01,...) can be entered. The selection of the appropriate action "date" or "day of year" computes the date (dd/mm/yy) or day (ddd) in the year 1996. The result is shown in a pop-up window.

The GETDATE REXX procedure is invoked to compute the result. The input fields are checked for validity. The week-day must be a three-character abbreviation: mon, tue, wed, thu, fri, sat, or sun. The calendar week must be numeric.

The application processing code (controlling procedures) must be coded explicitly. Two versions of the procedures are shown: as REXX procedures (GO4 and GO4X), and as the equivalent CLIST procedures (GO4C and GO4XC).

Initial Display:

```
 option help
                  - - - - - - - - - - - - - - - - - - - - - - - - - - -
  1  1. date                   Date Conversion
     2. day of year


 week-day . . . . . . . . wed  enter day of week
 calendar-week . . . . . . 8    enter calendar week
```

Result Pop-Up Display:

```
 21/02/1996  Result
```

18.2 GML DEFINITION

The GML (Graphic Markup Language) and DTL are equivalent. The GML (Graphic Markup Language) definition follows. The GML definition creates the five panels (the two display panels (PDTL4 and PDTL41) and three help panels (one general help (PDTL4H) and two field helps (PDTL4H1 and PDTL4H2)), the application-specific message (UMSG001) that is displayed for an invalid day-of-week entry, the key list entries (DEMOKEYS entry), and the command table entries (TESTCMD entry).

Note: To avoid overcomplicating the definitions, there is no coding for the help pull-down entries.

```
<!DOCTYPE DM SYSTEM ()>
<!-- PDTL4 panel definition -->

<HELP NAME=PDTLH4> Date Conversion
 <AREA>
  <INFO>
   <P> Convert week-day/week number (1996)
   <P> to date (dd/mm/yyyy) or day-of-year (ddd)
  </INFO>
 </AREA>
</HELP>

<HELP NAME=PDTLH41> Field-level Help: DAY
 <AREA>
  <INFO>
   <P> day of week:
   <P> 3 alphanumeric characters (sun,...,mon)
  </INFO>
 </AREA>
</HELP>

<HELP NAME=PDTLH42> Field-level Help: CALENDAR WEEK
```

```
   <AREA>
    <INFO>
     <P> week number of year
     <P> 1 or 2 numeric digits (1,...,52)
    </INFO>
   </AREA>
  </HELP>

  <KEYL NAME=demo>
   <KEYI KEY=f1 CMD=help FKA=no>
   <KEYI KEY=f3 CMD=exit FKA=yes>
   <KEYI KEY=f10 CMD=actions FKA=yes>
  </KEYL>

  <MSGMBR NAME=umsg00>
   <MSG SUFFIX=1> Day-of-week not mon,...,sun
  </MSGMBR>

  <VARCLASS NAME=dow TYPE='CHAR 3'>
   <CHECKL MSG=umsg001>
    <CHECKI TYPE=VALUES PARM1=EQ PARM2='mon tue wed thu fri sat sun'>
   </CHECKL>
  </VARCLASS>

  <VARCLASS NAME=cw TYPE='NUMERIC 2'>
  </VARCLASS>

  <VARCLASS NAME=any72 TYPE='ANY 72'>
  </VARCLASS>

  <VARLIST>
   <VARDCL NAME=day VARCLASS=dow>
   <VARDCL NAME=cw VARCLASS=cw>
   <VARDCL NAME=xdate VARCLASS=any72>
  </VARLIST>

  <CMDTBL APPLID=test>
   <!-- command definitions -->
   <CMD NAME=getdate>
    <CMDACT ACTION=passthru>
   </CMD>
  </CMDTBL>

  <PANEL NAME=PDTL4 HELP=PDTLH4 KEYLIST=demo>
   Date Conversion

  <!-- action bar definition -->
  <AB>

   <ABC PDCVAR=popt>option
    <PDC> date
     <ACTION RUN=GETDATE>
    <PDC> day of year
     <ACTION RUN=GETDATE>
   </ABC>

   <ABC>help
    <PDC> help for help
    <PDC> table of contents
```

```
      <PDC> index
     </ABC>

    </AB>

    <TOPINST>Enter 1996 date:

    <AREA>
     <DTACOL PMTWIDTH=25 ENTWIDTH=3 DESWIDTH=30>
      <DTAFLD DATAVAR=day HELP=PDTLH41 ENTWIDTH=3> week-day
      <DTAFLDD> enter day of week
      <DTAFLD DATAVAR=cw HELP=PDTLH42 ENTWIDTH=2> calendar-week
      <DTAFLDD> enter calendar week
     </DTACOL>
    </AREA>

   </PANEL>

   <PANEL NAME=PDTL41 WINDOW=YES DEPTH=FIT WIDTH=FIT>

   <AREA>
    <DTACOL DESWIDTH=10>
     <DTAFLD DATAVAR=xdate ENTWIDTH=10>
     <DTAFLDD> Result
    </DTACOL>
   </AREA>
   </PANEL>
```

18.3 GENERATED DISPLAY PANELS

To improve their readability, the generated panels have been slightly modified.
Normally hexadecimal attribute characters (e.g. X'01') are generated; these
hexadecimal codes have been replaced with special characters that are not used
elsewhere in the display panels.

18.3.1 PDTL4 Initial Display Panel

```
      )PANEL KEYLIST(DEMO,DEMO)
      )ATTR DEFAULT(%+_) FORMAT(MIX)
      | TYPE(AB)    /* action bar
      " TYPE(ABSL)  /* action bar separator line
      # TYPE(PT)    /* panel title
      ß TYPE(PIN)   /* panel instruction
      ( TYPE(FP)    /* field prompt
      } TYPE(NT)    /* Normal text
      [ TYPE(NEF)   /* Normal entry field
      } TYPE(DT)    /* Descriptive text
      )ABC DESC('option') MNEM(1)
      PDC DESC('date') MNEM(1) ACTION RUN(GETDATE)
      PDC DESC('day of year') MNEM(2) ACTION RUN(GETDATE)
      )ABCINIT
      .ZVARS=POPT
      )ABC DESC('help') MNEM(1)
      PDC DESC('help for help') MNEM(1)
      PDC DESC('table of contents') MNEM(1)
```

```
PDC DESC('index') MNEM(1)
)ABCINIT
.ZVARS=ZPDC
&ZPDC=' '
)BODY WINDOW(76,22) CMD()
)| option| help]
"-------------------------------------------------------------
}                              #Date Conversion]              }
}
ßEnter 1996 date:
}
{week-day . . . . . . . .[Z ]]enter day of week             }
{calendar-week . . . . . .[Z ]]enter calendar week          }
)INIT
.ZVARS = '( DAY CW)'
.HELP = PDTLH4
)PROC
VER (&DAY
LIST,mon,tue,wed,thu,fri,sat,sun MSG=UMSG001)
VER (&CW ENUM)
)HELP
FIELD(DAY) PANEL(PDTLH41)
FIELD(CW) PANEL(PDTLH42)
)END
```

18.3.2 PDTL41 Pop-Up Display Panel

```
)PANEL
)ATTR DEFAULT(%+_) FORMAT(MIX)
 # TYPE(PT)  /* panel title
 } TYPE(NT)  /* normal text
 [ TYPE(NEF) /* normal entry field
 } TYPE(DT)  /* descriptive text
)BODY WINDOW(24,5) CMD()
}          #}          }
}
[Z         ]]Result   }
)INIT
.ZVARS = '( XDATE)'
)PROC
)END
```

18.4 GENERATED HELP PANELS

Two help panels are generated:

·   A general help panel
·   Two field-help panels for the DOW and CW fields.

18.4.1 PDTL4H General Help Panel

```
)PANEL KEYLIST(ISPHELP,ISP)
)ATTR DEFAULT(%+_) FORMAT(MIX)
 # TYPE(PT) /* panel title
 } TYPE(NT) /* normal text
)BODY WINDOW(50,10) CMD()
```

```
}               #Date Conversion]              }
}
]Convert week-day/week number (1996)}          }
}
]to date (dd/mm/yyyy) or day-of-year (ddd)}    }
)PROC
)END
```

18.4.2 PDTL4H1 DOW Field-Help Panel

```
)PANEL KEYLIST(ISPHELP,ISP)
)ATTR DEFAULT(%+_) FORMAT(MIX)
 # TYPE(PT) /* panel title
 } TYPE(NT) /* normal text
)BODY WINDOW(50,10) CMD()
}               #Field-level Help: DAY]        }
}
]day of week:}                                 }
}
]3 alphanumeric characters (sun,...,mon)}          }
)PROC
)END
```

18.4.3 PDTL4H2 CW Field-Help Panel

```
)PANEL KEYLIST(ISPHELP,ISP)
)ATTR DEFAULT(%+_) FORMAT(MIX)
 # TYPE(PT) /* panel title
 } TYPE(NT) /* normal text
)BODY WINDOW(50,10) CMD()
}       #Field-level Help: CALENDAR WEEK]      }
}
]week number of year]                          }
}
]1 or 2 numeric digits (1,...,52)}             }
)PROC
)END
```

18.5 GENERATED MESSAGES

Up to ten messages are grouped in a single message entry. The message entry with
member name aaaaann contains the messages aaaaann0 through aaaaann9.

18.5.1 UMSG00 Message Entry

```
UMSG001 .TYPE=NOTIFY
'Day-of-week not mon,...,sun'
```

18.6 GENERATED KEYLIST

The keylists permit different key assignments for the various panels.

18.6.1 DEMOKEYS Table Entry

```
Variable   T   A   Value
KEYLISTN   K       TEST
KEY1DEF    N       HELP
KEY1LAB    N       HELP
KEY1ATR    N       NO
  ...
KEY3DEF    N       EXIT
KEY3LAB    N       EXIT
KEY3ATR    N       SHORT
  ...
KEY10DEF   N       ACTIONS
KEY10LAB   N       ACTIONS
KEY10ATR   N       SHORT
  ...
KEY13DEF   N       HELP
KEY13LAB   N       HELP
KEY13ATR   N       NO
  ...
KEY15DEF   N       EXIT
KEY15LAB   N       EXIT
KEY15ATR   N       SHORT
  ...
KEY22DEF   N       ACTIONS
KEY22LAB   N       ACTIONS
KEY22ATR   N       SHORT
  ...
KEYHELPN   S
```

Note: The non-significant entries are omitted from the shown list.

18.7 GENERATED COMMAND TABLE

The command table defines application-specific commands.

18.7.1 TESTCMD Table Entry

```
ZCTVERB    ZCTTRUNC  ZACTACT
GETDATE    0         PASSTHRU
```

18.8 GETDATE CODED PROCEDURE

```
/* REXX */
PARSE ARG popt cw day
day = TRANSLATE(day)
DayOfWeek = WORDPOS(day,"MON TUE WED THU FRI SAT SUN")
/* Jan 1, 1996 = Monday */
ddd = (cw-1)*7 + DayOfWeek
SELECT
  WHEN popt = 1 THEN DO /* date: dd/mm/yyyy */
    MonthDays = "31 29 31 30 31 31 30 31 30 31 30 31"
    mm = 1
```

```
       DO n = 1 TO 12 WHILE ddd > WORD(Monthdays,n)
         ddd = ddd - WORD(Monthdays,n)
         mm = mm+1
       END
       xdate = RIGHT(ddd,2,0)'/'RIGHT(mm,2,0)'/1996'
     END
     WHEN popt = 2 THEN DO /* day of year: nnn */
       xdate = ddd
     END
   END
   ADDRESS ISPEXEC 'VPUT (xdate)'
```

18.9 CODED PROCEDURES

18.9.1 Invocation Procedure

The invocation procedure is needed to set the application identifier (here TEST) and so activate the associated command table (TESTCMDS).

GO4 REXX:
```
    /* REXX */
    ADDRESS ISPEXEC "SELECT CMD(%GO4x) NEWAPPL(TEST)"
```

GO4C CLIST:
```
    PROC 0
    ISPEXEC SELECT CMD(%GO4XC) NEWAPPL(TEST)
```

18.9.2 Processing Procedure

GO4X REXX:
```
    /* REXX */
    SIGNAL ON NOVALUE
    ADDRESS ISPEXEC
    "DISPLAY PANEL(PDTL4)"
    IF RC = 0 THEN DO
      ADDRESS TSO zcmd popt cw day
      "ADDPOP"
      "DISPLAY PANEL(PDTL41)"
      "REMPOP"
    END
    NOVALUE:
      EXIT
```

GO4XC CLIST:

```
      PROC 0
      ISPEXEC DISPLAY PANEL(PDTL4)
      IF &LASTCC = 0 THEN DO
        IF &LENGTH(&zcmd) > 0 THEN DO
          &zcmd &popt &cw &day
          ISPEXEC ADDPOP
          ISPEXEC DISPLAY PANEL(PDTL41)
          ISPEXEC REMPOP
        END
      END
```

19

Graphical User Interface

19.1 INTRODUCTION

ISPF Version 4 introduced a GUI (Graphical User Interface, which is also referred to as the client/server interface). The GUI provides workstation support for ISPF mainframe applications, although not all features provided by OS/2 (or Windows 3.1) are available. The ISPF application processing is performed on the mainframe but the GUI provides a user-interface on the workstation. Other than supplying the GUI invocation parameter, no change needs to be made to the mainframe application. However, to provide maximum workstation-functionality, certain design considerations must be made. These design considerations do not affect the operation as a mainframe application.

19.2 MAINFRAME-WORKSTATION MAPPING

One of the most important considerations to be made for a GUI application is whether the application is to be run exclusively in GUI-mode or whether it is also to run as a native mainframe application. If the application is to run in both modes, the appropriate mappings should be made to adapt the application to the environment. To create a user-friendly GUI-application, workstation features should be used where possible. For example, action bars, push-buttons, checkboxes, pop-up displays, severity-related error messages. Provided the application has been designed with the appropriate features, the GUI automatically adapts the display to the environment. One exception is checkboxes, which are handled differently on the mainframe (multi-selection fields) and on the workstation. In this case the application should set dynamically the appropriate attribute.

ISPF Version 4.2 has introduced additional display elements, such as radio buttons, list boxes.

19.2.1 Action Bars

In GUI mode, action bars and the associated pull-down menus can be selected without any interaction with the mainframe (other than the original display).

To preserve the workstation-like character of the pull-down menu display and for user-friendliness, mnemonics should be specified for the action choices. Mnemonics are ignored in mainframe mode. In GUI-mode, the ALT-key used in conjunction with the mnemonic character selects the appropriate option.

Example:
```
)ABC DESC(file) MNEM(1)
 PDC DESC(open)
 PDC DESC(save) MNEM(1)
 PDC DESC('save as ...') MNEM(2)
 PDC DESC(close)
)ABC DESC(help)
```
f is used as mnemonic for the action bar choice. s and a (for save and save as, respectively) are used as mnemonic for the pull-down menu selections. The following GUI-mode display results:

```
file    help
open
save
save as ...
close
```

19.2.2 Pop-Up Windows

In GUI mode, pop-up windows (i.e. panels that are displayed when ADDPOP is active) are displayed in a dialogue box — the dialogue is modal, i.e. the pop-up window must be confirmed before control is returned to the original panel.

19.2.3 Pop-Up Messages

In GUI mode, pop-up messages are displayed in message boxes. Whereas in mainframe-mode the severity value (.TYPE=NOTIFY, WARNING, ACTION, or CRITICAL) is mapped to a colour, in GUI-mode the corresponding symbol (i for a notify message, ! for a warning, etc.) is shown with the message.

The .WINDOW parameter in the message definition causes the message to be displayed as a pop-up — the specified operand (NORESP or NOLRESP) determines whether the message is modal (RESP or LRESP) or modeless (NORESP or NOLRESP). The LRESP and NOLRESP operands specify that only the long message is to appear in the pop-up, otherwise both short and long messages appear in the pop-up.

Example:

```
CJMSG000 'Program Name Omitted' .WINDOW=LRESP .TYPE=ACTION
'Program name must be specified.'
```

19.2.4 Point-and-Shoot Fields

In GUI mode, point-and-shoot fields are automatically mapped to push buttons.

Both input and output variables, and text fields can be point-and-shoot fields. The PAS(ON) attribute is specified for input and output variables. The TYPE(PS) attribute is specified for text fields. A corresponding)PNTS section entry must be specified in both cases; a pseudo-variable (ZPSmmnnn) is used for text fields. This)PNTS section entry assigns a value to some variable.

Example:

```
)ATTR
> TYPE(PS)
] TYPE(VOI) PAS(ON)
)BODY

+Compiler:
     ]ASM      +Assembler
     ]CBL      +COBOL

>OK   >Cancel
)INIT
 &ASM = 'ASM'
 &CBL = 'COBOL'
)PNTS
 FIELD(ZPS00001) VAR(OPT) VALUE('OK')
 FIELD(ZPS00002) VAR(OPT) VALUE('NOK')
 FIELD(ASM) VAR(CLANG) VALUE('ASM')
 FIELD(CBL) VAR(CLANG) VALUE('COB')
)END
```

This panel defines two groups of point-and-shoot fields (push buttons):
·   The first group selects the required compiler: Assembler or COBOL. Depending on which field is selected (ASM or CBL), the CLANG variable is set to either ASM or CBL.
·   The second group specifies the required processing: OK or Cancel. Depending on which text field (ZPS00001 or ZPS00002 pseudo-variable) is selected, the OPT variable is set to either OK or NOK.

19.2.5 Push Buttons

In GUI-mode, push buttons are shown in three cases:
·   Function keys in the function key area. The FKA ON|OFF command controls whether function keys are shown.
·   The ENTER key is shown as a push button if text has been specified for the ZENTKTXT variable.
·   Point-and-shoot fields display as push buttons.

Example:
```
    )INIT
      &ZENTKTXT = OK
```
Display the ENTER key with OK as text.

19.2.6 Multi-Selection Fields (Checkboxes)

Mainframe multi-selection fields are equivalent to checkboxes on the workstation. In GUI-mode, a checkbox field has the CKBOX(ON) attribute. For mixed-mode applications, this attribute can be set dynamically based on the value of the ZGUI variable; in GUI-mode, ZGUI contains either the IP address or the LU address and is blank in 3270 mode. The ZGUI variable also can be used to set the appropriate prompt text.

Example:
```
    IF (&ZGUI NE '')
      .ATTR(field) = 'CKBOX(ON)'
      &PTEXT = 'Check required entries'
    ELSE
      &PTEXT = 'Select required entries with "/" '
```

19.3 GUI INVOCATION

The ISPSTART command with the GUI keyword is used to invoke a GUI application. The GUI keyword specifies the workstation's APPC network name or TCP/IP hardware-level IP address.

The FRAME keyword specifies the type of GUI window frame:

- STD   Standard. A GUI window can be resized.
- FIX   Fixed. A GUI window cannot be resized, but has max/min buttons.
- DLG   Dialogue. A GUI window cannot be resized and does not have max/min buttons. Pop-up panels are always displayed in dialogue frames.

The GUISCRW (width) and GUISCRD (depth) keywords specify the maximum panel size as displayed at the workstation.

19.4 GUI RESTRICTIONS

The GUI does not support the following features:

- Panels with graphical areas.
- Line-mode output (e.g. output from TSO commands) is written in the mainframe session.

19.5 EXAMPLE

The following example illustrates many of the aspects that should be taken into consideration for a GUI application.

The sample application is a simplified, but non-trivial, compile job generator:

· The CJPAN00 panel is displayed for the required parameters.

> Three input fields are present for the program, source file, and object (target) file. The source file and object file fields permit prompting. If the PROMPT command (PF4 key) is performed when the cursor is positioned in one of the fields, the associated procedure CJCMD11 is invoked to produce a list of all datasets for the current user. One of these datasets sets can be selected from the display (the selected dataset name is entered in the corresponding field in the CJPAN00 panel).

> · A set of checkboxes is used to specify any precompilers (either zero, one or both can be specified).

> · The first set of push buttons specifies the programming language (Assembler or COBOL). One of these buttons is pressed to initiate the processing.

> · A CANCEL push button can be used to terminate processing. The ZENTKTXT system variable is set to blank to eliminate the ENTER push button on the display.

> · Two pop-up menu selections are present (**file** and **help**). The **file** menu selection has three options: **view**, **output** and **exit**. The **view** option invokes ISPF BROWSE. The **output** option runs the CJXOUT command that invokes the CJCMD12 procedure. The CJCMD12 procedure displays a panel in which the SYSOUT class can be specified. For simplicity, no further of these options is shown. The **exit** option terminates the application.

· A skeleton (CJSKL) creates the required job control. The TSO SUBMIT command submits generated job-control. To avoid overcomplicating the skeleton, the precompiler information is only used to generate a job-control comment. Similarly, it is assumed that two job-control procedures (ASMCL and COBCL) are available — the procedure names are only illustrative.

· The CJKEYS keylist specifies the key processing for the CJPAN00 display panel and CJPAN11 scrollable panel.

· The CJCMDS command table specifies the application-specific commands.

Note: To avoid overcomplicating the example, the error processing is simplified.

Figure 19.1 shows the schematic processing for the application.

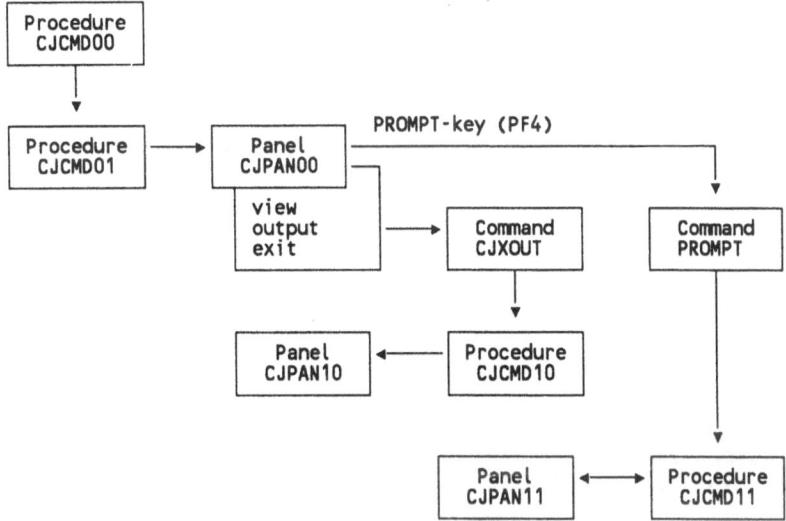

Figure 19.1 — Schematic application processing.

19.5.1 CJCMD00 Invocation Procedure

```
/* REXX */
"ISPSTART CMD(CJCMD01) GUI(LU:addr) TITLE(Compile Job) NEWAPPL(cj)"
```

Note: **addr** must specify the appropriate workstation address.

19.5.2 Processing Procedures

The sample application has three processing procedures:

- CJCMD01   Mainline processing.
- CJCMD11   Process the PROMPT command. Library Management services (see Chapter 17) are used to produce the dataset name list. The dataset name is entered into the corresponding panel field.
- CJCMD12   Process the Output pop-up menu selection.

19.5.2.1 CJCMD01 Processing Procedure.

```
/* REXX - CJCMD01 */
ADDRESS ISPEXEC
DO FOREVER
  "DISPLAY PANEL(CJPAN00)"
  IF rc > 0 THEN EXIT /* END-PFK pressed */
  IF opt = 'NOK' THEN EXIT /* CANCEL pressed */
  IF zcmd = 'PROMPT' THEN DO
    curfld = zcurfld /* prompt field */
    CALL cjcmd11 /* get dataset name */
```

```
        IF result /= '' THEN DO
          /* create REXX statement */
          stmt = curfld '=' result
          INTERPRET stmt
        END
        ITERATE
      END
    LEAVE
  END
  /* process skeleton */
  "FTOPEN TEMP"
  "FTINCL CJSKL"
  "FTCLOSE"
  "VGET (ztempf)"
  ADDRESS TSO "SUBMIT '"ztempf"'"
```

19.5.2.2 CJCMD11 Processing Procedure.

```
  /* REXX - CJCMD11 */
  ADDRESS ISPEXEC
  "VGET zuser"
  "LMDINIT LISTID(lid) LEVEL("zuser")"

  linelen = 47 /* line length on the dynamic area */
  xdsnlist = ''
  DO WHILE rc = 0
    "LMDLIST LISTID("lid") OPTION(LIST) DATASET(dsn)"
    IF rc = 0
      THEN xdsnlist = xdsnlist"(_)"LEFT(dsn,linelen-3)
  END

  "ADDPOP"

  dsn = ''
  pos = 1
  DO FOREVER
    SELECT
      WHEN zverb = 'DOWN' THEN DO
        pos = pos + (zscrolln*linelen)
        pos = MIN(pos,LENGTH(xdsnlist)-linelen)
      END
      WHEN zverb = 'UP' THEN DO
        pos = pos - (zscrolln*linelen)
        pos = MAX(pos,1)
      END
      OTHERWISE
    END
    dsnlist = SUBSTR(xdsnlist,pos)
    "DISPLAY PANEL(cjpan11)"
    IF rc > 0 THEN LEAVE
    PARSE VAR dsnlist . "(S)" dsn "(" .
    IF dsn /= '' THEN LEAVE
    "VGET (zverb zscrolln)"
  END
  "REMPOP"
  "LMDLIST LISTID("lid") OPTION(FREE)"
  "LMDFREE LISTID("lid")"
  RETURN dsn
```

19.5.2.3 CJCMD12 Processing Procedure.

```
/* REXX - CJCMD12 */
ADDRESS ISPEXEC
"ADDPOP"
"DISPLAY PANEL(cjpan10)"
"REMPOP"
```

9.5.3 Panels

The sample application has three panels:

- CJPAN00   The initial display panel. The panel performs validity checks, for example, prompt can be made only on the two dataset (file) name fields.
- CJPAN10   The output display panel — the SYSOUT class can be specified.
- CJPAN11   The dataset name list display panel.The CJPAN11 uses a scrollable dynamic area to display the dataset names.

19.5.3.1 CJPAN00 Display Panel.

```
)PANEL KEYLIST(pan00,cj)
/* CJPAN00
)ATTR
# TYPE(OUTPUT)
? TYPE(PT) /* panel title
a TYPE(AB) /* action bar
% TYPE(ABSL) /* action bar separator line
< TYPE(FP) /* field prompt
} TYPE(PS) /* point-and-shoot
[ TYPE(OUTPUT) PAS(ON) /* output; point-and-shoot
] TYPE(NEF) CAPS(ON) /* normal entry field
)ABC DESC(file) MNEM(1)
 PDC DESC(view) MNEM(1)
  ACTION RUN(ISRROUTE) PARM('BR1') /* browse
 PDC DESC(output) MNEM(1)
  ACTION RUN(cjxout)
 PDC DESC(exit) MNEM(2)
  ACTION RUN(EXIT)
)ABCINIT
 .ZVARS = PDCHOICE
 &PDCHOICE = ' '
)ABC DESC(help)
 PDC DESC(index)
)ABCINIT
 .ZVARS = PDCHOICE
 &PDCHOICE = ' '
)BODY EXPAND(//) CMD(ZCMD)
?/-/ Compile Job Generator /-/
 a file    a help
%-------------------------------------------------------------
+Command ===>_ZCMD                                           +
<Program . . . . ]PGMNAME +
<Source File . . ]SOURCE                                     +
<Object File . . ]OBJECT                                     +
<&PCTEXT
]Z+  <DB2-Precompiler
```

```
]Z+   <CICS-Precompiler
<Compiler:
+     [ASM      <Assembler
+     [COB      <COBOL
}Cancel+
)INIT
 .ZVARS = 'DB2 CICS'
 &ZENTKTXT = '' /* suppress ENTER-key
 &ZCMD = ''      /*clear command
 &ASM = 'ASM'
 &COB = 'COBOL'
 IF (&ZGUI NE '')
   .ATTR(DB2) = 'CKBOX(ON)'
   .ATTR(CICS) = 'CKBOX(ON)'
   &PCTEXT = 'Check precompiler box(es):'
 ELSE
   &PCTEXT = 'Enter "/" to select precompiler entries:'
)REINIT
 &ZCMD = ''      /*clear command
)PROC
 IF (&OPT NE NOK)
   IF (&ZCMD NE PROMPT)
     VER (&PGMNAME,NB,NAME,MSG=CJMSG002)
     VER (&SOURCE,NB,DSNAME,MSG=CJMSG002)
     VER (&OBJECT,NB,DSNAME,MSG=CJMSG002)
     IF (&ZGUI EQ '')
       &CHECK = '''/'''
       VER(&DB2,LISTV,&CHECK,MSG=CJMSG001)
       VER(&CICS,LISTV,&CHECK,MSG=CJMSG001)
   IF (&ZCMD EQ PROMPT)
     IF (.CURSOR NE SOURCE AND .CURSOR NE OBJECT) .MSG = CJMSG003
       &CURFLD = &ZCURFLD
       VPUT (CURFLD)
)PNTS
 FIELD(ASM) VAR(CLANG) VAL(ASM)
 FIELD(COB) VAR(CLANG) VAL(COB)
 FIELD(ZPS00001) VAR(OPT) VAL(NOK)
)END
```

19.5.3.2 CJPAN10 Display Panel.

```
)PANEL
/* CJPAN10
)ATTR
+ TYPE(TEXT)
# TYPE(OUTPUT)
? TYPE(PT) /*panel title
< TYPE(FP) /* field prompt
> TYPE(PS) /* point-and-shoot
| TYPE(OUTPUT) PAS(ON)
¬ TYPE(NEF) CAPS(ON) /* normal entry field
)BODY EXPAND(//) CMD() WINDOW(40,6)
?/-/ Compile Job Generator /-/
+Output:
<SYSOUT Class. . ¬Z+


>Cancel+
```

```
)INIT
.ZVARS = 'CLASS'
&ZENTKTXT = 'OK'
)PROC
&LIST = 'A ''*'''
VER(&CLASS,LISTV,&LIST,MSG=CJMSG001)
)PNTS
FIELD(ZPS00001) VAR(OPT) VAL(NOK)
)END
```

19.5.3.3 CJPAN11 Display Panel.

```
)PANEL KEYLIST(pan11,cj)
/* CJPAN11
)ATTR
} TYPE(DATAOUT) CAPS(ON)
{ TYPE(DATAIN) CAPS(ON)
% TYPE(TEXT)
_ TYPE(INPUT)
\ AREA(DYNAMIC) EXTEND(OFF) SCROLL(ON)
)BODY EXPAND(//) CMD() WINDOW(50,10)
%/-/ Compiler Job /-/
%                                    +SCROLL ===>_SAMT+
%Select a dataset:
\DSNLIST                                         \%
\                                                \%
\                                                \%
\                                                \%
\                                                \%

)INIT
IF (&SAMT = &Z) &SAMT = 'HALF'
)PROC
)END
```

19.5.4 CJMSG00 Message Member

```
CJMSG001 'Invalid input' .TYPE=ACTION .WINDOW=RESP
'Valid input: &LIST.'
CJMSG002 'Entry missing' .TYPE=ACTION .WINDOW=RESP
'Make mandatory entry.'
CJMSG003 'Non-prompt field' .TYPE=WARNING .WINDOW=RESP
'No prompt information available.'
```

The following display shows the form of a windowed error message (e.g. CJMSG002) as displayed in GUI mode.

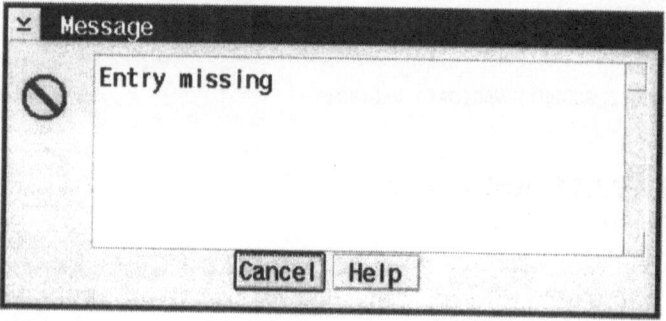

19.5.5 CJSKL Skeleton

```
)CM CJSKL
)SEL &DB2 NE &Z
//* DB2-Precompiler selected
)ENDSEL
)SEL &CICS NE &Z
//* CICS-Precompiler selected
)ENDSEL
)SEL &CLANG EQ ASM
//CMP EXEC ASMCL
)ENDSEL
)SEL &CLANG EQ COB
//CMP EXEC COBCL
)ENDSEL
//CMP.SYSIN DD DSN=&SOURCE,DISP=OLD
//LKED.SYSLMOD DD DSN=&OBJECT(&PGMNAME),DISP=OLD
```

19.5.6 CJKEYS Keylist.

The definition of the PAN00 keylist:

Key	Definition	Format	Label
F1	HELP	SHORT	help
F2	SPLIT	SHORT	split
F3	END	NO	end
F4	PROMPT	SHORT	prompt
F5	NOP	NO	NOP
F6	NOP	NO	NOP
F7	NOP	NO	NOP
F8	NOP	NO	NOP
F9	SWAP	SHORT	swap
F10	ACTIONS	NO	NOP
F11	NOP	NO	NOP
F12	NOP	NO	NOP

The definition of the PAN11 keylist:

Key	Definition	Format	Label
F1	HELP	SHORT	help
F2	SPLIT	SHORT	split
F3	END	NO	end
F4	NOP	NO	NOP
F5	NOP	NO	NOP
F6	NOP	NO	NOP
F7	UP	SHORT	up
F8	DOWN	SHORT	down
F9	SWAP	SHORT	swap
F10	NOP	NO	NOP
F11	NOP	NO	NOP
F12	NOP	NO	NOP

The following REXX procedure shows coding that can be used to generate the application keylist. For brevity, definitions are made only the first 12 function keys (PF13 through PF24 should be defined similarly). Similarly, not all the NOP function key definitions are shown.

```
/* REXX - Create keylist */
isptabl = "user.isptlib" /* table dataset name */
ADDRESS TSO "ALLOC F(ISPTABL) DA("isptabl") SHR REUS"
ADDRESS ISPEXEC
"TBCREATE cjkeys KEYS(KEYLISTN) ",
 " NAMES(KEY1DEF KEY1LAB KEY1ATR ",
 "       KEY2DEF KEY2LAB KEY2ATR ",
 "       KEY3DEF KEY3LAB KEY3ATR ",
 "       KEY4DEF KEY4LAB KEY4ATR ",
 "       KEY5DEF KEY5LAB KEY5ATR ",
 "       KEY6DEF KEY6LAB KEY6ATR ",
 "       KEY7DEF KEY7LAB KEY7ATR ",
 "       KEY8DEF KEY8LAB KEY8ATR ",
 "       KEY9DEF KEY9LAB KEY9ATR ",
 "       KEY10DEF KEY10LAB KEY10ATR ",
 "       KEY11DEF KEY11LAB KEY11ATR ",
 "       KEY12DEF KEY12LAB KEY12ATR) ",
 " REPLACE"

KEYLISTN = 'PAN00'
KEY1DEF = 'HELP'
KEY1LAB = 'help'
KEY1ATR = 'SHORT'
KEY2DEF = 'SPLIT'
KEY2LAB = 'split'
KEY2ATR = 'SHORT'
KEY3DEF = 'END'
KEY3LAB = 'end'
KEY3ATR = 'NO'
KEY4DEF = 'PROMPT'
KEY4LAB = 'prompt'
KEY4ATR = 'SHORT'
KEY5DEF = 'NOP'
KEY5LAB = 'NOP'
KEY5ATR = 'NO'
   ...
```

```
KEY9DEF = 'SWAP'
KEY9LAB = 'swap'
KEY9ATR = 'SHORT'
KEY10DEF = 'ACTIONS'
KEY10LAB = 'actions'
KEY10ATR = 'SHORT'
"TBADD cjkeys"

KEYLISTN = 'PAN11'
KEY1DEF = 'HELP'
KEY1LAB = 'help'
KEY1ATR = 'SHORT'
KEY2DEF = 'SPLIT'
KEY2LAB = 'split'
KEY2ATR = 'SHORT'
KEY3DEF = 'END'
KEY3LAB = 'end'
KEY3ATR = 'NO'
...
KEY7DEF = 'UP'
KEY7LAB = 'up'
KEY7ATR = 'SHORT'
KEY8DEF = 'DOWN'
KEY8LAB = 'down'
KEY8ATR = 'SHORT'
KEY9DEF = 'SWAP'
KEY9LAB = 'swap'
KEY9ATR = 'SHORT'
...
"TBADD cjkeys"
"TBSAVE cjkeys"
"TBCLOSE cjkeys"
```

19.5.7 CJCMDS Command Table.

Definition of the CJCMDS command table:

```
ZCTVERB   ZCTTRUNC  ZACTACT
PROMPT    0         PASSTHRU
CJXOUT    0         SELECT CMD(%CJCMD2)
```

The following REXX procedure shows coding that can be used to generate the application command table:

```
/* REXX - Create user commands */
isptabl = "user.isptlib" /* table dataset name */
SAY "CMDS being added"
ADDRESS TSO "ALLOC F(ISPTABL) DA("isptabl") SHR REUS"
ADDRESS ISPEXEC
"TBCREATE cjcmds NAMES(ZCTVERB ZCTTRUNC ZCTACT ZCTDESC) REPLACE"

ZTDESC = ''

ZCTVERB = 'PROMPT'
ZCTTRUNC = 0
ZCTACT = 'PASSTHRU'
"TBADD cjcmds"
```

```
ZCTVERB = 'CJXOUT'
ZCTTRUNC = 0
ZCTACT = 'SELECT CMD(%CJCMD2)'
"TBADD cjcmds"
"TBSAVE cjcmds"
"TBCLOSE cjcmds"
```

19.5.8 Sample Displays

The following display shows the form of the CJPAN00 as displayed on the mainframe:

```
------------------------ Compile Job Generator -------------
   file      help
------------------------------------------------------------
Command ===>
Program . . . .
Source File . .
Object File . .
Enter "/" to select precompiler entries:
     DB2-Precompiler
     CICS-Precompiler
Compiler:
     ASM       Assembler
     COBOL     COBOL
Cancel
```

The following display shows the same panel as displayed on a workstation:

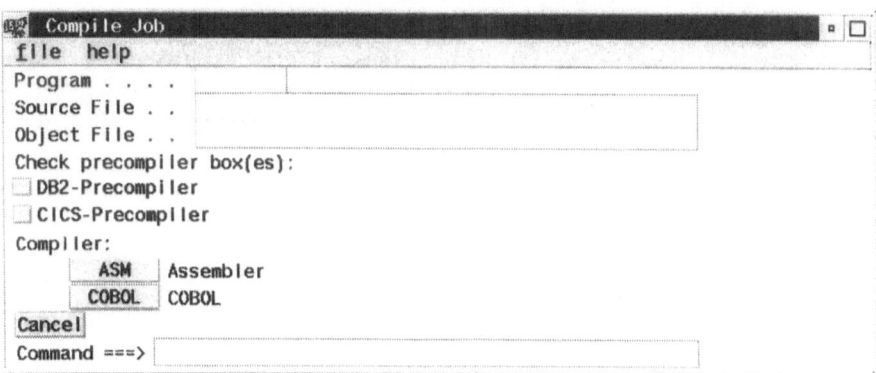

The following display shows the form of the CJPAN10 panel as displayed on the mainframe:

```
-------- Compile Job Generator --------
Specify output class:
SYSOUT Class. .

Cancel
```

The following display shows the form of the CJPAN11 panel as displayed on the mainframe:

```
----------------- Compiler Job ----------------
                            SCROLL ===> PAGE
Select a dataset:
_  TSOUSER
_  TSOUSER.APPC.CNTL
_  TSOUSER.APPC.EXEC
_  TSOUSER.APPC.LOAD
_  TSOUSER.APPC.OUTPUT
```

20

Test Facilities

20.1 INTRODUCTION

Although normally no problems arise in the development of ISPF applications, unexpected results can occur. This is especially true of program applications. The **Dialog Test option** as part of ISPF/PDF (PDF option 7) offers test facilities to assist in such circumstances. These test facilities only operate at the ISPF service level. Furthermore, the TSO test facility cannot be invoked in the ISPF environment. However, Section 20.4 shows how the ISPF environment can be invoked from TSO TEST.

The following ISPF test facilities are available:
- invoke function (selection panel, command procedure or program)
- display panel
- display content of the various dialogue variable pools
- display content of tables
- browse ISPF log
- invoke ISPF service
- trace variable or function
- set breakpoints on ISPF services.

20.2 TEST FACILITY INVOCATION

The test facility is invoked by calling PDF option 7; Figure 20.1 shows the selection panel in which it is displayed. The requested facility is selected by specifying the required option, e.g. option 1 displays the panel for function (selection panel, command procedure or program) invocation.

```
---------------- DIALOG TEST PRIMARY OPTION MENU ------------------
OPTION ===>

    1  FUNCTIONS        - Invoke dialog functions/selection menus
    2  PANELS           - Display panels
    3  VARIABLES        - Display/set variable information
    4  TABLES           - Display/modify table information
    5  LOG              - Browse ISPF log
    6  DIALOG SERVICES  - Invoke dialog services
    7  TRACES           - Specify trace definitions
    8  BREAKPOINTS      - Specify breakpoint definitions
    T  TUTORIAL         - Display information about Dialog Test
    X  EXIT             - Terminate dialog testing

Enter END command to terminate dialog testing.
```

Figure 20.1 - Primary selection (option 1)

20.3 TEST OPTIONS

ISPF provides the following test services:

1 Invoke function
2 Display panel
3 Display/modify variables
4 Display/modify table information
5 Browse ISPF log
6 Invoke ISPF service
7 Specify trace options
8 Specify breakpoints

20.3.1 Option 1 - Invoke Function

The input panel is displayed for specification of the required parameters. These parameters correspond with those for the ISPEXEC SELECT service. Figure 20.2 shows an example of a function selection where the command procedure TSCMD00 has been selected.

```
                        Invoke Dialog Function/Selection Panel
Command ===>
Invoke selection panel:
   PANEL  . .
   OPT  . . .


Invoke command:
   CMD  . . .


   LANG . . .                      (APL, CREX, or blank)
   MODE . . .                      (LINE, FSCR, or blank)


Invoke program:
   PGM  . . .
   PARM . . .


   MODE . . .                      (LINE, FSCR, or blank)


Invoke request:  (GUI mode only)
   WSCMD  . .




Options:
   Enter "/" to select option
      NEWAPPL                  ID . . .
      NEWPOOL
      PASSLIB
```

Figure 20.2 - Function selection (Option 1)

20.3.2 Option 2 - Display Panel

The input panel is displayed for specification of the required parameters. These parameters correspond with those for the ISPEXEC DISPLAY PANEL service. Figure 20.3 shows an example of a display panel selection where the panel TSPAN000 has been selected for display.

```
                        Display Panel
      Command ===>


      Panel name . . . . . . .
      Message id . . . . . . .            (Optional)
      Cursor field . . . . . .            (Optional)
      Cursor position . . . . .           (Optional)
      Message pop-up field . .            (Optional)


      Enter "/" to select option
         Display in window
```

Figure 20.3 - Panel display selection (Option 2)

20.3.3 Option 3 - Display/Modify Variables

The values of variables in the dialogue variable pools (function, shared and profile) are displayed as in a table display. Figure 20.4 shows a typical variable display panel. The usual scroll commands (e.g. UP, DOWN) are available. A particular variable (name) can be located with the following command:

     L varname

This locates the next (down) occurrence of the variable name relative to the current location. The command may be repeated to locate further occurrences of the variable.

New variables may be set into a dialogue variable pool by specifying the I (=insert) line operation:

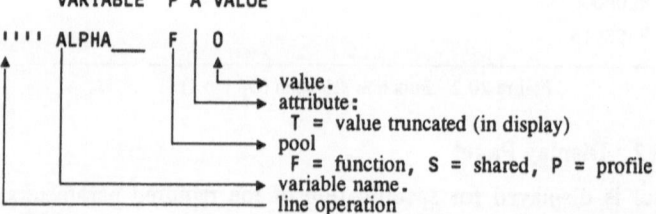

Similarly, the value of a variable may be changed, by overwriting the current value.

Note: A variable cannot be deleted, but its value may be set to blank.

```
                        Variables          Row 1 to 19 of 383
      Command ===>                          Scroll ===> PAGE


      Add, delete, and change variables. Underscores need not be blanked.
      Enter END command to finalize changes, CANCEL command to end
      without changes.


                                           Application . : ISR

          Variable P A Value
          Z        S N
          ZAPLCNT  S N 0000
          ZAPPLID  S N ISR
          ZCOLORS  S N 0007
```

Figure 20.4 - Variable display (Option 3)

20.3.4 Option 4 - Display/Modify Table Information

This option displays an input display panel used to specify the table name and the required function. Figure 20.5 shows a typical table selection panel. The following sub-options may be selected:

1   display row
2   delete row
3   modify row
4   add row
5   display structure
6   display status.

A specific row may be located by specifying either:
·   the row number;
·   values for one or more columns (the columns are selected for equal and all specified values must be satisfied in order that the row be selected).

Sub-options 5 and 6 retrieve general information pertaining to the table.

```
                              Tables
  Option ===>


  1 Display row        3 Modify row         5 Display structure
  2 Delete row         4 Add row            6 Display status


  Table Name  . .      Open tables  . .     (NOWRITE or WRITE or
                                             blank for no TBOPEN)
    Row identification:      Current row  . :
    By row number  . . *     (* = current row)
     Variable   Value        (Search for row if row number blank)



  DBCS column specification:


```

Figure 20.5 - Table selection (Option 4)

20.3.4.1 Display/Modify a Table Row. The panels displayed for the three sub-options pertaining to table rows have the same general structure:

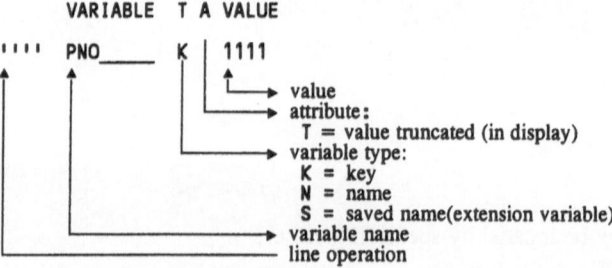

The following line operations are permitted:
- **I**   insert new extension variable in row
- **R**   replicate (duplicate) variable
- **D**   delete variable.

Note: The line operation may be immediately followed by a numeric replication factor, e.g. D4 deletes four entries.

A new value for a variable is entered in the VALUE column.

20.3.4.1 Table structure. The table structure is obtained by specifying sub-option 5.

The structure displays:
· the keys defined for the table
· the name fields defined for the table
· the number of rows currently in the table.

20.3.4.2 Table Status. The table status is obtained by specifying sub-option 6.

Example:

```
------------------- STATUS OF TABLE TEX01 --------------------
  COMMAND ===>


STATUS FOR THIS SCREEN   : OPEN     DATE CREATED       : 89/02/10
OPEN OPTION              : WRITE    TIME CREATED       : 12.27.02
TABLE ON DISK            : YES      LAST DATE MODIFIED : 89/03/15
LAST TABLE SERVICE       : TBSKIP   LAST TIME MODIFIED : 12.42.37
LAST SERVICE RETURN CODE : 00       LAST MODIFIED BY   : TSUSER01
CURRENT ROW POINTER      : 1            ORIGINAL ROW COUNT : 0
                                        CURRENT ROW COUNT  : 6
                                        MODIFIED ROW COUNT : 6
                                        UPDATE COUNT       : 4
```

20.3.5 Browse ISPF Log

The ISPF log, if defined, contains the log of important events which occurred during the current ISPF session, TRACE output and any messages which have been explicitly written to the log file using the LOG service. The standard PDF browse service is used to display the ISPF log, i.e. all browse facilities are available (scrolling, search for a particular string, etc.). Figure 20.6 shows a typical log output.

Note: The log file must have been previously defined using PDF option 0.2 (set ISPF PARAMETER OPTIONS, LOG/LIST defaults).

```
 BROWSE LOG - TSAB123.SPFLOG1.LIST -------- LINE 000000 COL 005 084
 COMMAND ===>                                   SCROLL ===> HALF
 *************************** TOP OF DATA ****************************
   TIME              *** ISPF TRANSACTION LOG ***


   12:52   START OF ISPF LOG - - - - SESSION # 1223 --------------
   12:53      TSO     - COMMAND -  - %TSCMD00
   12:53      TABLE IS NOT OPEN    - TBQUERY ISSUED FOR TABLE TEX01
```

Figure 20.6 - Typical log output

20.3.6 Invoke ISPF Service

This option is used to explicitly invoke an ISPF service. The service is invoked using control procedure syntax, except the ISPEXEC parameter is omitted. Figure 20.7 shows the invocation of the service request equivalent to ISPEXEC TBCLOSE TEX01.

```
                            Invoke Dialog Service
   Command ===>

   Enter dialog service and its parameters:
   ===> TBCLOSE TEX01


   Place cursor on choice and press enter to execute command.

   => TBOPEN TESTKEYS NOWRITE
```

Figure 20.7 - Example of explicit service invocation

20.3.7 Specify Trace Options

Two traces are available:
· functions
· variables.

The trace output is written to the ISPF log. Figure 20.8 shows the panel for the trace option specification.

Note: The title "function trace" is a misnomer, the function trace is actually a trace of ISPF service calls.

```
                             Traces
   Option ===>

   1   Function Traces    Monitor dialog service calls
   2   Variable Traces    Monitor dialog variable usage
```

Figure 20.8 - Trace option panel

The function trace specification has the following structure:

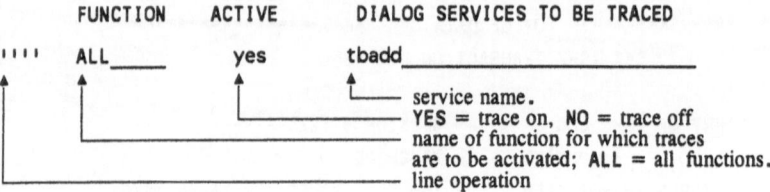

The following line operations are permitted:
- I insert new entry
- R replicate (duplicate) entry
- D delete entry.

Note: A line may specify more than one service and the names of services to be traced are separated by a comma (or a blank). The trace is made when any one of these services is invoked.

The variable trace specification has the following structure:

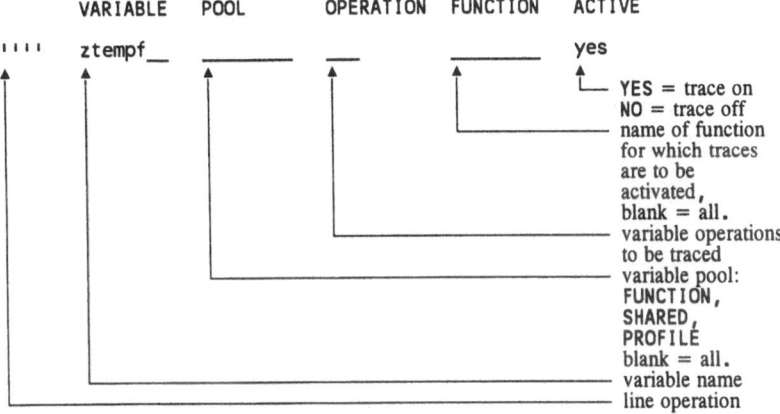

The following line operations are permitted:
- I insert new entry
- R replicate (duplicate) entry
- D delete entry.

20.3.8 Specify Breakpoints

Breakpoints can be specified to pause processing when a given service is invoked.

The breakpoint may be set:
- before
- after
- before and after

an ISPF service is invoked, or when an ISPF service sets a given return code. Furthermore, the breakpoint may be qualified with the names of required variables. The breakpoint is then effective only when the service is invoked with these variables. The command QUAL must be entered in order that variable names can be specified. If more than one name is entered on a line, all these names must occur in combination for the breakpoint to be activated.

Figure 20.9 shows an example of a breakpoint specification.

The breakpoint specification has the following structure:

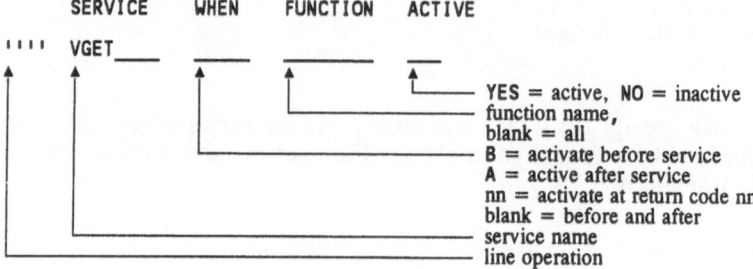

The following line operations are permitted:
   I   insert new entry
   R   replicate (duplicate) entry
   D   delete entry.

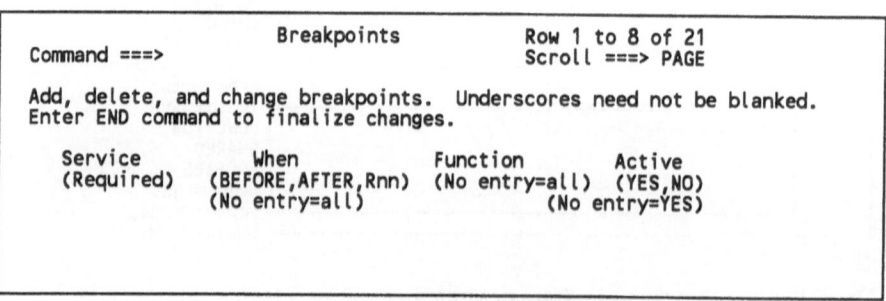

Figure 20.9 - Specification of a qualified breakpoint

An information panel (shown below) is displayed when the breakpoint is activated. This panel contains information concerning the breakpoint (service request, parameters, return code, etc.). The required continuation option must be specified.

The continuation options are:
   ·   invoke one of the eight standard functions (1-8)
   ·   cancel the test (option C)
   ·   continue after the breakpoint (option G).

20.4 INVOCATION OF ISPF FROM TSO TEST

The previous sections described how the ISPF/PDF test facility can be used to debug at the ISPF service level. These facilities are not always adequate to determine program errors. The TSO (interactive) test facility is normally used in such cases. Although the TSO TEST command cannot be invoked from the ISPF environment, the reverse situation is possible, i.e. ISPF can be invoked from the TSO TEST environment. Figure 20.10 describes the method used (output is printed bold).

```
1     TEST 'ISPF-library-name(ISPF)' CP
2     DATA
3     ISPF
4     ENDDATA
5     LOAD 'program-library-name(program-name)'
6     IJK57382I ENTRY POINT aaaaaa    AMODE=bb
7     TEST
          ...
         TSO test mode (set breakpoints, etc.)
          ...
8     go
```

Figure 20.10 - Invocation of ISPF from TSO TEST mode

Explanation:

1   ISPF is loaded as command processor (parameter CP) from ISPF-library-name, it is assumed that ISPF is an alias for ISPF.

2-4   Data statements for ISPF.

5   Load the program to be tested (program-name) from the load library program-library-name.

6   The TSO TEST facility displays the program's entry point address (aaaaaa).

7   The TEST message indicates that the TSO TEST mode is active. Breakpoints, etc. in the program to be tested should be entered at this stage. Note: This program is not currently active.

8   go passes control to ISPF.

The program to be tested is then invoked in the normal way (e.g. from a CLIST). Any breakpoints set in 7 are now activated and the usual TSO TEST commands used.

Appendix A

Syntax Notation

A.1 SYNTAX DESCRIPTION

This book uses two methods of describing syntax:
· syntax diagram,
· and syntax definition

A.1.1 Syntax Diagram

Syntax diagrams are read left to right, top to bottom.

▸▸—   Start of statement.

—▸◂   End of statement.

—▸   Statement is continued.

▸—   Statement continuation.

▸┬   Junction (branch-point). The principal path is the horizontal.

·   Mandatory items cannot be branched around.

Example:

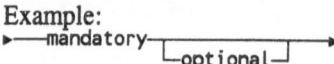

"mandatory" must be selected - it is on the horizontal path and cannot be branched around. At the following junction either the horizontal path (containing no entries) or the branch containing the entry optional can be taken - as there is a choice of paths the entry is optional.

·   If **one** of a number of mandatory items **must** be selected, then these items appear in a vertical stack.

Example:

Either "mandatory1" or "mandatory2" must be selected. The first junction offers two paths, one path with mandatory1 and one path with mandatory2 - each path contains an entry, and so one of the entries is mandatory.

·   Multiple options appear in a vertical stack, **one** of the specified options **may** be selected.

Example:

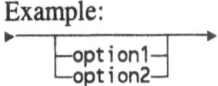

Either "option1" or "option2" may be selected. The first junction offers three paths: the horizontal path has no entry; the other two paths have the entries option1 or option2, respectively. Because the paths containing option1 and option2 need not be taken, these entries are optional.

·   Repetition is indicated by the following construction:

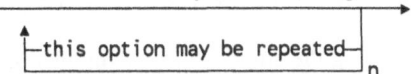

n at the right, if present, specifies the maximum number of times that the item **may** be repeated; the default value is unlimited.

Example:

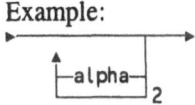

In this case the first junction is at the right-hand side of the diagram. This junction offers two paths, one horizontal to the end of the statement and one vertical. This vertical path has two subsequent paths, which contain either alpha or no entry. The value 2 indicates that up to two repetitions may be made. This means that either no entry, one alpha entry or two alpha entries may be specified.

·   If the repeat path contains an item, then this item is mandatory for repetitions.

Example:

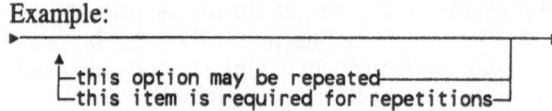

- An item written in upper case must be spelled exactly as shown, an item written in lower case is replaced by a valid entry (described in the text). An underlined entry is the default value.

Example:

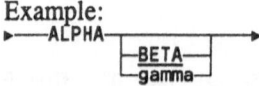

The first item is mandatory and must be ALPHA; the second item is optional, the default value is BETA. If an item is selected, then it must be a valid value for gamma.

- If an item is written italicised, then this is a parameter, the definition of which follows.

Example:
►——*logicaloperator*——►

logicaloperator:

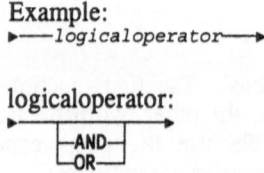

The parameter "logical-operator" may be replaced by one of the optional values: AND or OR.

A syntax diagram is formed by combining the simple elements defined above.

A.1.2 Syntax Definition

Syntax definitions specify the allowed operands and sequence for a service invocation, and make use of the following conventions:

[ ] Brackets enclose an optional item.

Example:
[ALPHA]
The item ALPHA is optional.

{ } Braces enclose a mandatory item.

Example:
{ALPHA}
The item ALPHA is mandatory.

...   Ellipsis indicate that multiple occurrences of the preceding element are permitted.

    Example:
    `[datasetname]...`
    The item `datasetname` may be repeated.

_   Underscore indicates that this is a default value.

    Example:
    `[ALPHA]`
    The item is optional, `ALPHA` is its default value.

| OR separates alternate items; one of the items so separated may be selected.

    Example:
    `[ALPHA | BETA]`
    Either `ALPHA` or `BETA` may be selected. If none is selected, `ALPHA` is used as the default value.

The same rules for upper and lower case apply as for syntax diagram.

A.2 FONT

A non-proportional font is used to depict commands, keywords or data set names.

Example:
The statement `TSO DELETE` is a command which invokes the `TSO` component `DELETE`.

Appendix B

Glossary and Acronyms

alphabetic   The set of characters containing the lower and upper case letters together with the three national characters: #, ə and $. An explicit note is made in those cases where the term alphabetic applies strictly to lower and upper case letters.

alphanumeric   The set of **alphabetic** characters together with the ten numeric digits.

APL   Acronym for A Programming Language. APL is a mathematical programming language.

application   An aggregate of dialogue components used to perform a self-contained unit of work.

ASCII   American Standard Code for Information Interchange. The principal character data coding for Personal Computers.

Assembler   Low-level programming language for low-level machine-dependent programming tasks.

batch   Application execution without man-machine interaction. Dialog Manager applications that do not require dialogue input can run in batch — the TSO monitor program runs as a batch program.

C   Mid-level programming language for low-level machine-independent programming tasks (Assembler replacement).

CICS™   Customer Information Control System, monitor system to provide on-line transaction processing facilities for programs.

CLIST   Procedure consisting of TSO commands and subcommands and control statements. CLISTs are also known as **command procedures**. The CLIST language has been largely superseded by the more powerful REXX language.

COBOL   COmmon Business Oriented Language. High-level commercial programming language.

command procedure   See CLIST and REXX.

command processor   A (dialogue) program entered as a command.

compiler   A software component which converts a source program into an object module.

CPI   Common Programming Interface. SAA components for program development. CPI components fall into two groups: languages and services. The CPI Dialog Interface is based on ISPF.

CPU   Central processing unit. Hardware component which controls the execution of program instructions.

CUA™   Common User Access™. IBM architecture for dialogue display. There have been several versions of CUA (89, 91, etc.).

dataset   IBM term for a file.

DB2™   DATABASE2™. IBM relational database package.

DBCS   Double-Byte Character Set. A set of pairs of characters used to represent characters in Far-East languages (Chinese, Japanese, Korean, etc.). Although ISPF provides DBCS support, this book does not discuss it.

DD   Data Definition. JCL statement that associates a ddname with a dataset or data stream.

Dialog Manager ISPF component which administers dialogue facilities. Dialog Manager is usually synonymous with ISPF.

dialogue   Man-machine interaction using a terminal directly attached to computer. Various levels of program systems (application program, terminal monitor program, etc.) control the dialogue.

display panel   Panel which is only to be used for display or data entry. See also **selection panel**.

DSORG   Data set organisation. The organisation of information in a data set.

DTL   Dialog Tag Language. A high-level proprietary language that can be used to create ISPF panels and associated entries.

EBCDIC   Extended Binary Coded Decimal Interchange Code. The principal character data coding on IBM mainframe computers.

FORTRAN   FORmula TRANslation. High-level scientific programming language.

function   The smallest dialogue application in the ISPF environment which can exist as a unit.

function pool   The pool of dialogue variables belonging to a function.

GDDM™   Graphic Data Display Manager. IBM product for creating and displaying graphic data.

help environment   Sub-environment within the ISPF environment entered by invoking the tutorial program. The help environment is used to provide on-line assistance.

help panel   Panel which is used for display or data entry within the help environment.

IBM™   International Business Machines Corporation, supplier of CICS, ISPF, PDF, MVS, etc. licensed products.

interpreter   A software component which directly executes a source program without producing an intermediate object module. An interpreter offers more flexibility than a compiler. However, this flexibility is bought at the cost of increased resource usage.

ISPEXEC   ISPF component which provides dialogue services for CLISTs and REXX execs.

ISPF   Interactive System Productivity Facility, IBM programming system to provide dialogue facilities. ISPF requires TSO, although TSO can run in batch.

ISPLINK   ISPF component which provides dialogue services for programs.

ISREDIT   ISPF component which provides edit services (edit macro).

JPA   Job Pack Area. An area of virtual storage that contains modules that are not in the link pack area but are needed for job execution.

library   A partitioned data set.

Linkage Editor   IBM program to combine one or more object modules into a load module. The Binder has superseded the Linkage Editor.

LINKLIB   A library or set of libraries that contains programs required for job execution. The LINKLIB does not need to be explicitly referenced by a task.

load module   Machine-readable Linkage Editor output in a form suitable for loading into virtual storage for execution.

logon   Connect terminal to telecommunications (e.g. VTAM) application program (e.g. TSO).

LPA   Link Pack Area. An area of virtual storage containing reenterable routines that can be used by all tasks in the system.

mainframe   Generic term for a large computer that uses a proprietary operating system. In the ISPF context a mainframe refers to a computer running MVS/TSO.

member   Independently named entry in a partitioned data set. A member can be directly accessed and processed as if it were a sequential data set.

MVS   Multiple Virtual Systems operating system.

NPT   Non-Programmable Terminal. A 'dumb' terminal as attached to a mainframe.

object module   Machine-readable compiler output.

OS/2™   Operating System/2™. IBM proprietary operating system for workstations.

panel   Form with which data is to be displayed on a VDU.

partitioned dataset   A data set comprising of members. Each member can be accessed directly by means of its (member) name. The member names and related information are contained in the index at the start of the partitioned dataset. PO (partitioned organisation) is a synonym for partitioned dataset.

Pascal   High-level programming language. Pascal was originally developed as a language used to teach programming.

PDF   Program Development Facility. IBM dialogue utility package to assist the programmer in program development, e.g. dataset services, compiler invocation dialogues. PDF is now part of ISPF.

PL/I   High-level programming language that combines many of the features of COBOL and FORTRAN.

profile pool   The pool of dialogue variables belonging to a particular application. The profile pool is retained across ISPF/TSO sessions.

QMF™   Query Management Facility. End-user interface to DB2.

RACF™   Resource Access Control Facility, IBM security package.

real storage   Storage that can be directly used for executable instructions and data. Virtual storage is mapped into real storage.

RECFM   Record format. The organisation of records in a block.

REXX   Restructured Extended Executor. REXX is a high-level programming language functionally similar to CLIST. However, the REXX language is more powerful than the CLIST language. A REXX program is often called an exec.

SAA™   Systems Application Architecture™. SAA is an IBM concept designed to provide a standard interface to the user (application developer).

SDF   Screen Development Facility. SDF is a tool to provide a common interface for the creation of panels independent of the target system. SDF does not provide any significant advantage for ISPF, as the panels are in an easily editable form.

selection panel   Panel which is used to invoke a new function.

sequential dataset   A file that is processed sequentially. PS (physical sequential) is a synonym for sequential dataset.

session   The dialogue environment for the current user. TSO is the lowest level session. The ISPF session is invoked from the user's TSO session.

shared pool   The pool of dialogue variables belonging to the current ISPF session.

skeleton   A data set containing fixed and variable data. Skeletons in the ISPF sense are used in conjunction with file tailoring.

source program   Input to a compiler or interpreter. A source program constitutes the "computer instructions" produced by the programmer. Source programs can exist in a number of levels of detail. **Low-level** languages (e.g. Assembler) require that the programmer has an intimate knowledge of the machine instructions available on the computer on which his program will run. **High-level** languages (e.g.

PL/I) remove much of this burden from the programmer and enable him to be more concerned with the procedure required to solve his program; such languages are often referred to as **procedure oriented** languages. So called **4th generation** languages (REXX execs offer certain features) are **problem oriented**. Modern high-level languages offer structuring facilities.

SPF   Structured Programming Facility, SPF was the forerunner to ISPF.

STEPLIB   A library or set of libraries that contains programs required for job execution. The STEPLIB applies only to the current step or TSO session and must be explicitly referenced. The TSO STEPLIB is defined in the TSO logon procedure.

table   A two dimensional array. A Dialog Manager table can exist as in a library.

TSO   Time Sharing Option, programming system to provide users with on-line access to computing system. TSO is now a standard MVS component.

userid   The unique code for the user when he logs onto the TSO system.

VDU   Visual Display Unit. Terminal unit with television-like display.

virtual storage   Addressable storage that appears to the user as real storage. Virtual storage contains the program instructions and data required for immediate processing.

VTAM™   Virtual Telecommunication Access Method. MVS subsystem used to administer data transfer between terminals and monitor subsystem (e.g. TSO).

Windows™   Microsoft™ operating system for personal computers.

workstation A synonym for a personal computer. In the ISPF context, a workstation is attached to the mainframe.

™ With the exception of Windows and Microsoft, which are registered trademarks of Microsoft, registered trademark of International Business Machines.

Index